Sixth Edition

ETHICS IN HUMAN COMMUNICATION

Sixth Edition

ETHICS IN HUMAN COMMUNICATION

Richard L. Johannesen
Northern Illinois University, Emeritus

Kathleen S. Valde
Northern Illinois University

Karen E. Whedbee
Northern Illinois University

WAVELAND
PRESS, INC.
Long Grove, Illinois

For information about this book, contact:
Waveland Press, Inc.
4180 IL Route 83, Suite 101
Long Grove, IL 60047-9580
(847) 634-0081
info@waveland.com
www.waveland.com

Contents

Preface

Our primary intentions in this book are: (1) to provide information and insights concerning a variety of potential perspectives for making ethical judgments about human communication; (2) to sensitize participants in communication to the inherency of potential ethical issues in the human communication process; (3) to highlight the complexities and difficulties involved in making evaluations of communication ethics; (4) to encourage individuals to develop thoughtfully their own workable approach to assessing communication ethics; and (5) to aid individuals in becoming more discerning evaluators of communication through enhancing their ability to make specifically focused and carefully considered judgments.

The first chapter treats only some of the standard topics of ethics such as definitions of ethics and morality, is versus ought, intent, sincerity, Aristotle's Doctrine of the Mean, and responsibility. Other now standard topics appear as discussions positioned at strategic points throughout various chapters and the appendix. These topics include the virtue/character ethics tradition, rationality, the deontological tradition (Kant's Categorical Imperative), the teleological tradition (utilitarianism—expanded in this edition), Ross's *prima facie* duties, situation ethics, absolute versus relative standards, the end as justification of means, feminist ethics, postmodern ethics, and the self as an ethical agent.

For this sixth edition, numerous changes have been made throughout. Major additions and deletions in chapter 1 result in significant updating. Major revisions and deletions also occur in chapters 6, 7, and 9. Chapters 2 and 12 reflect significant revision. All of the other chapters have undergone modest revision. Two new essays appear in the appendix of case studies, one on plagiarism and one on a role for shame in communication ethics.

The list of VHS and DVD resources on communication ethics has been updated. The significantly revised and updated bibliography of Sources for Further Reading has been shortened but still contains over 470 items and includes sections on journalism and the mass media and on character/virtue ethics. At various points throughout the book we continue to explore issues and standards relevant to print and electronic media: Internet ethics; formal codes of ethics for commercial advertising, public relations, journalism, and political communication; the "truth" standard in commercial advertising; propaganda and the demagogue; and the ethics of nonverbal communication (including pictorial images).

With this sixth edition, Richard Johannesen is pleased to welcome his friends and colleagues, Kathleen Valde and Karen Whedbee, as coauthors. Valde had primary revision responsibility for chapters 8 and 9. Whedbee had primary revision responsibility for chapters 5 and 6. Whedbee and Johannesen shared revision of chapter 7. All other revisions are Johannesen's.

Richard L. Johannesen
Kathleen S. Valde
Karen E. Whedbee

Acknowledgments

We are grateful to Neil and Carol Rowe of Waveland Press for their continued support of this book. We especially appreciate the guidance and patience of our superb editor, Jeni Ogilvie. We thank the various organizations for which we have reprinted part or all of their codes of ethics: American Advertising Association, American Association of Advertising Agencies, American Association of Political Consultants, Better Business Bureau, Committee on Decent Unbiased Campaign Tactics, Common Cause, International Association of Business Communicators, National Communication Association, Public Relations Society of America, and the Society of Professional Journalists. Some of the material in chapters 7, 11, 12, and the appendix is adapted from Johannesen, "Communication Ethics: Centrality, Trends, and Controversies," in *Communication Yearbook 25*, ed. William Gudykunst (Mahwah, NJ: Erlbaum, 2001), pp. 201–236.

1

Ethical Responsibility in Human Communication

Values can be viewed as conceptions of The Good or The Desirable that motivate human behavior and that function as criteria in our making of choices and judgments. Concepts such as material success, individualism, efficiency, thrift, freedom, courage, hard work, competition, patriotism, compromise, and punctuality are value standards that have varying degrees of potency in contemporary North American culture. But we probably would not view them primarily as *ethical* standards of right and wrong. Ethical judgments focus more precisely on degrees of rightness and wrongness, virtue and vice, and obligation in human behavior. In condemning someone for being inefficient, conformist, extravagant, lazy, or late, we probably would not also be claiming they are unethical. However, standards such as honesty, promise-keeping, truthfulness, fairness, and humaneness usually *are* used in making ethical judgments of rightness and wrongness in human behavior.

Ethical issues may arise in human behavior whenever that behavior could have significant impact on other persons, when the behavior involves conscious choice of means and ends, and when the behavior can be judged by standards of right and wrong.[1] If there is little possible significant, immediate, or long-term impact of our actions (physical or symbolic) on other humans, matters of ethics normally are viewed as minimally relevant. If we have little or no opportunity for conscious free choice in our behavior, if we feel compelled to do or say something because we are forced or coerced, matters of ethics usually are seen as minimally relevant to *our* actions.

Some philosophers draw distinctions between ethics and morals as concepts. Ethics denotes the general and systematic study of what ought to be the grounds and principles for right and wrong human behavior. Morals (or morality) denotes the practical, specific, generally agreed-upon, culturally transmitted standards of right and wrong. Other philosophers, however, use

1

the terms ethics and morals more or less interchangeably—as will be the case in this book.

Inherency of Potential Ethical Issues

Potential ethical issues are inherent in any instance of communication between humans to the degree that the communication can be judged on a right–wrong dimension, that it involves possible significant influence on other humans, and that the communicator consciously chooses specific ends sought and communicative means to achieve those ends. Whether a communicator seeks to present information, increase someone's level of understanding, facilitate independent decision making in another person, persuade about important values, demonstrate the existence and relevance of a societal problem, advocate a solution or program of action, or stimulate conflict—potential ethical issues inhere in the communicator's symbolic efforts. Such is the case for most human communication whether it is between two people; in small groups; in the rhetoric of a social movement; in communication from government to citizen; or in an advertising, public relations, or political campaign.

"Human beings always have a sense of the self, in the sense that they situate themselves somewhere in ethical space," contends philosopher Charles Taylor. "A human being exists inescapably in a space of ethical questions; she cannot avoid assessing herself in relation to some standards. To escape all standards would not be liberation but a terrifying lapse into total disorientation."[2] But some people ask, why worry at all about ethics in human communication? Indeed, to avoid consideration of ethics in communication, such persons may resort to various justifications: (1) everyone knows that this particular communication technique is unethical, so there is nothing to discuss; (2) since only success matters in communication, ethicality is irrelevant; (3) after all, ethical judgments are simply matters of individual personal opinion anyway, so there are no final answers; and (4) it is presumptuous, perhaps even unethical, to judge the ethics of others.[3]

Tension potentially exists between *"is"* and *"ought,"* between the actual and the ideal. What everyone is doing and what we judge they ought to do, what the majority says is ethical and what a few argue ought to be ethical, may differ. There may be a conflict between a communication technique we know is successful and the judgment that the technique ought not to be used because it is ethically suspect. We may overemphasize our understanding of the nature and effectiveness of communication techniques, processes, and methods at the expense of concern for the ethical use of such techniques. We should examine not only *how to*, but also *whether we ethically ought to*, employ methods and appeals. The question of "whether to" clearly is one not only of audience adaptation but also one of ethics. We may feel that ethical ideals are not realistically achievable and thus are of little usefulness. But Thomas

Nilsen reminds us that "we must always expect a gap between ideals and their attainment, between principles and their application." Nevertheless, he feels that "ideals reflect genuine beliefs, intentions, and aspirations. They reflect what we in our more calm and thoughtful moments think ought to be, however aware we may be of our actual . . . level of achievement. . . . Our ideals provide an ultimate goal, a sense of direction, a general orientation, by which to guide conduct."[4]

How participants in a human communication transaction evaluate the ethics of that transaction, or how outside observers evaluate its ethics, will differ depending on the ethical standards they employ. Some even may choose to ignore ethical judgments entirely. Nevertheless, *potential* ethical questions are there regardless of how they are resolved or answered.

Whether a communicator wishes it or not, communicatees generally will judge, formally or informally, the communicator's effort in part by those communicatees' relevant ethical standards. If for none other than the pragmatic reason of enhancing chances of success, the communicator would do well to consider the ethical criteria held by his or her audience.

Adaptation to the Audience

What are the ethics of audience adaptation? Most human communicators seek to secure some kind of response from receivers. To what degree is it ethical for communicators to alter their ideas and proposals in order to adapt to the needs, capacities, desires, and expectations of an audience? To secure acceptance, some communicators adapt to an audience to the extent of so changing their ideas that the idea is no longer really theirs. These communicators merely say what the audience wants them to say regardless of their *own* convictions. For example, in the words of one journalist, Bill Clinton "has been criticized throughout his career for trying to be all things to all people and saying whatever the person he is talking to wants to hear."[5] Other communicators, in contrast, go to the opposite extreme of making little or no adaptation to their audience. They do not take serious account of their audience. Their audience thus perceives the speaker, writer, or advertisement as unconnected to them or unconcerned about them. Some measure of adaptation in language choice, supporting materials, organization, and message transmission to reflect the specific nature of the audience is a crucial part of successful communication. No ironclad rule can be set down here.

The search is for an appropriate point between two undesirable extremes—the extreme of saying only what the audience desires and will approve and the extreme of complete lack of concern for and understanding of the audience. The search is for an appropriate point between too much adaptation to the audience and not enough. Both extremes are ethically irresponsible. This tension, this search for balance in audience adaptation, can be viewed as an example of Aristotle's Doctrine of the Mean (termed by others as the Golden Mean). For Aristotle, moral virtue usually represents a mean or intermediate point between two vices—the vice of excess and the vice of deficiency. For example, courage is a mean between foolhardiness and cowardice. Generosity is a mean between wastefulness and stinginess. Aristotle denies that the mean is a mathematically precise average or midpoint between extremes. Rather, the mean combines the right amount at the right time toward the right people in a right manner for the right motives. The mean is also relative to the person's status, specific situation, and strengths and weaknesses of character. A person generally disposed toward one extreme in an appropriate instance ought to tend toward the other extreme to redress the imbalance.[6] In this era of heightened awareness of ethnic, racial, religious, and sexual diversity, communicators face significant practical and ethical choices concerning the appropriate degree of audience adaptation.

The Importance of Ethics

Persons enrolled in communication courses frequently are preparing for careers in advertising, sales, law, journalism, business, or politics. But those interested in such careers may be surprised by the extremely negative perceptions that citizens have of the ethics and honesty of persons in those careers. The 2006 Gallup Poll of perceived honesty and ethics of 23 professions ranked the following 11, in descending order, as lowest in perceived ethicality: journalists, state governors, business executives, lawyers, stockbrokers, senators, congressmen, insurance salesmen, HMO managers, advertising practitioners, and, at the bottom, car salesmen (www.gallup.com; released December 14, 2006).

Evidence abounds that supports public concern over the decline of ethical behavior. A 2006 Gallup Poll of public perceptions of moral values in the United States found that 85 percent of respondents rated the current state of moral values as only fair/poor and 81 percent thought the level of moral values was getting worse (www.gallup.com; released May 25, 2006). A national firm that conducts background checks reviewed 2.6 million job applications in 2002 and found that 44 percent contained some lies (*New York Times*, December 28, 2002, p. C8). The Josephson Institute of Ethics conducted a 2006 national survey of over 33,000 high school students. The results show a puzzling contradiction. On the one hand, over 90 percent of those surveyed say that it is "important to me to be a person of good character," that "honesty and trust are essential in personal relationships," and that they are "satisfied with my own ethics and character." On the other hand, in stark contrast, 82 percent admitted they had lied to a parent (57 percent two or more times) and 62 percent lied to a teacher (35 percent two or more times) about something significant in the past year. Sixty percent admitted they cheated during a test at school this past year—35 percent cheated two or more times (www.josephsoninstitute.org; released October 15, 2006).

In his book, *The Cheating Culture* (2004), David Callahan documents a "pattern of widespread cheating throughout U.S. society," observes that people "not only are cheating in more areas but are feeling less guilty about it," and concludes that most of the cheating "is by people who, on the whole, view themselves as upstanding members of society." *The New Ethics: A Tour of the 21st Century Moral Landscape* (2004) is a wide-ranging analysis by Anita L. Allen. Her overview summary is one of pessimism and puzzlement: "Our contemporary ethical landscape is marked by . . . widespread ethical failure against the background of a culture rich with moral resources. We seem to have everything we need for exemplary character and conduct, and yet wrongdoing flourishes in every sector. Why are we not better? How can we become better?"[7]

"A society without ethics is a society doomed to extinction," argues philosopher S. Jack Odell. According to Odell, the "basic concepts and theories of ethics provide the framework necessary for working out one's own moral or ethical code." Odell believes that "ethical principles are necessary preconditions for the existence of a social community. Without ethical principles it would be impossible for human beings to live in harmony and without fear, despair, hopelessness, anxiety, apprehension, and uncertainty."[8]

A societal or personal system of ethics is not a magic or automatic cure-all for individual or collective ills. What can ethical theory and systematic reflection on ethics contribute? One answer is suggested by philosopher Carl Wellman:

> An ethical system does not solve all one's practical problems, but one cannot choose and act rationally without some explicit or implicit ethical system. An ethical theory does not tell a person what to do in any given situation, but neither is it completely silent; it tells one what to consider in making up one's mind what to do. The practical function of an ethical system is primarily to direct our attention to the relevant considerations, the reasons that determine the rightness or wrongness of any act.[9]

Freedom and Responsibility

American culture emphasizes dual concerns for maximizing latitude of freedom of communication and for promoting responsible exercise of such freedom. The current and future boundaries of freedom of communication in the United States are explored in such works as: *The System of Freedom of Expression, Freedom of Speech in the United States,* and *Speech and Law in a Free Society.*[10] Psychiatrist Thomas Szasz succinctly describes the interrelated and intertwined nature of freedom and responsibility.

> The crucial moral characteristic of the human condition is the dual experience of freedom of the will and personal responsibility. Since freedom

and responsibility are two aspects of the same phenomenon, they invite comparison with the proverbial knife that cuts both ways. One of its edges implies options: we call it freedom. The other implies obligations: we call it responsibility. People like freedom because it gives them mastery over things and people. They dislike responsibility because it constrains them from satisfying their wants. That is why one of the things that characterizes history is the unceasing human effort to maximize freedom and minimize responsibility. But to no avail, for each real increase in human freedom . . . brings with it a proportionate increase in responsibility. Each exhilaration with the power to do good is soon eclipsed by the guilt for having used it to do evil.[11]

African American legal scholar and social critic Stephen Carter describes the tension this way.

On the one hand, freedom unrestrained by clear moral norms begets anarchy. On the other hand, moral norms that have the force of law often stifle freedom. This tension is inevitable in a nation that wishes to be both moral and free. But nobody can (or should want to) sustain the tension indefinitely; sooner or later, on every question on which we might disagree, the side of freedom or the side of restraint will have its way.[12]

The freedom versus responsibility tension can appear when we, as individuals, carry to an extreme the now traditional view that the best test of the worth of our ideas is their ability to survive in the free and open public "marketplace" of ideas. We might take the mistaken view that, as individuals, we have no responsibility to test the ethicality of our communication means and ends before we present them. Rather we incorrectly assume that the logical and ethical soundness of our ideas need only be evaluated through their ability to survive in competition with other ideas and differing viewpoints in the marketplace. Such a view could lead each of us to ignore our ethical responsibilities as communicators because the marketplace will ultimately render the necessary judgments. However, we must remember that while we do have First Amendment protection of freedom of speech and press, each of us also has the responsibility to exercise that freedom in an ethical manner.[13]

We now turn to an actual example of freedom and responsibility in tension. In the early morning of April 16, 2007, a student at Virginia Tech University, armed with two handguns, shot and killed two students in a dormitory. A little over two hours later, the killer murdered 30 students and faculty in a classroom building before committing suicide. In the time between the murders, the killer mailed to NBC News a self-produced package of 27 video clips, 43 photos, and an 18,000-word hate-filled manifesto of his beliefs and complaints. After receiving the package two days later, NBC made copies for its own use and promptly turned over the multi-media diatribe to the FBI (*Chicago Tribune*, April 19, 2007, sec. 1, pp. 1, 10).

Quickly NBC, MSNBC, and, later, CNN broadcasted (and continually rebroadcasted) excerpts from the written document, some of the hate and profanity-filled video clips, and photos showing the killer brandishing two handguns, holding a gun to his head, and holding a knife to his throat. The multi-media materials seemed intended by the killer to depict himself as a victim of societal forces beyond his control and as a hero, even a martyr, for the downtrodden. Very soon, controversy arose in the public press about whether NBC (and other media) had acted responsibly and ethically in giving such prominence to the killer's self-serving material. (For a chronology of events, see *Newsweek*, April 30, 2007, pp. 22–29.)

Don Wycliff, a well-respected Chicago journalist, approved of NBC's decisions. No "secondhand account" could have captured the killer's "mental and emotional" mind-set "as well as his writing, those photographs, and that frightful, appalling videotape." NBC, he felt, was justified, even obligated, to broadcast the material. Wycliff concluded: "They did the right thing. They did what a good news organization is supposed to do: responsibly inform the people about matters of genuine public importance" (*Chicago Tribune*, April 22, 2007, sec. 2, p. 7).

In contrast, a number of writers of letters-to-the-editor in the *Chicago Tribune* (April 21, 2007, sec. 1, pp. 24–25; April 28, 2007, p. 29) represent the viewpoint that while NBC has the right to freedom of the press, in this case it was ethically irresponsible in the way it exercised that right. Here, in summary form, are just four of their arguments. First, NBC's airing of the killer's own material gave him exactly the widespread publicity he sought. Second, broadcasting the material could encourage others to emulate the killer. Third, NBC's coverage should have centered more on the victims' lives and the impact of their deaths on others. Fourth, NBC's coverage caused unnecessary trauma and pain for the relatives and friends of those massacred. One letter writer believed that NBC's irresponsible coverage "proves that ratings trump ethics." Another writer concluded: "Yes there is free speech in the United States, but along with that, the media have a responsibility to exercise good judgment in their reporting and maintain some sense of decorum."

Consider, now, your own viewpoint on the freedom versus responsibility tension as manifested in this case. From your own memory of network television coverage of the Virginia Tech shootings, to what degree were the national broadcast media, especially NBC, MSNBC, and CNN, acting ethically or irresponsibly in exercising their press freedom? Why?

As communicators, our ethical responsibilities may stem from a position or role we have earned or been granted, from commitments (promises, pledges, agreements) we have made, from established ethical principles, from relationships we have formed, or from consequences (effects, impacts) of our communication on others. Responsibility includes the elements of fulfilling duties and obligations, of being held accountable as evaluated by agreed-upon standards, and of being accountable to our own conscience. But an essential element of responsible communication, for both sender and receiver, is the exercise of thoughtful and caring judgment. That is, the responsible communicator reflectively analyzes claims, soundly assesses probable consequences, and conscientiously considers relevant values (both abstract principles and personal relationships). In a sense a responsible communicator is *response-able*. She or he exercises the ability to respond (is responsive) to the needs and communication of others in sensitive, thoughtful, fitting ways.[14]

Feminist philosopher Margaret Urban Walker provides an apt summary:

> We can be responsible for specific tasks or goals, roles with discretionary powers, acts and failures to act, outcomes and upshots of actions (not always controllable or foreseen), contributions to outcomes that are not ours alone, and attitudes, habits, and traits. Specific distributions of responsibility roughly map out this complex terrain of who must account, how far and for what, to whom.[15]

From time to time, however, we or others attempt to evade ethical responsibility or accountability by using one or more excuses such as: (1) I was just following orders; I was told to do it; (2) it was part of my job to do it; (3) everyone else is doing it; (4) what I did won't make any difference anyhow; (5) it's not my problem or my responsibility; or (6) nobody else knew about it.[16]

The concern for ethically responsible communication finds apt expression in the words of Dag Hammarskjöld, a former Secretary General of the United Nations:

> Respect for the word—to employ it with scrupulous care and an incorruptible heartfelt love of truth—is essential if there is to be any growth in a society or in the human race.
>
> To misuse the word is to show contempt for man. It undermines the bridges and poisons the wells. It causes Man to regress down the long path of his evolution.[17]

The Intentional and the Sincere

Whether communicators seem *intentionally* and *knowingly* to use particular content or techniques is a factor that most of us take into account in judging degree of communication ethicality. If a dubious communication behavior seems to stem more from accident, from an unintentional slip of the tongue, or even from ignorance, often we are less harsh in our ethical assessment. For most of us, it is the intentional use of ethically questionable tactics that merits our harshest condemnation. As an example, Nicholas Rescher believes that there is no moral or ethical issue when persons unintentionally or accidentally use unsound evidence or illogical reasoning. But he sees the intentional use of faulty reasoning as quite different. "Undoubtedly, the person who sets out *deliberately to deceive* others by means of improper reasoning is morally culpable."[18]

In contrast, it might be contended that in argumentative and persuasive situations, communicators have an ethical obligation to double-check the soundness of their evidence and reasoning before they present it to others; sloppy preparation is not an adequate excuse to lessen the harshness of our ethical judgment. A similar view might be advanced concerning elected or appointed government officials. If they use obscure or jargon-laden language that clouds the accurate and clear representation of ideas, even if that use is not intended to deceive or hide, they are ethically irresponsible. Such officials, according to this view, should be obligated to communicate clearly and accurately with citizens in fulfillment of their governmental duties.

In *Moralities of Everyday Life*, the authors note that usually "there is a close relationship between responsibility and intent—we are responsible for what we intend to do, what we are trying to do." Nevertheless they argue the position that "people are responsible for all that they cause so long as they can see that they cause it and can do otherwise. We may feel responsible only for what we intend; we are responsible for all that we do."[19]

As a related question we can ask, does *sincerity* of intent release a communicator from ethical responsibility concerning means and effects? Could we say that *if* Adolf Hitler's fellow Germans judged him to be sincere, they should not assess the ethics of his persuasion? In such cases, evaluations are probably best carried out if we appraise sincerity and ethicality separately. For example, a communicator sincere in intent may be found to utilize an unethical strategy. Or communication techniques generally considered ethical might be used by an insincere person. Wayne Booth reminds us that "sincerity is more difficult to check and easier to fake than logicality or consistency, and its presence does not, after all, guarantee very much about the speaker's case."[20] And Peter Drucker describes the different meanings of sincerity in Western and Eastern cultures. Westerners view sincerity as "words that are true to convictions and feelings" whereas people from Eastern cultures define sincerity as "actions that are appropriate to a specific relationship and make it harmonious and of optimum mutual benefit."[21]

Components of Morality and Integrity

The research program of James Rest and his colleagues on moral development suggests that moral action typically is the outcome of four complex and interrelated psychological processes.[22] They may occur in varying sequences and varying degrees of strength but all must be present in significant strength for the moral act to occur. *Moral sensitivity* involves interpreting the situation, recognizing it as one embodying ethical issues, using empathy and role-taking to understand how the act might affect all concerned, and imagining cause-effect sequences of events. *Moral judgment* involves deciding, after reflection and in light of relevant ethical standards, which act would be most morally justifiable. *Moral motivation* involves a degree of commitment to doing the moral act, preferring ethical standards when in conflict with other values (selfish gain, immediate self-satisfaction, etc.), and taking personal moral responsibility for consequences of the act. *Moral character* involves persistence, backbone, courage, toughness, energy, focus, and strength of conviction necessary for actually performing the behaviors necessary to accomplish the act. A person may possess the first three components in a situation, but if that person's character is weak rather than strong, the ethical act probably will not occur. Of course lack of sufficient strength for any one of the four components can result in moral failure in a situation.

In some senses, Rest's components leading to a moral act harmonize with the elements of "integrity" defined by Stephen Carter. For him, a person of integrity takes time and effort to deliberate about the right thing to do, actually does the right thing despite personal hardship, and is willing to explain what was done and to justify it.[23] Margaret Urban Walker elaborates her view of integrity as a "morally admirable quality."[24] She sees "integrity as a kind of *reliability*: reliability in the accounts we are prepared to give, act by, and stand by, in moral terms, and dependable responsiveness to the ongoing fit among our accounts, the ways we have acted, and the consequences and costs our actions have in fact incurred." Integrity as reliability, she believes, includes engaging in actions that are reasonably consistent and coherent ethically, providing sensible ethical justifications for these actions, keeping short-term and long-term promises, recognizing that sometimes we may be expected to account for consequences we did not control, and being willing to try to restore reliability after an action of dubious or failed ethicality.

Ethics and Personal Character

An emphasis on duties, obligations, rules, principles, and the resolution of complex ethical dilemmas has dominated the contemporary philosophy of ethics. This dominant emphasis has been true whether as variations on Immanuel Kant's Categorical Imperative, on John Rawls's depersonalized veil of ignorance to determine justice, on statements of intrinsic ultimate goods, or on Jeremy Bentham's or John Stuart Mill's utilitarian views. The past several decades, however, have witnessed a growing interest among ethicists in a largely ignored tradition that goes back at least as far as Plato's and Aristotle's philosophies of ethics. This largely bypassed tradition typically is called virtue ethics or character ethics. Most ethicists of virtue or character see that perspective as a crucial complement to the current dominant ethical theories. Ethicists describe virtues variously as deep-rooted dispositions, habits, skills, or traits of character that incline persons to perceive, feel, and act in ethically right and sensitive ways. Also, they describe virtues as learned, acquired, cultivated, reinforced, capable of modification, capable of conflicting, and ideally coalesced into a harmonious cluster.

Ethical communication is not simply a series of careful and reflective decisions, instance by instance, to communicate in ethically responsible ways. Deliberate application of ethical rules sometimes is not possible. Pressure may be so great or a deadline so near for a decision that there is not adequate time for careful deliberation. We may be unsure what ethical criteria are relevant or how they apply. The situation may seem so unique that applicable criteria do not readily come to mind. In such times of crisis or uncertainty, our decision concerning ethical communication stems less from deliberation than from our formed "character." Furthermore, our ethical character influences the terms with which we describe a situation and whether we believe the situation contains ethical implications.[25]

Consider the nature of moral character as described by ethicists Richard DeGeorge and Karen Lebacqz. According to DeGeorge:

> As human beings develop, they tend to adopt patterns of actions, and dispositions to act in certain ways. These dispositions, when viewed collectively, are sometimes called character. A person who habitually tends to act as he morally should has a good character. If he resists strong temptation, he has a strong character. If he habitually acts immorally, he has a morally bad character. If despite good intentions he frequently succumbs to temptation, he has a weak character. Because character is formed by conscious actions, in general people are morally responsible for their characters as well as for their individual actions.[26]

Lebacqz believes:

> Indeed, when we act, we not only *do* something, we also shape our own character. Our choices about what to do are also choices about whom to be. A single lie does not necessarily make us a liar; but a series of lies may. And so each choice about what to *do* is also a choice about whom to *be*—or, more accurately, whom to become.[27]

Ideally, according to Cunningham's interpretation of Aristotle's Doctrine of the Mean, a person of soundly formed moral character generally will, upon reflection, choose the right thing to do because it is right in the circumstances, not because it is right by avoiding excess or deficiency. The right thing to do turns out to be an intermediate or mean position somewhere between excess and deficiency. Right, as a virtue, is determined not in comparison to excess or deficiency; rather excess and deficiency as vices are determined in comparison to the right thing to do. For Aristotle, a person of sound moral character generally lives a life of right action in the realm of the mean rather than slipping into excess or deficiency.[28]

In Judeo-Christian or Western cultures, good moral character usually is associated with habitual embodiment of such virtues as courage, temperance, wisdom, justice, fairness, generosity gentleness, patience, truthfulness, and trustworthiness. Other cultures may praise additional or different virtues that they believe constitute good ethical character. Instilled in us as habitual dispositions to act, these virtues guide the ethics of our communication behavior when careful or clear deliberation is not possible.

When we evaluate a person's ethical character in light of a specific communication or action, there are five issues or dimensions that may aid us in reaching a judgment. These issues may apply in varying degrees to a wide variety of persons, such as family, friends, coworkers, business leaders, leaders of volunteer or social organizations, or elected and appointed government officials. That is, these issues apply to anyone in whom we place our trust and whom we assume to have certain responsibilities in their roles.

First, we consider the *citizen–politician issue*. Should the ethical standards we expect of politicians be the same or higher than those for the average citizen? Why? Second, the *private–public dimension* warrants consideration. Is the behavior that is ethically at issue relevant to the duties or responsibilities the person has in the public realm? Or is the behavior purely a personal and private matter and not appropriate for public examination? Third for consideration is the *past–present dimension*. Should we be most concerned about behavior in the recent past? Or should unethical behavior in the past also be of concern? How far past is past? Should we overlook a "youthful indiscretion" but worry more about unethical behavior of the mature person? Fourth, we must consider the *once–pattern issue*. Should we overlook a one-time unethical behavior ("we all make mistakes") while taking very seriously evidence of a pattern or habit of unethical behaviors? What if the one-time mistake is intentional rather than unintentional? Is evidence of a pattern of unethical behavior a sign of a serious character flaw, such as poor judgment or hypocrisy (such as saying one thing and doing the opposite)? Fifth, the *dimension of trivial–serious* must be evaluated. Is the unethical behavior trivial and minor or is it serious and significant? Should we make allowances for minor ethical mistakes but not make allowances for major, serious, clearly harmful ethical errors? A careful consideration of these five issues/dimensions may help us reach clearer and more precise judgments about a person's ethical character (even our own) when that character is in question because of unethical communication or action.

We explore implications of character ethics for communication in organizations later in chapter 9, and the role of virtue ethics and character in political communication is examined at length in an essay in the appendix.

Implied Ethical Contracts

There are some general unspoken assumptions, some implicit expectations, which seem to characterize most instances of public discourse.[29] The speaker or writer believes that a problem or need exists that can be solved or satisfied through communication with other persons. The communicator also believes that the subject is important to a number of persons whose aid can be sought and that the matter cannot be resolved by himself or herself alone. The subject is perceived as important enough to the communicator that she or he is willing to risk public evaluation, and both communicator and audience are assumed to be willing to open themselves to the possibilities to change—to altering their own views or actions. How should this implied general contract influence a communicator's and receiver's ethical judgments? More precisely, are there some relevant ethical guidelines imbedded in this implied contract? Might one be that dogmatic inflexibility is ethically suspect?

In most public and private communication, a fundamental implied and unspoken assumption is that words can be trusted and people will be truthful. Unless there are reasons to be skeptical, we expect people to mean what they say. Also, even if persons do not know the absolutely certain "ultimate truth" about something, we expect those persons to say what they believe to be true and not to say as true what they believe to be false. An observation by Jeffrey Olen concerning journalism applies equally well to human communication generally. We "don't ordinarily enter into explicit agreements to be truthful with one another. . . . The moral prohibition against lying provides, in effect, an implicit agreement, allowing us to expect the truth from one another." Philosopher Warren Shibles agrees: "Strictly speaking, we usually do not have a contract with people not to lie. It is just implied or assumed that we will not lie." Trust in some degree of truthfulness, argues, Sissela Bok in *Lying*, is a *"foundation* of relations among human beings." We must trust the words of others if we are to trust that they will treat us fairly, not harm us, and have our welfare at heart. "If there is no confidence in the truthfulness of others . . . how, then, can they be trusted?" Bok stresses: "*Whatever* matters to human beings, trust is the atmosphere in which it thrives."[30]

Beyond a general implied ethical contract, various types of communication settings, communicator roles, and each specific situation may have unspoken expectations that help define the ethical relationship between communicator and audience.[31] The phrases "information age" and "information society" have become commonplace. The book *Ethics of Information Management* explores ethical responsibilities for "information professionals" in key roles: information *givers* who provide information; information *orchestrators* who gather, process, store, and disseminate information and who also serve as information gatekeepers; and information *takers* who receive and use information. Furthermore, *stakeholders* are affected by the information-related actions of these professionals. The authors of this book describe an "unwritten agreement" among professionals in these roles:

> An implied covenant exists between the givers, takers, orchestrators, and stakeholders in an information society. Givers should provide valid information, orchestrators should handle it with fidelity, and takers should use it only for the purpose agreed on for its collection. All should conduct their activities in a way that helps rather than harms stakeholders.[32]

Now consider a hypothetical example reflective of role and situation. Imagine that you are an audience member listening to a speaker, call him Mr. Bronson, representing the American Cancer Society. His aim is to persuade you to contribute money to the research efforts sponsored by the American Cancer Society. Suppose that, with one exception, all of the evidence, reasoning, and motivational appeals he employs are valid and above ethical suspicion. But at one point in the speech Mr. Bronson *consciously* chooses to use a set of *false* statistics to scare the audience into believing that, during their lifetime, there is a much greater probability of their getting some form of cancer than there actually is.

To promote analysis of the ethics of this persuasive situation, consider these issues: If the audience, or society at large, views Mr. Bronson's persuasive end or goal as worthwhile, does the worth of his end justify his use of false statistics as a means to help achieve that end? Does the fact that he *consciously* chose to use false statistics make a difference in your evaluation? If he used the false statistics out of ignorance, or out of failure to check his sources, how might your ethical judgment be altered? Should he be condemned as an unethical *person*, as an unethical *speaker*, or as one who in this instance used a *specific* unethical technique?

Carefully consider the standards you would employ to make your ethical judgment. Are they purely pragmatic? In other words, should Mr. Bronson avoid false statistics because he might get caught? Are they societal in origin? If he gets caught, his credibility as a *representative* would be weakened with this and future audiences. Or his getting caught might weaken the credibility of *other* American Cancer Society representatives.

Should his communication ethics be criticized because he violated an implied agreement of trust and honesty between you and him? Your expectations concerning honesty, accuracy, and relevancy of information probably would be different for him as a representative of the American Cancer Society in contrast to the stereotypical used car dealer. You might not expect a representative of such a humanitarian society to use questionable techniques, and thus you would be especially vulnerable.

Approaches to Ethical Judgment

What ethical standards should be used by communicator and communicatee in judging choices among communicative techniques, contents, and purposes? What should be the ethical responsibilities of a communicator in contemporary society? Obviously, answers to these questions are ones we should face squarely. We should formulate meaningful ethical guidelines, not inflexible rules, for our communication behavior and for evaluating the communication of others.

The study of communication ethics should encompass both individual ethics and social ethics. What are the ethical virtues of character and the central ethical standards that should guide individual choices? What are the ethical standards and responsibilities that should guide the communication of organizations and institutions—public and private, corporate, governmental, or professional? For an ethically suspect communication practice, where should individual and collective responsibility be placed? The study of communication ethics should suggest standards both for individual, daily, and context-bound communication choices and also for institutional/systemic policies and practices.

One purpose of this book is to make us more discerning receivers and consumers of communication by encouraging ethical judgments of communication that are specifically focused and carefully considered. In making judgments of the ethics of our own communication and the communication to which we are exposed, our aim should be specific rather than vague assessments, and carefully considered rather than reflex-response, "gut level" reactions.

The following framework of questions is offered as a means of making more systematic and firmly grounded judgments of communication ethics.[33] At the same time we should bear in mind philosopher Stephen Toulmin's observation that "moral reasoning is so complex, and has to cover such a variety of types of situations, that no one logical test . . . can be expected to meet every case."[34] In underscoring the complexity of making ethical judgments, in *The Virtuous Journalist*, Klaidman and Beauchamp reject the "false premise that the world is a tidy place of truth and falsity, right and wrong, without the ragged edges of uncertainty and risk." Rather they argue: "Making moral judgments and handling moral dilemmas require the balancing of often ill-defined competing claims, usually in untidy circumstances."[35]

1. Can I *specify exactly* what ethical criteria, standards, or perspectives are being applied by me or others? What is the concrete grounding of the ethical judgment?

2. Can I justify the *reasonableness* and *relevancy* of these standards for this particular case? Why are these the most appropriate ethical criteria among the potential ones? Why do these take *priority* (at least temporarily) over other relevant ones?

3. Can I indicate clearly in what respects the communication being evaluated *succeeds or fails in measuring up* to the standards? What judgment is justified in this case about the *degree* of ethicality? Is the most appropriate judgment a specifically targeted and narrowly focused one rather than a broad, generalized, and encompassing one?

4. In this case to whom is *ethical responsibility owed*—to which individuals, groups, organizations, or professions? In what ways and to what extent? Which responsibilities take precedence over others? What is the communicator's responsibility to herself or himself and to society-at-large?

5. *How do I feel about myself* after this ethical choice? Can I continue to "live with myself" in good conscience? Would I want my parents or spouse to know of this choice? Would I feel ashamed of myself?

6. Can the ethicality of this communication be justified as a *coherent reflection of the communicator's personal character?* To what degree is the choice ethically "out of character"?

7. If called upon *in public to justify* the ethics of my communication, how adequately could I do so? What generally accepted reasons or rationale could I appropriately offer?

8. *Are there precedents or similar previous cases* to which I can turn for ethical guidance? Are there significant aspects of this instance that set it apart from all others?

9. How thoroughly have *alternatives been explored* before settling on this particular choice? Might this choice be less ethical than some of the workable but hastily rejected or ignored alternatives?

There are, of course, other possible frameworks for ethical decision making, some especially useful for journalism and the mass media.[36] In particular you are encouraged to read more extensively about one suggested by Rushworth Kidder, former reporter and editor for a national newspaper and founder of the Institute for Global Ethics. In paraphrased form, here are nine "checkpoints" that Kidder believes illuminate "the underlying structure of ethical decision making."[37] First, recognize there is a moral issue and of what it consists. Second, determine the moral agent or agents who have the responsibility for decision or action. What are their responsibilities? Third, carefully gather and consider the relevant facts of the situation. Fourth, determine if the ethical issue clearly is one of a choice between right and wrong, ethical or unethical. Fifth, determine if the ethical issue may be a choice between two competing ethical, good, or right things to do (such as truth versus loyalty, individual versus community, short-term versus long-term, justice versus mercy). Sixth, apply some resolution principles—such as utilitarianism, consequences, categorical rules, or caring—to reveal more clearly what is at stake in the situation. Seventh, if the issue seems to be a dilemma between two good or two bad options, diligently explore all possible alternatives to develop a more acceptable third option. Eighth, make a decision. Ninth, after the action is taken, evaluate the action again to learn possible lessons.

Also of interest is the TARES test proposed by Sherry Baker and David Martinson. They explain at length five principles to judge the ethics of professional persuasion, such as advertising, public relations, or promotional campaigns.[38] These are not absolute rules but are prima facie duties that generally hold true, all other things being equal. Occasionally principles may conflict in a particular situation and an ethical choice of priorities must be made. TARES is an acronym for the five principles summarized here: *Truthfulness* of the message (honesty, trustworthiness, nondeceptiveness). *Authenticity* of the persuader (genuineness, integrity, ethical character, appropriate loyalty). *Respect* for the persuadee (regard for dignity, rights, well-being). *Equity* of the content and execution of the appeal (fairness, justice, nonexploitation of vulnerability). *Social responsibility* for the common good (concern for the broad public interest and welfare more than simply selfish self-interest, profit, or career).

Forecast

Throughout this book we present a variety of starting points and materials to aid in analyzing ethics in human communication. Certainly they are not to be viewed as the "last word" on the subject or as the only possible ones. Rather they should stimulate our thinking and encourage reflective judgment.

In chapters 2 through 6 we explore seven perspectives for ethical assessment of human communication. Each perspective represents a major ethical viewpoint or conceptual "lens" that scholars intentionally, and others often unknowingly, use to analyze specific issues and instances. As categories, these perspectives are not mutually exclusive of each other and they are not in any priority. These perspectives should not be taken as exhaustive of possible stances; probably each of us could think of others. For each perspective, the essential elements—the sources of grounding—for that general perspective are briefly explained. Examples—versions—of each perspective are then analyzed. Versions simply are illustrative, not exhaustive.

In chapter 7, we explore some fundamental ethical issues and problems facing us individually and collectively as communicators. Chapters 8 and 9 discuss standards that have been suggested specifically for interpersonal communication, small group discussion, and communication in organizations. Chapter 10 discusses the pros and cons of formal codes of ethics, together with examples of formal codes from advertising, public relations, political communication, and journalism. Chapter 11 surveys some contributions to communication ethics from feminist theory, and chapter 12 examines ethical standards and issues in intercultural and multicultural communication. An appendix contains reprints of essays in which one or more of the ethical perspectives in this book are reflected or applied. A list of relevant video and Internet resources is provided. An extensive bibliography of Sources for Further Reading is categorized according to the chapters in the book, but it also contains special concluding sections on ethics in mass communication and on ethical character/virtue ethics.

Through examination of various perspectives, issues, problems, examples, and case studies, this book seeks to aid students and teachers of human communication. The goal is exploration of ethical responsibilities in contemporary communication—whether that communication is oral or written, whether it is labeled informative, persuasive, or rhetorical, whether it is labeled interpersonal, public, or mass.

Notes

[1] See, for example, Carl Wellman, *Morals and Ethics*, 2d ed. (Englewood Cliffs, NJ: Prentice-Hall, 1988), pp. xiii–xviii, 267.

[2] Charles Taylor, "The Dialogical Self," in *Rethinking Knowledge*, Robert F. Goodman and Walter R. Fisher, eds. (Albany: State University of New York Press, 1995), pp. 57–66.

[3] For one attempt to side-step ethical issues, see Theodore Levitt, "Are Advertising and Marketing Corrupting Society? It's Not Your Worry," *Advertising Age* (October 6, 1958): 89–92; a

rebuttal to this position is Clyde Bedell, "To the Extent Advertising and Marketing are Corrupting Society—You'd Better Worry!" *Advertising Age* (October 27, 1958): 101–102.

[4] Thomas R. Nilsen, *Ethics of Speech Communication*, 2d ed. (Indianapolis: Bobbs-Merrill, 1974), p. 15.

[5] David Maraniss, "The Comeback Kid's Last Return," *Washington Post National Weekly Edition*, September 2–8, 1996, pp. 8–9. For further discussion of the audience adaptation ethical issue, see Wayne C. Booth, *The Rhetoric of RHETORIC* (Malden, MA: Blackwell, 2004), pp. 50–54.

[6] This explanation of the Golden Mean is indebted to Clifford G. Christians et al., *Media Ethics: Cases and Moral Reasoning*, 6th ed. (New York: Addison Wesley Longman, 2001), pp. 12–13. Also see Aristotle, *Nicomachean Ethics*, in *The Basic Works of Aristotle*, ed. Richard McKeon (New York: Random House, 1941), pp. 952–964 (1103a–1109b).

[7] David Callahan, *The Cheating Culture: Why More Americans Are Doing Wrong to Get Ahead* (New York: Harcourt, 2004), pp. 12–14; Anita L. Allen, *The New Ethics: A Tour of the 21st-Century Moral Landscape* (New York: Miramax, 2004), p. xii.

[8] Odell in John C. Merrill and S. Jack Odell, *Philosophy and Journalism* (New York: Longman, 1983), pp. 2, 95.

[9] Wellman, *Morals and Ethics*, p. 305.

[10] See, for example: Thomas I. Emerson, *The System of Freedom of Expression* (New York: Random House, 1970); Franklyn S. Haiman, *Speech and Law in a Free Society* (Chicago: University of Chicago Press, 1981); Thomas L. Tedford and Dale Herbeck, *Freedom of Speech in the United States*, 5th ed. (State College, PA: Strata, 2004).

[11] Thomas Szasz, *The Theology of Medicine* (Baton Rouge: Louisiana State University Press, 1977), p. xiii. Also see J. Vernon Jensen, *Ethical Issues in the Communication Process* (Mahwah, NJ: Erlbaum, 1997), pp. 9–10.

[12] Stephen L. Carter, *Civility: Manners, Morals, and the Etiquette of Democracy* (New York: Basic Books, 1998), p. 207.

[13] Adapted from Alexander Meiklejohn, *Political Freedom* (New York: Harper & Brothers, 1948, 1960), pp. 73–74.

[14] This discussion of responsibility is based on: J. Roland Pennock, "The Problem of Responsibility," in *Nomos III, Responsibility*, Carl J. Friedrich, ed. (New York: Liberal Arts Press, 1960), pp. 3–27; Ludwig Freund, "Responsibility—Definitions, Distinctions, and Applications in Various Contexts," in Ibid., pp. 28–42; H. Richard Niebuhr, *The Responsible Self* (New York: Harper and Row, 1963), pp. 47–89, 151–154; Edmund L. Pincoffs, "On Being Responsible for What One Says," paper presented at Speech Communication Association convention, Houston, December 1975; Kurt Baier, "Responsibility and Freedom," in *Ethics and Society*, Richard T. DeGeorge, ed. (Garden City, NY: Anchor Books, 1966), pp. 49–84. Also see Michael S. Pritchard, *On Becoming Responsible* (Lawrence: University Press of Kansas, 1991); John Martin Fischer, "Recent Work on Moral Responsibility," *Ethics*, 110 (October 1999): 93–139.

[15] Margaret Urban Walker, *Moral Understandings: A Feminist Study in Ethics* (New York: Routledge, 1998), pp. 93–100, espec. 94.

[16] Thomas A. Bivins, "Responsibility and Accountability," in *Ethics in Public Relations: Responsible Advocacy*, Kathy Fitzpatrick and Carolyn Bronstein, eds. (Thousand Oaks, CA: Sage, 2006), pp. 31–35. Also see Tamera B. Murdock and Jason M. Stephens, "Is Cheating Wrong? Students' Reasoning about Academic Dishonesty," in *The Psychology of Academic Cheating*, Eric M. Anderman and Tamera B. Murdock, eds. (Burlington, MA: Elsevier Academic Press, 2007), pp. 229–251.

[17] Dag Hammarskjöld, *Markings* (New York: Alfred A. Knopf, 1964), p. 112.

[18] Nicholas Rescher, *Dialectics: A Controversy-Oriented Approach to the Theory of Knowledge* (Albany: State University of New York Press, 1977), pp. 78–82; also see Glen H. Stamp and Mark L. Knapp, "The Construct of Intent in Interpersonal Communication," *Quarterly Journal of Speech*, 76 (August 1990): 282–299.

[19] John Sabini and Maury Silver, *Moralities of Everyday Life* (New York: Oxford University Press, 1982), pp. 65–66.

[20] Wayne C. Booth, *Modern Dogma and the Rhetoric of Assent* (Notre Dame: University of Notre Dame Press, 1974); also see Arnold M. Ludwig, *The Importance of Lying* (Springfield, IL: Charles C. Thomas, 1965), p. 227.

21 Peter Drucker, *The Changing World of the Executive* (New York: Times Books, 1982), p. 249.

22 The following summary is paraphrased from James Rest et al., *Postconventional Moral Thinking* (Mahwah, NJ: Erlbaum, 1999), pp. 100–103; James Rest and Darcia Narvaez, eds., *Moral Development in the Professions* (Hillsdale, NJ: Erlbaum, 1994), pp. 22–25; James Rest, *Moral Development: Advances in Theory and Research* (New York: Praeger, 1986), pp. 3–18. Also see Rushworth M. Kidder, *Moral Courage* (New York: Wm. Morrow, 2005), pp. 7, 35–38, 72.

23 Carter, *Civility,* p. 274; Stephen L. Carter, *Integrity* (New York: Basic Books, 1996), pp. 7–12.

24 Walker, *Moral Understandings,* pp. 115–120.

25 Karen Lebacqz, *Professional Ethics* (Nashville: Abingdon Press, 1985), pp. 77–91; Steven Klaidman and Tom L. Beauchamp, *The Virtuous Journalist* (New York: Oxford University Press, 1987), pp. 17–20; Stanley Hauerwas, *Truthfulness and Tragedy* (Notre Dame: University of Notre Dame Press, 1977), pp. 20, 29.

26 DeGeorge, *Business Ethics,* 3rd ed. (New York: Macmillan, 1990), p. 94.

27 Lebacqz, *Professional Ethics,* p. 83.

28 Stanley B. Cunningham, "Getting It Right: Aristotle's 'Golden Mean' as Theory Deterioration," *Journal of Mass Media Ethics,* 14 (1999): 5–15. Also see W. D. Ross, *Aristotle: A Complete Exposition of His Works and Thought* (New York: Meridian Books, 1959), p. 191; J. O. Urmson, "Aristotle's Doctrine of the Mean," *American Philosophical Quarterly,* 10 (1973): 223–230, espec. 226; Aristotle, *Nicomachean Ethics,* at 1128a, 3–5.

29 Roderick P. Hart, Gustav W. Friedrich, and Barry Brummett, *Public Communication,* 2d ed. (New York: Harper and Row, 1983), pp. 13–15; Caroll Arnold, *Criticism of Oral Rhetoric* (Columbus, OH: Chas. E. Merrill, 1974), pp. 38–43.

30 Jeffrey Olen, *Ethics in Journalism* (Englewood Cliffs, NJ: Prentice-Hall, 1988), pp. 2–4; Warren Shibles, *Lying* (Whitewater, WI: Language Press, 1985), p. 145; Sissela Bok, *Lying* (New York: Vintage Books, 1979), pp. 32–33.

31 For elaboration of this viewpoint see Olen, *Ethics in Journalism,* pp. 4–31, 79–80, 101–102; B. J. Diggs, "Persuasion and Ethics," *Quarterly Journal of Speech,* 50 (December 1964), 359–373; Robert D. Murphy, *Mass Communication and Human Interaction* (Boston: Houghton Mifflin, 1977), pp. 81–104; Kathleen Hall Jamieson, *Dirty Politics* (New York: Oxford University Press, 1992), p. 59; James E. Porter, "The Role of Law, Politics, and Ethics in Corporate Composing: Toward a Practical Ethics for Professional Writing," in *Professional Communication,* Nancy R. Blyler and Charlotte Thralls, eds. (Newbury Park, CA: Sage, 1993), p. 134; Michael J. Cody and Richardson R. Lynn, *Honest Government: An Ethics Guide for Public Service* (Westport, CT: Praeger, 1992), p. 36.

32 Richard O. Mason, Florence M. Mason, and Mary Culnan, *Ethics of Information Management* (Thousand Oaks, CA: Sage, 1995), pp. xiv–xv, 28, 33.

33 For some of these questions I have freely adapted the discussions of H. Eugene Goodwin, *Groping for Ethics in Journalism,* 2d ed. (Ames: Iowa State University Press, 1987), pp. 14–15; Christians et al., *Media Ethics,* pp. 22–25.

34 Stephen Toulmin, *An Examination of the Place of Reason in Ethics* (England: Cambridge University Press, 1950), p. 148.

35 Klaidman and Beauchamp, *The Virtuous Journalist,* p. 20.

36 For example, see Clifford G. Christians et al., *Media Ethics: Cases and Moral Reasoning,* 7th ed. (New York: Pearson/Allyn & Bacon, 2005), pp.1–30; Larry Z. Leslie, *Mass Communication Ethics: Decision Making in Postmodern Culture,* 2nd ed. (Boston: Houghton Mifflin, 2004), chapter 12; Thomas Bivins, *Mixed Media: Moral Distinctions in Advertising, Public Relations, and Journalism* (Mahwah, NJ: Erlbaum, 2003), pp. 172–187.

37 Rushworth M. Kidder, *How Good People Make Tough Choices* (New York: Marrow, 1995), espec. pp. 180–186. Also see Sherry Baker, "Applying Kidder's Ethical Decision-Making Checklist to Mass Media Ethics," *Journal of Mass Media Ethics,* 12 (1997): 197–210.

38 Sherry Baker and David L. Martinson, "The TARES Test: Five Principles for Ethical Persuasion," *Journal of Mass Media Ethics,* 16 (2001): 148–175.

2

Political Perspectives

A political system (system of government) usually contains within its ideology an implicit and explicit set of values and procedures accepted as crucial to the health and growth of that governmental system. Once these essential political values are identified for a political system, they can be employed as criteria for evaluating the ethics of communicative means and ends within that particular system. The assumption is that communication should foster realization of these values and that communication techniques and tactics that retard, subvert, or circumvent these fundamental political values should be condemned as unethical.

As used here, the scope of the label "political perspective" ranges far beyond just the communication of presidents, politicians, political campaigns, or a particular political party. Any communication on public issues and public policy broadly defined, whether military, economic, social, or political, whether national, state, or local, could be assessed by one or more of the following political perspectives.

Naturally each different system of government could embody differing values leading to differing ethical judgments. Within the context of U.S. representative democracy, for instance, various analysts pinpoint values and procedures they view as fundamental to the optimum functioning of our political system and, thus, as values that can guide ethical scrutiny of communication therein. As we will see, among these values considered central to the optimum functioning of representative democracy are: the intrinsic dignity and worth of all persons; equal opportunity for fulfillment of individual potential; enhancement of citizen capacity to reach rational decisions; access to channels of public communication; access to relevant and accurate information on public issues; maximization of freedom of choice; toleration of dissent; honesty and clarity in presenting values relevant to problems and policies; honesty in presenting motivations and consequences; thoroughness, accuracy, and fairness in presenting evidence and alternatives; and recognition that the societal worth of an end or goal seldom should be the primary justification of the ethics of the means used to achieve that end.

21

Four Moralities

In proposing "An Ethical Basis of Communication," Karl Wallace develops a political perspective.[1] He isolates four values that he believes are basic to the welfare of our political system: respect, or belief in the dignity and worth of the individual; fairness, or belief in equality of opportunity; freedom coupled with responsible exercise of freedom; and belief in each person's ability to understand the nature of democracy. Citizens, to implement these values, should promote freedom of speech, press, and assembly, should encourage general diffusion of information necessary for decision making, and should ensure width and diversity of public channels of communication. Wallace outlines four "moralities" or ethical guidelines rooted in these democratic values. These are statements of communication behavior necessary to foster the values.

First, we should develop the *habit of search* stemming from recognition that during the moments we are communicating we are the primary, if not the sole, source of arguments and information on the subject at hand. Our message should reflect thorough knowledge of our subject, sensitivity to relevant issues and implications, awareness of essential and trustworthy opinions and facts, and awareness that most public issues are complex rather than one-sided. As an individual test for this ethical guideline we could ask ourselves: Can I answer squarely, without evasion, any relevant question a hearer or reader might ask?

Second, we should cultivate the *habit of justice* by selecting and presenting fact and opinion fairly. The communicator, according to Wallace, should not distort or conceal data that his or her audience would need in justly evaluating the argument. The communicator should avoid substituting emotionally loaded language and guilt-by-association for sound argument. As a personal test we can ask: In the selection and presentation of my materials, am I giving my audience the opportunity to make fair judgments?

Third, communicators should habitually *prefer public to private motivations.* Responsible public communicators should uniformly reveal the sources of their information and opinion. We should assist our audience in weighing any special bias, prejudices, and self-centered motivations inherent in source material. As the test question we can ask: Have I concealed information about either my source materials or my own motives that, if revealed, would damage my case?

Finally, Wallace urges us to cultivate the *habit of respect for dissent* by allowing and encouraging diversity of argument and opinion. A communicator will seek cooperation and compromise where appropriate and justified by conscience. But Wallace feels we should not "sacrifice principle to compromise," and we should "prefer facing conflict to accepting appeasement." He offers as a test question: Can I freely admit the force of opposing evidence and argument and still advocate a position that represents my convictions?

To aid our analysis of Wallace's ethical guidelines, we will suggest several questions: Where might points of ambiguity arise in application of these standards? To what extent are these four ethical standards actually observed by contemporary communicators, such as in political campaigns, advertisements, and public relations? Wallace's guidelines seem designed primarily for scrutiny of public communication, such as a public speech, newspaper editorials, or political advertisements. To what degree are these "moralities" also appropriate for ethical assessment of private, interpersonal communication, such as an interview, small group discussion, dormitory "bull session," or letter between friends? A good source to stimulate thought on this question is Ernest Bormann's examination of ethical implications of small group discussion in *Small Group Communication*. Bormann relies heavily on Wallace's insights and perspectives.[2]

Wallace also stresses consideration of both means and ends. He is concerned that we have exalted the end of success in communication over the means used to achieve it. Of special importance is his fear that communicators' lack of concern for use of ethical techniques and appeals may undermine confidence by breeding distrust and suspicion. To what degree should we believe that the fostering of public confidence in the truthfulness of public communication is a necessary goal for our society?

Degree of Rationality

Franklyn Haiman offers one version of a "degree of rationality" political perspective for judging communication ethics. The fundamental democratic value upon which he bases his approach is enhancement of the human capacity to reason logically. He believes a prime necessity for the adequate functioning of our political system is encouragement of this human rational capacity. The ethical standard advocated by Haiman is the degree of rationality, the degree of conscious free choice, reflected in and promoted by any specific communication technique or appeal.[3]

Condemned as unethical in Haiman's view (particularly in political campaigning, governmental communication, and advertising) are techniques that influence the receiver "by short-circuiting his conscious thought processes and planting suggestions or exerting pressures on the periphery of his consciousness which are intended to produce automatic, non-reflective behavior." Haiman sees these techniques as unethical communicative approaches that attempt to circumvent the human "mind and reason in order to elicit non-reflective, semi-conscious, or unconscious responses." What are some examples from contemporary politics and advertising that probably would fail Haiman's suggested test for ethical communication?

Along with some critics, Haiman suspects the ethics of motivational and emotional appeal as a persuasive technique. But unlike some, he carefully attempts to describe conditions under which such appeals may be considered ethical. As a guide, Haiman suggests that "there is no more effective way in the long run" to motivate a person than to help him or her consciously focus on emotions, needs, values, and desires, which are relevant to the issue at hand and "to show him, clearly and rationally, how he can best fulfill them." But as a basic principle he emphasizes "that to the extent that a persuader seeks to gain uncritical acceptance of his views, whatever extent that may be, he is in violation of democratic ideals." In later writings, Haiman modified his degree-of-rationality political perspective to take into account specific situational justifications for the ethical use of various techniques of the rhetoric of protest and confrontation.[4]

We can consider several questions related to a political perspective such as Haiman's. Should we believe that emotional appeals are inherently unethical or that they should be judged in the context of how and why they are used? Do all emotional appeals short-circuit human logical reasoning processes? How easy is it to label an appeal as either logical or emotional? How might logical and emotional appeals be intertwined in one argument?

Significant Choice

In his book, *Ethics of Speech Communication*, and in several essays, Thomas Nilsen propounds an essentially political perspective for judging communication ethics.[5] Values essential to the optimum functioning of U.S. democracy are the intrinsic worth of the human personality, reason as an instrument of individual and societal development, self-determination as the means to individual fulfillment, and human realization of individual potentialities. Necessary democratic procedures include unrestricted debate and discussion; varied forms of public address, parliamentary procedure, and legal procedure; freedom of inquiry, criticism, and choice; and publicly defined rules of evidence and tests of reasoning.

From this basis Nilsen develops ethical guidelines, not fixed criteria, for a view that he labels "significant choice." The ethical touchstone, he believes, should be "the degree of free, informed, and critical choice," which is fostered by communication on matters significant to us. Ethical communication techniques are those that foster significant choice.

> It is choice making that is voluntary, free from physical or mental coercion. It is choice based on the best information available when the decision must be made. It includes knowledge of various alternatives and the possible long- and short-term consequences of each. It includes awareness of the motivations of those who want to influence, the values they serve, the goals they seek. Voluntary choice also means an awareness of the forces operating within ourselves.[6]

In public discourse, where relationships are relatively impersonal and the issues public, the good is served by communications that preserve and strengthen the processes of democracy, that provide adequate information, diversity of views, and knowledge of alternative choices and their possible consequences. It is served by communications that provide significant debate, applying rational thought to controversial issues, recognizing at the same time the importance and relevance of feeling and personal commitment. Further, the good is served by communications that foster freedom of expression and constructive criticism, that set an example of quality in speech content, in language usage, and in fair play and civility.[7]

The ethical issues are whether the information presented is the most relevant available and is as complete as the particular circumstances make feasible. Further, since selection of material is inevitable, it must be made clear to the listeners what principles of selection are operating, what biases or special interests characterize the speaker, and what purposes are being served by the information given. Definitions must be adequate; statistical units must be defined and the assumptions underlying their use made explicit. The listeners must not be led to believe that they are getting a more complete and accurate picture than they really are. In addition, the subject must be placed in the proper perspective as far as its individual and social importance is concerned. In brief, the speaker must provide for the listener as adequate a grasp of the truth of the situation as is reasonably possible under the circumstances.[8]

In discussing the ethical demands for telling the truth, Nilsen develops a position he terms "the truth of the situation." As a basic assumption, he holds that the "truth of discourse" never is absolute and always is a matter of degree. In communication, the *truth* in some ultimate and absolute sense is not possible. Such an assumption seems similar to that of contemporary philosophers W. V. Quine and J. S. Ullian who urge our awareness "that we have less than the whole truth about even those matters we understand best. Such awareness can never be misplaced since 'the whole truth' about anything is but a fanciful ideal."[9]

"Although we can only reach an approximation of the truth," Nilsen contends, "this approximation should be as close as possible." For humans to communicate truthfully, some fundamental demands must be met: good intentions; ability to appraise evidence objectively and to employ rigorous reasoning; knowledge of facts, values, purposes and feelings; and, most important, exercise of disinterested good will.[10]

Every utterance expresses a part of a vastly larger whole of possible meaning. What is relevant from the larger whole of meaning depends upon several things: the needs, desires, and expectations of the auditors; the purposes and value assumptions of both speaker and listeners; the attitudes, needs, and values of the larger community of which the speaker and listeners are a part; the alternatives open; the possible consequences of the various alternatives and the relationship of these consequences to the values of those concerned."[11]

If a speaker is to tell the truth, he must attempt to arouse in the mind of his listeners as clear, accurate, and complete a picture or conception of his subject as possible. Since he cannot say all there is to say about it, he must select certain parts or aspects to describe, the aspects must be those which are relevant for the listeners—that is, those which will provide the information needed for informed and constructive response. Moreover, since purposes, values, and feelings have much to do with the meanings the speaker intends and the listeners receive, the speaker must make clear his own values, purposes, and feelings, and adapt his discourse to compensate for the influence that the listeners' values and feelings will have on the meanings they discern in the words used. Again, the truth that needs to be told is determined by what the listeners need to know and feel in order to make the most informed, constructive response. At the level of human interaction truth and values are intertwined. The truth of discourse refers, not simply to empirically verifiable statements, but to a complex pattern of meanings relating a listener to some part of the world he experiences.[12]

Kathleen Hall Jamieson employs a type of significant-choice political perspective in her book, *Dirty Politics: Deception, Distraction, and Democracy* (1992). In her chapter on argument, engagement, and accountability in political discourse, she posits two preconditions for citizens to make adequate ethical judgments about political communication: "the time to consider options and with it the ability of a conscious agent to grant informed consent." She believes: "In two centuries of political speech we have developed norms for appropriate discourse and additionally some sense of the ideal to which it should aspire." Ethical political argument, Jamieson contends, should allow differing sides to be heard, should be scrutinized for accuracy, relevance, and fairness of evidence, should not distort evidence from its context, should allow a right of reply for persons attacked, should grant the integrity and goodwill of opponents, should assume that advocates must take responsibility for their claims, should avoid name-calling, guilt by association, and other personalized attacks, and should strive toward consensus as much as possible. In a later book, *Everything You Think You Know About Politics... and Why You're Wrong* (2000), Jamieson expands on these norms of responsibility in public discourse. She also elaborates on "civility" as a desirable standard for most types of public communication.[13]

Ground Rules for Political Controversy

Sidney Hook presents a framework for evaluating the ethics of public communication on societal controversies, including political campaign persuasion and the rhetoric of protest.[14] Rooted in the values of our democratic society, his political perspective condemns as unethical communication techniques that "tend to poison instead of refreshen" the life blood of that system. Such techniques, Hook feels, characteristically aim, not at establishing the truth or making a case, but merely at discrediting persons. He questions the ethics of communication tactics that suppress relevant evidence, foster refusal to listen to opposing views, and fanatically make the holding of a particular idea synonymous with patriotism.

What might be an instance where a method questioned by Hook would be ethically justifiable? What might be an example where the issue is the qualifications and competency of a person? What might be conditions under which it would be ethical to suppress relevant evidence?

Hook elaborates ten "ground rules" or ethical guidelines for scrutinizing communication on controversial public issues. In abbreviated form they are as follows:

1. Nothing and no one is immune from criticism.

2. Anyone involved in a controversy has an intellectual responsibility to inform himself of the available facts.

3. Criticism should be directed first at policies, and against persons only when they are responsible for policies, and against their motives or against their purposes only when there is some independent evidence of their character, not derived from the consequences of their policies.

4. Because certain words are legally permissible, they are not therefore morally permissible.

5. Before impugning an opponent's motives, even when they legitimately may be impugned, answer his arguments.

6. Do not treat an opponent of a policy as if he were therefore a personal enemy of the country or a concealed enemy of democracy.

7. Since a good cause may be defended by bad arguments, after answering those bad or invalid arguments, present positive evidence in behalf of your own position, or for your own alternatives.

8. Do not hesitate to admit lack of knowledge or to suspend judgment if the evidence is not decisive either way.

9. Only in pure logic and mathematics and not in human affairs can you demonstrate that something is impossible. Because something is logically possible, it is not therefore probable. The phrase "it is not impossible" really is a preface to an irrelevant statement about human affairs. In human affairs, especially in politics, the question always is one of the balance of probabilities. The evidence of probabilities must include more than abstract possibilities.

10. When we are looking for truth of fact or wisdom of policy, the cardinal sin is refusal to discuss, or the taking of action that blocks discussion, especially when it takes the form of violence.

Consider the following questions as aids in your assessment of Hook's ground rules. In what ways do you agree or disagree with his suggested standards? To what extent, for example, should the axiom "nothing and no one is immune from criticism" apply to criticism of a president's foreign policy in time of declared war? What ethical justification, if any, might there be for communication techniques that block discussion?

Hook urges that ethical standards for judging societal controversy be enforced not by law but by voluntary self-discipline. To what degree do you feel that the ethics of public communication can or should be enforced by law? Examine the adequacy and/or necessity of such legal enforcement of ethics as regulations governing advertising set by the Federal Trade Commission and the Federal Communications Commission.

A Synthesis of Textbook Standards

Traditional American textbook discussions of the ethics of persuasion, communication, and argument often include lists of standards suggested for evaluating the ethicality of an instance of persuasion. Such criteria sometimes are rooted, implicitly if not explicitly, in what we earlier in this chapter described as a type of political perspective. That is, the criteria stem from a commitment to values and procedures deemed essential to the health and growth of the U.S. political governmental system of representative democracy.

What follows is our synthesis and adaptation of a number of such typical traditional lists of ethical criteria for persuasion.[15] Within the context of our own society, the following criteria are not necessarily the only or best ones possible; they are suggested as general guidelines rather than inflexible rules; and they may stimulate discussion on the complexity of judging the ethics of communication. Consider, for example, under what circumstances there may be justifiable exceptions to some of these criteria. How might other cultures and other governmental systems embrace basic values that lead to quite different standards for communication ethics? Also bear in mind that one difficulty in applying these criteria in concrete situations stems from different standards and meanings people may have for such key terms as: distort, falsify, rational, reasonable, conceal, misrepresent, irrelevant, and deceive.

1. Do not use false, fabricated, misrepresented, distorted, or irrelevant evidence to support arguments or claims.

2. Do not intentionally use unsupported, misleading, or illogical reasoning.

3. Do not represent yourself as informed or as an "expert" on a subject when you are not.

4. Do not use irrelevant appeals to divert attention or scrutiny from the issue at hand. Among the appeals that commonly serve such a purpose are: "smear" attacks on an opponent's character; appeals to hatred and bigotry; derogatory insinuations—innuendos; God and Devil terms that cause intense but unreflective positive or negative reactions.

5. Do not ask your audience to link your idea or proposal to emotion-laden values, motives, or goals to which it actually is not related.

6. Do not deceive your audience by concealing your real purpose, by concealing self-interest, by concealing the group you represent, or by concealing your position as an advocate of a viewpoint.

7. Do not distort, hide, or misrepresent the number, scope, intensity, or undesirable features of consequences or effects.

8. Do not use "emotional appeals" that lack a supporting basis of evidence or reasoning, or that would not be accepted if the audience had time and opportunity to examine the subject themselves.

9. Do not oversimplify complex, gradation-laden situations into simplistic two-valued, either-or, polar views or choices.

10. Do not pretend certainty where tentativeness and degrees of probability would be more accurate.

11. Do not advocate something in which you do not believe yourself.

Public Confidence in
Truthfulness of Public Communication

Whether public communication takes the form of messages from government to governed, political candidate to voter, news media to citizen, or advertiser to consumer, at least a minimal degree of mutual confidence and trust is desirable. Yet now we witness a crisis in public confidence in truthfulness of public communication. By truthfulness as used here we do not mean an ultimate, absolutely certain truth. We are speaking of public confidence in reliable information in the form of accurate data and highly probable conclusions. Such public confidence generally is viewed as a value or goal integral to the optimum functioning of U.S. representative democracy, but it is a goal being less and less attained.

Democratic decision making through vigorous public debate and responsible functioning of our economic system assume maximum access to accurate and trustworthy information. Strong democratic processes, for example, are rooted in adequacy of information, diversity of viewpoints, and knowledge of potential strengths, weaknesses, and effects of alternative choices. These requisites for responsible communication in our political system have been stressed by several of the "political perspectives" already examined.

Weakening of public trust in communication from the government, political candidates, news media, and advertisers is evident. Citizens today complain more and more of "managed news" and a "credibility gap" in communication from the federal government. Statements made by the federal government as factual and dependable on one occasion have a way of becoming "inoperative" on a later occasion. Citizens tend to dismiss as untrue, without analysis, much governmental communication. During political campaigns voters also dismiss many speeches and political advertisements, often characterized by gross hyperbole, as "mere campaign oratory." They have so little confidence in campaign persuasion that they feel a substantial portion of it is not worthy of careful scrutiny.

What are some of the actual and potential consequences flowing from weakened public confidence in truthfulness of public communication? Sincere human communication is thwarted and democratic decision-making processes are hampered. Alienation from the "system" and polarization of attitudes increase. Distrust and suspicion poison a widening variety of human communication relationships.

We should combat the growing assumption, by us or by others, that most public communication *inherently* is untrustworthy. Just because a communication is of a certain type or comes from a certain source (government, political candidate, news media, advertiser), it must not be rejected *automatically, without evaluation*, as tainted or untruthful. But we are *not* saying that we should believe everything we read or hear. Analysis and evaluation are our central concern.

Clearly, always we should exercise caution in acceptance and care in evaluation. Using the best evidence available to us, we should reach a reflective judgment of a message. But to condemn a message as untruthful *solely because* it stems from a suspect source and *before directly* assessing it is to exhibit decision-making behavior detrimental to our political system. Rejection of the message, if such be our judgment, should come *after*, not *before*, our understanding and evaluation of it. As with a defendant in a courtroom, an instance of public communication should be presumed ethically innocent until we, or experts we acknowledge, have proven it guilty.

Other Political Systems

Other political systems to some extent espouse fundamental values differing from those central to representative democracy. Thus, they may present different frames of reference for assessing the ethics of communication within that system and may view as ethical techniques that we judge unethical.

In Germany, under Hitler's Nazi influence, the ends of national survival and National Socialism justified any persuasive means.[16] The soundness of political persuasion was measured, not by objective truth, but solely by effectiveness of results. Nazi persuasion frequently reflected either/or oversimplification, inconsistency, questionable premises, faulty analogies, innuendo, and appeals to power, fear, and hate. Joseph Goebbels, the Minister of Propaganda, felt that lies were useful when they could not be disproved and that the source of propaganda should be concealed when revelation might risk failure. Hitler's own oratory, not bounded by logic, plausibility or accuracy, reveals lies, slander, verbal smokescreens to conceal intent, and scapegoat counterattacks. Immediately we recognize that some of these communication tactics characterize public discourse on the contemporary American political scene. These tactics are not generally accepted as ethical in the context of our political values.

Communism in the former Union of Soviet Socialist Republics (USSR) espoused values that gave a special ethical slant to communication techniques and purposes within Soviet society.[17] Values propagated include supreme love of nation, trust in the Party, hatred toward enemies specified by the Party, and promotion of class strife. A communicator need not be impartial and display an objective concern for events. The person may, for example, define terms to suit his or her purposes rather than the facts, and he or she may introduce spurious or irrelevant issues. In the Soviet communist perspective, words were tools to achieve Party approved ends, not means to communicate in the search for truth. Communist ethical standards for judging communication flowed from and were subordinated to the interest of the class struggle as formulated by the Party.

Some Twenty-First Century Proposals

As the Twenty-First Century began, scholars of communication and political theory continued to explore ethical standards for communication on public issues and public policy very broadly defined. In other words, they continued to discuss the ethics of public discourse. Often they identified again the central values mentioned at the start of this chapter as crucial to the health and growth of American representative democracy. Then they identified guidelines for ethically responsible public communication that would foster those values. We will summarize a few of the suggestions made by several of these scholars.

In "Seven Characteristics of the 'Ethical' Communicator," Robert White argues that the ethical public communicator promotes freedom of expression, demands public communication outlets open to all viewpoints, takes the initiative in speaking out on public issues, and encourages citizen participation in public decision making. The ethical public communicator places the collective common good of the community or nation above selfish private personal interests. And such a communicator seeks the "truth" defined to include accurate factual statements, values that *should* be followed rather than those that happen to be popular, wisdom that has endured across cultures and centuries, and "consensus which emerges out of a moment of profound intercultural dialogue in which *all* moral claims—including the oppressed and the marginal—are heard and discussed."[18]

Mortimer Sellers identifies civility, sincerity, community, and toleration as values crucial for optimum functioning of representative democracy in our republic. Sellers terms them "ideals of public discourse" and describes ethical communication that promotes them.[19] *Civility* "requires listening to the arguments made by others in public discussion, trying to understand them, and responding as if they were made in good faith by making reasoned responses even to incoherent or transparently self-interested views." Civility "does not mean that all perceptions and insights are equally valid, but that all equally deserve to undergo the test of sincere public discourse." *Sincere* discourse is truly committed to the common good of the persons affected. Sincerity "entails listening to and considering the observations of others, without necessarily endorsing them." Also, insincere discourse deprives decision makers of the honest information they need to make wise choices. *Community* requires public consideration of views of all members of the community. Persons in positions of power must genuinely consider the views of people they govern or control. *Toleration* includes overlooking those violations of the ideals of public discourse that are minimally harmful to public communication. Toleration involves ignoring trivial or minor intolerances held by others so that a workable degree of public discourse can continue. But persons in positions of power who violate the values of civility, sincerity, and community in their discourse should not be tolerated by less powerful communicators. Those less powerful should respond with public outrage and condemnation.

In the context of a democracy where widespread and wise public deliberation on public issues are essential to its optimum functioning, David Rife suggests some principles of "good" public discourse.[20] By "good" he seems to mean both effective and ethical. *Grounded rationality* involves discourse that not only proposes claims with supporting evidence but also is rooted in concrete human relationships and experiences and also is sensitive to the role of emotion in establishing relationships. *Reflexivity* requires "constant reflection" on a proposition's or argument's basic values, terms, and assumptions to see if they are clear and still acceptable in the current instance. Also, procedures within our public policy institutions should actively promote such constant re-examination. *Reciprocity* means that "individuals actively engage with rather than simply tolerate the views of others. Unlike respect, which requires an active appreciation of alternative views, reciprocity merely guarantees that individuals will concede the existence of those views, and commit to engage with them." *Radical differences* means that persons should have the right to speak in the voice of any or all of the many and varied groups to which they belong, whether racial, religious, sexual, generational, occupational, or others. *Moderation* requires that communicators acknowledge the limitations of their claims and the fact that their personal experiences may not always be generalizable to the situations of other people.

What are your reactions to these proposals for the century ahead? How do they differ from the four moralities, degree of rationality, and significant choice approaches discussed at the beginning of this chapter? How do the ethical guidelines in these proposals either supplement or challenge ethical standards in the earlier approaches? Are there any ethical guidelines in the proposals with which you disagree? Why?

Notes

[1] Karl R. Wallace, "An Ethical Basis of Communication," *The Speech Teacher*, 4 (January 1955): 1–9.

[2] Ernest G. Bormann, *Small Group Communication: Theory and Practice*, 3rd ed. (New York: Harper and Row, 1990), chapter 11.

[3] Franklyn S. Haiman develops his "degree of rationality" political perspective in two sources: "Democratic Ethics and the Hidden Persuaders," *Quarterly Journal of Speech*, 44 (December 1958): 385–392; "A Re-Examination of the Ethics of Persuasion," *Central States Speech Journal*, 3 (March 1952): 4–9.

[4] Franklyn S. Haiman, "The Rhetoric of the Streets: Some Legal and Ethical Considerations," *Quarterly Journal of Speech*, 52 (April 1967): 99–114. "The Rhetoric of 1968: A Farewell to Rational Discourse," reprinted in Richard L. Johannesen, *Ethics in Human Communication*, 2nd ed. (Long Grove, IL: Waveland Press, 1983), pp. 177–197.

[5] Thomas R. Nilsen's viewpoint of "significant choice" is elaborated in his *Ethics of Speech Communication*, 2nd ed. (Indianapolis: Bobbs-Merrill, 1974); "Free Speech, Persuasion and the Democratic Process," *Quarterly Journal of Speech*, 44 (October 1958): 235–243; "Ethics and Argument," in *Perspectives on Argument*, Gerald R. Miller and Thomas R. Nilsen, eds. (Chicago: Scott, Foresman, 1966), pp. 176–197; "The Ethics of Persuasion and the Marketplace of Ideas Concept," in *The Ethics of Controversy: Politics and Protest*, Donn W. Parson and Wil Linkugel, eds. (Lawrence, KS: The House of Usher, 1968), pp. 7–49. For an application of Nilsen's "significant choice" view, see Ralph E. Dowling and Gabrielle Grinder, "An Ethical Appraisal of Ronald Reagan's Justification for the Invasion of Granada," in *Warranting Assent*, Edward Schiappa, ed. (Albany: State University of New York Press, 1995), pp. 103–124.

[6] Nilsen, *Ethics of Speech Communication*, p. 45.

[7] Ibid., p. 18.

[8] Ibid., p. 72.

[9] W. V. Quine and J. S. Ullian, *The Web of Belief* (New York: Random House, 1970), p. 90.

[10] Nilsen, *Ethics of Speech Communication*, ch. 2.

[11] Ibid., p. 34.

[12] Ibid., p. 27.

[13] Kathleen Hall Jamieson, *Dirty Politics: Deception, Distraction, and Democracy* (New York: Oxford University Press, 1992), pp. 203–236. Also see Kathleen Hall Jamieson, *Everything You Think You Know About Politics . . . and Why You're Wrong* (New York: Basic Books, 2000), pp. 55–69.

[14] Sidney Hook, "The Ethics of Political Controversy," in *The Ethics of Controversy*, Parson and Linkugel, eds., pp. 50–71. For a much briefer earlier version see Hook, "The Ethics of Controversy," *The New Leader* (February 1, 1954), pp. 12–14. This 1954 version is reprinted in *Hook, Philosophy and Public Policy* (Carbondale: Southern Illinois University Press, 1980), pp. 117–123.

[15] For example, see: E. Christian Buehler and Wil A. Linkugel, *Speech Communication for the Contemporary Student*, 3rd ed. (New York: Harper and Row, 1975), pp. 30–36; Robert T. Oliver, *The Psychology of Persuasive Speech*, 2nd ed. (New York: Longmans, Green, 1957), pp. 20–34; Wayne Minnick, *The Art of Persuasion*, 2nd ed. (Boston: Houghton Mifflin, 1968), pp. 278–287; Henry Ewbank and J. Jeffery Auer, *Discussion and Debate*, 2nd ed. (New York: Appleton-Century-Crofts, 1951), pp. 255–258; Bert E. Bradley, *Fundamentals of Speech Communication*, 5th ed. (Dubuque, IA: William C. Brown Co., 1988), pp. 23–31; Robert C. Jeffrey and Owen Peterson, *Speech: A Text With Adapted Readings*, 3rd ed. (New York: Harper and Row, 1980), ch. 1.

[16] Adolf Hitler, *Mein Kampf*, trans. Ralph Manheim (Boston: Houghton Mifflin, 1943), pp. 80–81, 106–107, 177–179, 231–232, 342; Z. A. B. Zeman, *Nazi Propaganda* (London: Oxford University Press, 1964), pp. 25–26, 37, 86; Ernest K. Bramstead, *Goebbels and National Socialist Propaganda* (East Lansing: Michigan State University Press, 1965), pp. 56, 174, 193–195, 455–457; Ross Scanlan, "Adolf Hitler and the Technique of Mass Brainwashing," in *The Rhetorical Idiom*, Donald Bryant, ed. (Ithaca, NY: Cornell University Press, 1958), pp. 201–220; Haig

Bosmajian, "Nazi Persuasion and the Crowd Mentality," *Western Speech*, 29 (Spring 1965): 68–78; Leonard W. Doob, "Goebbels' Principles of Propaganda," *Public Opinion Quarterly*, 14 (1950): 419–442; Adolf Hitler, *My New Order*, ed. with commentary by Raoul de Roussy de Sales (New York: Reynal and Hitchcock, 1941), pp. xiv, 7–9.

[17] Jack H. Butler, "Russian Rhetoric: A Discipline Manipulated by Communism," *Quarterly Journal of Speech*, 50 (October 1964): 229–239; Robert T. Oliver, *Culture and Communication* (Springfield, IL: Charles C. Thomas, 1962), pp. 88, 104; Alex Inkeles, *Public Opinion in Soviet Russia: A Study In Mass Persuasion* (Cambridge: Harvard University Press, 1962), pp. 6, 22–25, 123, 317–320, 325–327, 337–338; Stefan Possony, *Wordsmanship: Semantics as a Communist Weapon* (Washington, DC: U.S. Government Printing Office, 1961), pp. 2, 14–15; Ithiel de Sola Pool, "Communication in Totalitarian Societies," in Pool et al., eds., *Handbook of Communication* (Chicago: Rand-McNally, 1973), pp. 466–468; Paul Kecskemeti, "Propaganda," in *Handbook of Communication*, pp. 849–850; V. M. Tepljuk, "The Soviet Union: Professional Responsibility in Mass Media," in *Communication Ethics and Global Change*, Thomas W. Cooper et al., eds. (New York: Longman, 1989), pp. 109–123. Also see Richard DeGeorge, *Soviet Ethics and Morality* (Ann Arbor: University of Michigan Press, 1969).

[18] Robert A. White, "The Seven Characteristics of the 'Ethical' Public Communicator: Protecting the Quality of Democratic Communication," in *Media Ethics*, Bart Pattyn, ed. (Leuven, Belgium: Peeters, 2000), pp. 283–304.

[19] Mortimer Sellers, "The Ideals of Public Discourse," in *Civility and Its Discontents*, Christine T. Sistare, ed. (Lawrence: University Press of Kansas, 2004). Also see Ronald C. Arnett and Pat Arneson, *Dialogic Civility in a Cynical Age* (Albany: State University of New York Press, 1999), pp. 12, 77, 279–304.

[20] David M. Ryfe, "The Principles of Public Discourse: What Is Good Public Discourse?" in *Public Discourse in America: Conversation and Community in the Twenty-First Century*, Judith Rodin and Stephen P. Steinberg, eds. (Philadelphia: University of Pennsylvania Press, 2003), pp. 163–177. Also see James F. Klumpp, "Freedom and Responsibility in Constructing Public Life: Toward a Revised Ethic of Discourse," *Argumentation*, 11 (February 1997): 113–130. For an application of a representative democracy political perspective, see Richard L. Johannesen, "An Ethical Assessment of the Reagan Rhetoric: 1981–1982," in *Political Communication Yearbook 1984* (Carbondale: Southern Illinois University Press, 1985), pp. 226–241, reprinted in Johannesen, *Ethics in Human Communication*, 5th ed. (Long Grove, IL: Waveland Press, 2002), pp. 250–267.

Human Nature Perspectives

Human nature perspectives, as considered here, focus on the essence of human nature. Answers are sought to the question: What makes a human essentially human? Unique characteristics of human nature that set humans apart from animals are identified. Such characteristics then can be employed as standards for judging the ethics of human communication. The assumption is that uniquely human attributes should be enhanced, thereby promoting fulfillment of maximum individual potential. A determination could be made of the degree to which a communicator's appeals and techniques either foster or undermine the development of a fundamental human characteristic. In light of such criteria, a technique that *de*humanizes, makes a person less than human, is unethical.

Any particular characteristically human attribute could be used in a largely absolute way to assess the ethics of communication regardless of situation, culture, religion, or governmental form. In taking such an absolutist view it could be argued that a human is essentially human no matter the context. Wherever found, a person might be assumed to possess the uniquely human attribute(s) worthy of nurture. Christopher Lyle Johnstone observes that a difficulty in most human nature "approaches to communication ethics is that they are inclined to concentrate upon only one aspect of human nature (e.g. reason, symbolism, persuadability, etc.) at the expense of other equally essential aspects (e.g. imagination, the capacity for humor, curiosity, etc.)."[1]

Skepticism concerning the use of human nature as a basis for ethical norms comes from philosophers Kai Nielsen and Richard Bernstein. Nielsen contends: "Even if we were to find certain characteristics that all humans, and only humans, possess, this of itself would not establish anything of a normative nature; it would not follow that it would be a good thing to have that yearning satisfied. We often 'yearn' for what is not good. . . . It may be that we ought to try to develop potentialities not yet distinctive of the human animal." Bernstein observes: "Philosophers, scientists, and theologians radically disagree whether there is such a thing as human nature, about what constitutes human nature, and about the relevance of claims about human nature for explaining or grounding morality."[2]

Human Rational Capacity

Aristotle's view of human nature, as interpreted and applied by Lawrence Flynn, provides one perspective for evaluating the ethics of communication.[3] Aristotle, according to Flynn, emphasized the capacity for reason as a uniquely human attribute. (Note that the stress on reason here is related more to human nature than to the values central to any particular political system, such as in Haiman's "degree of rationality" approach examined in chapter 2.) A truly human act, from Aristotle's viewpoint, stems from a rational person who is conscious of what he or she does and freely chooses to do it. The ethics of communication are judged by the interrelated criteria of (1) communicator intent, (2) nature of the means employed, and (3) accompanying circumstances, as these three factors combine to enhance or undermine human rationality and choice-making ability. While Aristotle apparently held some human actions to be unethical inherently, other human behaviors depend for their ethicality on the above mentioned criteria. But Aristotle did reject the notion that the end justifies the means when the means is unethical. Thus, a worthy end or intent would not justify the use of unethical communicative means.

A more recent interpretation of Aristotle's ethical standards for rhetoric is provided by Robert Rowland and Deanna Womack.[4] Their analysis of Aristotle's *Rhetoric, Nicomachean Ethics,* and *Politics* leads them to refute as partial and oversimplified the view that Aristotle advocated the use of rational appeals only and condemned as unethical any use of emotional or nonlogical appeals. Also they question the interpretation that claims Aristotle took a stance wherein achievement of effect is paramount and any emotional appeals that might promote success are approved.

According to Rowland and Womack, Aristotle did assume that the capacity for rationality is a defining characteristic of humans and thus a necessary part of rhetoric, but Aristotle also recognized the emotional nature of humans and believed that emotional appeal is necessary to motivate humans to good actions. Logic by itself normally will not energize people to act. Emotional appeal by itself risks becoming extreme in intensity, thus undercutting the role of reason. Especially ethically suspect are appeals to our "vegetative appetites" such as sex and food. In contrast, other emotions, such as fear or anger, involve cognitive, reflective, responses to situations and thus are more susceptible to the influence of reason. Both reason and emotion can be used unethically. Deceptive practices, whether logical or emotional, are unethical for Aristotle because, in Rowland and Womack's words, "reason cannot function without accurate information."

As an art or theory of discovering all available means of persuasion for a given situation, rhetoric is morally neutral in Aristotle's view, but as application or practice, rhetoric becomes in varying degrees either ethical or unethical. In Rowland and Womack's interpretation of Aristotle, ethical rhetoric as practice represents a mean between the extremes of pure logic on the one hand and of irrational appeals to our animal instincts, to nonreflective emotional states, or to harmful passions on the other hand. Their interpretation would seem to point toward an Aristotelian ethic for rhetoric summarized as follows: The sound, relevant, integrated use of both reason and emotion in the service of practical wisdom and the general public good.

Thomas Garrett argues that a person becomes more truly human in proportion to his or her behavior becoming more conscious and reflective.[5] Because of the human capacity for reason and because of the equally distinctive fact of human dependence on other people for development of potential, Garrett suggests there are several ethical obligations for advertisers. As humans we are obliged, among other things, to behave rationally ourselves, to help others behave rationally, and to provide truthful information. Suggestive advertising, in Garrett's view, is that which seeks to bypass human powers of reason or to some degree render them inoperative. Such advertising is unethical not just because it uses emotional appeal, feels Garrett, but because it demeans a fundamental human attribute and makes people less than human.

Should perspectives stressing human rational capacity be applied in judging the ethics of advertising and public relations? Why or why not? What are some examples of advertisements or sales approaches that clearly seem to be ethical (or unethical) when evaluated by this perspective?

Human Symbol-Using Capacity

In a tentative, probing spirit, Henry Wieman and Otis Walter offer another human nature perspective for scrutinizing communication ethics. They find the "unique nature of the human being" rooted in "two complicated and interlocking processes which generate all capacities that we call 'human.'"[6] In these capacities, they contend, "should lie the ultimate standard of ethics" for assessing human communication.

One fundamentally human attribute, according to Wieman and Walter, is the symbol-using capacity. This capacity, some might say compulsion, to transform the raw data of sensory experience into symbols is viewed as uniquely human. Not only can we convert immediate sensory data into symbols, we also can use symbols to refer to other symbols (such as conceptions of goals, values, ideals) and to pass on accumulated knowledge and insight from one generation to another. This power of symbolization, believe Wieman and Walter, is responsible for the genesis and continued growth of the human personality and for the creative works of humanity.

A second peculiarly human quality, and one that provides a principle to guide our ethical use of symbols, is the "unique need of human beings for other human beings." This need, labeled by Wieman and Walter as "appreciative understanding," is more than the gregariousness of animals. It stimulates development of the "mind" and "self" as human conceptions. Fulfillment of the need for mutual, appreciative understanding does not mean, they note, approval of everything someone else does or says. "One cannot, however, justly disapprove anything until after one has first achieved an understanding of it."

The ethical standard advocated by Wieman and Walter is clear: communication is ethical to the degree that it enhances human symbol-using capacity, fulfills the need for mutual appreciative understanding, and promotes mutuality of control and influence. Such communication requires, in part, valid and honest evidence and reasoning along with solutions that are of most benefit to humanity. To what extent can their suggested standard be functionally and unambiguously applied? What might be some examples of communication that would be ethical by this standard but condemned as unethical by criteria and perspectives outlined elsewhere in this book?

Various contemporary scholars share the assumption of Wieman and Walter that the capacity to use symbols is a uniquely human trait. In her *Philosophy in a New Key*, Susanne Langer argues that "symbolism is the recognized key to that mental life which is characteristically human and above the level of sheer animality." She believes that the basic "need of symbolization, . . . which other creatures probably do not have," is obvious in humans, functions continuously, and is the fundamental process of the human mind.[7]

Kenneth Burke, in *Language as Symbolic Action*, makes the human symbol-using capacity the foundation of his definition of man: "Man is the symbol-using (symbol-making, symbol-misusing) animal, inventor of the negative (or moralized by the negative), separated from his natural condition by instruments of his own making, goaded by the spirit of hierarchy (or moved by the sense of order), and rotten with perfection." In another book Burke asserts that the function of rhetoric is to induce "cooperation in beings that by nature respond to symbols."[8] In *Philosophy of Rhetoric*, I. A. Richards assumes that language is "no mere signalling system. . . . It is the instrument of all our distinctively human development, of everything in which we go beyond the other animals."[9]

Evidence is accumulating, however, based on research with chimpanzees and gorillas who have learned nonoral languages (such as gestural sign language used by the deaf), that *symbol generation and utilization*, as opposed to rote learning of signals, *may not be* a solely human ability. The status of the debate on this issue remains unresolved. The evidence and research methods of studies showing that chimpanzees essentially have a humanlike symbolic capacity have been both vigorously attacked and stoutly defended. If the capacity for symbol using eventually is proven to be a characteristic that humans share to a significant degree with at least some other animals, what might be the implications of continuing to use it as a standard for assessing the ethics of human communication? Because its uniqueness is diminished, should it play a very minimal role in evaluation of communication ethics?[10] Because some animals seem to share this important and creative ability, should we broaden our concern for ethical communication to include such animals?[11]

Kant's Categorical Imperative

To better understand several of the following versions of a human nature perspective, a brief discussion of Immanuel Kant's Categorical Imperative is in order.[12] An eighteenth-century German philosopher, Kant believed that the uniquely human capacity was a sense of conscience (moral will, moral reason). To varying degrees, in Kant's view, all humans possess rationality and a sense of right and wrong; universal moral law as apprehended by conscience must be obeyed by all rational beings. Moral imperatives are categorical—without conditions, exceptions, or extenuating circumstances. A lie, for example, always is unethical. Moral imperatives are right in themselves, not because of their consequences. Kant's is a deontological or duty-bound ethic. We have a duty to obey universal and absolute principles.

As touchstones to guide ethical behavior, Kant presented two forms of his Categorical Imperative. First: "Act only on that maxim which you can at the same time will to become a universal law." We must ask ourselves, is the ethical principle that I am using to justify my choice a principle that I would want everyone to follow? Is the ethical standard that I am following in a particular case one that I would agree should apply to everyone? Second: "Always act so that you treat humanity, whether in your own person or in another, as an end, and never merely as a means." Humans must not be treated simply or solely as things (means to an end), but always also as persons worthy of dignity and respect in themselves.

This simplified extraction from Kant's ethical theory will suffice for present purposes. Bear in mind, however, that his ethical theory as a whole is extremely complex and that it somewhat modified as it evolved over time.[13]

Humans as Persuaders

"What is distinctively human at the most fundamental level is the capacity to persuade and be persuaded." Assuming this basic premise, contemporary philosopher Henry W. Johnstone, Jr., develops an ethic for rhetoric (persuasion).[14] Other specifications of the essence of human nature (language-using, political, rational, etc.), Johnstone believes, presuppose the capacity for persuasion. He also believes that what is distinctively human ought to be fostered and perpetuated. Johnstone wants to locate an ethic for rhetoric in the rhetorical process itself. He wants to avoid evaluating the ethics of persuasion by standards external to persuasion, standards derived from the surrounding culture, religion, or political system.

As the foundation of his ethic for rhetoric, Johnstone offers his Basic Imperative: "So act in each instance as to encourage, rather than suppress, the capacity to persuade and be persuaded, whether the capacity in question is yours or another's." Responsible rhetoric is a self-perpetuating rhetoric. People should not employ persuasion to block or foreclose persuasive responses on the part of others. Sullen obedience, inarticulate anger, and refusal to continue listening are examples of such blocking tactics. Tactics like these are "dehumanizing and immoral" because they break the chain of persuasion.

The most ethically responsible rhetoric, in Johnstone's view, is that which addresses others "with love." The spirit of love in persuasion, he believes, means that we are not motivated primarily by selfish personal interests. Instead, when persuading "with love" we respect the truth, respect the other persons participating, and respect those participants' need to know the truth.

Flowing from his Basic Imperative, Johnstone presents duties to ourselves and to others. These duties are ethical standards for assessing an instance of persuasion. Toward ourselves we have the duties of resoluteness and openness. *Resoluteness* means that I must not agree with or give in to the arguments or appeals of others in an unthinking, uncritical, automatic fashion. I must advocate my own position and use my own capacities for persuasion to assess propositions urged by others. *Openness* means I must listen carefully to ideas others present and must not be impassive, self-centered, or simply turn a deaf ear. Toward others we have the duties of gentleness and compassion. *Gentleness* means that I must address others through persuasion rather than violence, either physical violence or symbolic coercive violence. *Compassion* means that I must listen to others more for the sake of their own welfare and interests than for the sake of my own interests.

Communicative Competence and the Ideal Speech Situation

The German philosopher and social critic, Jürgen Habermas, is working toward a comprehensive theory of "communicative competence." How language, as a distinctively human capacity, functions to foster mutual understanding, shared knowledge, mutual trust, and interpersonal relationships is a major focus of his theory. The details of his complex theory, and various shortcomings of it, can be examined in several secondary sources.[15] But for our purposes, two central concepts of his theory of communicative competence have potential as standards for ethical communication. The first concept involves the basic assumptions that undergird all normal human communication. The second concept involves the essential elements of an ideal communication situation. You are urged to consider to what degree these two views might appropriately function as ethical guides.[16]

Habermas identifies four assumptions that underlie all normal human communication. For everyday communication to function smoothly and without question, each participant must assume that the communication of other participants meets these four expectations. While any particular utterance may stress only one expectation, all four assumptions are present to some degree. First, participants assume that all statements made are capable of being comprehended; statements are in a grammatical and semantical form capable of being understood by others. Second, participants assume that the statements are true representations of existing, agreed-upon, factual states of affairs. Third, participants assume that statements sincerely and accurately reflect the actual intentions of others. Fourth, participants assume that statements are appropriate; that is, they are in harmony with relevant shared social values and rules. Could we, then, adapt Habermas's assumptions and suggest that ethical communication aiming at mutual understanding and trust must meet the tests of comprehensibility, truth, sincerity, and appropriateness?

Habermas also outlines four constituent elements of what he terms the "ideal speech situation," the system where communication is free from (or minimally subject to) constraints and distortions. For both private and public communication, the ideal speech situation can be approximated when four requirements are met. First, participants must have equal opportunity to initiate and continue communicative acts. Second, participants must have equal opportunity to present arguments, explanations, interpretations, and justifications; no significant opinions should go unexamined. Third, participants must have equal opportunity to express honestly personal intentions, feelings, and attitudes. Fourth, participants must have equal opportunity to present directive statements that forbid, permit, command, etc. In an attempt to adapt Habermas's view, we could explore how adequately these four elements of the ideal speech situation might serve as ethical standards for communication.

In *Moral Consciousness and Communicative Action*, Habermas emphasizes the fundamental ethical principles of justice and solidarity.[17] Justice requires equal respect and equal rights for individuals while solidarity demands "empathy and concern for the well-being of one's neighbor." These principles are rooted in the fact that humans are unique in the social and communicative construction of their "selves." At another point Habermas cites Thomas McCarthy's revision of Kant's Categorical Imperative as fitting the theory of communicative action: "Rather than ascribing as valid to all others any maxim that I will to be a universal law, I must submit my maxim to all others for purposes of discursively testing its claims to universality. The emphasis shifts from what each can will without contradiction to be a universal law, to what all can will in agreement to be a universal norm." In Seyla Benhabib's words, the "core idea behind communicative ethics" is the "generation of reasonable agreement about moral principles via an open-ended moral conversation."

<hr>

An Epistemic Ethic

Epistemology is the study of the origin, nature, methods, and limits of human knowledge. If rhetoric is viewed broadly as intentional human attempts to influence through symbols, one traditional conception of rhetoric's function is to describe it as transmitting or utilizing knowledge (facts, reality) previously discovered or derived through other processes (science, religion, philosophy). According to this view, reality exists "out there" completely independent of humans. Reality simply is waiting to be discovered and transmitted by humans as facts in a completely neutral, objective manner or as raw material to achieve a persuasive purpose.

In contrast, some contemporary scholars of rhetoric develop a conception of *rhetoric as epistemic, rhetoric as generative of knowledge*.[18] They are exploring the extent to which rhetoric functions to *construct* or *create* reality. According to this view, the only meaningful reality for humans is a symbolically, rhetorically constructed reality. Humans *in interaction* with their environment (empirical phenomena, concepts, other humans) *give or create* the significance and meaning of the sensations they experience. Some scholars even describe the doing of science as a process of symbolically constructing reality. Richard Gregg summarizes the "rhetoric as epistemic" viewpoint in its most inclusive sense: "All areas of knowledge are human symbolic constructs guided by various human purposes in light of various needs. There are some areas, of course, where objectives or procedures are more clearly defined or agreed upon than others, or where there can be clearly established authoritative bodies which legitimate knowledge claims."[19]

Although he acknowledges a number of useful conceptions of rhetoric, Barry Brummett believes that in a fundamental sense rhetoric best is viewed as "advocacy of realities." He asserts a significant ethical implication of such a stance. "Thus, rhetoric in process is doubly ethical: it is the result of a choice on the part of the rhetor as to the reality advocated and the method of doing so, and it urges choice rather than complete and necessary acceptance on the part of the audience. Truth that is rhetorically made encourages choice and awareness of alternative realities."[20]

Robert Scott argues that one unique capacity of humans is their ability to *generate or create* knowledge *in and during* the actual process of communication (Scott uses the term *rhetoric as equivalent to persuasion*.) Communication, he believes, is not *solely* the *transmission* of knowledge somehow previously established or of prior immutable truth. Truth is contingent and derives from communication interaction in the form of cooperative inquiry. He explains: "Insofar as we can say that there is truth in human affairs, it is in time; it can be the result of a process of interaction at a given moment. Thus rhetoric may be viewed not as a matter of giving effectiveness to truth but of creating truth."[21]

While the rhetoric-as-epistemic view admits no *a priori* knowledge, or no reality completely independent of humans, Scott does not believe that this particular type of relativism necessitates abandonment of ethical and logical standards.

> Relativism, supposedly, means a standardless society, or at least a maze of differing standards, and thus a cacophony of disparate, and likely self-ish, interests. Rather than a standardless society, which is the same as saying no society at all, relativism indicates circumstances in which standards have to be established cooperatively and renewed repeatedly.[22]

From these assumptions about a uniquely human capacity, Scott derives three ethical guidelines for judging communication. First, we should tolerate divergence of viewpoints and the right of others to self-expression. We spoil our own potentiality for *knowing*, says Scott, if we fail to respect the integrity of the expression of others. Second, we should consciously strive toward maximum participation in the communication transaction at hand. "Inaction, the failure to take on the burden of participating in the development of contingent truth," Scott believes, "ought to be considered ethical failure." Third, in our own communication we should strive to achieve good consequences. But also we should accept responsibility for all undesired and undesirable consequences of our communication so far as they can be known.

How adequate are Scott's suggested ethical guidelines as criteria for assessing both interpersonal and public communication? How easily could they be applied in concrete situations? Note that Scott's first guideline is one also proposed in some of the political perspectives examined in chapter 2, specifically those of Wallace and Nilsen. This commonality illustrates again, as with the rationality criterion, that a specific ethical standard may become associated with several ethical perspectives. In fact, Scott's second ethical guideline is one also associated with "presentness" as a characteristic of the dialogical perspective to be discussed in chapter 4.

Human Capacity for Value Judgment

The capacity to create and sustain values and to apply them in rendering value judgments is seen by Ralph Eubanks as the central characteristic of human nature.[23] Our "essential nature" is that of the "valuing creature." Humans strive to fulfill their personalities through the values they advocate and embody. For Eubanks, to live as a human being "is to choose between better and worse on the basis of values." Such beliefs lead Eubanks "inexorably" to a human nature perspective on symbolic behavior.

What ethical standards for communication behavior stem from this viewpoint? First, Eubanks endorses the second form of Immanuel Kant's

Categorical Imperative: "Act so as to treat humanity, whether in your own person or that of another, always as an end and never as a means only."[24] Second, to promote the "primacy of the person" in our communication transactions, we should adhere to the "civilizing values" of *health, creativity, wisdom, love, freedom with justice, courage,* and *order.*

Third, in our communication we should respect the imperative of *civility.* In our verbal and nonverbal symbolic behavior, we should exemplify the so-called "dialogical" attitudes of genuineness, directness, nonpossessive warmth, and so forth. (This dialogical stance will be explained at length in the following chapter.) Civility requires that we avoid communication practices that "violate the intrinsic worth" of other people, practices such as deception, verbal obscenity, and irrelevant attacks on an opponent's character.

Fourth, the "ethical demand of *veracity,* or truthfulness," is crucial. Through communication we not only transmit established knowledge, but we also create or construct knowledge. Eubanks favorably cites the "epistemic ethic" proposed by Robert Scott (and previously explained in this chapter). A "major affront to human dignity" Eubanks believes, would be the violation of the "very process by which wisdom is transmitted and knowledge generated." Hiding the truth, falsifying evidence, or using faulty reasoning are among the tactics condemned as unethical.

A Humanistic Ethic for Rhetoric

The "commitment to the idea that humanness is good—that human nature has worth," is the starting point for Christopher Lyle Johnstone's "humane ethic" for rhetoric.[25] Such a commitment assumes that we should seek out, nurture, and actualize the multiple essential elements of human nature. Our choices of communication means and ends can be assessed for ethicality, in general, by the degree to which they humanize or dehumanize us. By "rhetorical" Johnstone means "those dimensions of discourse that function to induce judgment or provoke decision," those communicative elements that influence a receiver's "coming-to-judgment." Rhetoric offers "grounds for legitimate choice" by combining feeling, imagining, inference making, and value judgment. Johnstone, too, sees rhetoric as having an epistemic function, a function of generating reliable knowledge in and through the rhetorical process. Human nature flowers at its fullest not in isolation but in relationship and interaction with the environment and other humans.

Based on these fundamental assumptions, Johnstone develops a humanistic ethical stance applicable to rhetoric. He describes a "general sense" of the obligations of such an ethic.

> To be *humane* suggests that one's conduct is guided by a respect for and a tenderness toward others' beings. It suggests a prizing of these beings and a desire to protect and nourish them. In the first instance, therefore, a

humanist ethic requires that the individual be responsive in his or her actions to the impact they might have on the humanity of those affected by the act. It demands, finally, that one conduct oneself so as to maximize opportunities for cultivating in oneself and in others an awareness and appreciation of humanness.

As an ethical orientation appropriate for evaluating the "attitudes" of participants in communication, Johnstone endorses the "dialogical" stance that we will explore in the following chapter. Such a spirit of dialogue is characterized in part by such qualities as mutuality, open-heartedness, directness, spontaneity, honesty, lack of pretense, nonmanipulative intent, and loving responsibility of one human for another.

What ethical guidelines does Johnstone offer to assess the ethicality of the "content" of rhetoric? How should we assess the ethics of the evidence, reasoning, and appeals we use to justify the choices we advocate? Humane rhetoric should include in its arguments "an analysis of the human foundations of the values argued from." "A humanizing argument," he believes, "will articulate the fundamental commitments upon which it draws." Concludes Johnstone:

> The "good reasons" upon which choice can be made, therefore, will articulate, clarify, and affirm those human features that are most to be valued: our resourcefulness, our capacity for loving, our receptiveness to and inclination toward beauty, our emotional resilience and range of sensitivities, our capacities for foresight and self-control, our imagination, our curiosity, our capacity for wonder, our powers of passionate attachment, to name but a few. These are features that humanists have always embraced. These are among the characteristics of human nature that must be known and prized if we are to live humane lives.

Natural and Social Science Contributions

The field of evolutionary ethics is one in which pro and con positions have emerged as to whether, or to what degree, scientific evidence demonstrates that our moral capacity is rooted in biological, genetic, or developmental evolution.[26] Mark Johnson examines the implications of cognitive science for ethics and develops the central thesis that "human beings are fundamentally *imaginative* moral animals." He argues that the "quality of our moral understanding and deliberation depends crucially on the cultivation of moral imagination." What is needed, he contends, "is a new empirically responsible moral philosophy" that is "grounded in what the cognitive sciences teach us about concepts, understandings, and reasoning."[27]

James Q. Wilson explores insights from the biological and social sciences to contend that humans have a natural "moral sense" formed from the interactions of their innate human nature with family experiences and culture. In all people to some but differing degrees, the moral sense shapes how we believe that we and others ought to behave. Among the examples of the moral sense, Wilson lists sympathy, fairness, self-control, duty, and integrity.[28]

In his book, *The Moral Animal: The New Science of Evolutionary Psychology*, Robert Wright offers a summary so provocative that it warrants complete quotation.[29]

> Altruism, compassion, empathy, love, conscience, the sense of justice— all of these things, the things that hold society together, the things that allow our species to think so highly of itself, can now confidently be said to have a firm genetic basis. That's the good news. The bad news is that, although these things are in some ways blessings for humanity as a whole, they didn't evolve for the "good of the species" and aren't reliably employed to that end. Quite the contrary: it is now clearer than ever how (and precisely why) the moral sentiments are used with brutal flexibility, switched on and off in keeping with self-interest; and how naturally oblivious we are to this switching. In the new view, human beings are a species splendid in the array of their moral equipment, tragic in their propensity to misuse it, and pathetic in their constitutional ignorance of the misuse.

The Machine Question

At the beginning of this chapter, we noted a philosopher's skepticism about using unique characteristics of human nature as a basis for ethical norms. Later we mentioned research that questions whether the capacity to generate and manipulate symbols for communication is unique to humans. Now we briefly summarize what David Gunkel terms "The Machine Question" in the final chapter of his book, *Thinking Otherwise: Philosophy, Communication, Technology.*[30]

Gunkel objects to the human-centered focus of traditional ethics in Western civilization. That is, he objects to using uniquely human capacities as the uniform test to determine the "Others" toward whom we have ethical responsibilities. Must the Others to whom we are ethically responsible be similar to humans in essential characteristics? Gunkel's answer is no. The "machine question" he explores focuses on autonomous self-regulating machines such as cyborgs, "chatterbots" that communicate with humans, software that functions in virtual space, embodied robots that function in medicine and manufacturing, and machines that "think" with "intelligence" quite differently than humans. He argues that such machines, regardless of similarities or differences with human nature, warrant moral status as autonomous ethical agents.

Gunkel's work on this issue can generate a number of related questions: What is our ethical responsibility as humans toward such machines? What is the ethical responsibility of such machines toward us as humans? What happens when the ethical standards of humans and such machines conflict: Who decides which standards should prevail? How should the decision be reached? Gunkel's complete argument is thorough, detailed, and complex. Here we simply attempt to focus your attention on the fact that such a revolutionary "machine question" is being debated.

Notes

[1] Christopher Lyle Johnstone, "Ethics, Wisdom, and the Mission of Contemporary Rhetoric: The Realization of Human Being," *Central Slates Speech Journal*, 32 (Fall 1981): 180, n. 12.

[2] Kai Nielsen, "On Taking Human Nature as the Basis for Morality," *Social Research*, 29 (Summer 1962): 157–177; Richard J. Bernstein, "Response," in *Universalism vs. Relativism*, Don Browning, ed. (Lanham, MD: Rowman & Littlefield, 2006), p. 171.

[3] Lawrence J. Flynn, S. J., "The Aristotelian Basis for the Ethics of Speaking," *The Speech Teacher*, 6 (September 1957): 179–187.

[4] Robert C. Rowland and Deanna Womack, "Aristotle's View of Ethical Rhetoric," *Rhetoric Society Quarterly*, 15 (Winter–Spring, 1985): 13–32. Also see Marlene K. Sokolon, *Political Emotions: Aristotle and the Symphony of Emotions* (DeKalb: Northern Illinois University Press, 2006).

[5] Thomas M. Garrett, S. J., *An Introduction to Some Ethical Problems of Modern American Advertising* (Rome: The Gregorian University Press, 1961), pp. 39–47.

[6] Henry N. Wieman and Otis M. Walter, "Toward an Analysis of Ethics for Rhetoric," *Quarterly Journal of Speech*, 43 (October 1957): 266–270. For another version see Otis M. Walter and Robert L. Scott, *Thinking and Speaking*, 4th ed. (New York: Macmillan, 1979), pp. 235–239. For an application to mass media ethics, see Jerry Harvill, "Oikonomia: The Journalist as Steward," *Journal of Mass Media Ethics*, 3, no. 1, (1988): 65–76.

[7] Susanne Langer, *Philosophy in a New Key* (New York: New American Library Mentor Book, 1948), pp. 34, 45.

[8] Kenneth Burke, *Language as Symbolic Action* (Berkeley: University of California Press, 1966), pp. 3–22; Burke, *A Rhetoric of Motives* (New York: Prentice-Hall, 1950), p. 43.

[9] I. A. Richards, *The Philosophy of Rhetoric* (New York: Oxford University Press Galaxy Book, 1965), p. 131.

[10] For analyses, including ones denying that chimpanzees have demonstrated a human capacity for symbol use, see: Thomas Sebeok and Jean Umiker-Sebeok, eds., *Speaking of Apes: A Critical Anthology of Two-Way Communication with Man* (Bloomington: Indiana University Press, 1980); Linda Haupe and Meridith Richards, "Defining Man Through Language: A Theoretical and Historical Perspective," *Pavlovian Journal of Biological Science*, 14 (October-December 1979): 234–242; Thomas A. Sebeok and Robert Rosenthal, eds., *The Clever Hans Phenomenon: Communication with Horses, Whales, Apes, and People* (New York: New York Academy of Sciences, 1981), pp. 26–129; David Premack, *Gavangi! Or the Future History of the Animal Language Controversy* (Cambridge, MA: MIT Press, 1986); R. Allen Gardner, Beatrix T. Gardner, and Thomas E. Van Cantfort, eds., *Teaching Sign Language to Chimpanzees* (Albany: State University of New York Press, 1989); Sue Savage-Rumbaugh and Roger Levin, *Kanzi: The Ape at the Brink of the Human Mind* (London: Doubleday, 1994); Roger Fouts and Stephen Turkel Mills, *Next of Kin: My Conversations with Chimpanzees* (New York: Living Planet Books, 1997); Pär Segerdahl, William Fields, and Sue Savage-Rumbaugh, *Kanzi's Primal Language: The Cultural Initiation of Primates into Language* (Hampshire, UK: Palgrave Macmillan, 2005); Donna Haraway, *Simians, Cyborgs, and Women: The Reinvention of Human Nature* (New York: Routledge, 1991).

[11] Social scientists R. Harré and P. F. Secord take this latter position. *The Explanation of Social Behavior* (Totowa, NJ: Littlefield, Adams and Co., 1973), p. 96.

[12] This discussion is based on Radoslav A. Tsanoff, *Ethics*, Rev. Ed. (New York: Harper & Row, 1955), pp. 107, 167–168; Brendan E. A. Liddell, *Kant on the Foundation of Morality* (Bloomington: Indiana University Press, 1970), pp. 42–49, 119–120, 133, 155–157, 200, 227, 247; Clifford G. Christians, Kim B. Rotzoll, and Mark Fackler, *Media Ethics*, 2nd. ed. (New York: Longman, 1987), pp. 11–12.

[13] This complexity and development is captured in Alan W. Wood, *Kant's Ethical Thought* (Cambridge, UK: Cambridge University Press, 1999).

[14] Henry W. Johnstone, Jr., "Toward an Ethics for Rhetoric," *Communication*, 6, no. 2 (1981): 305–314. Also see Johnstone, *Validity and Rhetoric in Philosophical Argument* (University Park, PA: Dialogue Press of Man and the World, 1978), pp. 41–43, 84–85, 133; Molly Wertheimer, "Johnstone's Versions of Rhetoric," in *Dimensions of Argument*, George Ziegelmueller and Jack Rhodes, eds. (Annandale, VA: Speech Communication Association, 1981), pp. 865–874; Johnstone, Jr., "Bilaterality in Argument and Communication," in *Advances in Argumentation Theory and Research*, J. Robert Cox and Charles A. Willard, eds. (Carbondale: Southern Illinois University Press, 1982), pp. 95–103. For applications of Johnstone's view, see two essays in Edward Schiappa, ed., *Warranting Dissent: Case Studies in Argument Evaluation* (Albany: State University of New York Press, 1995): Jeffrey L. Courtright, "'I Respectfully Dissent': The Ethics of Dissent in Justice O'Connor's *Metro Broadcasting, Inc. v. FCC* Opinion," pp. 125–152; and Kathryn M. Olson, "Aligning Ethicality and Effectiveness in Arguments: Advocating Inclusiveness Percentages for the New Lutheran Church," pp. 81–102.

[15] See, for example, Thomas McCarthy, *The Critical Theory of Jürgen Habermas* (Cambridge, MA: MIT Press, 1978); Jane Braaten, *Habermas's Critical Theory of Society* (New York: State University of New York Press, 1991); Larry J. Ray, *Rethinking Critical Theory* (Newbury Park, CA: Sage, 1993).

[16] The sources drawn upon for the following descriptions are: Jürgen Habermas, *Communication and the Evolution of Society*, trans. Thomas McCarthy (Boston: Beacon Press, 1979), ch. 1; Thomas McCarthy, "Translator's Introduction," in Jürgen Habermas, *Legitimation Crisis* (Boston: Beacon Press, 1975), pp. vii–xxiv; Brant R. Burleson and Susan L. Kline, "Habermas's Theory of Communication: A Critical Explication," *Quarterly Journal of Speech*, 65 (December 1979): 412–428; Thomas Farrell, "The Ideality of Meaning of Argument: A Revision of Habermas," in *Dimensions of Argument*, Ziegelmueller and Rhodes, eds., pp. 905–926; Susan L. Kline, "The Ideal Speech Situation: A Discussion of Its Presuppositions," in Ibid., pp. 927–939. Also see Habermas, *Legitimation Crisis*, pp. 95, 120; Ronald Beiner, *Political Judgment* (Chicago: University of Chicago Press, 1983), pp. 25–30; J. Torpey, "Ethics and Critical Theory: From Horkheimer to Habermas," *Telos*, 69 (Fall 1986): 68–84.

[17] Jürgen Habermas, *Moral Consciousness and Communicative Action*, trans. Christian Lenhardt and Shierry Weber Nicholson (Cambridge, MA: MIT Press, 1990), pp. 56–67, 200. Also see Seyla Benhabib and Fred Dallmayr, eds., *The Communicative Ethics Controversy* (Cambridge, MA: MIT Press, 1990), espec. p. 345; Kenneth Baynes, "Communicative Ethics, the Public Sphere, and Communication Media," *Critical Studies in Mass Communication*, 11 (December 1994): 315–326; Niels Thomassen, *Communicative Ethics in Theory and Practice* (New York: St. Martin's Press, 1992).

[18] Richard B. Gregg, "Rhetoric and Knowing: The Search for Perspective," *Central States Speech Journal*, 32 (Fall 1981): 133–144; C. Jack Orr, "How Shall We Say: 'Reality Is Socially Constructed Through Communication?'" *Central States Speech Journal*, 29 (Winter 1978): 263–274; Michael C. Leff, "In Search of Ariadne's Thread: A Review of the Recent Literature on Rhetorical Theory," *Central States Speech Journal*, 29 (Summer 1978): 73–91; Walter Weimer, "Science as a Rhetorical Transaction," *Philosophy and Rhetoric*, 10 (Winter 1977): 1–19; Peter L. Berger and Thomas Luckman, *The Social Construction of Reality* (Garden City, NY: Doubleday, 1966), pp. 38, 89, 96, 119–120, 140–142; Richard Gregg, *Symbolic Inducement and Knowing* (Columbia: University of South Carolina Press. 1984); Richard A. Cherwitz and James W. Hikens, *Communication and Knowledge* (Columbia: University of South Carolina Press, 1986).

[19] Gregg, "Rhetoric and Knowing," 141.

[20] Barry Brummett, "Some Implications of 'Process' or 'Intersubjectivity': Postmodern Rhetoric," *Philosophy and Rhetoric*, 9 (Winter 1976): 21–51.

[21] Robert L. Scott, "On Viewing Rhetoric as Epistemic," *Central States Speech Journal*, 18 (February 1967): 9–17.

[22] Scott, "On Viewing Rhetoric as Epistemic: Ten Years Later," *Central States Speech Journal*, 27 (Winter 1976): 258–266. Also see Jeffrey L. Bineham, "From Within the Looking-Glass: The Ontology of Consensus Theory—Bineham's Rejoinder," *Communication Studies*, 49 (Fall 1989): 182–188.

[23] Ralph T. Eubanks, "Reflections on the Moral Dimension of Communication," *Southern Speech Communication Journal*, 45 (Spring 1980): 297–312. Also see Eubanks, "Axiological Issues in Rhetorical Inquiry," *Southern Speech Communication Journal*, 44 (Fall 1978): 11–24; Virgil L. Baker and Ralph T. Eubanks, *Speech in Personal and Public Affairs* (New York: David Makay Co., 1965), preface and ch. 6.

[24] Immanuel Kant, *Fundamental Principles of the Metaphysics of Morals*, trans. Thomas Abbott (Indianapolis, IN: Library of Liberal Arts/Bobbs-Merrill. 1949), p. 46.

[25] Lyle Johnstone, "Ethics, Wisdom, and the Mission of Contemporary Rhetoric: The Realization of Human Being," *Central States Speech Journal*, 32 (Fall 1981): 177–188.

[26] Larry Arnhart, *Darwinian Natural Right: The Biological Ethics of Human Nature* (Albany: State University of New York Press, 1998), pp. 29–36, 120–160; Michael Bradie, *The Secret Chain: Evolution and Ethics* (Albany: SUNY Press, 1994); Matthew H. Nitecki and Doris V. Nitecki, eds., *Evolutionary Ethics* (Albany: SUNY Press, 1993); Paul Thompson, ed., *Issues in Evolutionary Ethics* (Albany: SUNY Press, 1995); Edward O. Wilson, *Consilience: The Unity of Knowledge* (New York: Knopf, 1998).

[27] Mark Johnson, *Moral Imagination: Implications of Cognitive Science for Ethics* (Chicago: University of Chicago Press, 1993), pp. 1, 11–12. Also see Alvin I. Goldman, "Ethics and Cognitive Science," *Ethics*, 103 (January 1993): 337–360.

[28] James Q. Wilson, *The Moral Sense* (New York: The Free Press, 1993). Also see Mary Midgley, *The Ethical Primate: Humans, Freedom, and Morality* (London: Routledge, 1994); Steven Pinker, *The Blank Slate: The Modern Denial of Human Nature* (New York: Viking, 2002); Michael S. Gazzaniga, *The Ethical Brain* (New York: Dana Press, 2005).

[29] Robert Wright, *The Moral Animal: The New Science of Evolutionary Psychology* (New York: Pantheon, 1994), pp. 12–13. Also see Frans de Waal, *Good Natured: The Origins of Right and Wrong in Humans and Other Animals* (Cambridge, MA: Harvard University Press, 1996), pp. 217–218.

[30] David J. Gunkel, "The Machine Question: Ethics, Alterity, and Technology," in *Thinking Otherwise: Philosophy, Communication, Technology*, David J. Gunkel, ed., (Lafayette, IN: Purdue University Press, 2007), chapter 6. Also see David Gunkel and Debra Hawhee, "Virtual Alterity and the Reformatting of Ethics," *Journal of Mass Media Ethics*, 18 (2003): 173–193; Jeffrey T. Nealon, *Alterity Politics: Ethics and Performative Subjectivity* (Durham, NC: Duke University Press, 1998).

4

Dialogical Perspectives

The term "dialogue" means many things to many people. In the political arena the give and take of debate is known as public dialogue. Religious leaders of divergent faiths exchange views in ecumenical dialogue. Educational experts encourage classroom dialogue through group discussion and question and answer exchanges. Classicists examine Plato's dialogues and dramatists write dialogue for their plays. Communication researchers remind us that human communication is not a one-way transmission but a two-way dialogic transaction. Race relations experts urge expanded dialogue between persons of diverse ethnic heritages.

Another view of dialogue has emerged from such fields as philosophy, psychiatry, psychology, and religion.[1] Proponents discuss the concept of communication as dialogue, often contrasting it with the concept of communication as monologue. Characteristics of dialogical communication are treated by various scholars under a variety of labels: authentic communication, facilitative communication, therapeutic communication, nondirective therapy, presence, participation, existential communication, encounter, self-disclosing communication, actualizing communication, supportive communication, helping relationship, caring relationship, and loving relationship. So, too, various labels are used to designate the features of monological communication: defensive communication, manipulative communication, inauthentic communication, directive communication, and so forth.

Focus of Dialogical Perspectives

Dialogical perspectives for evaluating communication ethics focus on the *attitudes toward each other* held by the participants in a communication transaction. Participants' attitudes are viewed as an index of the ethical level of that communication. The assumption is that some attitudes (characteristic of dialogue) are more fully human, humane, and facilitative of self-fulfillment than are other attitudes (characteristic of monologue). Dialogical attitudes are held to best nurture and actualize each individual's capacities and potentials, whatever they are. The techniques and presentation of a communication participant could be scrutinized to determine the degree to which they reveal ethical dialogical attitudes or unethical monological attitudes toward other participants.

Among contemporary existentialist philosophers, Martin Buber is the primary one who places the concept of dialogue at the heart of his view of human communication and existence. His writings on dialogue have served as a stimulus for other scholars.[2] Another existentialist philosopher who finds dialogue, or its equivalent, fundamental to our understanding of humanity is Karl Jaspers.[3] The principle of dialogue appears in the conceptions of desirable human communication described by such psychologists and psychiatrists as Carl Rogers, Erich Fromm, Paul Tournier, Jack Gibb, Everett Shostrom, Sidney Jourard, David Johnson, and Abraham Maslow.[4] Other scholars, such as Reuel Howe, Georges Gusdorf, Milton Mayeroff, John Powell, and Floyd Matson and Ashley Montagu, also elaborate some features of the concept.[5] Significant conceptions of dialogue are found in the works of Mikhail Bakhtin and Hans-Georg Gadamer.[6]

Martin Buber's analysis of two primary human relationships or attitudes, I-Thou and I-It, significantly influenced the concept of communication as dialogue. According to Buber, the fundamental fact of human existence is "man with man," person communicating with person. Interaction between humans through dialogue promotes development of self, personality, and knowledge. For Buber, meaning and our sense of "self" are constructed only in the realm of the "between" of relationships; our becoming "persons" rather than self-centered individuals arises only in the "between" of dialogic relationships.

Buber sees personal relationships on an I-It to I-Thou continuum with roughly five positions (see chart). This continuum ranges from I-It monologue at its most manipulative and self-centered at one extreme; through degrees of I-It monologue that simply measure, observe, or classify others; through degrees of "technical dialogue" or impersonal communication that focus on objective understanding of information; through degrees of I-Thou dialogue characterized by authenticity, inclusion, presentness, confirmation, and partial mutuality; and, finally, at the other extreme, to fully mutual but rare dialogic relations or moments (typically in contexts of marriage or friendship).[7]

In the I-Thou or dialogical relationship, the attitudes and behavior of each communication participant are characterized by such qualities as mutuality, open-heartedness, directness, honesty, spontaneity, frankness, lack of pretense, nonmanipulative intent, communion, intensity, and love in the sense of responsibility of one human for another.[8] In dialogue, although interested in being understood and perhaps in influencing, a communicator does not attempt to *impose* his or her own truth or view on another and is not interested in bolstering his or her own ego or self-image. Each person in a dialogic

Martin Buber's Monologue–Dialogue Continuum

I-It   I-Thou

◄──►

Monologue	Monologue	Impersonal Communication/ "Technical Dialogue"	Partially Mutual Dialogue	Fully Mutual Dialogue
manipulative; self-centered	objectifies persons as things or objects	focuses on objective understanding of information	awareness of roles; occurs in public and private	full awareness of other person; typically marriage and friendship

authenticity, confirmation, inclusion, presentness

relationship is accepted as a unique individual. One becomes totally aware of the other person rather than functioning as an observer or onlooker.

The essential movement in dialogue, according to Buber, is turning toward, being outgoing toward, and reaching for the other. And a basic element in dialogue is "seeing the other" or "experiencing the other side." A person also does not forego his or her own convictions and views but strives to understand those of others and avoids imposing his or her own on others. For Buber, the increasing difficulty of achieving genuine dialogue between humans of divergent beliefs represents the central problem for the fate of humankind.

Carl Rogers provides a second major influence for the concept of communication as dialogue. Differences between the views of Rogers and Buber are debated.[9] Nevertheless, the processes characteristic of Rogers's client-centered, nondirective approach to psychotherapy, of his person-centered view of communication, are similar in important respects to Buber's conception of dialogic communication. In fact, after extensive comparison, Maurice Friedman concludes: "Rogers's emphases upon the I-Thou relationship in therapy, healing through meeting, acceptance, empathy, unconditional positive regard, and congruence are not only compatible with Buber's philosophy of dialogue but could be strengthened, clarified, and made more consistent within that framework."[10] In Rogers's language, therapists who are "transparently real" or "congruent" are genuine and honest in expressing their feelings at the moment toward the client, realizing that those feelings expressed must be relevant to the relationship. Through "empathic understanding" the therapist attempts to assume the internal frame of reference of the client and attempts to perceive both the world and the client through the client's own eyes. Although therapists temporarily set aside their own ideas and values, *complete* therapist-client identification does not occur, for therapists ultimately retain their own sense of personhood and self-identity.

The therapist holds "unconditional positive regard" for the client; this is a generally nonevaluative, nonjudgmental attitude that actively accepts the patient as a worthy human being for whom the counselor has genuine respect. The therapist prizes the client's feelings and opinions. He or she trusts clients and sees them as individual persons having worth in their own right. While the therapist may offer negative "reactions" to the client, expressing the therapist's personal viewpoint toward the client's behavior or beliefs, the therapist avoids "evaluations" that condemn the fundamental worth of the client as a human being or that apply to the client a set of external, absolute, value standards.

Dialogue versus Expressive Communication

Some writers imply that Buber's and Rogers's views of communication are synonymous with "expressive" communication. In expressive communication, the writers contend, we always reveal every gut feeling, do our own thing, do what comes naturally, let the chips fall where they may, and are totally honest without considering the consequences to others in the situation.[11] However, Rogers makes clear that congruence or transparency does not mean simply expressing every feeling or attitude experienced at the moment in a relationship. Rogers's description of congruence explicitly excludes expression of feelings that are irrelevant or inappropriate to that particular relationship or situation.[12] Buber's view of dialogue clearly would exclude unrestrained expressivism. Dialogue involves a genuine concern for the welfare and fulfillment of the other and a conscious choice making in response to the demands of specified situations. For example, dialogue requires sensitivity to the role responsibilities of such relationships as teacher–pupil, therapist–client, doctor–patient, clergy–parishioner, and parent–child.[13]

Characteristics of Dialogue

We now can summarize the characteristics of dialogue fundamental to the process. These are the major attitudinal dimensions that most scholars writing on dialogue, under various labels, identify to some degree as typifying communication as dialogue. In this summary, we have relied heavily on Martin Buber's terminology and explanations.[14]

Remember that dialogue manifests itself more as a stance, orientation, or quality in communication rather than as a specific method, technique, or format. We can speak of an attitude of dialogue in human communication. As categories, these characteristics are not mutually exclusive, not completely separate from each other; there may be margins of overlap. Other writers might choose different language to describe essentially the same characteristics. Furthermore, the categories are not intended in any particular rank order of importance.

There is another important point to bear in mind. Even the characteristics of dialogue can be abused and used irresponsibly. Blunt honesty, for example, could be employed to humiliate others in order to satisfy our own ego and sense of self-importance.

Authenticity. One is direct, honest, and straightforward in communicating all information and feelings that are *relevant and legitimate* for the subject at hand. But we avoid simply letting ourselves go and saying everything that comes to mind. We strive to avoid facade, projecting a false image, or "seeming" to be something we are not. The communication filters formed by inappropriate or deceptive roles are minimized. But the legitimate expectations of an appropriate role can be honestly fulfilled. In judging appropriateness, we would consider both our own needs and those of other participants.

Inclusion. One attempts to "see the other," to "experience the other side," to "imagine the real," the reality of the other's viewpoint. Without giving up our own convictions or views, without yielding our own ground or sense of self, we imagine an event or feeling from the side of the other. We attempt to understand factually and emotionally the other's experience.

Confirmation. We express nonpossessive warmth for the other. The other person is valued for his or her worth and integrity as a human. A partner in dialogue is affirmed as a person, not merely tolerated, even though we oppose her or him on some specific matter. Others are confirmed in their right to their individuality, to their personal views. Confirmation involves our desire to assist others to maximize their potential, to become what they can become. The spirit of mutual trust is promoted. We affirm others as unique persons without necessarily approving of their behavior or views.

Presentness. Participants in a dialogue must give full concentration to bringing their total and authentic beings to the encounter. They must demonstrate willingness to become fully involved with each other by taking time, avoiding distraction, being communicatively accessible, and risking attachment. One avoids being an onlooker who simply takes in what is presented or an observer who analyzes. Rather, what is said to us enters meaningfully into our life; we set aside the armor used to thwart the signs of personal address. The dialogic person listens receptively and attentively and responds readily and totally. We are willing to reveal ourselves to others in ways appropriate to the relationship and to receive their revelation.

Spirit of Mutual Equality. Although society may rank participants in dialogue as of unequal status or accomplishment, and although the roles appropriate to each partner may differ, participants themselves view each other as persons rather than as objects, as things, to be exploited or manipulated for selfish satisfaction. The exercise of power or superiority is avoided. Participants do not impose their opinion, cause, or will. In dialogic communication, agreement of the listener with the speaker's aim is secondary to independent, self-deciding participation. Participants aid each other in making responsible decisions regardless of whether the decision be favorable or unfavorable to the particular view presented.

Supportive Climate. One encourages the other to communicate. One allows free expression, seeks understanding, and avoids value judgments that stifle. One shows desire and capacity to listen without anticipating, interfering, competing, refuting, or warping meanings into preconceived interpretations. Assumptions and prejudgments are minimized.

Characteristics of Monologue

In elaborating their view of communication as dialogue, many writers discuss the concept of communication as monologue. To illuminate dialogue, they contrast it with monologue as a usually undesirable type of human communication. Monologue frequently is equated with persuasion and propaganda. Such an equation is open to debate depending upon how persuasion and propaganda are defined. The relation of ethics and propaganda will be examined in chapter 7. Matson and Montagu contend that "the field of communication is today more than ever a battleground contested by two opposing conceptual forces—those of *monologue and dialogue.*"[15]

At the minimum, a human treated as an It in monologue simply is observed, classified, measured, or analyzed as an object, not encountered as a whole person.[16] The communication is nonpersonal or impersonal. More frequently, according to Buber, the I-It relation, or monological communication, is characterized in varying degrees by self-centeredness, deception, pretense, display, appearance, artifice, using, profit, unapproachableness, seduction, domination, exploitation, and manipulation.[17] Communicators manipulate others for their own selfish ends. They aim at power over people and view them as objects for enjoyment or as things through which to profit. The monological communicator is interested in the personal attributes of receivers only to the extent that he or she can capitalize on those attributes to achieve selfish ends. In monologue we are primarily concerned with what others think of us, with prestige and authority, with display of our own feelings, with display of power, and with molding others in our own image.

Buber describes typical examples of monologue disguised as dialogue:

> A *debate* in which the thoughts are not expressed in the way in which they existed in the mind but in the speaking are so pointed that they may strike home in the sharpest way, and moreover without the men that are spoken to being regarded in any way present as persons; a *conversation* characterized by the need neither to communicate something, nor to learn something, nor to influence someone, nor to come into connexion with someone, but solely by the desire to have one's own self-reliance confirmed by marking the impression that is made, or if it has become

unsteady to have it strengthened; a *friendly chat* in which each regards himself as absolute and legitimate and the other as relativized and questionable; a *lover's talk* in which both partners alike enjoy their own glorious soul and their precious experience—what an underworld of faceless spectres of dialogue![18]

Writers such as Matson and Montagu, Howe, Gusdorf, Gibb, Shostrom, Jaspers, Meerloo, Greenagel and Rudinow use much the same vocabulary as Buber to explain the nature of monologue.[19] A person employing monologue seeks to command, coerce, manipulate, conquer, dazzle, deceive, or exploit. Other persons are viewed as "things" to be exploited solely for the communicator's self-serving purpose; they are not taken seriously as persons. Choices are narrowed and consequences are obscured. Focus is on the communicator's message, not on the audience's real needs. The core values, goals, and policies espoused by the communicator are impervious to influence exerted by receivers. Audience feedback is used only to further the communicator's purpose. An honest response from a receiver is not wanted or is precluded. Monological communicators persistently strive to impose their truth or program on others; they have the superior attitude that they must coerce people to yield to what they believe others ought to know. Monologue lacks a spirit of mutual trust, and it displays a defensive attitude of self-justification.

Buber believes that some I-It relations in the form of an impersonal type of monologue often are unavoidable in human life (such as in routine, perfunctory interactions). For example, in impersonal, pragmatic exchanges of information (that Buber terms "technical dialogue") where understanding of each other as unique individuals is not expected or appropriate, dialogue would not be the goal. In Buber's view, I-It relations, especially in the form of exploitative monologue, become evil when they predominate our life and increasingly shut out dialogue. In contrast, Howe contends that any monologue (nondialogue) relation always is unethical because it exploits.[20]

In his article "On Using People," Don Marietta questions the view that human communication never should be of the I-It type and never should reflect attitudes of participants being "used" as things and means.[21] He rejects misinterpretations of the second version of Kant's Categorical Imperative that urge us to treat others and ourselves always as ends and never as means. Rather, Kant said humans should not be treated "merely" (or solely) as means. He argues that some institutionalized communication transactions, such as the type that occurs when we pay for an item at a drugstore counter, do not ethically demand full dialogue. As minimal ethical standards, such routine and relatively impersonal interactions demand honesty and civility. But making all human relationships as personal as marriage or close friendship "would be intolerable." In all human communication, contends Marietta, persons should not be used solely as means. In communication a person is ethically justified in using another person as a means "if the relationship is such that the used person is not prevented from realizing his own ends in that relationship." For Marietta, a communicator ethically could "use" another person to satisfy his or her own ends as long as the other person also has the opportunity to satisfy his or her own ends, and as long as the other person is not systematically subjected to harm in areas of psychological vulnerability.

Humans as Persons and Objects

John Stewart suggests characteristics of both personal and impersonal communication in which we relate to others primarily as persons or primarily as objects.[22] Persons each are unique biologically and psychologically, are actors capable of choice among means and ends, are beings whose feelings and emotions are not readily measurable and quantifiable, and are reflective in the sense of being aware of life's meaning and time flow. In contrast, when we communicate with others primarily as objects, we see them as essentially similar and interchangeable, as responding without choice to external stimuli, as measurable and quantifiable in all important respects, and as unreflective and unaware of their "self" or their "place" in human existence. In addition, Stewart argues that only persons are *addressable*, while objects are not. Objects can be *talked* about and even animals can be *talked to*. But only persons can be *talked with*. Only persons can engage in mutually responsive communication.

Stewart contends, however, that not all objectifying communication is undesirable. For some relationships, dialogic communication is not possible, appropriate, or expected. While not all our communication can be dialogic, believes Stewart, more of it could be. Stewart concludes:[23]

> The ethic which emerges from this perspective on persons is grounded in response-ability. Since each communication contact has person-building potential, ethical communication is communication which promotes realization of that potential. Such communication is responsive, attentive to and concretely guided by as much as possible of one's own and the other's humanness, that is, uniqueness, choice-making, more-than-spatiotemporal aspects, and reflexivity.

Dialogue and Persuasion

Some writers on the nature of monologue, by equating monologue and persuasion, contend that all attempts at persuasion are unethical. Is it inherently unethical to attempt to persuade others, to ask them to adopt your viewpoint?

Buber, and some others to varying degrees, believe that even in dialogue we may express disagreement with other persons, may seek to influence them, or may attempt to suggest the inadequacy of what those persons are believing or doing. But always, according to Buber, the communicative influence must be exerted in a noncoercive, nonmanipulative manner that respects the free choice and individuality of the receiver.[24]

In a speech in 1953 in Frankfurt, Germany, Martin Buber, himself a Jew of German origin, reflected the dialogic attitudes of inclusion and confirmation toward Germans who participated in, who ignored, or who resisted Nazi atrocities. Buber stood his own ground in condemning those who committed atrocities while at the same time attempting to understand the circumstances and motives of those who knew of atrocities but did not resist or those who were uninformed but did not investigate rumors.[25]

Persuaders could, we contend, present their best advice for the solution to a problem in as sound and influential a way as possible, always admitting that it may not be the only solution and that ultimately the audience has the right of independent choice. A communicator can advise rather than coerce or command.[26] While the communicator may express judgments of policies and behaviors, judgments of the intrinsic worth of audience members *as persons* are avoided.

Richard M. Weaver feels that all humans are "born rhetoricians" who by nature desire to persuade and be persuaded. "We all need," says Weaver, "to have things pointed out to us, things stressed in our own interest.[27] Monologue is most properly viewed as only one (although usually unethical and undesirable) species of persuasion; monologue, we would contend, should not be equated with *all* types of persuasion.

Some scholars perceive dialogue and monologue as mutually exclusive opposites. Certainly Matson and Montagu describe them as polar phenomena. Buber, however, sees any human relationship as involving greater or lesser degrees of dialogical and monological attitudes. He rejects a conception of communication as either all dialogic or all monologic, and he realizes that "pure" dialogue seldom occurs.[28]

Conditions and Contexts for Dialogue

Under what conditions and in what communication contexts and situations can dialogue function most effectively? We could speculate that dialogue seems most likely to develop in private, two-person, face-to-face, oral communication settings that extend, even intermittently, over lengthy periods of time. If this is true, dialogue would most frequently occur in such relationships as husband–wife, parent–child, doctor–patient, psychotherapist–client, counselor–counselee, clergy–parishioner, continuing small-group discussions, and sensitivity-training sessions. It is also true, however, that Martin Buber and Carl Rogers believed that dialogue, either fully or partially mutual, frequently occurs during brief periods or "dialogic moments" in longer interactions or established relationships.[29]

Privacy seems desirable for dialogue, but perhaps not absolutely necessary. While dialogue may be most likely when only two people are involved, it would seem possible for dialogue to occur in small groups. Although face-to-face oral communication seems requisite for optimum dialogue, communicators can reflect dialogical attitudes toward receivers in writing or in mass media situations.

Buber believes that dialogue to some degree is possible in virtually any realm of human interaction. He believes that many role-oriented relationships, such as student–teacher, doctor–patient, therapist–client, and parishioner–pastor, can be conducted authentically in partial mutuality with dialogic attitudes between participants. Buber also contends that partially mutual dialogue can occur in the arenas of politics and business. For example, he says that the leader of a business enterprise could "practice the responsibility of dialogue" (both through individual actions and through structuring the organization) by treating employees as persons rather than numbers, servants, or interchangeable parts. Employees within an organization ("in the factory, in the shop, in the office, in the mine, on the tractor, at the printing-press") can participate in moments of partially mutual dialogue with each other.[30]

Indeed, several scholars have advocated the desirability of a dialogical ethical approach to guide the public relations practices of organizations. At length they describe how ethical public relations practice should embody attitudes of dialogue rather than monologue.[31] You are urged to read these provocative arguments and judge for yourself how adequately they have made their case for the applicability of dialogue to public relations.

Despite the unplanned nature of dialogue, and although "genuine dialogue cannot be arranged beforehand," Buber believes nevertheless that "one can hold oneself free and open for it" and can be "at its disposal."[32] Perhaps this is what Thomas Nilsen means by choosing to open ourselves to dialogue:[33]

> I can choose whether I will consider the other's self-determining choice more important than his acceptance of mine; I can choose whether I will turn to the other and seek to meet him; to perceive him in his wholeness and uniqueness; I can choose whether I will value him as a person above all else. I can choose to try to relate to him as honestly as I can rather than put on a front so that he cannot relate to me.

Dialogical Attitudes in Public and Written Communication

Dialogue flowers most easily in private, interpersonal communication settings, but public communicators (in speeches, essays, editorials, and mass media appeals) *could* hold and reflect honest, sincere dialogical attitudes toward their audiences.[34] In fact, public communicators in speech or writing often do reveal varying degrees of dialogue or monologue. Several textbooks on written rhetoric advocate insights from Carl Rogers.[35] Mahatma Gandhi, the famous advocate of nonviolent political change in India, reflected major attitudinal elements of dialogue in a public address to an international conference.[36] Martin Buber's ninety-minute public conversation with Carl Rogers at the University of Michigan can be seen as embodying moments of genuine dialogue, and, after the event, Buber came to hold the view that dialogical attributes can be located in public communication.[37]

Consider the somewhat monological attitudes that a newspaper reader perceived in the nationally syndicated opinion column of Carl Rowan:[38]

> Carl Rowan so often writes as if there can be just no viewpoint other than his own. His recent column on amnesty was a case in point. I am not writing to take issue with his position, but to chide him for his attitude toward those who disagree with him. . . . Let Rowan plump for his convictions. . . . But let him refrain from disparagement—to the point of contempt—toward those who disagree with him.

Another example of monological arrogance was Secretary of State James Baker's explanation in 1990 of the need to send American troops to the Gulf War: "To bring it down to the average American citizen, let me say it means jobs." Syndicated news columnist Mona Charen wondered: "Bring it 'down to the average American'? Is that how this administration sees the people? Too simpleminded or too selfish to understand anything beyond their pocketbooks?"[39]

Several scholars of rhetoric explore monological and dialogical communicator attitudes toward audience from the metaphorical vantage point of rhetoric as love.[40] Richard M. Weaver analyzes Plato's *Phaedrus* from a rhetorical viewpoint and concludes that, among other things, it is a commentary on rhetoric in the guise of the metaphor of love. Weaver's perception of the *Phaedrus* allows him to explain three kinds of lovers (the nonlover, the evil lover, and the noble lover), which he in turn equates with the neutral speaker, the evil speaker, and the noble speaker.[41] Each of the lover-speakers exhibits characteristic attitudes toward the audience. The neutral speaker's attitudes are prudence, disinterest, objectivity, moderation, blandness, and cold rationality. The evil or base speaker reflects attitudes of exploitation, domination, possessiveness, selfishness, superiority, deception, manipulation, and defensiveness. The evil communicator, according to Weaver, frequently subverts clear definition, causal reasoning, and an "honest examination of alternatives" by "discussing only one side of an issue, by mentioning cause without consequence or consequence without cause, acts without agents or agents without agency." The noble speaker described by Weaver exalts the intrinsic worth of the audience and reflects essentially dialogical attitudes: respect, concern, selflessness, involvement, and a genuine desire to help the audience actualize its potentials and ideals.

Through the metaphorical prism of love, Wayne Brockriede probes the nature of argumentation and of arguers as lovers. Using a sexual metaphor, Brockriede identifies three stances of arguer toward other arguers: rape, seduction, and love.[42] Several writers supplement Brockriede's analysis by suggesting additional stances: flirtation, romance, and lust. Emory Griffin develops categories roughly similar to those of Weaver and Brockriede: nonlover, smother lover, legalistic lover, flirt, seducer, rapist, and true lover.[43] (See our later discussion of Griffin's view in chapter 6.)

The rhetorical rapist, according to Brockriede, assumes a unilateral relationship with the audience, sees them as objects, victims, or inferior human beings, and intends to manipulate or violate them. The rapist's attitudes toward the audience are superiority, domination, coercion, and contempt. The attitudes of rhetorical rape often manifest themselves, feels Brockriede, in the courtroom, political campaign, business meeting, legislative chamber, and competitive intercollegiate debate.

The rhetorical seducer, according to Brockriede, is often found in the fields of politics and advertising and also assumes a unilateral relationship with the audience. The rhetorical seducer's attitudinal tone is deceptive, insincere, charming, beguiling, and indifferent to the identity, integrity, and rationality of the audience. Characteristically, says Brockriede, the rhetorical seducer employs logical fallacies (such as begging the question and the red herring), misuses evidence (such as withholding information and quoting out of context), and bedazzles with appeals, language, and presentation that lower the audience's reflective guard.

In contrast, the rhetorical lover represents the desirable (dialogical) argumentative stance. A bilateral or power parity relationship is sought by the rhetorical lover who views the audience as persons rather than objects or victims. The attitudes of speaker toward audience characterizing the rhetorical lover are equality, respect, willingness to risk self-change, openness to new ideas and arguments, and a genuine desire to promote free choice in the audience. Brockriede believes that the attitudes of rhetorical love frequently are found in communication between friends, actual lovers, philosophers, and scientists.

Toward an Ethic for Rhetoric

Some conceptions of mature and responsible rhetoric or argument appear similar at a number of points to a dialogic ethic. The conceptions further open the possibility that dialogic attitudes may be applicable to some degree, or in part, in public communication. To stimulate discussion of this possibility, we offer here a synthesis of standards for sound and ethical rhetoric derived from Douglas Ehninger, Walter Fisher, Wayne Brockriede, and Henry W. Johnstone, Jr.[44] Ethical rhetoric:

1. serves the ends of self-discovery, social knowledge, or public action more than personal ambition;
2. avoids intolerance and acknowledges audience freedom of choice and freedom of assent;
3. is reflexive in including self-scrutiny of one's own evidence, reasoning, and motives;

4. is attentive to data through use of accurate, complete, and relevant evidence and reasoning and through use of appropriate field-dependent tests for soundness of evidence and reasoning;

5. is bilateral, meaning it includes mutuality of personal and intellectual risk, openness to the possibility of self-change, and openness to scrutiny by others;

6. is self-perpetuating. Disagreement on a subject leaves open the possibility of deliberation on other subjects and of later deliberation on the disputed subject. Also, human capacities for persuasion, in ourselves and in others, are nurtured through what Henry W. Johnstone terms the habits of resoluteness, openness, gentleness, and compassion (see our summary in chapter 3);

7. embodies an attitude of reasonableness, including willingness to present reasons in support of our views, tolerance of presentation of reasons by others, respect for the intrinsic worth of the other person as a human, and avoidance of personalizing the controversy;

8. manifests what Walter R. Fisher terms the "logic of good reasons." Such a logic of value judgment embodies five key questions. (a) What are the implicit and explicit values embedded in a message? (b) Are the values appropriate to the nature of the decision that the message bears upon? (c) What would be the effects of adhering to the values in regard to one's concept of oneself, to one's behavior, to one's relationships with others and society, and to the processes of rhetorical transaction? (d) Are the values confirmed or validated in one's personal experience, in the lives or statements of others whom one admires and respects, and/or in a conception of the best audience that one can conceive? (e) Even if an immediate need for belief or action has been demonstrated, would an outside observer/critic assess the values offered or assumed in the message as the ideal basis for human conduct?

Dialogical Ethics and Significant Choice

Some scholars advocate that dialogue, as a more desirable type of communication behavior, should be *substituted* for persuasion. Such a position usually is taken when persuasion is defined as synonymous with unethical monologue. Other scholars, in contrast, see dialogue as a *supplement* to traditional theory, practice, and ethics of persuasion.

Although Thomas Nilsen's *Ethics of Speech Communication* primarily develops a political perspective centering on the concept of "significant choice" (see our earlier discussion in chapter 2), he also offers some supplementary dialogical standards for assessing the ethics of interpersonal communication.[45] Nilsen feels interpersonal communication, where "the impact of personality on personality is more immediate" than in public communication, must meet the ethical standards both of significant choice and of dialogue. "Morally right speech," says Nilsen, "is that which opens up channels for mind to reach mind, heart to reach heart." Such speech creates conditions "in which the personality can function most freely and fully." Nilsen believes that ethical interpersonal communication fosters the dignity of the individual personality, optimizes the sharing of thought and feeling, promotes feelings of belonging and acceptance, and fosters cooperation and mutual respect.

Nilsen suggests that the following attitudes be encouraged for achievement of ethical interpersonal communication: (1) respect for a person as a person regardless of age, status, or relationship to the speaker; (2) respect for the other person's ideas, feelings, intentions, and integrity; (3) permissiveness, objectivity, and open-mindedness, which encourage freedom of expression; (4) respect for evidence and the rational weighing of alternatives; and (5) careful and empathic listening prior to agreeing or disagreeing.

Paul Keller and Charles Brown offer a dialogical perspective for interpersonal communication as a supplement to more traditional political perspectives for judging the ethics of persuasion.[46] In fact, they build their view in part on Nilsen's analysis of values fundamental to the U.S. political system. As basic democratic values they adhere to the intrinsic worth of the human personality and the process of self-determination as means of individual fulfillment. They see "signs concerning the attitude of speaker and listener toward each other" as more valid ethical indexes than are indications of loyalty to rationality or to some conception of universal truth.

Keller and Brown would demand that a speaker be sensitive to listener freedom of choice and be willing to tolerate a listener response contrary to the one sought. If a speaker attempts to influence others and the suggestion or advice is rejected by listeners, the speaker is unethical to the degree that his subsequent communication with them reflects such attitudes as anger, despondency, appeal of sympathy, withdrawal, or unconcern. Ethical standards for interpersonal communication are violated, believe Keller and Brown, to the degree that a speaker shows hostility toward listeners or in some way tries to subjugate them.

In her article, "Nixon and the Strategy of Avoidance," Karen Rasmussen applies standards of significant choice, dialogue, and rhetorical seduction to evaluate the ethics of Richard M. Nixon's public communication during the 1972 presidential campaign. You may wish to develop your own assessment of how adequately and appropriately she applies these standards.[47]

Guidelines for Applying Dialogical Standards

Dialogue has been criticized for being too idealistic and unrealistic, for being inappropriate in some communication situations, for being promoted by some as the only acceptable mode of human communication, and for being ineffective in addressing harmful power imbalances such as entrenched racism.[48] In defense of dialogue, however, Anderson, Baxter, and Cissna remind us:

> Dialogue scholars tend to acknowledge, with Buber, that this phenomenon exists in moments rather than extended states, that it cannot be lionized, that it cannot become business as usual, and that it cannot be planned precisely or made to happen. Further, life presents many situations that do not demand dialogic responses, and faith in dialogue will not necessarily lead to rosy results. . . . However, this suggests neither that dialogue is the only valid model for communication, nor that message dissemination techniques are inappropriate or unworthy of study.[49]

And Julia Wood urges: "Yet for dialogue to be possible, people—particularly those who enjoy relative privilege—must take responsibility for identifying and reducing socially determined asymmetries that dictate who gets to speak, what forum and forms of speech are deemed legitimate, whose speech counts, and to whom it counts."[50]

Note that when two basic dialogical attitudes come into conflict, situational factors (such as will be discussed in chapter 5) may influence ethical judgment. A choice may have to be made and a temporary hierarchy of priorities established. In a specific communication situation, for example, the attitude of concern for the psychological welfare of a close friend might take precedence over an attitude of total frankness and blunt honesty. In another specific communication situation, an urgent need to prevent physical violence or harm may be a higher priority than being attentive and accessible.

Remember that communicator attitudes toward receivers are revealed *both* through verbal elements (word choice, overt meaning) *and* through nonverbal elements (eye contact, facial expression, gestures, posture, vocal tone and quality, etc.). Consider whether dialogical and monological attitudes seem most clearly and easily revealed through verbal or nonverbal cues.

John Makay and William Brown list ten conditions for dialogue, which we also might use as ethical guides for determining the degree to which dialogical attitudes reveal themselves in a human communication transaction:[51]

1. Human involvement from a felt need to communicate
2. An atmosphere of openness, freedom, and responsibility
3. Dealing with the real issues and ideas relevant to the communicator
4. Appreciation of individual differences and uniqueness
5. Acceptance of disagreement and conflict with the desire to resolve them
6. Effective feedback and use of feedback
7. Mutual respect and, hopefully, trust
8. Sincerity and honesty in attitudes toward communication
9. A positive attitude for understanding and learning
10. A willingness to admit error and allow persuasion

Consider some of the popular interactive media such as e-mail, chat rooms, blogs, cell phone text messaging, and Microsoft Xbox. For example, blogs (short for Web logs) facilitate extensive participation between blogger and users. One 2005 estimate indicated that 8 million American adults have created their own blogs, almost 32 million indicated they read blogs, and over 14 million say they have responded to a blog. Blog activity has been compared to a conversation or a seminar.[52] How might we apply dialogical ethical standards to communication via blogs or other such interactive media?

The ethical standard implied in most conceptions of communication as dialogue seems clear. Human communication achieves maximum ethicality in appropriate situations to the degree that it reflects and fosters participant attitudes of authenticity, inclusion, confirmation, presentness, mutual equality, and supportiveness. A communicator's choices in seeking understanding or influence can be assessed for the extent to which they reveal dialogical attitudes, impersonal attitudes, or unethical, exploitative, monological attitudes.[53]

Notes

[1] For an earlier analysis than appears in this chapter, see Richard L. Johannesen, "The Emerging Concept of Communication as Dialogue," *Quarterly Journal of Speech*, 57 (December 1971): 373–382. For additional analyses, see John Stewart, "Foundations of Dialogic Communication," *Quarterly Journal of Speech*, 64 (April 1978): 183–201; Ronald C. Arnett, *Communication and Community: Implications of Martin Buber's Dialogue* (Carbondale: Southern Illinois University Press, 1986); Rob Anderson, Kenneth R. Cissna, and Ronald C. Arnett, eds., *The Reach of Dialogue: Confirmation, Voice, and Community* (Cresskill, NJ: Hampton Press, 1994).

[2] The major works by Martin Buber relevant to communication as dialogue are: *I and Thou*, trans. Ronald Gregor Smith, 2nd ed. (New York: Scribner's, 1958): *Between Man and Man*, trans. Ronald Gregor Smith (New York: Macmillan paperback, 1965), especially pp. 1–39, 83–103; *The Knowledge of Man*, ed. Maurice S. Friedman, trans. Friedman and Ronald Gregor Smith (New York: Harper and Row, 1965), especially pp. 72–88, 110–120, 166–184; and *Pointing the Way*, trans. Maurice S. Friedman (New York: Harper Torchbook, 1963), especially pp. 83, 206, 220–239. The standard analysis of Buber's concept of dialogue is Maurice S. Friedman, *Martin Buber: The Life of Dialogue* (New York: Harper Torchbook, 1960), especially pp. 57–97, 123–126, 176–183. See also Paul E. Pfuetze, *Self, Society, Existence: Human Nature and Dialogue in the Thought of George Herbert Mead and Martin Buber* (New York: Harper Torchbook, 1961), pp. 139–206; Rob Anderson, Leslie A. Baxter, and Kenneth N. Cissna, eds., *Dialogue: Theorizing Difference in Communication Studies* (Thousand Oaks, CA: Sage, 2004).

[3] Among the works of Karl Jaspers, see particularly *Philosophy*, trans. E. B. Ashton, vol. 2 (Chicago: University of Chicago Press, 1970), pp. 56–69, 76–77, 97, 101.

[4] Among the works of Carl Rogers, see *Client-Centered Therapy* (Boston: Houghton Mifflin, 1951), pp. 19–64; *On Becoming a Person* (Boston: Houghton Mifflin, 1961), pp. 16–22, 31–69, 126–158, 338–346, 356–359; Rogers and Barry Stevens, *Person to Person* (Lafayette, CA: Real People Press, 1967), pp. 88–103; "The Necessary and Sufficient Conditions of Therapeutic Personality Change," *Journal of Consulting Psychology*, 21 (February 1957): 95–103. For the other sources see: Erich Fromm, *The Art of Loving* (New York: Harper, 1956), pp. 7–31; Paul Tournier, *The Meaning of Persons*, trans. Edwin Hudson (New York: Harper and Row, 1957), pp. 123–159, 191, 196, 203, 209; Jack R. Gibb, "Defensive Communication," *Journal of Communication*, 11 (September 1961): 141–148; Everett L. Shostrom, *Man, the Manipulator* (New York: Bantam Books, 1968); Sidney M. Jourard, *The Transparent Self*, 2nd ed. (Princeton, NJ: Van Nostrand, 1971); David W. Johnson, *Reaching Out: Interpersonal Effectiveness and Self-Actualization*, 2nd ed. (Englewood Cliffs, NJ: Prentice-Hall, 1981); Abraham Maslow, *Motivation and*

Personality, 2nd ed. (New York: Harper and Row, 1970), ch. 11: Maslow, *Toward a Psychology of Being*, 2nd ed. (Princeton, NJ: Van Nostrand Insight Book, 1968), chs. 6 and 7; Maslow, *The Farther Reaches of Human Nature* (New York: Viking 1971), pp. 17–18, 41–73, 260–266, 347.

5 Reuel Howe, *The Miracle of Dialogue* (New York: Seabury Press, 1963), pp. 6, 36–83; Georges Gusdorf, *Speaking (La Parole)*, trans. Paul T. Brockelman (Evanston, IL: Northwestern University Press, 1965), pp. 57, 84–85, 101–104; Milton Mayeroff, *On Caring* (New York: Harper and Row, 1971); John Powell, S. J., *Why Am I Afraid to Tell You Who I Am?* (Chicago: Argus Communications, 1969); Floyd Matson and Ashley Montagu, eds., *The Human Dialogue* (New York: Free Press, 1967), pp. 1–11.

6 Kenneth H. Cissna and Rob Anderson, "Communication and the Ground of Dialogue," in Anderson, Cissna, and Arnett, eds., *The Reach of Dialogue*, pp. 9–30; "Studies in Dialogue," entire issue of *Southern Communication Journal*, 65 (Winter-Spring 2000). Also see Jeffrey W. Murray, *Face to Face: Emmanuel Levinas and (the) Communication (of) Ethics* (Lanham, MD: University Press of America, 2003).

7 Buber, *I and Thou*, pp. 34, 46, 48; Buber, "Interrogation of Martin Buber," in *Philosophical Interrogations*, Sydney and Beatrice Rome, eds. (New York: Holt, Rinehart, and Winston, 1964), pp. 28, 37–38, 57; Buber, *Between Man and Man*, pp. 19, 61–62, 97, 101; Buber, "Replies to My Critics," in *The Philosophy of Martin Buber*, Paul Arthur Schlipp and Maurice Friedman, eds. (La Salle, IL: Open Court Press, 1967), pp. 691–692. Also see John Stewart and Karen Zediker, "Dialogue as Tensional Ethical Practice," *Southern Communication Journal*, 65 (Winter–Spring, 2000): 240–241, note #1.

8 This description of Buber's conception is based on: Buber, *Between Man and Man*, pp. 5–10, 20–21, 82, 96–101, 202–205; Buber, *Knowledge of Man*, pp. 76–77, 86; Buber, *Pointing the Way*, p. 222; Friedman, *Martin Buber*, pp. 57, 81–89, 97, 180–181. Also see Dan Avnon, *Martin Buber: The Hidden Dialogue* (Lanham, MD: Rowman and Littlefield, 1998), pp. 39–40, 149–155.

9 Ronald C. Arnett, "Toward a Phenomenological Dialogue," *Western Journal of Speech Communication*, 45 (Summer 1981): 201–212; Rob Anderson, "Phenomenological Dialogue, Humanistic Psychology, and Pseudo-Walls: A Response and Extension," *Western Journal of Speech Communication*, 46 (Fall 1982): 344–357; accompanied by a reply by Arnett, "Rogers and Buber: Similarities, Yet Fundamental Differences": 358–372; Ronald C. Arnett, "What Is Dialogic Communication? Friedman's Contributions and Clarification," *Person-Centered Review*, 4 (February 1989): 42–60.

10 See, for example, Rogers, *Client-Centered Therapy*, pp. 19–64; Rogers, *On Becoming a Person*, pp. 16–22, 31–69, 126–158, 338–346; 356–359; Rogers and Stevens, *Person to Person*, pp. 88–103; Rogers in *Buber, The Knowledge of Man*, p. 170; Rogers, *A Way of Being* (Boston: Houghton Mifflin, 1980), chs. 1, 6, 7; Maurice Friedman, "Carl Rogers and Martin Buber: Self Actualization and Dialogue," *Person-Centered Review*, 1 (November 1986): 409–435.

11 Roderick P. Hart and Don M. Burks, "Rhetorical Sensitivity and Social Interaction," *Speech Monographs*, 38 (June 1972): 76, 84, 87, 89–90. For a contrasting view, see Allan Sillars, "Expression and Control in Human Interaction," *Western Speech*, 38 (Fall 1974): 269–277. Also see Donald K. Darnell and Wayne Brockriede, *Persons Communicating* (Englewood Cliffs, NJ: Prentice-Hall, 1976), chs. 2, 11, 12. For a critique of Hart and Burks's mistaken equating of dialogue and expressive communication, see Gerald Fulkerson, "The Ethics of Interpersonal Influence: A Critique of the Rhetorical Sensitivity Construct," *Journal of Communication and Religion*, 13 (1990): 1–14.

12 Rogers, *On Becoming a Person*, pp. 51, 61, 118.

13 Buber, *Knowledge of Man*, pp. 31–33, 75–77, 85–86, 171–173; Buber, *I and Thou*, pp. 131–134; Buber, *Between Man and Man*, pp. 95–101; Buber in Sydney and Beatrice Rome, eds., *Philosophical Interrogations*, p. 66. Also see three books by Maurice Friedman: *The Hidden Human Image* (New York: Delacorte, 1974), pp. 274–285; *Touchstones of Reality* (New York: Durton, 1972), p. 307; *To Deny Our Nothingness* (New York: Delacorte, 1967), p. 25; and Donald L. Berry, *Mutuality: The Vision of Martin Buber* (Albany: State University of New York Press, 1983), pp. 41–68.

14 See the writings by Martin Buber and Carl Rogers cited in prior footnotes. For a somewhat similar yet different set of dialogical characteristics or elements, see Kenneth N. Cissna and Rob Anderson, *Moments of Meeting: Buber, Rogers, and the Potential for Public Dialogue* (Albany:

State University of New York Press, 2002), pp. 9–11, 237–238. For interpretations of Buber on dialogue, see Maurice Friedman's two books: *Touchstones of Reality*, chs. 16, 17, 18; *To Deny Our Nothingness*, chs. 16, 19. Also see Alexander S. Kohanski, *An Analytical Interpretation of Martin Buber's I and Thou* (Woodbury, NY: Barron's Educational Series, 1975). Concerning Buber's views on lying and deception, see Virginia Shabatay, "Deception and the Relational: Martin Buber and Sissela Bok—Against the Generation of the Lie," in *Martin Buber and the Human Sciences*, Maurice Friedman, ed. (Albany: State University of New York Press, 1996), pp. 207–214. Bear in mind that Buber also describes the communication relationship of a human I with God, the Eternal Thou. His view of dialogic I-Thou communication between humans derives from his assumptions about the nature and significance of human communication with God and God with humans. See Buber, *I and Thou*, pp. 75–120; Friedman, *Martin Buber*, chs. 12, 24, 25; Kohanski, *Analytical Interpretation of Martin Buber's I and Thou*, pp. 100–147.

[15] Matson and Montagu, *The Human Dialogue*, p. viii.

[16] Kohanski, *Analytical Interpretation of Martin Buber's I and Thou*, pp. 48, 168, 174.

[17] This description of the I-It relation is based on Buber, *I and Thou*, pp. 34, 38, 43, 60, 105, 107; Buber, *Knowledge of Man*, pp. 82–83; *Between Man and Man*, pp. 19–20, 23, 29–30, 95; Friedman, *Martin Buber*, pp. 57–58, 63, 82, 123–124, 180.

[18] Buber, *Between Man and Man*, pp. 19–20.

[19] Matson and Montagu, *The Human Dialogue*, pp. 3–10; Howe, *The Miracle of Dialogue*, pp. 18–56, 84–88; Gusdorf, *Speaking*, pp. 106–108. Gibb, "Defensive Communication"; Shostrom, *Man, the Manipulator*; Jaspers, *Philosophy*, Vol. 2, pp. 49, 60, 80–84, 90; Joost Meerloo, *Conversation and Communication* (New York: International Universities Press, 1952), pp. 94–97, 133–143; Frank Greenagel, "Manipulation and the Cult of Communication in Contemporary Industry," in *Communication-Spectrum* 7, Lee Thayer, ed. (National Society for the Study of Communication, 1968), pp. 237–245; Joel Rudinow, "Manipulation," *Ethics*, 88 (July 1978): 338–347.

[20] Buber, *I and Thou*, pp. 34, 46, 48; Buber, *Between Man and Man*, p. 19; Ronald C. Arnett, *Dwell in Peace: Applying Nonviolence to Everyday Relationships* (Elgin, IL: Brethren Press, 1980), pp. 129–131; Howe, *Miracle of Dialogue*, pp. 38–39.

[21] Don E. Marietta, "On Using People," *Ethics*, 82 (April 1972): 232–238. Also see Arthur Flemming, "Using a Man as a Means," *Ethics*, 88 (July 1978): 283–298; for a contrasting view, see John R. S. Wilson, "In One Another's Power," Ibid., 299–315. Nancy Davis, "Using Persons and Common Sense," *Ethics*, 94 (April 1984): 387–406.

[22] John Stewart, ed., *Bridges Not Walls*, 9th ed. (New York: McGraw-Hill, 2006); Stewart and Carol Logan, *Together: Communicating Interpersonally*, 5th ed. (New York: McGraw-Hill, 1998), chs. 1 and 2.

[23] John Stewart, "Communication, Ethics, and Relativism: An Interpersonal Perspective," paper presented at Speech Communication Association convention, New York City, November 1980.

[24] Buber, *Knowledge of Man*, pp. 69–79. See also Rogers, *On Becoming a Person*, p. 358; Shostrom, *Man, the Manipulator*, p. 51.

[25] Buber, *Pointing the Way*, pp. 232–233; Arnett, *Dwell in Peace*, pp. 114–116.

[26] On the advisory function of rhetoric see Karl R. Wallace, "Rhetoric and Advising," *Southern Speech Journal*, 29 (Summer 1964): 279–284; Walter R. Fisher, "Advisory Rhetoric," *Western Speech*, 29 (Spring 1965): 14–19; B. J. Diggs, "Persuasion and Ethics," *Quarterly Journal of Speech*, 50 (December 1964): especially pp. 363–364.

[27] Richard M. Weaver, "Language Is Sermonic," in *Contemporary Theories of Rhetoric: Selected Readings*, Richard L. Johannesen, ed. (New York: Harper and Row, 1971), pp. 175–176.

[28] Buber, *Between Man and Man*, pp. 36, 97.

[29] Kenneth H. Cissna and Rob Anderson, "Theorizing about Dialogic Moments: The Buber–Rogers Position and Postmodern Themes," *Communication Theory*, 8 (February 1998): 63–104; Cissna and Anderson, *Moments of Meeting*.

[30] Buber, *I and Thou*, pp. 49, 131–134; Buber, *Between Man and Man*, pp. 35–38, 98–100; Buber, *The Knowledge of Man*, pp. 171–173; Buber, "Interrogation of Martin Buber," pp. 66–68. For example, see Eric M. Eisenberg, H. L. Goodall, Jr., and Angela Tretheway, *Organizational Communication: Balancing Creativity and Constraint*, 5th ed. (Boston: Bedford/St. Martins, 2007), pp. 39–53.

[31] Ron Pearson, "Business Ethics as Communication Ethics: Public Relations Practice and the Idea of Dialogue," in *Public Relations Theory*, Carl H. Botan and Vincent Hazelton, Jr., eds. (Hillsdale, NJ: Erlbaum, 1989), pp. 111–131; Pearson, "Beyond Ethical Relativism in Public Relations: Coorientation, Rules and the Idea of Communication Symmetry," in *Public Relations Research Annual*, Vol. 1, James E. Grunig and Larissa A. Grunig, eds. (Hillsdale, NJ: Erlbaum, 1989), pp. 67–86; Carl Botan, "A Human Nature Approach to Image and Ethics in International Public Relations," *Journal of Public Relations Research*, 5 (1993): 71–81; Carl Botan, "Ethics in Strategic Communication Campaigns: The Case for a New Approach to Public Relations," *Journal of Business Communication*, 34 (April 1997): 188–202; Michael L. Kent and Maureen Taylor, "Toward a Dialogic Theory of Public Relations," *Public Relations Review*, 28 (February 2002): 21–37.

[32] Buber, *Knowledge of Man*, p. 87; Buber, *Pointing the Way*, p. 206.

[33] Thomas R. Nilsen, "Dialogue and Group Process," paper presented at the 1969 convention of the Speech Association of America.

[34] For one innovative discussion, see George E. Yoos, "A Revision of the Concept of Ethical Appeal," *Philosophy and Rhetoric*, 12 (Winter 1979): 41–58. Also see Jeanine Czubaroff, "Dialogical Rhetoric: An Application of Martin Buber's Philosophy of Dialogue," *Quarterly Journal of Speech*, 86 (May 2000): 168–189; Cissna and Anderson, *Moments of Meeting*.

[35] Richard E. Young, et al., *Rhetoric: Discovery and Change* (New York: Harcourt, Brace and World, 1970), ch. 12; Maxine Hairston, *A Contemporary Rhetoric*, 3rd ed. (Boston: Houghton Mifflin, 1982). For a critical view of Rogers, see Phyllis Lassner, "Feminist Responses to Rogerian Argument," *Rhetoric Review*, 8 (Spring 1990): 220–231.

[36] Michael J. Beatty et al., "Elements of Dialogic Communication in Gandhi's Second Round Table Conference Address," *Southern Speech Communication Journal*, 44 (Summer 1979): 386–398. Also see V. V. Ramana Murti, "Buber's Dialogue and Gandhi's Satyagraha," *Journal of the History of Ideas*, 24 (1968): 605–613. For other discussions of dialogic attitudes in formal communication settings, see Donald G. Douglas, "Cordell Hull and the Implementation of the 'Good Neighbor Policy,'" *Western Speech*, 34 (Fall 1970): 288–299; William D. Thompson and Gordon C. Bennett, *Dialogue Preaching: The Shared Sermon* (Valley Forge, PA: Judson Press, 1969); Gary L. Cronkhite, *Public Speaking and Critical Listening* (Menlo Park, CA: Benjamin/Cummings, 1978), pp. 36–43.

[37] Rob Anderson and Kenneth N. Cissna, *The Martin Buber–Carl Rogers Dialogue: A New Transcript with Commentary* (Albany: State University of New York Press, 1997), pp. 117–119. Also see Kenneth N. Cissna and Rob Anderson, "Dialogue in Public: Looking Critically at the Buber–Rogers Dialogue," in *Martin Buber and the Human Sciences*, Maurice Friedman, ed. (Albany: SUNY Press, 1996), pp. 191–206; Rob Anderson and Kenneth N. Cissna, "Criticism and Conversational Texts: Rhetorical Bases of Role, Audience, and Style in the Buber–Rogers Dialogue," *Human Sciences*, 19 (1996): 85–118.

[38] Kathleen Kaufman, letter to the editor, *Chicago Daily News*, April 23, 1973.

[39] Mona Charen, "Unfamiliarity Breeds Contempt for Modest George," *Chicago Tribune*, November 19, 1990, sec. 1, p. 21.

[40] The following discussion of the views of rhetorical theorists is adapted from a more extensive examination of speaker attitude toward audience as a conceptual framework for rhetorical criticism: Richard L. Johannesen, "Attitude of Speaker Toward Audience: A Significant Concept for Contemporary Rhetorical Theory and Criticism," *Central States Speech Journal*, 25 (Summer 1974).

[41] Richard M. Weaver, *The Ethics of Rhetoric* (Chicago: Regnery, 1953), pp. 3–26.

[42] Wayne Brockriede, "Arguers as Lovers," *Philosophy and Rhetoric*, 5 (Winter 1972): 1–11.

[43] Darnell and Brockriede, *Persons Communicating*, pp. 162–169; Karen Rasmussen, "Nixon and the Strategy of Avoidance," *Central States Speech Journal*, 24 (Fall 1973): 193–202; Emory A. Griffin, *The Mind Changers: The Art of Christian Persuasion* (Wheaton, IL: Tyndale House, 1976), ch. 3.

[44] Douglas Ehninger, "Argument as Method: Its Nature, Its Limitations and Its Uses," *Speech Monographs*, 37 (June 1970): 101–110: Darnell and Brockriede, *Persons Communicating*, chs. 7,

11; Walter R. Fisher, "Toward a Logic of Good Reasons," *Quarterly Journal of Speech*, 64 (December 1978): 376–384; Fisher, "Rationality and the Logic of Good Reasons," *Philosophy and Rhetoric*, 13 (Spring 1980): 121–130; Henry W. Johnstone, Jr., "Towards an Ethics of Rhetoric," *Communication*, 6, no. 2 (1981): 305–314; Johnstone, Jr., *Validity and Rhetoric in Philosophical Argument* (University Park, PA: The Dialogue Press of Man and the World, 1978), chs. 11, 17; Johnstone, Jr., "Bilaterality in Argument and Communication," in *Advances in Argumentation Theory and Research*, J. Robert Cox and Charles A. Willard, eds. (Carbondale: Southern Illinois University Press, 1982), pp. 95–102.

45 Thomas R. Nilsen, *Ethics of Speech Communication*, 2nd ed. (Indianapolis: Bobbs-Merrill, 1974), pp. 19, 88–94.

46 Paul W. Keller and Charles T. Brown, "An Interpersonal Ethic for Communication," *Journal of Communication*, 18 (March 1968): 73–81. A later expanded version is Brown and Keller, *Monologue to Dialogue An Exploration of Interpersonal Communication*, 2nd ed. (Englewood Cliffs, NJ: Prentice-Hall, 1979), ch. 11.

47 Karen Rasmussen, "Nixon and the Strategy of Avoidance," *Central States Speech Journal*, 24 (Fall 1973): 193–202.

48 John Durham Peters, *Speaking into the Air: A History of the Idea of Communication* (Chicago: University of Chicago Press, 1999), pp. 33–62; Mark Lawrence McPhail, "Race and the (Im)Possibility of Dialogue," in *Dialogue: Theorizing Difference in Communication Studies*, Rob Anderson, Leslie A. Baxter, and Kenneth N. Cissna, eds. (Thousand Oaks, CA: Sage, 2004), pp. 210, 216–217; Kevin Stoker and Kati A. Tusinski, "Reconsidering Public Relations' Infatuation with Dialogue: Why Engagement and Reconciliation Can Be More Ethical than Symmetry and Reciprocity," *Journal of Mass Media Ethics*, 21 (2006): 156–176. Also see Julia T. Wood, "Foreword: Entering into Dialogue," in *Dialogue*, Anderson, Baxter, and Cissna, eds., pp. xix, xxii.

49 Rob Anderson, Leslie A. Baxter, and Kenneth N. Cissna, "Texts and Contexts of Dialogue," in *Dialogue*, Anderson, Baxter, and Cissna, eds., pp. 15–16. Also see Ronald C. Arnett and Pat Arneson, *Dialogic Civility in a Cynical Age* (Albany: State University of New York Press, 1999), pp. 12, 286.

50 Julia T. Wood, "Foreword: Entering in to Dialogue," p. xx. Also see Scott C. Hammond, Rob Anderson, and Kenneth N. Cissna, "The Problematics of Dialogue and Power," *Communication Yearbook*, 27 (2003): 125–157.

51 John J. Makay and William R. Brown, *The Rhetorical Dialogue* (Dubuque, IA: William C. Brown Co., 1972), p. 27. For a detailed discussion of these conditions, see John J. Makay and Beverly A. Gaw, *Personal and Interpersonal Communication: Dialogue with the Self and with Others* (Columbus, OH: Charles E. Merrill Co., 1975), ch. 8.

52 "A Primer: Blogs and Blogging," *Media Ethics*, 16 (Spring 2005): 14–16.

53 See Stewart and Zediker, "Dialogue as Tensional Ethical Practice," 224–242; Michael Gardiner, "Alterity and Ethics: A Dialogical Perspective," *Theory, Culture, and Society*, 13 (1996): 121–143.

5

Situational Perspectives

Situational perspectives focus regularly and primarily on the *elements of the specific communication situation at hand*. Virtually all perspectives (those mentioned in this book and others) make some allowances, on rare occasion, for the modified application of ethical criteria due to special circumstances. However, an extreme situational perspective routinely makes judgments only in light of *each different context*. Criteria from broad political, human nature, dialogical, or religious perspectives are minimized; absolute and universal standards are avoided.

Among the concrete situational or contextual factors that may be relevant to making a purely situational ethical evaluation are: (1) the role or function of the communicator for the audience (listeners or readers); (2) audience standards concerning reasonableness and appropriateness; (3) degree of audience awareness of the communicator's techniques; (4) degree of urgency for implementation of the communicator's proposal; (5) audience goals and values; (6) audience standards for ethical communication.

Two analysts of communication ethics offer their negative judgments of an extreme or "pure" situational perspective. "When the matter of ethics" is reduced to pure situationism, argues John Merrill, "it loses all meaning as ethics." "If every case is different, if every situation demands a different standard, if there are no absolutes in ethics, then we should scrap the whole subject . . . and simply be satisfied that each person run his life by his whims or 'considerations' which may change from situation to situation."[1] Bert Bradley concludes:[2]

> It appears . . . that situation ethics has an unsettling ability to justify a number of diverse decisions. It is not difficult to see how situation ethics can be used to rationalize, either consciously or unconsciously, decisions and actions that stem from selfish and evasive origins.
>
> An extremely vulnerable aspect of situation ethics is that it requires a high degree of sophistication in reasoning, objectivity in analysis, and an unusual breadth of perspective to exist in combination within a single individual. These attributes rarely occur singly in human beings.

71

Situational Ethics and
Public Relations Professionals

Despite such concerns and criticisms, situational ethics requires our attention because of its pervasive influence within the field of communication. For example, situational ethics has been described as "the dominant moral value in the decision-making process of U.S. public relations."[3] David L. Martinson explains that most public relations practitioners have little background in moral philosophy, and as a result, they tend not to think deeply about their moral responsibilities. When confronted with an ethical dilemma, the tendency is to set aside moral rules and principles in order to "just deal" with the situation. "Many undoubtedly respond by 'doing what needs to be done'—leaving 'worries' about ethical questions until 'later.'" In this extreme form, situational ethics makes every situation exceptional, and thus undermines moral rules and principles. Martinson rejects this attitude saying that "individuals—particularly those who claim to be professionals—must come to ethical decision making in something at least approaching a systematic fashion."[4]

However, Martinson also warns against overreacting in the other direction. Even if one rejects an extreme situational perspective on communication ethics, the opposite extreme—rigid adherence to moral principles and rules without any attention to the situation—is equally problematic. He explains, "The context or situation is a critical consideration in making the moral judgment . . . even those who abhor situational ethics still must take situation or context into account." So, for example, public relations professionals do have a presumptive moral responsibility to tell the truth. Even so, there may be exceptional situations in which rigid adherence to this principle of truth telling would lead to morally harmful results. Failure to pay attention to the specific context or situation would be to "place the letter of the law above the spirit of the law."

Martinson advises that public relations practitioners pay attention not only to moral rules and principles but also to the ways in which those rules and principles apply (or don't apply) in particular situations. He reminds us that to suggest "that circumstances are a consideration in applying ethical principles is a far cry from contending that 'each situation is unique . . . (and) so moral principles are useless.'" Ultimately, he concludes:[5]

> In considering circumstances, one must apply the same rules—principles—to himself or herself that he or she would apply to others. (If, for example, one would want to defend, as ethical, telling a lie under a particular extreme circumstance, that individual would have to agree that others would also be acting ethically if they were to lie to him or her *under the identical circumstances*.)

Diggs's Situational Perspective

B. J. Diggs also offers a partially situational approach to communication ethics. He primarily focuses on the "contextual character of the ethical standards" that should govern persuasion.[6] Diggs believes that a persuader's role or position, as defined by the specific situation, audience, and society, should determine what criteria are appropriate for judging the ethics of means and ends. In trying to persuade us, a friend, lawyer, or salesperson each would be subject to somewhat different ethical standards. Even generally accepted universal or societal ethical norms, says Diggs, often depend for their interpretation and application on the nature of the persuader's specific role with the audience.

Within his situational viewpoint stressing the nature of a persuader's specific role, Diggs suggests various guidelines for assessment of ethics. We should consider the degree to which we or another person: (1) has a *right* to communicate on the subject (has adequate knowledge of the subject and of audience needs and responsibilities); (2) has an *obligation* to communicate on the subject (perhaps due to role or possession of vitally needed information); (3) uses morally right communicative means; (4) urges the wise and right course; (5) and demonstrates good reasons for adopting the view advocated.[7] How valuable as guidelines are these considerations suggested by Diggs?

Diggs also notes that the receiver or persuadee can share in the blame for unethical persuasion. Being gullible, too open-minded, or being too closed-minded, Diggs argues, can allow the success of unethical persuasion. Do you agree with Diggs? Who should bear the prime responsibility for the ethical level of persuasion in a society—the persuader, the audience, or both?

Fletcher's Christian Situation Ethics

In 1966, Joseph Fletcher, a professor of social ethics at an Episcopal theological school, published his controversial book, *Situation Ethics: The New Morality.*[8] Obviously Fletcher's view also could be discussed in the following chapter on religious perspectives. It is included here because it fits significantly but not completely the criteria of a situational perspective, discussed at the beginning of the chapter. One premise of his Christian situation ethics is that ethical judgments of human behavior, including communication, should be made in light of specific situational factors rather than according to prescriptive or absolute standards. Another premise of his Christian situation ethics is that there is *one* absolute ethical criterion to guide situational evaluations— namely, *love* for fellow humans in the form of genuine affection for them and concern for their welfare. This loving relationship is similar in some respects to attitudes characteristic of dialogue as examined previously in chapter 4.[9]

To aid in the ethical evaluation of human behavior, Fletcher outlines four general situational elements that easily could be used to judge communication ethics: What is the end or goal sought? What means or methods are used to achieve the end? What motive(s) generate the effort? What are the foreseeable immediate and remote consequences of the end and means?[10]

Three quotations summarize Fletcher's concept of Christian situation ethics.[11]

> The situationist enters into every decision-making situation armed with the ethical maxims of his community and its heritage, and he treats them with respect as illuminators of his problems. Just the same he is prepared in any situation to compromise them or set them aside in the situation if love seems better served by doing so.

> Christian situation ethics has only one norm or principle or law . . . that is binding and unexceptionable, always good and right regardless of the circumstances. That is "love"—the *agape* of the summary commandment to love God and the neighbor. Everything else without exception, all laws and rules and principles and ideals and norms, are only *contingent*, only valid *if they happen* to serve love in any situation.

> As the Christian situationist sees it, his faith answers for him three questions of the seven always to be asked. These are his "universals." He knows the *what*; it is love. He knows the *why*; for God's sake. He knows the *who*; it is his neighbors, people. But only in and of the situation can he answer the other four questions: When? Where? Which? How?

Alinsky's Situational Perspective

In *Rules for Radicals*, Saul Alinsky, a noted community organizer, presents an essentially situational perspective for evaluating the ethics of communication and persuasion as forces for societal change. He does espouse the democratic political values of equality, justice, peace, cooperation, educational and economic opportunity, freedom, right of dissent, and the preciousness of human life.[12] But Alinsky constantly stresses that situational and contextual ethical judgments of communication are necessary for actualizing these goals. The communicator persuading in behalf of significant societal change, believes Alinsky, must view truth and all values as relative.[13] In the revised edition of *Reveille for Radicals*, Alinsky argues pragmatically: "We must accept open-ended systems of ethics and values, not only to meet constantly changing conditions but also to keep changing ourselves, in order to survive in the fluid society that lies ahead of us. Such systems must be workable in the world *as it is* and not unrealistically aimed toward the world *as we would like it to be*."[14]

Alinsky develops eleven rules for ethical judgment of means and ends, including communicative means and ends, in societal agitation and protest.[15] Note the distinctly situational nature of many of these rules, particularly the third, fourth, fifth, and eighth. To what extent should we accept Alinsky's view as a desirable and workable ethical perspective? In paraphrased and condensed form, Alinsky's rules are:

1. One's concern with the ethics of means and ends varies inversely with one's personal interest in the issue. When our interest is minimal or when we are far from the scene of conflict, we can afford the luxury of morality.

2. The judgment of the ethics of means is dependent upon the political position of those sitting in judgment. (For illustration of this variability, refer to the diverse political perspectives that we examined in chapter 2.)

3. In war the end justifies almost any means. Alinsky does not mean solely military combat. "A war is not an intellectual debate, and in the war against social evils there are no rules of fair play."[16]

4. Judgment must be made in the context of the times in which the action occurred and not from any other chronological vantage point.

5. Concern with ethics increases with the number of means available and vice versa. Moral questions may enter when we have the opportunity to choose among equally effective alternative means.

6. The less important the end desired, the more one can afford to engage in ethical evaluations of means.

7. Generally, success or failure is a mighty determinant of ethics. A successful outcome may allow the suspect means to be rationalized as ethical.

8. The morality of a means depends upon whether the means is being employed at a time of imminent defeat or imminent victory. The same means used when victory is assured may be judged immoral, but when used in desperate circumstances may be acceptable.

9. Any effective means automatically is judged by the opposition as unethical.

10. You do what you can with what you have and clothe it with moral garments. Leaders such as Churchill, Gandhi, Lincoln, and Jefferson always covered naked self-interest in the clothing of "moral principles" such as "freedom," "equality of humankind," "a law higher than man-made law," and so on.

11. Goals must be phrased in powerful general terms such a "Liberty, Equality, Fraternity," "Of the Common Welfare," "Pursuit of Happiness," or "Bread and Peace." (In this connection we profitably might examine the contemporary use of slogans and phrases that reflect potent value commitments: Duty, Honor, Country; Law and Order; Law and Order with Justice; Freedom Now!; All Power to the People; Peace with Honor.)[17]

Alinsky also offers a number of "rules" for utilizing "power tactics" to aid the "have-nots" in taking power away from the "haves." In most cases, these rules can be applied to tactics and techniques of protest communication. Apart from the situational perspective in which they are rooted, what might be some other ethical perspectives and sets of standards that appropriately could be applied to assess the ethics of these rules? Do *you* believe that any of these rules or tactics are unethical and, if so, why? Alinsky discusses these rules at length in *Rules for Radicals;* they are presented here in condensed and partially paraphrased form:[18]

1. Power is not only what you have but what the enemy thinks you have.

2. Never go outside the experience of your people.

3. Whenever possible go outside the experience of the enemy. Attempt to cause confusion, fear, and retreat.

4. Make the enemy live up to their own book of rules. They will be unable to do so and you can expose them.

5. Ridicule is man's most potent weapon. The opposition finds it almost impossible to counterattack ridicule, is infuriated, and then overreacts to your advantage.

6. A good tactic is one that your people enjoy.

7. A tactic that drags on too long becomes a drag.

8. Keep the pressure on, with different tactics and actions.

9. The threat is usually more terrifying than the thing itself.

10. The major premise for tactics is the development of operations that will maintain a constant pressure on the opposition.

11. If you push a negative hard and deep enough it will break through into its counterside. Mistakes made by the enemy can be converted to your advantage.

12. The price of a successful attack is a constructive alternative. If the opposition finally admits the problem, you must have a solution ready.

13. Pick the target, freeze it, personalize it, and polarize it. Select your target from the many available, constantly focus on it, attack a concrete person who represents the opposing institution, and force a choice between all good and all bad.

Ethical Issues in Social Protest Situations

Is the use of so-called "obscene" and "profane" words ethical in some public communication situations? In North American culture, such words often are viewed as acceptable (if not ethical) in certain clearly specified private or semiprivate communication settings. Such words are not severely frowned upon, for instance, in an Army barracks, in some family settings, and between some close friends.

But what of public communication settings in such forms as public speeches, newspaper editorials, and argumentative essays? During the 1960s and 1970s, communicators who engaged in social protest often utilized obscenity and profanity to express deep emotion or to further some more ultimate goal. What ethical judgment should be made of such use in protest and according to what standards? Sidney Hook, as part of his political perspective (discussed in chapter 2), judged as unethical the use of obscenity in protest "by certain radical student groups" because such language is "incompatible with the whole process of democracy, and tends to destroy it."[19] To what extent would you agree or disagree with this judgment?

J. Dan Rothwell concludes his analysis of the serious functions that obscenity can serve in protest rhetoric with this provocative summary:

> Neither denunciation nor suppression of its use is an adequate response to the fact of verbal obscenity; the students of rhetoric must seek to understand the purposes and effects of this rhetorical strategy. Despite centuries of negative criticism, verbal obscenity has become a more frequent rhetorical device. It is successful in creating attention, in discrediting an enemy, in provoking violence, in fostering identification, and in providing catharsis. . . . Hoping it will go away will not make it so. It is time to accept verbal obscenity as a significant rhetorical device and help discover appropriate responses to its use.[20]

Communicators whose aim is persuasion usually seek to generate between themselves and their audience an end-state variously described as consensus, agreement, or identification. But on occasion some communicators see *promotion of conflict, unrest,* and *tension* as desirable for a healthy and growing society. In specific situations, such communicators view aggressive, abrasive, nonconciliatory (sometimes coercive) techniques of protest rhetoric as pragmatically and ethically justifiable.[21] Franklyn Haiman, in his lecture, "The Rhetoric of 1968: A Farewell to Rational Discourse," not only describes the characteristics of protest rhetoric but also assesses the effectiveness of such rhetoric and uses a largely situational perspective to justify much of it ethically.[22]

Herbert W. Simons argues that "inciting or exacerbating conflict may be just as ethical as working at preventing, managing, or resolving it." Rather than assuming that coercive and confrontative rhetoric necessarily is evil, Simons urges that we evaluate users of such rhetoric open-mindedly "in light of the ends they sought to achieve, the conditions under which they took action, and the consequences of their acts on themselves, on other interested parties, and on the system as a whole."[23]

Protesters often present an ethical rationale for their use of extreme rhetorical tactics. Frequently they argue that society must be awakened to a crucial problem, that the true evil nature of an opponent must be exposed, or that the traditional channels and types of public communication and decision making are inadequate for certain groups or in certain contexts. This latter point concerning the inadequacy of traditional modes of public persuasion is an assumption held by many protesters and by some analysts of confrontation rhetoric. It is an assumption sometimes used for ethical justification without accompanying evidence that this assumption is true in a given instance.[24]

As proof of the inadequacy of traditional channels and types of public communication and decision making, and thus as support for the ethicality of extreme and less traditional persuasive techniques, practitioners and analysts of confrontation rhetoric sometimes cite one or more of the following reasons for inciting confrontation and conflict.

1. Traditional methods are too slow and cumbersome to meet pressing societal problems.

2. Some segments of the citizenry do not have ready access to the traditional channels, perhaps due to high cost, ethnic discrimination, or Establishment control.

3. The Establishment simply refuses to listen. (Note that some protesters assume that an answer of "no" can be taken as absolute proof of refusal to listen; they assume that willingness to listen is proven only by acceptance of *their* viewpoint.)

4. The Establishment cannot be trusted. (Note that mutual trust is a basic element in many traditional modes of communication.)

5. Traditional modes have become masks for perpetuating injustice. When delay of decision is the Establishment goal, for example, a "study committee" is appointed to "investigate" the problem.

6. Some citizens lack facility with words and must turn to nonverbal and fragmentary means to symbolize their grievance. (Note that skill in word use is a requisite for effective utilization of most traditional channels.)

7. Traditional modes emphasize reasoned discourse, which seems increasingly irrelevant to the great moral issues. (Note that rationality and reasonableness are assumed in the Anglo-American heritage of rhetorical theory. See the discussion of this point in chapter 7.)

8. Traditional modes lead to negotiation and compromise, which are unacceptable outcomes in light of the protesters' "nonnegotiable" demands and clear perception of moral truth. Protesters would be co-opted by the assumption of conciliation inherent in traditional rhetoric.

In what ways would you agree or disagree with the above reasons as support for the ethics of extreme protest rhetoric? What concrete ethical guidelines *should* be used as most appropriate for scrutinizing the rhetoric of social protest and confrontation? For instance, are the situational and political perspectives more appropriate than the human nature and dialogical perspectives? Why? What are other alternatives?

"Moralistic preferences for order, civility, rationality, and decorum are still merely preferences. Such preferences may mask injustice, ignore the marginalized, and even become rationales for the powerful." These assumptions by Steven Goldzwig undergird his defense of such "demagogic" strategies and tactics as threats, shattering of consensus, polarization, vilification, and conspiracy appeals as sometimes necessary, effective, and ethical modes of agitation in social protest efforts.[25] He urges development and application of new ethical standards to more adequately evaluate the ethics of social protest agitation. As one suggestion, he proposes suspending ethical judgment of a "demagogue" until the "ultimate purpose" of the suspect tactic can be determined. An additional possibility is to employ a "situational ethic in which hyperbole, emotional appeals, suggestion, innuendo, name-calling, and guilt by association" might be viewed in a more favorable ethical light under certain circumstances. Consideration of "ends, means, motives, short- and long-term consequences, the duty to communicate or not communicate, and the employment of good reasons" are among Goldzwig's possible relevant ethical criteria.

Notes

[1] John C. Merrill, *The Imperative of Freedom* (New York: Hastings House, 1974), chs. 8–10, espec. pp. 170–173.

[2] Bert E. Bradley, *Fundamentals of Speech Communication: The Credibility of Ideas*, 3rd ed. (Dubuque, IA: William C. Brown Co., 1981), pp. 27–29.

[3] Cornelius B. Pratt, "Critique of the Classical Theory of Situational Ethics in U.S. Public Relations," *Public Relations Review*, 19, no. 3 (1993): 219.

[4] David L. Martinson, "Public Relations Practitioners Must Not Confuse Consideration of the Situation with 'Situational Ethics,'" *Public Relations Quarterly*, 42 (1997–98): 39–40.

[5] Ibid., 42–43. Martinson's quotation is of James A. Jaska and Michael S. Pritchard, *Communication Ethics*, 2nd ed. (Belmont, CA: Wadsworth, 1994), p. 21.

[6] B. J. Diggs, "Persuasion and Ethics," *Quarterly Journal of Speech*, 50 (December 1964): 359–373. For a response by Howard H. Martin questioning some facets of Diggs's position, and for Diggs's reply, see *Quarterly Journal of Speech*, 51 (October 1965): 329–333.

[7] On the concept of "good reasons," see Karl R. Wallace, "The Substance of Rhetoric: Good Reasons," *Quarterly Journal of Speech*, 49 (October 1963): 239–249; Walter R. Fisher, "Toward a Logic of Good Reasons," *Quarterly Journal of Speech*, 64 (December 1978): 376–384.

[8] Joseph Fletcher, *Situation Ethics: The New Morality* (Philadelphia: Westminster Press, 1966). See also Fletcher, *Moral Responsibility: Situation Ethics at Work* (Philadelphia: Westminster Press, 1967). For some pro and con evaluations of Fletcher's view, see Harvey Cox, ed., *The Situation Ethics Debate* (Philadelphia: Westminster Press, 1968).

[9] For example, see Fletcher, *Situation Ethics*, pp. 51, 79, 103.

[10] Ibid., pp. 127–128.

[11] Ibid., pp. 26, 30, 142. Also see pp. 33 and 151.

[12] Saul D. Alinsky, *Rules for Radicals: A Practical Primer for Realistic Radicals* (New York: Random House, 1971), pp. xxiv, 3, 12, 22, 46–47. For further evaluation of Alinsky's position on social agitation, see the interview with him in *Playboy*, March 1972, pp. 59–79, 169–178.

[13] Alinsky, *Rules for Radicals*, pp. 7, 11–12, 79.

[14] Saul D. Alinsky, *Reveille for Radicals* (New York: Vintage Books, 1969), p. 207.

[15] Alinsky, *Rules for Radicals*, pp. 214–247.

[16] Alinsky, *Reveille for Radicals*, pp. 132–133.

[17] For a penetrating analysis of the persuasive functions of potent value concepts ("god terms" and "devil terms"), see Richard M. Weaver, *The Ethics of Rhetoric* (Chicago: Regnery, 1953), ch. 9.

[18] Alinsky, *Rules for Radicals*, pp. 126–164.

[19] Sidney Hook, "The Ethics of Political Controversy," in *The Ethics of Controversy: Politics and Protest*, Donn W. Parson and Wil Linkugel, eds. (Lawrence, KS: The House of Usher, 1968), p.

61. Also see Thomas R. Nilsen, *Ethics of Speech Communication*, 2nd ed. (Indianapolis: Bobbs-Merrill, 1972), pp. 65–68.

[20] J. Dan Rothwell, "Verbal Obscenity: Time for Second Thoughts," *Western Speech*, 35 (Fall 1971): 231–242. Also see Haig Bosmajian, "Obscenity and Protest," in *Dissent: Symbolic Behavior and Rhetorical Strategies*, Haig Bosmajian, ed. (Boston: Allyn & Bacon, 1972), pp. 294–306; J. Dan Rothwell, *Telling It Like It Isn't* (Englewood Cliffs, NJ: Prentice-Hall 1982), ch. 4.

[21] See, for example, Herbert W. Simons, "Persuasion in Social Conflicts: A Critique of Prevailing Conceptions and a Framework for Future Research," *Speech Monographs*, 39 (November 1972): espec. 238–240; Parke G. Burgess, "Crisis Rhetoric: Coercion vs. Force," *Quarterly Journal of Speech*, 59 (February 1973): espec. 69–73; Franklyn S. Haiman, "The Rhetoric of the Streets: Some Legal and Ethical Implications," *Quarterly Journal of Speech*, 53 (April 1967): 99–114; Alinsky, *Rules for Radicals*, pp. 59, 62; Kenneth Keniston, *Youth and Dissent* (New York: Harvest Book, 1971), pp. 319, 336, 388–389.

[22] Haiman's lecture is reprinted in Johannesen, *Ethics in Human Communication*, 2nd ed. (Long Grove, IL: Waveland Press, 1983), pp. 177–190. On the nature and characteristics of protest and confrontation rhetoric, see, for example, John W. Bowers, Donovan Ochs, and Richard J. Jensen, *The Rhetoric of Agitation and Control*, 2nd ed. (Long Grove, IL: Waveland Press, 1993); Charles Stewart et al., *Persuasion and Social Movements*, 5th ed. (Long Grove, IL: Waveland Press, 2007).

[23] Simons, "Persuasion in Social Conflicts," pp. 238–240.

[24] For two efforts to document the existence of this assumed inadequacy of traditional channels and types of public persuasion, see Howard Zinn, *Disobedience and Democracy* (New York: Vintage Books, 1968), pp. 7, 53–68, 105; Ruth McGaffey, "A Critical Look at the Marketplace of Ideas," *The Speech Teacher*, 21 (March 1972): 115–122. For other inquiries, see Stanley Ingber, "The Marketplace of Ideas: A Legitimizing Myth," *Duke Law Journal* (February 1984): 1–91; Paul H. Brietzke, "How and Why the Marketplace of Ideas Fails," *Valpariso University Law Review,* 32 (1997): 951–969.

[25] Steven R. Goldzwig, "A Social Movement Perspective on Demagoguery: Achieving Symbolic Realignment," *Communication Studies*, 40 (Fall 1989): 202–228.

Religious, Utilitarian, and Legalistic Perspectives

Religious Perspectives: General Nature

Religious perspectives on communication ethics are rooted in the basic assumptions of a religion about the relation of The Divine/The Eternal to humans and the world and about the relation of humans and the world to The Divine/The Eternal. In the light of such assumptions, various world religions emphasize moral and spiritual values, guidelines, and rules that can be employed as standards for evaluating the ethics of communication. One source for ethical criteria would be the sacred literature of a particular religion, such as the Bible, Koran, or Talmud.[1] Furthermore, interpretations stemming from a religion may present standards for ethical communication.

The Old Testament clearly admonishes Jews and Christians against use of lies and slander. God commands Moses, "You shall not steal, or deal falsely, nor lie to one another." The Psalmist reports, "Let not slander be established in the land." In the New Testament, Christians are told, "Let everyone speak the truth with his neighbor. . . ." Jesus warns, "I tell you, on the Day of Judgment men will render account for every careless word they utter; for by your words you will be justified and by your words you will be condemned."[2]

A Christian Ethic for Persuasion

The source of human religiousness is a person's creation in the image of God. This premise underlies a religious perspective on persuasion and communication developed by Charles Veenstra and Daryl Vander Kooi.[3] Because humans are created in God's image, they are endowed with a uniquely human capacity for ethical judgment, they honor God through worship and the quality of their relationships with other persons, and they have the capacities for creative thought and communication not possessed by other creatures. Veenstra and Vander Kooi derive a number of "principles" for a Christian ethic of persuasion and communication. First, humans deserve full respect as reflections of God's image. We should communicate with others in the same loving and respectful spirit we worship God.

Second, honesty should be practiced in all aspects of persuasion. Persuaders should be open with audiences concerning their intentions and accurate with audiences concerning all facts relevant to ideas, policies, or products.

> Honesty necessitates careful documentation of facts, solid information, cogent reasoning, clear statistics, quoting within context, appropriate emotional appeals, use of genuine experts, etc. If the persuader fully respects the persuadee, he will not try to bypass the persuadee's ability to think, to weigh alternatives, to choose, since these abilities make up part of the image of God in that persuadee.

However, the requirement for honesty does not demand full and complete disclosure at all times. Tactfulness and sensitivity to others' feelings should guide implementation of the principle of honesty. In addition, receivers of communication have the ethical responsibility to be honest in their feedback, that is, in their expression of interest and attention, feelings, judgments, and disagreements.

Third, only the best language should be employed. As a guiding question, they ask: "Is this the best language I can use to show respect for the image of God in a person?" Profanity and obscenity clearly would be unethical. Fourth, the genuine needs of an audience should be determined and an attempt made to meet those real needs. Needs should not be manufactured where none actually exist. Appeals to genuine needs should not be confused with appeals to audience wants and preferences. Fifth, communication techniques and appeals should be appropriate for the subject, the participants, and the situation. Techniques and appeals should be relevant to the genuine needs being addressed. In Christian evangelism, for example, conversion should stem from commitment of both heart and mind, from both emotional and logical appeals.

The Mass Media and Christian Morality

"Authentic Christian morality" is a concept developed by Kyle Haselden as a standard for evaluating the morality of communication, especially mass communication.[4] Two other possible "Christian" standards are examined by Haselden and rejected: Christian legalism and Christian situation ethics. Christian legalism, according to Haselden, assumes that the Ten Commandments, the teachings of Jesus and his disciples, and church doctrines derived from them, provide a "detailed, inflexible, always appropriate moral code," which is "adequate for all times, places, persons, and circumstances." This legalist approach fails, he argues, because it externalizes and mechanizes morality; takes a negative, restrictive, static stance; emphasizes trivialities, and predetermines the range of future decisions; and "precludes the Working of the Holy Spirit."

In chapter 5 we examined the nature of Joseph Fletcher's Christian situation ethics in which love is the sole standard to be used in judging what is ethical in the context of each specific, unique situation. Haselden finds this view defective because it too easily fosters unprincipled behavior; unrealistically disconnects each act and situation from tradition, law, and revelation; and utilizes an inadequate definition of love simply as benevolence or good will.

Authentic Christian morality, according to Haselden, strives to secure the freedom, the latitude of choice, necessary to transform people into persons (as opposed to treating them as things, animals, or machines). God's will for humans, as exemplified in Jesus Christ, stresses love as the force leading to the experience of oneness. But this love goes beyond simple benevolence to include sexual, aesthetic, and parental love. Indeed this love combines and transforms all of these into a oneness within appropriate ethical guidelines. Haselden also contends that "it is not possible to be a genuine Christian without participating in authentic morality" and that "it is possible to participate in genuine morality without being a Christian or even a theist."

Haselden applies ethical criteria rooted in his concept of authentic Christian morality. In the course of his ethical scrutiny, he assesses the degree of morality of various mass media: books, magazines, radio, television, films, and commercial advertising.[5] Concerning the philosophy that guides the commercial advertising industry, Haselden concludes that it is "antithetical to almost everything we have been taught as Christians." As guidelines for exploring ethical issues in mass communication, Haselden suggests several sets of questions:[6]

> Are we really concerned about the effect of that medium on people or are we concerned about its effect on things secondary to people? Does our deepest focus fall on the national image, static customs, honored institutions, memories of how much better things and people were in the old days, organized religion, our personal fear of painful change, or on people?
>
> So the question that we should ask about the impact of the media of mass communication on our society is whether they help people become persons or prevent their being persons. Do they facilitate and promote man's emergence as true man—integrated, independent, and responsible—or do they transform man into a receptacle, a puppet, an echo?
>
> Do modern forms of communication help man to be his full self? Do they discover and encourage the unfolding of his latent possibilities? Or, do they reduce all men to a stale pattern of conformity, blighting those individual traits that add charm and possibility to the whole society? Does mass communication inevitably mean the emergence of a mass mind, an intellectual ant heap, an amorphous religiosity, and a collective ethic? Will the media eventually standardize all human behavior at the level of the lowest conduct in the society, or will they enrich the general tone and character of the people?

An Ethic for Christian Evangelism

An ethic for the Christian who seeks to persuade others to commit themselves to Christianity has been developed by Emory Griffin.[7] Employing the metaphorical imagery of love and courtship, he finds in the Bible, in Plato's *Phaedrus*, and in Soren Kierkegaard's *Philosophical Fragments* bases for his viewpoint. Griffin describes the communication practices of the ethical Christian lover-persuader and of various unethical lover-persuaders. Each type of persuader is described in part by the degree to which they implement the twin requirements of *love* (genuine concern for the consequences of an act upon other persons) and *justice* (adherence to universal rules of Christian conduct).

The *true lover*, the ethical Christian persuader, is both loving and just. Such persuaders care more about the welfare of others than about their own egos. They use appeals that respect the human rights of others, including the right to say no. The *nonlover* attempts to avoid persuasion by taking a nonmanipulative, detached, uninvolved stance. Indeed, Griffin sees this type as even more unethical than various false lovers because nonlovers are uncaring about their own beliefs or about other persons.

Various types of false lover-persuaders deny to others the free choice of whether to accept Christ. The *flirt* sees people simply as souls to be counted. The evangelist "who is more concerned about getting another scalp" for his or her collection than for the welfare of others exemplifies the Christian flirt. The *seducer* employs deception, flattery, and irrelevant appeals to success, money, patriotism, popularity, or comfort to entice the audience. Because the religious seducer induces decisions for the wrong reasons, she or he is unethical. The *rapist* uses psychological coercion virtually to force a commitment. Intense emotional appeals, such as guilt, effectively "remove the element of conscious choice." The *smother* lover overwhelms others with love, so much so that he or she will not take no for an answer. Smother lovers believe that they know what is best for everyone else, treat everyone identically, and ignore the uniqueness of each person. Their persuasion is unethical, believes Griffin, because it fails to respect the free choice of others. Finally, the *legalistic lover* lacks genuine love and persuades purely "out of a sense of obligation or duty." The legalistic lover may go through the motions when there is no genuine need, when he or she no longer feels personally motivated, or even when relevant human needs are being ignored.

Oral Roberts's Controversial Fund-Raising Appeal

On two weekends in January 1987, evangelist Oral Roberts recounted on his syndicated television program an encounter with God the previous year. God told him that Roberts would not be allowed to live beyond March 1987 unless he raised $8 million to be used for 69 scholarships for medical students at Oral Roberts University to allow them to serve in medical clinics overseas. In an emotion-laden plea to his viewers, Roberts asked: "Will you help me extend my life?" Roberts's chief spokeswoman, Jan Dargatz, defended Roberts's motives to reporters but conceded that his "methods have hit the fan." Dargatz said that Roberts sincerely believed the fund drive was a do-or-die effort and believed it "from the very core of his being." The Rev. John Wolf, senior minister of Tulsa's All Souls Unitarian Church, condemned the appeal as "emotional blackmail" and as an "act of desperation" (account taken from Bruce Buursma, *Chicago Tribune*, January 17, 1987, sec. 1, pp. 1, 10). Another news report revealed that in 1986 Roberts had made a similar appeal. Roberts told a Dallas audience that his "life is on the line" and that God "would take me this year" if he did not raise necessary funds to finance "holy missionary teams." "Because if I don't do it," Roberts said, "I'm going to be gone before the year is out. I'll be with the Father. I know it as much as I'm standing here." Roberts failed to raise the necessary money (*Chicago Tribune*, February 26, 1987, sec. 1, p. 4).

Now attempt to assess the ethicality of Roberts's appeals. Particularly bring to bear the ethic for Christian evangelism developed by Emory Griffin. Is Roberts's appeal best characterized as that of the true lover, nonlover, flirt, seducer, rapist, smother lover, or legalistic lover? Why? How might versions of the human nature or the dialogical ethical perspectives apply? What about the issues of conscious intent, sincerity, habits of character, and good ends justifying dubious means? How might these issues influence your ethical evaluations? Finally, consider the Christian ethic for persuasion proposed by Veenstra and Vander Kooi. How relevant is it and how might it apply?

Several Asiatic Religious Perspectives

Several Asian religions also provide examples of religious perspectives for accepting or shunning certain communication appeals.[8] The Confucian religion generally has tended to shun emotional appeals and stress fact and logic. But within the Confucian religious mainstream, various tributaries and rivulets have occurred. A sixteenth-century scholar named Yulgok developed a view that approved appeals to any or all of seven passions (joy, anger, sorrow, fear, love, hatred, and desire) as means of persuading people to adopt the four principles of charity, duty to neighbors, propriety, and wisdom. The School of Rites, a sixteenth-century variation of Confucianism, emphasized ritualistic patterns of human behavior. Thus, depth of understanding, the policy advocated, and the facts of the matter were less crucial than proper modes of procedure. Taoist religion stresses empathy and insight, rather than reason and logic, as roads to truth. Citing facts and demonstrating logical conclusions are minimized in favor of feeling and intuition.

In the Buddhist religion, communication is a crucial dimension of ethical behavior. "Speech is so important to the successful practice of Buddhism that the Buddha accorded it the same prominence as the mind and the body." [9] The Buddha warned against four major types of unethical communication: lying, duplicity, harsh speech, and idle speech.[10]

Lying includes deceit, defamation, misrepresentation, falsification, fabrication, and distortion. A lie of commission states as true something we know to be false, while a lie of omission involves failing to say something true that we know we should say. Lies demonstrate disrespect for persons lied to, often damage the trust others have in us, and undermine their accurate sense of true and false, right and wrong. When we lie, we also show disrespect for ourselves and waste precious time and energy maintaining the lie. Usually the lie necessitates a sequence of further lies. Lying weakens our own moral character and may become habitual.

Duplicity can mean speaking with a "forked tongue" by saying one thing to one person and the opposite to another person in order to create confusion or disharmony. Duplicity also can mean pretending to have certain feelings or views but acting in light of real but concealed beliefs. Often duplicity may involve insincere flattery to manipulate others for selfish personal gain. *Harsh speech* intentionally hurts others and causes pain or suffering, such as through vicious teasing. *Idle speech* offers nothing of value to others and wastes their time. Such idle speech may include ill-timed speech, disorganized and rambling speech, pointless speech, thoughtless speech, and unreasonable speech. Contemporary Christians often test their moral decisions by asking, "What would Jesus do?" In a similar vein, contemporary Buddhists are urged: 'If you have trouble knowing how to speak, try to imagine what the Buddha would say if he were in your situation."[11]

Shared Perspectives

J. Vernon Jensen examines the ancient Eastern and Western religions of Hinduism, Buddhism, Taoism, Confucianism, Judaism, Christianity, and Islam and finds that, despite significant differences in core values, views of the deity, and sacred truths, these seven world religions share some commonalities concerning communication ethics.[12] Generally, these religions stress individual responsibilities more than rights, and they typically employ negatively worded statements to identify specifically what not to do. Jensen isolates a core of six ethical standards for communication held in common by these religious traditions: (1) tell the truth and avoid lies; (2) do not slander anyone; (3) do not blaspheme, dishonor, and profane the sacred persons, symbols, or rituals central to the religion; (4) avoid communication that demeans other persons or life in general by being "evil, shameful, foolish, clever, cunning, glib, or vain"; (5) aim habitually to embody ethical virtues in your character as preparation for ethical communication and aim to become trustworthy—to earn trust; and (6) go beyond traditional notions of communicating to inform, persuade, and please in order to aim at "edifying" others, that is, showing them how close to excellence humans can become. Jensen argues in conclusion: "One need not be a 'believer' to appreciate the power of the values expressed in these various traditions, and with a reasonable amount of filtering, we would learn from them to our benefit."

Utilitarian Perspectives: General Nature

Utilitarianism is an ethical standard which holds that "actions are right in proportion as they tend to promote happiness, wrong as they tend to produce the reverse of happiness."[13] So whenever we are faced with a moral dilemma, we are obligated to choose the course of action that will allow us to maximize happiness and minimize unhappiness. A key feature of utilitarianism is that it establishes a consequentialist (or "teleological") standard of evaluation: The morality or immorality of an action is a function—not of anything inherent in the action itself—but of the good and bad outcomes (or consequences) of the action.

Applied to communication, the central question posed by a utilitarian ethic would be this: In comparison to alternatives, will a specific communication act (or strategy) be productive of more happiness than unhappiness for all people affected by the act (or strategy)? So, for example, a utilitarian would say that there is nothing inherently or categorically unethical about lying. In any particular situation, lying is likely to be wrong not because of something inherent within the act itself but because the act is likely to produce harmful consequences for the people involved. (For example, the person lied to would be denied information that might be essential to making good deliberative choices; the reputation of the liar would be harmed if the lie is discovered; a relationship of trust would be damaged, and so forth. Again, the act is wrong not because of something inherent in the act but because of the *outcomes* of the act.) Even so, we might imagine situations in which a lie would produce more short-term and long-term benefits than the truth. If we could reliably predict in a particular situation that the benefits of the lie would outweigh any harms, then, according to the utilitarian standard, the lie would be morally permissible. Stated in simple terms, the utilitarian adopts, in effect, a standard of "no harm, no foul."

Like utilitarianism, egoism is also a form of consequentialism that obligates us to do those actions that will bring about the "greatest happiness." However, in egoism, the individual is obligated to do those actions that maximize *his or her own* individual happiness. In utilitarianism, the individual is obligated to do those actions that maximize the happiness of *everyone*. In other words, unlike egoism, utilitarianism strives not only to maximize happiness but also to distribute that happiness as widely and equally as possible through-out the community. As Geoffrey Scarre explains, utilitarianism is a *universalist* and an *egalitarian* ethical standard. Everyone's interests count equally, and no individual ought to be treated as having more moral significance than any other.[14] When describing this feature of utilitarianism, many people will refer to Jeremy Bentham's famous formula "the greatest happiness of the greatest number."[15] We should note, however, that strictly speaking, this formula pushes the point too far. Taken literally, "the greatest happiness of the greatest number" demands that we pursue two ultimate standards simultaneously. The problem with this is that we can easily imagine situations in which those two standards would come in conflict. Sometimes we have to choose between an action that will produce less happiness for a larger population or more happi-ness for a smaller population. Which should we choose? Any coherent ethical theory would need to provide some answer. In traditional theories of utilitari-anism, "the greatest happiness principle" is usually advocated as the ultimate standard of moral conduct and the "greatest number" is adopted as a kind of secondary aim, assuming that, in most situations, happiness will tend to be greater when it is distributed widely throughout the community.[16]

Setting aside this complication, another controversial issue associated with utilitarianism arises because the concept of "happiness" is not as simple as it may at first appear. For some people, happiness may refer only to a plea-surable mental state. For others, happiness will also include a diverse array of activities and relations necessary for human flourishing. To be happy, we may require not only simple enjoyment, but also health, wealth, security, reputa-tion, friendship, spiritual fulfillment, and so forth. Thus, in these more nuanced versions, the utilitarian standard likely will be applied in combina-tion with other ethical perspectives. For example, "happiness" frequently will be rooted in considerations associated with political perspectives (as discussed in chapter 2), with human nature perspectives (as discussed in chapter 3), or with religious perspectives (discussed earlier in this chapter). More generally, because utilitarians reject the concept of categorical moral duties (moral obli-gations that hold regardless of the consequences), the principle of utility might also be associated with a kind of situational ethic (as discussed in chapter 5).

Among communication professionals utilitarianism is widely accepted and applied. Clifford G. Christians argues that, for the last century, utilitari-anism has been especially attractive to those who work in the media: "The mainstream press and the policies of advertising agencies, codes of ethics, and media textbooks are dominated by various strands of it."[17] For media professionals who strive to present all sides of an issue fairly and impartially, utilitarianism provides a standard for negotiating conflicts among individuals and groups who may subscribe to diverse religious and cultural traditions.

Even so, as Christians explains, despite its appeal, utilitarianism is not without serious problems. First, utilitarianism depends on our ability to pre-dict the outcomes of actions and to weigh anticipated costs and benefits. Fre-quently, however, the consequences of our actions are so complicated and intertwined, and our foresight about the future is so imperfect, that it is impossible to make such predictions. So, for example, those who apply the standard of utility may be inclined to overestimate the *short-term* costs and benefits of an action while misjudging the *long-term* consequences. The short-term benefits to a journalist of getting a scoop over competitors may be offset by increased long-term public hostility toward an overly aggressive press corps. Second, by focusing attention on the *future* consequences of actions, utilitarianism does not provide adequate attention to commitments and promises that emerge out of the actions and relationships of our *past*. Focusing only on what actions will produce the most good in the future, it provides inadequate weight to the importance of the ordinary range of human personal relationships and obligations. Through our cultural and biographical circumstances, we all enter into relationships with others: promisee to promisor, creditor to debtor, employee to employer, husband to wife, child to parent, friend to friend, and so forth. These relationships frequently involve moral claims that may demand attention, regardless of any calculated harms and benefits in the future. So for example, if, in the past, I have engaged in some action that harmed someone, I acquire a duty to make up for that earlier wrong. This duty of doing justice for past wrongs may require me to ignore any calculations of benefits in the future.

Levels of Moral Thinking

In *Well-Being: Its Meaning, Measurement and Moral Importance* James Griffin outlines a response to the sorts of concerns raised by Clifford G. Christians and by other critics of utilitarianism.[18] Griffin points out that it would be unwise and counterproductive to apply the principle of utility routinely on an individual, case-by case basis. In other words, if we spent our days calculating the benefits and harms of each proposed individual act, we would never be able to find time to actually do anything. Furthermore, our knowledge of any individual situation inevitably will be imperfect and partial. Frequently, we engage in an action with best intentions, but the action turns out to have unintended and harmful side-effects that we never predicted. These sorts of considerations don't mean utilitarianism is inherently flawed, but it does mean that we need to reconsider the ways in which we apply the principle of utility in our everyday lives.

Griffin distinguishes between four major levels of moral thinking.[19] At the first and deepest level of moral thinking, we need to have an *ideal criterion* for right and wrong. Thus, a utilitarian would say that the ultimate and ideal standard of right and wrong is the greatest happiness principle: We have an obligation to maximize happiness and minimize unhappiness. But for every individual, day-to-day life is far from the ideal. We do not have time, full access to the facts, or a capacity for detachment that would allow us to make reliable predictions about the consequences of our individual actions. Thus, we need to distinguish the ideal criterion of right and wrong from more commonplace forms of moral thinking.

This brings us to the next two levels of moral thinking: The *practical decision procedure* and the *reflective decision procedure*. When time is short, information is limited, and self-interested motives are strong, we are better off following practical, prima facie moral rules. In general, our experience has taught us that lying does tend to lead to more harmful consequences than telling the truth. In general, when a person breaks a promise this tends to diminish rather than increase happiness. Thus, in our practical, everyday, moral lives, we would be well advised to follow common moral rules such as "tell the truth" and "don't break your promises." On the other hand, there are moments in our lives when our time (while not unlimited) is sufficient to allow for more reflective consideration of these prima facie moral rules. In reflective moral thinking we have an opportunity to "go behind" practical, everyday rules of morality in order to decide on their exceptions and to clarify their amendments. When we find ourselves free of the restrictions of time and information that are characteristic of our everyday lives, we have an opportunity for re-examining our moral convictions: Under what circumstances might lying be morally permissible? Is it ever permissible to break a promise?

The practical and the reflective levels of moral thinking are for individuals who, in their ordinary lives, are attempting to answer the question, "what should *I* do?" In the fourth level of moral thinking, Griffin asks a different question: "What should *we* as a group or as a society do?" The change in scale imposes new limitations on our knowledge and it requires a new decision procedure, distinct from the other three forms of moral thinking. The difficulty of *political decision making* is that a few individuals are charged with making decisions for a larger community. Since most of the people affected by the decisions are likely to be strangers to the deliberator, how does the deliberator determine what sorts of things would make them happy? Politics also brings with it limitations in trust: Can ordinary citizens depend on officeholders to look out for their interests? What sorts of rules are needed to prevent officeholders from confusing their own selfish interest with the larger interests of the community? Thus, in politics, we need new rules, many of which will be imposed by force of law, which will allow us to cope with variations in the deliberator's moral reliability.

The "social utility" approach discussed next represents another variation in the utilitarian ethic for communication. Readers might consider how this approach reflects one or more of Griffin's four levels of moral thinking.

The Social Utility Approach

In a number of sources, William S. Howell (sometimes with Winston Brembeck) has developed a "social utility" approach to communication ethics. Howell offers this approach as applicable for both public persuasion and for intimate communication, for both communication *within* a given culture and for intercultural communication *between* people of different cultures.[20]

This social utility approach stresses usefulness to the people affected and the survival potential for groups involved. Ethically adequate communication, for Howell, "assesses the short-range and long-range consequences of the communicative act, including the benefits to and negative effects on the group and on particular individuals." Ethical communication should "benefit most of the people involved" with "minimum harm to individuals." Standards of "benefit" and of "harm" are rooted in a "culture's ongoing value system, and thus can be described as *cultural-specific*. What is useful in one culture may well be detrimental in another." Among the questions that might be asked in applying the social utility approach are: Is there a revealed or concealed penalty to be paid? Could injury to one or a few individuals outweigh group gains?

That the ethics of communication is a function of context is an assumption basic to Howell's view. Universal standards for communication ethics are inappropriate. "Circumstances and people exert powerful influences. To say it differently, applied ethics constitute a necessarily open system. The environment, the situation, the timing of an interaction, human relationships, all affect the way ethical standards are applied." While not approving universal standards, Howell claims that the social utility approach is a framework that can be applied universally.

Howell suggests six criteria that should be met by any useful and workable system of communication ethics. First, the system protects the fabric of its culture. A society's intricately woven fabric of values and basic assumptions should be preserved. "Whatever strengthens or protects the fabric of a culture is ethical. What strains, weakens, or tears it is unethical." Second, ethical responsibilities are shared by both communicator and communicatee. "What the receiver does with the message he receives can contribute as much to the ethical qualities of a communication as the intent and strategies of the sender." Third, it must be both pragmatic and idealistic, both workable and desirable. "Operationally, ideals are useful as goals, to establish directions that are necessary to effect change." But, Howell believes, "instead of trying to assess only the *goodness* of an ideal, let the further criterion, 'Does it work?' be emphasized." The ideal is operationally effective if it modifies behavior significantly in the direction of the moral goal it embodies. Fourth, the system of ethics is sensitive to the gap between verbalization and action, between words and deeds. It must allow "for the human capacity to say one thing and do something else." Fifth, it accepts relativity in the application of ethical principles, even when a principle is almost universally agreed to. The ethics of communication is a function of context. Sixth, social utility is the standard to be considered in every ethical decision.

Legalistic Perspectives: General Nature

A legalistic perspective would take the general position that illegal human communication behavior also is unethical. That which is not specifically illegal is viewed as ethical. In other words, legality and ethicality are made synonymous. Such an approach certainly has the advantage of allowing simple ethical decisions. We would only need to measure communication techniques against current laws and regulations to determine whether a technique is ethical. We might, for example, turn for ethical guidance to the regulations governing advertising set forth by the Federal Trade Commission or the Federal Communications Commission. Or we might use Supreme Court criteria, or state legislation, defining obscenity, pornography, libel, or slander to judge whether a particular message is unethical on those grounds.

However, many people would feel uneasy with this legalistic approach to communication ethics. They would contend that obviously there are some things that presently are legal but that are ethically dubious. And some social protestors for civil rights and against the Vietnam War during the 1960s and 1970s admitted that their actions then were illegal but contended they were justifiable on ethical and moral grounds. Richard DeGeorge and Joseph Pichler, contemporary philosophers, contend that "morality is broader than legality. Not everything that is immoral can or should be made illegal."[21] Chief Justice Warren Burger spoke for a unanimous Supreme Court in 1974 in the case of *Miami Herald v. Tornillo*. "A responsible press is an undoubtedly desirable goal, but press responsibility is not mandated by the Constitution and like many other virtues it cannot be legislated."

A scholar of public relations, Kathy Fitzpatrick, agrees with the standard view that law and ethics are not synonymous. "Law is about what people *must* do, while ethics is about what people *should* do. . . . Ethics begins where law ends." The law does not encompass the full scope of ethical behavior. At the same time, however, Fitzpatrick contends that four principles central to Supreme Court First Amendment free speech decisions can serve as baselines or minimum starting points to evaluate the ethics of public relations practices. "The fundamental marketplace principles of access, process, truth, and disclosure provide an ethical floor on which public relations practice standards can be built."[22]

How should we answer the question, to what degree can or should we enforce ethical standards for communication through government law or regulation? What degrees of soundness might there be in two old but seemingly contrary sayings? "You can't legislate morality." "There ought to be a law." In the United States, very few ethical standards for communication are codified in governmental laws or regulations. As indicated earlier, F.C.C. or F.T.C. regulations on the content of advertising and laws and court decisions on obscenity and libel represent the governmental approach. But such examples are rare compared to the large number of laws and court decisions specifying the boundaries of freedom of speech and press in our society. Rather, our society applies ethical standards for communication through the more indirect avenues of group consensus, social pressure, persuasion, and formal-but-voluntary codes of ethics.

Politics and Advertising

On occasion, proposals are made to pass legislation that would promote ethical political campaign communication by regulating the content of political speeches, politically sponsored television programs, televised political advertisements, or the reporting of public opinion polls. For example, without mentioning possible conflicts with freedom-of-speech provisions of the First Amendment, Brembeck and Howell maintain that government regulation "of the content of politically sponsored programs could safeguard against unethical and vicious practices."[23]

In the mid-1970s, the New York state legislature passed a Fair Campaigning Code that prohibited attacks on candidates based on race, sex, religion, or ethnic background and prohibited misrepresentations of a candidate's qualifications, position, or party affiliation. In January 1976, the U.S. Supreme Court, by a summary action, affirmed a lower court decision that these provisions of the New York code were unconstitutional under the First Amendment, were overbroad and vague in meaning and possible application, and created a substantial "chill" that probably would deter use of protected free speech.[24]

Robert Spero explains that unethical content of televised political advertisements presently cannot be banned or regulated through government law because it is viewed as ideological or as political speech protected by the First Amendment. "When political speech turns up in the form of a television commercial, freedom of speech is extended implicitly to whatever the candidate wishes to say or show, no matter how false, deceptive, misleading, or unfair it may be."[25]

As part of its Code of Professional Ethics and Procedures, the American Association of Public Opinion Research has established "standards for minimal disclosure" to guide professional public opinion pollsters in conducting polls and presenting results. Consider whether these standards appropriately might be applied to news media in reporting polls and to politicians in publicizing poll results:

1. Who sponsored the survey and who conducted it

2. The exact wording of the questions asked, including the text of any preceding instruction or explanation to the interviewer or respondent that might reasonably be expected to affect the response

3. A definition of the population under study and a description of the sampling frame used to identify this population

4. A description of the sampling selection procedure, giving a clear indication of the method by which the respondents were selected by the researcher, or whether the respondents were entirely self-selected

5. Size of sample and, if applicable, completion rates and information on eligibility criteria and screening procedures

6. A discussion of the findings, including, if appropriate, estimates of sampling error, and a description of any weighting or estimating procedures used

7. Which results are based on parts of the sample, rather than the total sample

8. Method, location, and dates of the data collection

Actually an earlier version of these standards formed the basis for a "Truth-in-Polling Act" proposed numerous times but never passed in the U.S. House of Representatives—a law intended to govern news media reports of polls.[26]

Concerning advertising ethics, Burton Leiser believes that because "the law does not always conform with standards of moral right," advertisers who are "concerned with doing what is right need not set the limits of their conduct at the bounds" set by the law. Harold Williams issues a reminder to his professional advertising colleagues.[27]

> What is legal and what is ethical are not synonymous, and neither are what is legal and what is honest. We tend to resort to legality often as our guideline. This is in effect what happens when we turn to the lawyers for confirmation that a course of action is an appropriate one.
>
> We must recognize that we are getting a legal opinion, but not necessarily an ethical or moral one. The public, the public advocates, and many of the legislative and administrative authorities recognize it even if we do not.

Problems with Legalistic Perspectives

John Stuart Mill, the nineteenth-century British utilitarian philosopher and a leading advocate of maximum freedom of speech, identified a number of public communication practices that he felt were ethically dubious. Included in his catalogue of ethically suspect techniques were: the hiding of facts and arguments, misstating elements of a case, misrepresenting an opponent's views, invective or name-calling, sarcasm, unfair personal attacks, and stigmatizing opponents unfairly as bad or immoral. Nevertheless, Mill felt that the law should not "presume to interfere with this controversial misconduct." For Mill, "law and authority have no business" regulating such communication behavior.[28]

Consider the following five problems that may result from attempts to enforce ethical standards for communication through government laws and regulations.[29] First, oversimplified and superficial judgments may be made of complex situations. Second, regulation of unethical communication techniques may have a harmful "chilling effect" on use of other less ethically doubtful techniques. People feel less free to speak their minds for fear of legal action. Third, legal regulation of the content of communication may undermine human capacities for communication and reason by violating our right to learn the maximum we are capable of learning, by narrowing our range of choices, and by constricting our access to ideas and knowledge. Fourth, legal regulation tends to remove from receivers, the audience, the necessity for choice and judgment. Rather than fostering mutually shared ethical responsibilities for communication, regulation tends to focus responsibility on the communicator while minimizing audience responsibility. Finally, governmental regulation of almost anything, including communication content, has a tendency to expand to include ever-widening spheres of behavior, spheres that most citizens might not want regulated by law.

Franklyn Haiman, scholar of the First Amendment and communication ethics, explores where our society should "draw the line against writing morality into law" for both physical and communicative behaviors.[30] He proposes three criteria as guides. First, a "moral standard concerning a particular behavior" should be codified in legislation only when there is a "near-unanimous consensus in society that the conduct in question is immoral." Second, laws that codify ethical standards must embody credibility and fairness by being realistically enforceable and by not being subject to capricious or unequal enforcement. Finally: "A free society will always draw the line between what it considers immoral and what it makes illegal as close as possible to the more serious, direct, immediate, and physical of the harms, and it will leave to the operations of social pressure, education, and self-restraint the control of behaviors whose harm to others is less serious, less direct, less immediate, and less physical."

Consider the adequacy of Haiman's guidelines. Describe, if you can, a type of communication that you believe not only to be unethical but also should be regulated by law. How well would the communication you condemn as unethical, and the law regulating it, measure up to the three tests? What revisions or modifications of Haiman's guidelines might you suggest? Why?

Notes

[1] Arnold D. Hunt, Marie T. Crotty, and Robert B. Crotty, *Ethics of World Religions*, rev. ed. (San Diego, CA: Greenhaven Press, 1991).

[2] All quotations are from the Revised Standard Version. See Leviticus, 19:11; Psalms, 140:11; Proverbs, 21:6; Psalms, 59:12; Zechariah, 8:16; Ephesians, 4:25; Matthew, 12:36–37.

[3] Charles D. Veenstra and Daryl Vander Kooi, "Ethical Foundations for 'Religious' Persuasion: A Biblical View," *Religious Communication Today*, 1 (September 1979): 43–48; for a more extensive development of this position, see Veenstra, "A Reformed Theological Ethics of Speech Communication," unpublished PhD dissertation, University of Nebraska, 1981, ch. 4; Veenstra, "Communication Ethics: A Christian Approach," *Equid Novi*, 15, no. 1 (1994): 71–85.

[4] Kyle Haselden, *Morality and the Mass Media* (Nashville, TN: Broadman Press, 1968), espec. chs. 1, 2, and 10.

[5] Ibid., chs. 3, 6, 7, 8.

6 Ibid., pp. 36, 41, 43.

7 Emory A. Griffin, *The Mind Changers: The Art of Christian Persuasion* (Wheaton, IL: Tyndale House, 1976), ch. 3. For an extensive discussion of ethical issues and standards for evangelistic persuasion, see the entire issue of *Cultic Studies Journal*, 2 (Fall/Winter 1985).

8 Robert T. Oliver, *Culture and Communication* (Springfield, IL: Charles C. Thomas, 1962), pp. 111–117, 133–135. Also see Oliver, *Communication and Culture in Ancient India and China* (Syracuse: Syracuse University Press. 1971), pp. 76–77, 124, 145–149, 176, 181, 193; D. Lawrence Kincaid. ed., *Communication Theory: Eastern and Western Perspectives* (San Diego, CA: Academic Press, 1987); William G. Kirkwood, "Truthfulness as a Standard for Speech in Ancient India," *Southern Communication Journal*, 54 (Spring 1989): 213–234; Hunt, Crotty, and Crotty, *Ethics of World Religions*, pp. 136, 141, 144–146; C. A. Cua, *Moral Vision and Tradition: Essays in Chinese Ethics* (Washington, DC: Catholic University of America Press, 1998), ch. 13.

9 Yun Hsing, *Being Good: Buddhist Ethics for Everyday Life*, trans. Tom Graham. (New York: Weatherhill, 1998), p. 23.

10 Ibid., pp. 8, 15–25, 63–64, 86–89,107, 153.

11 Ibid., p. 24.

12 J. Vernon Jensen, "Ancient Eastern and Western Religions as Guides for Contemporary Communication Ethics," in *Proceedings of the Second National Communication Ethics Conference, June 11–14, 1992*, James A. Jaksa, ed. (Annandale, VA: Speech Communication Association, 1992), pp. 58–67. Also see Jensen, *Ethical Issues in the Communication Process* (Mahwah, NJ: Erlbaum, 1997), pp. 19–23.

13 John Stuart Mill, *Utilitarianism in Collected Works of John Stuart Mill* Vol. X, ed. John Robson (Toronto: University of Toronto Press, 1963–1991), p. 210. See also Thomas K. Hearn, Jr., ed., *Studies in Utilitarianism* (New York: Meredith, 1971). This anthology reprints the classic statements on utilitarianism by Jeremy Bentham and John Stuart Mill as well as more recent interpretations. Also see Jonathan Glover, ed., *Utilitarianism and Its Critics* (New York: Macmillan, 1990).

14 Geoffrey Scarre, *Utilitarianism* (London and New York: Routledge, 1996), pp. 23–25.

15 Jeremy Bentham, *A Fragment on Government* (1776), Preface, sect. 2. See also, David Baumgardt, *Bentham and the Ethics of Today* (Princeton: Princeton University Press, 1952), p. 505.

16 For further analysis of the "greatest number" principle, see Scarre, *Utilitarianism*, pp. 24–25. See also James Griffin, *Well-Being: Its Meaning, Measurement and Moral Importance* (Oxford: Clarendon Press, 1986), pp. 151–155.

17 Clifford G. Christians, "Utilitarianism in Media Ethics and Its Discontents," *Journal of Mass Media Ethics*, 22, nos. 2 & 3 (2007): 113–131.

18 Griffin, *Well-Being*, pp. 200–202.

19 Ibid., pp. 246–249.

20 Winston L. Brembeck and William S. Howell, *Persuasion: A Means of Social Influence*, 2nd ed. (Englewood Cliffs, NJ: Prentice-Hall, 1976), ch. 10; Howell, *The Empathic Communicator* (1982, reissued 1986 by Waveland Press, Long Grove, IL), ch. 8; Howell, "Foreword," in *Ethical Perspectives and Critical Issues in Intercultural Communication*, Nobleza Asuncion-Lande, ed. (Falls Church, VA: Speech Communication Association, n.d.) pp. viii–x; Howell, "Ethics of Intercultural Communication," paper presented at Speech Communication Association convention, November 15, 1981. See also, Patricia Freeman, "An Ethical Evaluation of the Persuasive Strategies of Glenn W. Turner of Turner Enterprises," *Southern Speech Communication Journal*, 38 (Summer 1973): 347–361, where Freeman uses the "social utility" perspective as one basis for ethical judgment.

21 Richard T. DeGeorge and Joseph A. Pichler, eds., *Ethics, Free Enterprise, and Public Policy* (New York: Oxford University Press, 1978), p. 7.

22 Kathy Fitzpatrick, "Baselines for Ethical Advocacy in the 'Marketplace of Ideas,'" in *Ethics in Public Relations: Responsible Advocacy*, Kathy Fitzpatrick and Carolyn Bronstein, eds. (Thousand Oaks, CA: Sage, 2006), pp. 1–18.

23 Brembeck and Howell, *Persuasion*, p. 344.

24 *United States Law Week*, 44 (January 13, 1976): 3390.

[25] Robert Spero, *The Duping of the American Voter: Dishonesty and Deception in Presidential Television Advertising* (New York: Lippincott and Crowell, 1980), ch. 9.

[26] *Code of Professional Ethics and Practices and AAPOR's Procedures*, (Ann Arbor, MI: American Association of Public Opinion Research, 1991), pp. 4–5; Lucien N. Nedzi, "Public Opinion Polls: Will Legislation Help?" *Public Opinion Quarterly*, 35 (1971): 336–341.

[27] Burton M. Leiser, "The Ethics of Advertising," in *Ethics, Free Enterprise, and Public Policy*, DeGeorge and Pichler, eds., p. 181; Harold N. Williams, "What Do We Do Now, Boss? Marketing and Advertising," *Vital Speeches of the Day*, 40 (February 15, 1974): 285–288.

[28] John Stuart Mill, *On Liberty* (New York: Appleton-Century-Crofts, 1947), pp. 53–54. Also see Franklyn S. Haiman, *Speech and Law in a Free Society* (Chicago: University of Chicago Press, 1981), pp. 232–233.

[29] Sidney Hook, "The Ethics of Political Controversy," in *The Ethics of Controversy: Politics and Protest*, Donn Parson and Wil Linkugel, eds. (Lawrence, KS: The House of Usher, 1968), p. 53; Haselden, *Morality and the Mass Media*, chs. 4, 5, 9; Lee Thayer, "Ethics, Morality, and the Media," in *Ethics, Morality and the Media*, Thayer et al., eds., pp. 16, 39–40; Haiman, *Speech and Law in a Free Society*, pp. 207–208, 277–278. Richard T. Kaplar and Patrick Maines, "The Role of Government in Undermining Journalistic Ethics," *Journal of Mass Media Ethics*, 40, no. 4 (1995): 236–247; Stephen L. Carter, *Civility* (New York: Basic Books, 1998), pp. 207–225.

[30] Franklyn S. Haiman, *"Speech Acts" and the First Amendment* (Carbondale: Southern Illinois University Press, 1993), pp. 81–86.

7

Some Basic Issues

In previous chapters we surveyed seven potential perspectives for evaluating the ethics of human communication—the religious, utilitarian, legalistic, political, human nature, dialogical, and situational perspectives. With this information in hand, we now examine a variety of questions that underscore difficult issues related to ethical problems in human communication. As creators of messages, and as receivers constantly bombarded with complex verbal and nonverbal messages, we continually face resolution of one or another of these fundamental issues. We hope that the raising of these issues will stimulate you to consider them at length on your own to reach your own position on them.

Absolute and Relative Standards

To what degree should ethical criteria for judging human communication be *inflexible, universal,* and *absolute* or to what degree should they be *flexible, situation-bound,* and *relative?*[1] Surely the more absolute our standards are the easier it is to render simple, clear-cut judgments. But in matters of human interaction and public decision making, the ethics of communicative means and ends seldom are simple. Several cautions probably are worth remembering. Usually the choice is not between an absolute standard or an extremely relativistic one; for most of us most of the time the applicable ethical standard is one that to *some degree* is relative and context-bound.[2]

Should ethical standards vary for communication in different fields, such as advertising, education, law, politics, and religion? Jurgen Ruesch argues that "there is no single set of ethical rules that control communication." Instead, he contends, "we have to specify what purposes the communication serves."[3] Based on this assumption, Ruesch suggests that differing sets of ethical standards might have to apply for such different areas as: (1) the interpretive, manipulative, and exhortative communication of advertisers, propagandists, and public relations experts; (2) the representational communication of scientists; (3) the political communication of government and candidates; and (4) the personal communication of individuals.

Also worth remembering is the fact that ethical criteria, which we assume to be obviously appropriate and valid, may be viewed as irrelevant by other persons. Consider the following observation concerning some of the ethical and value standards implied in assumptions central to our view of communication in Anglo-American and Western European culture.[4]

> When we think of influencing people, we think of free men [and women] who have the right to cast free ballots; we think of rational beings, beset by emotionalism, but finally "available" to persuasion that is factually and logically sound. We think of propositions that are worthy of discussion because they are based on probabilities, concerning which various speakers may reasonably present various interpretations. And with our emphasis on the sovereignty of the people and the doctrine of the "greatest good for the greatest number," we accept (sometimes with bad grace) the conclusion finally rendered by majority vote. It is honestly and fundamentally difficult for us to realize that *no single one of these presumptions is universal.* . . . It is my belief that we shall have to stop using rhetoric in the singular and commence using it in the plural.

In making ethical evaluations of communication, we should avoid snap judgments, carefully examine the relevant circumstances to determine which might influence our judgment and to what degree, consider the welfare of everyone involved, and utilize the ethical perspectives most appropriate for the instance.

Maximum or Minimum Standards

Should guidelines for assessing the ethics of human communication be stated as *minimum* criteria to be met in order to maintain ethicality? Or should they be stated as *maximum* ideals we are *obliged* to strive for? After surveying scholars representing both views, Thomas Nilsen offers his belief that communicators have an obligation to follow the better of two "good" criteria.[5] What is *your* view? Ethicists also discuss ethical behavior termed *superogatory.* Superogatory ethical communication would be above and beyond the call of duty. Such behavior, while ethically desirable, is not required.

The End as Justification of Means

In assessing the ethics of human communication, does the *end* justify the *means?* Does the necessity of achieving a goal widely acknowledged as worthwhile justify the use of ethically questionable techniques? A number of scholars remind us that the communicative means employed can have cumulative impacts and effects on audience thought and decision-making habits apart from and in addition to the specific end that the communicator seeks. No matter the purpose they serve, the arguments, appeals, structure, and language we choose do shape the audience's values, thinking habits, language patterns, and level of trust.[6]

Concerning advertising and public relations, John Marston contends that a "good end cannot be held to justify a bad means. . . . Public relations, like democracy itself, is a way of achieving agreement through understanding and persuasion. The way is just as important as the ends sought at any particular moment by fallible human beings; and indeed it may be more important, because democracy lives by the road it travels."[7] Because advertising is so powerful and widespread, semanticist S. I. Hayakawa believes "it influences more than our choice of products; it also influences our patterns of evaluation. It can either increase or decrease the degree of sanity with which people respond to words."[8]

"The kinds of persuasion exercised on people are important elements in their logical and moral training." This contention is central to the view of B. J. Diggs in his essay on "Persuasion and Ethics."[9] Robert Oliver expands a similar line of reasoning: "An audience that is induced to accept shoddy reasoning or falsification of facts to support a right conclusion has, at the same time, suffered the adverse effect of becoming habituated to false pleading." This process, feels Oliver, probably would make "listeners more vulnerable, on another occasion, to demagoguery exercised in a bad cause."[10]

To say that the end does not *always* justify the means is different from saying that ends *never* justify means. The communicator's goal is best considered as one of a number of potentially relevant ethical criteria from among which the most appropriate standards (perspectives) are selected. Under some circumstances, such as threat to physical survival, the goal of personal or national security *temporarily may take* precedence over other criteria. Arthur Sylvester, former Assistant Secretary of Defense for Public Affairs, evoked divided citizen reactions with his assertion that "it is the government's inherent right to lie if necessary to save itself when faced with nuclear disaster; that is basic."[11] In general, however, we best can make mature ethical assessments by evaluating the ethics of communicative techniques apart from the worth and morality of the communicator's specific goal. We can strive to judge the ethics of means and ends *separately*. In some cases we may find ethical communication tactics employed to achieve an unethical goal. In other cases unethical techniques may be used in the service of an entirely ethical goal. On this point, Winston Brembeck and William S. Howell offer a worthwhile warning. "Methods themselves must meet many ethical standards (for example, humanitarian and social). The zealous proponent of a good cause must continually review his methods to be sure that he is not slipping into practices he himself would condemn when used for a 'lesser' purpose."[12]

Although discussed in the context of journalistic ethics, the six questions suggested by Warren Bovée can serve as useful probes to unravel the degree of ethicality embedded in almost any particular means–end relationship.[13] Here are the questions in paraphrased form: (1) Is the means truly unethical/morally evil or just distasteful, unpopular, unwise, or ineffective? (2) Is the end truly good or does it simply appear good to us because we desire it? (3) Is it probable that the ethically bad or suspect means actually will achieve the good end? (4) Is the same good achievable using other more ethical means if only we are willing to be creative, patient, determined, and skillful? (5) Is the good end clearly and overwhelmingly better than the probable bad effects of the means used to attain it? Bad means require justification whereas good means do not. (6) Will the use of the unethical means to achieve a good end withstand the test of publicity? For instance, could the use of the unethical means be justified to those most affected by them or to those most capable of impartially judging them?

Consider this report in the *Chicago Tribune* (April 12, 2000, sec. 1, p. 3):

> More than one-third of doctors surveyed nationwide admit deceiving insurance companies to help patients get the care they need. Their tactics included exaggerating the severity of an illness to help patients avoid being sent home early from the hospital, listing an inaccurate diagnosis on bills and reporting non-existent symptoms to secure insurance coverage. . . . More than one-quarter, 28.5 percent, said it is necessary to "game" the system to provide high-quality care.

Does the end of securing high-quality care for patients justify use of such deceptive communication tactics? Why or why not?

The Ethics of Lying

Is it ever ethical to lie? To this question, some people would respond with a resounding no, never! Others would respond with less certainty. Some would say that it depends on the meaning or definition of a lie. Some would say it depends on the intent and circumstances of the lie. For example, if we are telling a "little white lie" to spare the feelings of a friend who at the moment is emotionally unstable, that communication may not be defined as a "real" lie or may be viewed as justified by intent and circumstances.

Making ethical judgments of lies often is a complex rather than a simple matter. No detailed and exhaustive treatment will be presented here. Instead we simply will sketch some issues, viewpoints, and sources that should be useful to you in investigating the subject further. Contemporary philosopher Charles Fried contends that lying (asserting as true what we believe to be false) always is wrong because it demonstrates disrespect for persons as beings capable of rational judgments and of free and intentional choice. At the same time, Fried believes that "withholding a truth which another needs may be perfectly permissible" because withholding truth is not defined as lying. Utilitarian Carl Wellman observes that the "most useful rule for any society to have is not simply, 'Acts of lying are always wrong,' but something more like, 'Lying is wrong except to save a human life or to spare hurt feelings over unimportant matters.'"[14]

What do we mean by a lie? What is the nature and scope of the human behavior we term lying? Here are two views of the nature and boundaries of lying. George Yoos reminds us that definitions of a lie are culture-bound. Interpretations of what a lie is and expectations concerning appropriateness of deceptive behavior differ from society to society. At length Yoos describes a broad spectrum of behavior that can be termed lying.[15]

> Our looks, our actions, and even our silence can lie. Reports, promises, and even apologies lie. We lie by implication and suggestion. What is first needed in order to understand the phenomena of lying is to analyze the wide variety of deliberate deceptions that take place by means of speech acts other than the giving of information, for to lie is not just to say only what is clear-cut and false. An analysis of lying involves, among other things, an analysis of motives, beliefs, and intentions. In sum, lying is not just simply misinforming or inaccurately reporting what it is that is the case. Lying extends to all sorts of statements and behaviors that may be misleading, deceptive, and confusing.

In his book, *The Lies of George W. Bush*, David Corn provides this detailed opening summary of his exhaustive analysis. Note how widely and inclusively the definitional net of lying is cast by Corn, who raises issues of intent, awareness, seriousness, overtness, and repetition.[16]

> George W. Bush is a liar. He has lied large and small. He has lied directly and by omission. He has misstated facts, knowingly or not. He has misled. He has broken promises, been unfaithful to political vows. Through his campaigns for the presidency and his first years in the White House, he has mugged the truth—not merely in honest error, but deliberately, consistently, and repeatedly to advance his career and agenda. . . . This president has treated the truth in the manner his predecessor treated an intern.

In *Lying: Moral Choice in Public and Private Life,* Sissela Bok distinguishes between intentional deception and intentional lying. Deception is the larger, more encompassing category of which lying is a subcategory. When we "communicate messages meant to mislead" others, to "make them believe what we ourselves do not believe," then we are engaged in intentional deception. Deception may come not only through words but also through gestures, disguise, action and inaction, and even silence. Bok defines a lie as "any intentionally deceptive message which is *stated*."[17] Although lies usually are oral or written, they could be in other symbol systems such as Morse code or sign language. In her book, she explores the functioning and assessment of lying in varied contexts: white lies, lies in a crisis or for the public good, lying to liars and to enemies, lying to protect confidentiality, lying for the welfare of others, lies in social science research on humans, lies to the sick and dying.

Bok assumes there always is a negative presumption against lying. She argues that lying always carries an "initial negative weight," that "truthful statements are preferable to lies in the absence of special considerations," and that "lying requires explanation, whereas truth ordinarily does not." Her basic assumption is that trust in some degree of truthfulness is a "*foundation* of relations among human beings; when this trust shatters or wears away, institutions collapse. . . . *Whatever* matters to human beings, trust is the atmosphere in which it thrives."[18]

The "moral presumption against lying," contends Joseph Kupfer, rests on two lines of argument that demonstrate ultimate negative effects on the "character" of the liar. First, lying causes immediate restriction of the freedom of the deceived. Lying inclines the liar toward a general disrespect for persons—toward abuse of the uniquely human capacity for language as necessary for understanding and reflective choice. Second, lying involves the self-contradiction of "repudiating in speech what we believe." Liars disguise their "real selves" from others by contradicting their real beliefs and thus who they really are. This self-opposition threatens the integration or coherence of the liar's personality. By disguising the self, the liar rejects an opportunity for self-knowledge; reactions of others useful for self-definition are possible only in response to truthful self-disclosure of beliefs. Both of the negative effects on the liar—an attitude of disrespect for persons and a threat to coherence of personality—weaken the moral character of the liar.[19]

Lies, says Bok, add to the power of the liar and diminish the power of those deceived by altering their choices in several ways. First, the lie may obscure or hide some objective the deceived person sought. Second, the lie may obscure or eliminate relevant alternatives that should be considered. Third, the lie may misinform concerning benefits and costs of probable consequences. Finally, lies may mislead concerning the level of confidence or certainty we should have about our choice.

What excuses typically are offered to make a particular lie permissible? What excuses do we offer to minimize, or even remove, the blame for something that normally would be a fault? Sometimes we contend that what is labeled a fault is not actually one. Sometimes we admit that a fault happened, but argue that we are not responsible for it and thus not blameworthy. Sometimes we are bold enough to admit both that the fault happened and that we are responsible, but we argue we still are not blameworthy because we did it in the name of some higher good. Among the higher goods frequently used to justify a lie are: avoiding harm to ourselves or others; producing benefits for others; promoting fairness and justice; and protecting the truth by counteracting another lie, by furthering some more important truth, or by preserving the confidence of others in our own truthfulness. Consider when and how often you have heard the following rationalizations for cheating, described by J. Barton Bowyer, also applied to excuse lying: (1) I need it; (2) they deserve it; (3) it won' t matter anyway; and (4) no one will know anyhow.[20]

At one point, Bok outlines a three-level procedure for determining whether a lie is justifiable. The justification procedure moves from the private to public spheres to foster increasing assurance that the lie is justified.[21] First, we scrutinize our own conscience through internal testing to ensure that the decision is carefully weighed. Second, we examine precedents, consult with friends, elders and colleagues, and seek the advice, directly or through their writings, of experts on ethics. Third, and most crucial, Bok contends that there should be opportunity for public debate among the public at large. For example, public scrutiny might occur prior to policy decisions such as use of deception in experiments on human subjects, entrapment by police in "sting" operations, or use of unmarked police cars to trap speeders. The decision, or potential decision, to deceive deliberately should be scrutinized by reasonable persons of all allegiances, including representatives of those potentially to be affected. In the course of such public debate, the availability of alternative nondeceptive means must be explored. The moral reasons for and against the lie should be evaluated from the viewpoint of the deceived and others affected by it. From the viewpoint of reasonable people outside the specific deceptive situation, additional potential harms should be weighed: an uncondemned liar may find lying all the easier on subsequent occasions; observers may be encouraged to imitate the lying; trust central to the human communication process may be weakened.

In *The Varnished Truth: Truth Telling and Deceiving in Ordinary Life,* David Nyberg takes issue with many of the assumptions and arguments by Sissela Bok and takes a much broader view of the necessity and ethicality of some lying and deception.[22] Nyberg considers deception to be "normal rather than abnormal" and to be "an essential property of language and not merely some kind of perversion of it." It is not a question, in his view, of whether deception ever is acceptable but rather "how we may deceive whom about what and for how long." We have not, he argues, "diligently trained ourselves to deceive thoughtfully and judiciously, charitably, humanely, and with discretion. . . . Truth telling," he contends, "is morally overrated."

For Nyberg, deception is an "essential component of our ability to organize and shape the world, to resolve problems of coordination among individuals who differ, to cope with uncertainty and pain, to be civil and to achieve privacy as needed, to survive as a species, and to flourish as persons." In order to avoid misunderstanding of his position, he does "repudiate all harmfully exploitative deceptions. . . ." But it is a "mistake to despise and reject all other forms of deception, too, just because we have had experience with these contemptible ones." And Nyberg argues that while truth telling is a natural obligation in most voluntary relationships, persons in involuntary relationships have to decide what degree of truth telling is reasonable. Consider whether the voluntary/involuntary dichotomy suggested by Nyberg is as clear as implied. Following his reasoning, joining a social club is voluntary while being assigned by your boss to a problem-solving work group without your approval is involuntary. But is the parent–child relationship voluntary or involuntary? Normally voluntary on the parent's part but involuntary on the child's part? From Nyberg's viewpoint, for whom would the obligation for truth telling be expected and for whom would that obligation evolve?

The Ethics of Intentional Ambiguity and Vagueness

Language that is of doubtful or uncertain meaning might be a typical definition of ambiguous language. Ambiguous language legitimately is open to two or more interpretations.[23] Vague language lacks definiteness, explicitness, or preciseness of meaning. Clear communication of intended meaning usually is one major aim of an ethical communicator, whether that person seeks to enhance receiver understanding or seeks to influence belief, attitude, or action. Textbooks on oral and written communication typically warn against ambiguity and vagueness; often they directly or indirectly take the position that intentional ambiguity is an unethical communication tactic. One textbook on argument, for example, condemns as sham or counterfeit proof the use of equivocation, vagueness, and ambiguity because they "are attempts to avoid or circumvent the proof process." A textbook for the beginning course in English admonishes: "The writer is responsible for supplying all the meaning, and he is seriously at fault when he leaves the reader to grope even for a moment."[24]

A different viewpoint is offered for consideration by Lee Williams and Blaine Goss:[25]

> One must be careful not to equate untruthfulness with ambiguity, or to confuse ambiguity in informative speaking with ambiguity in persuasive speaking. To encode a vague message is not necessarily to encode a lie or untruthful statement. Indeed, vagueness is not even a necessary condition for lying to occur, for there are many lies which explicitly identify their referents. We must remember that all words contain some degree of vagueness, and instead of being inherently bad, vagueness, like rhetoric, appears to be an amoral means which can be applied to produce many different ends.

Most people probably would agree that intentional ambiguity is unethical in situations where accurate instruction or efficient transmission of precise information is the acknowledged purpose. Even in most so-called persuasive communication situations, intentional ambiguity would be ethically suspect. However, in some situations communicators may feel that the intentional creation of ambiguity or vagueness is necessary, accepted, expected as normal, and even ethically justified.[26] Such might be the case, for example, in religious discourse, in some advertising, in some legal discourse, in labor-management bargaining, in political campaigning, or in international diplomatic negotiations.

We can itemize a number of specific purposes for which communicators might feel that intentional ambiguity is ethically justified: (1) to heighten receiver attention through puzzlement; (2) to allow flexibility in interpretation of legal concepts; (3) to use ambiguity on secondary issues to allow for precise understanding and agreement on the primary issue; (4) to promote maximum receiver psychological participation in the communication transaction by letting them create their own relevant meanings; (5) to promote maximum latitude for revision of a position in later dealings with opponents or with constituents by avoiding being "locked-in" to a single absolute stance.[27]

In his Law *Dictionary for Non-Lawyers,* Daniel Oran warns against the use of vague language but also explains:[28]

> Some legal words have a "built-in" vagueness. They are used when the writer or speaker does not want to be pinned down. For example, when a law talks about "reasonable speed" or "due care," it is deliberately imprecise about the meaning of the words because it wants the amount of speed allowed or care required to be decided situation-by-situation, rather than by an exact formula.

What is your personal assessment of the ethicality of such intentional vagueness? On what ethical grounds would you defend or condemn such vagueness?

In political communication, whether during campaigns or by government officials, several circumstances might be used to justify intentional ambiguity ethically. First, a president, or presidential candidate, often must communicate to multiple audiences through a single message via a mass medium such as television or radio. Different parts of the message may appeal to specific audiences while at the same time intentional ambiguity in some message elements avoids offending any of the audiences.[29] Lewis Froman describes a second circumstance. A candidate "cannot take stands on specific issues because he [or she] doesn't know what the specific choices will be until he [or she] is faced with the necessity for concrete decision. Also, specific commitments would be too binding in a political process that depends upon negotiation and compromise."[30] Third, groups of voters increasingly make decisions whether to support or oppose a candidate on the basis of that candidate's stand on a single issue of paramount importance to those groups. The candidate's position on a variety of other public issues often is ignored or dismissed. "Single-issue politics" is the phrase frequently used to characterize this trend. A candidate intentionally may be ambiguous on one emotion-packed issue in order to get a fair hearing for stands on many other issues.[31]

In some advertising, intentional ambiguity seems to be understood as such by consumers and even accepted by them. In your opinion, what might be some ethical implications of the TV ad for a popular beer, in which Sergio Garcia, a famous professional golfer, is acting as a kind of secret agent? He sneaks into a plush party to meet a sultry, sexy-looking date. She: "What took you so long?" He: "Tough drive." He: "How's your game?" She (*in a sexy voice*): "Oh, there's nothing like a good up and down."

A balanced and flexible view on the ethics of intentional ambiguity and vagueness is offered by Thomas Nilsen:[32]

This is not to say that vagueness and ambiguity are wrong in themselves. To a certain extent they cannot be avoided. There are also instances of their legitimate use. If a speaker seeks to stimulate his [or her] listeners to feelings of national pride (certainly an acceptable purpose if done with prudence), he must realize that for different people different aspects of their national life are cause for pride, and the speaker can rightfully permit each listener to identify with that which is most meaningful to him [or her]. Where rigorous thought is needed, however, where decisions are being made on specific issues, such personal interpretations may be highly misleading, and the speaker has an ethical obligation to minimize them. If ambiguity is unavoidable, it should be made explicit. Where vagueness is unavoidable, the speaker should not claim more specificity than the terms warrant.

Ethics, Emotional Appeals, and Rationality

Is the use of so-called "emotional appeals" in communication inherently unethical? What should be the ethical standards guiding appeals to an audience's emotions, motives, drives, needs, and desires? Our North American culture traditionally has viewed with suspicion the expression of or capitalization on emotion in public communication. Appeal to emotion in interpersonal communication usually has been judged less harshly. The Aristotelian heritage in rhetorical theory has perpetuated the primacy of reason and logic over emotion in selecting ethical persuasive strategies.[33] On this point you may wish to refer back to the "degree of rationality" political perspective discussed in chapter 2. One generalization that emerges from contemporary social science research on communication is that receivers of messages find it difficult to categorize appeals or supporting materials as either logical or emotional in exactly the same manner intended by the communicator. Differing audiences may view the same appeal differently. A given technique, such as a set of statistics indicating the high probability of falling victim to cancer during our lifetime, may be perceived as possessing both rational and emotional components. On a related point, Ivan Preston observes that although an outside observer may judge an advertising message as irrational, from the viewpoint of the receiving consumer the message may be evaluated as rational in light of his or her own values and goals.[34]

Oliver notes the cultural variability of standards for assessing rationality:[35]

> People in separate cultures and separate nations are concerned about *different* problems; and they have different systems of thinking about them. What seems important to us is not necessarily important to everyone. Our logic may not be theirs; our very faith in rationality may be countermatched by their faith in irrationality. What we consider proof of a particular proposition, they may consider irrelevant.

"There are many logics," observe John Condon and Fathi Yousef, "each being a system with its own assumptions and consistent in itself, and different cultures will express different logics." They caution us "against criticizing statements from other societies which rely on different authorities, derive from different perceptions of the world, and follow a logic which is different from our own."[36] Marshall McLuhan offers provocative hypotheses concerning the impact of visual, print orientation on Western culture's conception of rationality:[37]

> Connected sequential discourse, which is thought of as rational, is really visual. It has nothing to do with reason as such. Reasoning does not occur on single planes or in continuous, connected fashion. The mind leapfrogs. It puts things together in all sorts of proportions and ratios instantly. To put down thoughts in coded, lineal ways was a discovery of the Greek world. It is not done this way, for example, in the Chinese world. But to deny that the Chinese have access to reason would be ridiculous.

Even within contemporary American culture, there are differing conceptions of what is rational or reasonable.[38] Winston Brembeck and William S. Howell recognize: "Methods of critical thinking are culture bound. Within a culture, approved norms exist that function as universals." They outline values that they believe function as "universals of thoughtful deliberation in America": orderliness; clarity and directness; concreteness and specificity; accuracy; unity and coherence.[39] Other scholars explore the possibility that standards for "reasonable" communication vary between different fields of discourse, such as public issues, philosophy, religion, natural science, law, historiography, or the arts. There may be standards for reasonableness in discourse agreed upon by experts *within* particular fields but that differ *between* fields.[40]

The ethicality of so-called emotional and logical appeals depends primarily on which specific technique is used, in what manner, and in what context. The need to dichotomize communicative appeals into either a logical or an emotional category does not seem very compelling. A communicative technique can be assessed for ethicality in and of itself regardless of how it is labeled. Note, too, that a specific "emotional appeal" may be viewed as nonrational (different from reason) without necessarily being irrational (contrary to reason).

If we do, nevertheless, wish to evaluate the ethics of a communication technique that we perceive as an "emotional appeal," the following guidelines are suggested within the context of "mainstream" North American culture. Assuming that the appeal is ethical in light of other *relevant* perspectives, the "emotional" technique is ethical if it is undergirded by a substructure of sound evidence and reasoning to support it. Presentation of this substructure could accompany the appeal in the message, or the substructure could exist apart from the message and be produced upon the request of a critic. When a *sound* proposal is linked to satisfaction of *relevant* audience emotions, values, and motives, then the appeal probably is ethical. If the audience is asked to view the emotional appeal not as proof or justification but as an *expression* of the communicator's internal emotional state, it probably is ethical. Generally, the emotional appeal is ethically suspect when it functions as *pseudoproof,* giving the appearance of sound evidence, or when it functions to short-circuit the receiver's capacity for free, informed, critical choice.[41]

The Truth Standard in Commercial Advertising

Commercial advertising in the United States typically has been viewed as persuasion that argues a case or demonstrates a claim concerning the actual nature or merit of a product. To such attempts at arguing the quality of a product, ethical standards rooted in truthfulness and rationality have been applied. For instance, are the evidence and reasoning supporting the claim clear, accurate, relevant, and sufficient in quantity? Are the motivational and emotional appeals directly relevant to the product?[42]

But what if the primary purpose of most commercial advertisements, especially on television, is not to prove a claim? Then what ethical standards we apply may stem from whatever alternative view we hold of advertising's nature and purpose. In *Advertising Age,* J. R. Carpenter observed: "Specific claims can be argued on the basis of facts. Logic can be questioned. . . . But it is difficult to challenge image, emotion, style."[43] Some advertisements function primarily to capture and sustain consumer attention, to announce a product, or to create consumer awareness of the name of a product.[44] What ethical criteria are most appropriate for such attention-getting advertisements?

Some analysts view commercial advertising as a type of poetic game.[45] The following poetic techniques are used in combination to invite consumers to participate in a recreational, feel-good, emotionally satisfying experience: making the commonplace significant, connotation, ambiguity, metaphor, fantasy, and aesthetically pleasing structure. If there is such a thing as commercial advertising-as-poetic, what ethical standards should we use to judge this kind of poetry?

Neither poets nor advertisers, argues Theodore Levitt, focus on the literal functionality of things they depict. "Instead," he contends, "each celebrates a deep and complex emotion" symbolized through "creative embellishment—a content which cannot be captured by literal description alone." Levitt views advertising as commercial poetry. Neither poetic descriptions nor advertisements make any "pretense of being the things themselves." He admits that there are tasteless and intentionally deceptive advertisements and he condemns advertising that "dulls our senses and assaults our sensibilities." But advertisements are the symbols of human aspirations. "They are not the real thing, nor are they intended to be, nor are they accepted as such by the public."[46]

In *The Responsive Chord,* Tony Schwartz leaves the impression that truth is completely irrelevant as a standard for electronic media, especially for commercial and political television advertisements.[47] He assumes that "the question of truth is largely irrelevant when dealing with electronic media content." Argues Schwartz:

> Electronic communication deals primarily with effects. The problem is that no "grammar" for electronic media effects has been devised. Electronic media have been viewed merely as extensions of print, and therefore subject to the same grammar and values as print communication. The patterned auditory and visual information on television or radio is not "content." Content is a print term, subject to the truth-falsity issue. Auditory and visual information on television or radio are stimuli that affect a viewer or listener. As stimuli, electronically mediated communication cannot be analyzed in the same way as print "content." A whole new set of questions must be asked, and a new theory of communication must be formulated.

Since "truth is a print ethic, not a standard for ethical behavior in electronic communication," Schwartz feels that critics and regulatory agencies should assess the ethics of advertising not by standards of truth and clarity of content but by evaluating effects of advertisements on receivers.[48] In a later writing, Schwartz attempts to clarify his position by contending that truth is a relevant but not a major standard for judging electronic media ethics. It is interesting to note, however, that in his evaluation of *political* broadcast advertising, he employs such truth-related standards as accuracy, factual verifiability, and use of a factual foundation to support implications.[49]

What ethical evaluation of effects and consequences would you make of an advertisement for Fetish perfume in *Seventeen* magazine, a magazine whose readers include several million girls ages 12–15? The ad pictures an attractive female teenager looking very seductively straight at the young female reader. The written portion of the ad says: "Apply generously to your neck so he can smell the scent as you shake your head 'no.'" Consider that this ad exists in a larger cultural context where acquaintance rape is a societal problem, where women and girls are clearly urged to say "No!" to unwanted sexual advances, and where men and boys too often still believe that "no" really means "yes." What harmful individual and societal consequences may stem from ads that negatively stereotype persons or groups on the basis of age (old and confused), sex (women as sex objects), or culture/ethnicity (backward; inarticulate)? Frequent exposure to such ads may influence the way we perceive and treat such stereotyped people and the way the stereotyped people view themselves and their own abilities.[50]

Ethics and Propaganda

Is propaganda unethical? The answer to this question in part depends on how propaganda is defined. Numerous, often widely divergent, definitions abound.[51] Originally the term *propaganda* was associated with the efforts of the

Roman Catholic Church to persuade people to accept the Church's doctrine. Such efforts were institutionalized in 1622 by Pope Gregory XV when he created the Sacred Congregation for Propagating the Faith. The word propaganda soon came to designate not only institutions seeking to propagate a doctrine but also the doctrine itself and the communication techniques employed.

Today one cluster of definitions of propaganda presents a *neutral* position toward the ethical nature of propaganda. A definition combining the key elements of such neutral views might be: propaganda is a campaign of mass persuasion. According to this view, propaganda represents an organized, continuous effort to persuade a mass audience primarily using the mass media.[52] Propaganda thus would include advertising and public relations efforts, national political election campaigns, the persuasive campaigns of some social reform movements, and the organized efforts of national governments to win friends abroad, maintain domestic morale, and undermine an opponent's morale both in hot and cold war. Such a view stresses communication channels and audiences and categorizes propaganda as one species of persuasion. Just as persuasion may be sound or unsound, ethical or unethical, so too may propaganda.

Another cluster of definitions of propaganda takes a *negative* stance toward the ethical nature of propaganda. Definitions in this cluster probably typify the view held by many "average" American citizens. A definition combining the key elements of such negative views might be: Propaganda is the intentional use of suggestion, irrelevant emotional appeals, and pseudoproof to circumvent human rational decision-making processes.[53] Such a view stresses communication techniques and sees propaganda as *inherently* unethical.

Jacques Ellul, the noted French social and political analyst, has written at length on propaganda. In his book, *Propaganda,* Ellul offers this definition: "a set of methods employed by an organized group that wants to bring about active or passive participation in its actions of a mass of individuals, psychologically unified through psychological manipulations and incorporated in an organization." He does not view propaganda simply as a campaign of mass persuasion. Rather he sees propaganda as so pervasive and powerful in all aspects of contemporary technological societies that it is an injurious "menace which threatens the total human personality."[54]

In a lengthy essay, Ellul focuses precisely on the ethical implications of propaganda.[55] Contrary to the conventional wisdom on the limitations of propaganda, Ellul argues that, even in the long run, the clearest and most obvious factual evidence cannot overcome the self-contained delusional world constructed by modern propaganda. Ellul outlines three reasons why he believes propaganda is so pervasive and potent that it destroys, literally obliterates, any possibility of ethics. First, propaganda is a self-justifying process whereby a descriptive state of what *is* (power) evolves into a value judgment of what *ought* to be (this power is right and just). Second, because propaganda focuses on the instantaneousness of the immediate and the present, it destroys the sense of history (continuity of generations) and of philosophy (critical reflection on experiences) necessary for moral existence. Third, because propaganda undercuts our powers of conscious choice making and because it fosters a situation in which we each remain completely alone while still belonging to a collective mass, it destroys the kinds of mutual, thoughtful, interpersonal communication (reciprocal participation, encounter, dialogue) necessary for building an ethical existence.

Communication scholar Stanley Cunningham undertakes a philosophical reconstruction in his book, *The Idea of Propaganda*. For him, propaganda is "an inherently unethical social phenomenon" because it undermines the significant values of truth and truthfulness, reasoning and knowledge, because it sidesteps voluntary choice and human agency, and because it "exploits and reinforces society's moral weakness." Because propaganda violates the normal communication expectations (implied ethical contracts) of trust, truthfulness, and understanding, it is best characterized as "counterfeit or pseudocommunication." He provides a description of the "deep-structured constituents and the enabling conditions" that mark propaganda.[56]

Propaganda, contends Cunningham, is constituted by a "complex array" of deficiencies or shortcomings that undermine justified knowledge. We paraphrase those characteristics here. Propaganda plays on complexity and stimulates confusion; exploits expectations; poses as valid information and accepted knowledge; constructs belief systems that include tenacious convictions that defy questioning; offers false or artificial assurances and certainties; distorts perceptions; disregards truth and truthfulness as values necessary for accurate knowledge and understanding; subverts "rationality, reasoning, and a healthy respect for rigor, evidence, and procedural safeguards"; promotes ignorance and passive acceptance of unexamined beliefs; and uses truths and information as mere instruments rather than as ethical ideals in themselves.

Are the traditional "propaganda devices" always to be viewed as unethical? Textbooks in such fields as journalism, communication, and social psychology often discuss the traditional list: name-calling, glittering generality, transfer, testimonial, plain folks, card-stacking, and band wagon.[57] Such a list does *not* constitute a surefire guide, a "handy dandy" checklist, for exposure of unethical persuasion. The ethics of at least some of these techniques depends on how they are employed in a given context.

The plain folks technique, for example, stresses humble origins and modest backgrounds shared by the communicator and audience. The communicator emphasizes to his or her audience, although usually not in these words, that "we're all just plain folks." In his "whistle-stop" speeches to predominantly rural, Republican audiences during the 1948 presidential campaign, Democrat Harry Truman typically used the plain folks appeal in the introductions of his speeches to establish common ground. He used the device to accomplish one of the purposes of the introductory segment of most speeches—namely, establishment of rapport; he did not rely on it for proof in the main body of his speeches. If a politician relied primarily on the plain folks appeal as pseudoproof *in justifying* the policy he or she advocated, such usage could be condemned as unethical. Furthermore, Truman really was the kind of person who could legitimately capitalize on his actual plain folks background. A politician of more privileged and patrician background, such as Edward Kennedy, could be condemned for using an unethical technique if he were to appeal to farmers and factory workers by saying "you and I are just plain folks."

Ethics and the Demagogue

Today the label "demagogue" frequently is used to render a negative ethical judgment of a communicator. Too often the label is left only vaguely defined; the criteria we are to use to evaluate a person as a demagogue are unspecified. In ancient Greece, a demagogue simply was a leader or orator who championed the cause of the common people.

Consider the following hypothetical description of a politician: He is the perfect example of a demagogue, combining true-believer certainty, raw pursuit of power, blue-collar populism, Chameleon-like adaptability, and blunt, sometimes crude, persuasive appeals.[58] Are each of the characteristics listed a truly appropriate criterion for judging a demagogue? Are there any appropriate criteria omitted? Would you label this politician as a demagogue?

You now are invited to consider the following five characteristics collectively as possible appropriate guides for determining to what degree a persuader merits the label demagogue.[59]

1. A demagogue wields popular or mass leadership over an extensive number of people.

2. A demagogue exerts primary influence through the medium of the spoken word—through public speaking, whether directly to an audience or via radio or television.

3. A demagogue relies heavily on propaganda, defined in the negative sense of intentional use of suggestion, irrelevant emotional appeals, and pseudoproof to circumvent human rational decision-making processes.

4. A demagogue capitalizes on the availability of a major contemporary social cause or problem.

5. A demagogue is hypocritical; the social cause serves as a front or persuasive leverage point while the actual primary motive is selfish interest and personal gain.

Several cautions are in order in applying these guidelines. A communicator may reflect each of these characteristics to a greater or lesser degree and only in certain instances. A communicator might fulfill only several of these criteria (such as items 1, 2, and 4) and yet not be called a demagogue; characteristics 3 and 5 seem to be central to a conception of a demagogue. How easily and accurately can we usually determine a communicator's actual motivations? Should we limit the notion of a demagogue solely to the political arena? An excellent collection of case studies that you may want to examine is Reinhard Luthin's *American Demagogues.*

Ethics and Nonverbal Communication

The process of communication includes not only verbal expression but also nonverbal expression. In *The Importance of Lying*, Arnold Ludwig underscores the ethical implications of nonverbal communication: "Lies are not only found in verbal statements. When a person nods affirmatively in response to something he does not believe or when he feigns attention to a conversation he finds boring, he is equally guilty of lying. . . . A false shrug of the shoulders, the seductive batting of eyelashes, an eyewink, or a smile may all be employed as nonverbal forms of deception."[60] Even silence may carry ethical implications.[61] For instance, if to be responsible in fulfillment of our role or position demands that we speak out on a subject, to remain silent might be judged unethical. On the other hand, if the only way that we can persuade others successfully on a subject is to employ unethical communication techniques or appeals, the ethical decision probably would be to remain silent.

Do the ethical standards commonly applied to verbal communication also apply appropriately to nonverbal elements in communication? Should there be a special ethic for nonverbal communication in place of, or in addition to, the ethical criteria for assessing human use of language? For instance, what ethical standards should govern eye contact, facial expression, tone of voice, or gestures? How should the ethics of silence be judged? In attempting to answer these questions, we should note that an ethic of nonverbal communication is complicated by the fact that many nonverbal signals are unintentional or semiconscious. To the extent that a nonverbal element reflects lack of conscious choice or intent, should we consider that element as outside the realm of ethical scrutiny? Or, because some nonverbal cues often are less consciously controlled by the communicator than words and because they usually are assumed by receivers to be more believable than words as keys to real sender intent and meaning, should we view nonverbal elements as *better* indexes than words of the ethical level of communication?[62]

Another type of nonverbal communication that raises a variety of ethical concerns is the use of photographic images. Anyone who believes that "pictures don't lie" is forgetting the fact that every decision a photographer makes involves subjective choices that may "distort" what others perceive as "objective reality": What should be included in the frame of the photograph? What should be left out of the frame? Should the subject matter of the photograph be staged? Should it be spontaneous? What angle should be used? Should the viewer look up or look down on the subject? Should zoom and contrast enhancement be used to reveal elements of the picture that would not have been visible otherwise? How should the photo be cropped? What discursive captions should accompany the photograph? With each decision comes the possibility for manipulation and distortion.[63] Further, as Jim Lewis, a writer for *Slate Magazine*, explains, the shift from film to digital photography has made it even more difficult to distinguish between photographic truth and illusion:

> Even the cheapest chip-based pocket camera lets you set white balance, color effects, aspect ratio, and a dozen other parameters and automatically interpolates pixels based on its best guess as to what came through the lens; and such tweaking isn't tampering, because the image doesn't exist until these decisions are made.[64]

Photographs have potential to influence in powerful ways the beliefs and emotions of viewers. For example, in 1862 Matthew Brady shocked the nation with his photographs of the corpses of soldiers who had been killed during the Battle of Antietam. A critic who saw the original photo exhibit commented in *The New York Times* that Brady's pictures served an important journalistic purpose. They brought home "the terrible reality and earnestness" of the Civil War in a way that would not have been possible in descriptive words or in drawings. However, the critic also worried about whether this journalistic value really justified the emotional trauma caused to those who recognized in the photos the face of a beloved son, father, or husband.[65] In the twenty-first century, journalists, government officials, and members of the military still struggle with these same moral problems. Should the images of wounded soldiers be published? What about photographs of flag-draped coffins of American troops killed in battle? Should pictures of civilian casualties of war be published? Can the public understand the sacrifices of soldiers without seeing the circumstances of their service? Should this public understanding come at the price of violating the privacy of the casualties and of their families?[66]

Media coverage of the terrorist attacks on the World Trade Center on September 11, 2001, yielded many vivid pictures that were burned into our memories. An Associated Press photographer produced one especially emotional image of a man falling headfirst down the side of the still-standing North Tower. No captions identified the man, but with the telephoto lens and digital enhancement, the man's face could be recognized by those who knew him. The picture did help to reinforce the personal impact of the terrorist attack in a way that would not have been possible in words. But the cost of this public understanding of the event was to intensify the grief and violate the privacy of family members and friends of the victim. Did the photo have legitimate news value? Or did it merely feed into the public's seemingly unlimited appetite for glimpses into the intimate details of the grief of others—a process that some scholars refer to as the "pornography of grief"?[67]

Ethical concerns also arise when people attempt to manipulate the subject matter of a photograph in order to achieve some preconceived persuasive purpose. For example, in September 2000, the University of Wisconsin at Madison published a recruiting brochure for prospective students. On the cover, they wanted to include a picture that would invite students to a racially diverse campus. University officials later admitted that they spent several months looking for the right picture, but they had no luck. They decided to solve their problem by creating a photograph that would suit their needs. They took a picture of a crowd of white students who were cheering at a football game. They then used digital software to insert a picture of a black student into the crowd.

The altered photograph was not as convincing as the university had hoped, however. When journalists at the *Daily Cardinal* (the campus newspaper) saw the photo, they immediately became suspicious because the black student looked as if he was sitting in the sunlight while the rest of the crowd appeared to have been sitting in the stands on a cloudy day. Passing the photograph around, someone recognized the black student. When contacted, he was startled because he had never attended any football games. At this point, the reporters confronted the university and asked for an explanation. University officials admitted publicly that they had "doctored" the photograph. They apologized but explained that they had meant no harm. They only wanted to create a photo that would reflect a racially diverse student population. For many critics of the university, this apology seemed a poor excuse for their nonverbal lie. The incident invites us to reflect on the ethical implications of image manipulation: Did the university's apparently good intentions justify their use of nonverbal deception? Also, one might wonder, what if the university had attempted to achieve the same end by using different means? Imagine if, instead of doctoring the picture, university officials had invited a group of racially diverse students to the football game and asked them all to sit together in order to be photographed. Would a "staged" photograph be any more honest than the "doctored" photograph? Or again, what if the university had hired a photographer to attend football games and specifically requested that the photographer take pictures which included students of color? Would this selective framing of the event be morally acceptable? Communication professionals need to remember that photographs can be manipulated in many different ways. Where is the line between ethical and unethical manipulation?[68]

To explore further ethical standards for nonverbal communication, you are urged to read several sources that are especially rich in more extended case studies. The book *Image Ethics: The Moral Rights of Subjects in Photographs, Film and Television* (1988) is an anthology of original essays that explore "ethical and moral issues surrounding the use of the camera," especially the "moral rights of those individuals and groups whose images are used by photographers, filmmakers, and video producers." This book also highlights the tension between freedom and responsibility:[69]

> Photography, film, and television confer enormous power to create images that combine verisimilitude and visual impact. . . . These powers are appropriately protected under our Constitution as an essential free-

dom in a democratic society, but they should also entail responsibilities. There is . . . the need for all concerned to pause and contemplate the moral implications of the images they produce and distribute.

Image Ethics in the Digital Age (2003) is a more recent work also edited by Larry Gross, John Stuart Katz, and Jay Ruby.[70] It includes essays that explore the ethical implications of new digital technologies on image creation and distribution. For instance, there is a general trend in the new media industries (and in the Internet) to weaken the boundaries between journalism, entertainment, and advertising. This can be seen, for example, in digitally superimposed advertising that allows sports viewers to see different corporate logos in the backgrounds of televised playing fields. New technologies also tend to blur the boundaries between the public sphere and the private sphere. Reality TV, webcams, and closed-circuit surveillance cameras seem specially created to reinforce our collective voyeuristic urges. The anthology also includes essays dealing with copyright law and the use of new technologies to prevent unlicensed use and distribution of graphic and photographic images.

Finally, another useful anthology is *Images that Injure: Pictorial Stereotypes in the Media* (2002).[71] Included are essays that explore the origins and effects of stereotypes as they appear in newspapers, magazine advertisements, television, film, and the Internet. The intentional or unintentional use of stereotypes perpetuates oversimplified, and frequently negative, depictions of individuals because of their membership in various groups. The book surveys numerous stereotypical images, including those based on race and ethnicity, gender, age, physical disability, and sexual orientation. As well, the book includes several essays on post-9/11 stereotyping in the media.

Ethics and Ghostwriting

Is a communicator unethical when utilizing a ghostwriter?[72] Can a speaker or writer ethically use a person, or staff, to write his or her message, to write parts of the message, to contribute ideas, or to do research? Nationally prominent figures such as Franklin D. Roosevelt, Adlai E. Stevenson II, John F. Kennedy, Richard M. Nixon, and Ronald Reagan relied heavily on ghostwriters to write their speeches. Rhetorical critics stress that these politicians also frequently played an extensive role in the creation of their own speeches. Were they, nevertheless, unethical in using speechwriters? We can analyze the ethics of ghostwriting through exploration of a number of interrelated questions.

First, what is the communicator's intent and what is the audience's degree of awareness? Clearly condemned by some critics is the communicator who deceives the audience by pretending to author his or her own messages when, in fact, they are ghostwritten. However, if the audience is fully aware that ghostwriting is a normal circumstance, such as for presidents, senators, or corporation executives, then no ethical condemnation may be warranted. Everyone seems aware, for example, that certain classes of speakers use ghostwriters and make no pretense of writing all of each of their speeches.

Second, does the communicator use ghostwriters to make himself or herself appear to possess personal qualities that he or she really does not have? Eloquent style, wit, coherence, and incisive ideas are qualities all communicators desire; but some communicators can obtain them only with the aid of ghostwriters. We must consider the extent to which ghostwriters are used to improve a communicator's image without unethically distorting his or her true character.

Third, what is the communicator's role and what are the surrounding circumstances? Pressures of time and duty are invoked to sanction the necessity of ghostwriters for some communicators. In a speech communication course or an English composition course, most people agree that the student is entirely responsible for creating his or her own message. Training in analysis, research, and composition is subverted when a student relies on someone else to do all or part of his or her work. However, the president of the United States, a senator, a college president, or corporation head may, because of job demands and lack of time, be unable to avoid using ghostwriters. But what about a college professor, state senator, or local executive? Are they unethical when they use a ghostwriter? Should clergy use a ghostwriter? Although a minister has written his or her own sermon, is he or she ethical if he or she repeats the same speech again and again over the years, even though the nature and needs of the congregation change? Some critics would argue that when the president of the United States speaks, not as the head of the executive branch, as in a State of the Union message, but as an individual politician, as in a presidential campaign, he or she should avoid using ghostwriters.

Fourth, to what extent do the communicators actively participate in the writing of their messages? Adlai E. Stevenson II and Franklin D. Roosevelt participated extensively in the writing of their major addresses, even though each of them used a staff of speechwriters. They are not often ethically condemned for employing ghostwriters; their speeches accurately reflected their own style and intellect. But what of the ethics of the speakers who let their ghostwriter research and write the entire speech and then simply deliver it?

Finally, does the communicator accept responsibility for the message he or she presents? Some argue that even if communicators did not write their message, or help write it, they still are ethical as long as they accept responsibility for the ethics and accuracy of its contents. When their statement is criticized, communicators should not disclaim authorship and "pass the buck" to their ghostwriters.

By fully exploring these five issues, we should be able to assess perceptively the ethics of a communicator who employs ghostwriters. Depending on the standards we employ, our judgment may not always be clear-cut. Through such analysis, however, we may avoid oversimplification inherent in most either/or evaluations.[73]

Secrecy

What is a secret? In her book, *Secrets,* Sissela Bok argues that "anything can be secret as long as it is kept intentionally hidden, set apart in the mind of its keeper as requiring concealment." Bok probes the nature of the concept, examines the need for and the dangers of secrecy, and illuminates varied contexts for secrecy and revelation such as personal relations, gossip, business, government, whistle-blowing, leaking of information, social science research, undercover police operations, and investigative journalism. In *Lying,* Bok advocated a negative ethical presumption against all lying—any specific lie needed adequate justification. In *Secrets,* however, Bok holds a "neutral" view of secrecy—not all secrets are wrong and not all secrets need justification. "Secrecy may accompany the most innocent as well as the most lethal acts; it is needed for human survival, yet it enhances every form of abuse."[74]

Bok does explain two assumptions that undergird her analysis of secrecy. First she assumes *equality* as a principle: "Whatever control over secrecy and openness we conclude is legitimate for some individuals should, in the absence of special considerations, be legitimate for all." Her second assumption is the desirability for *"partial individual control* over the degree of secrecy or openness about personal matters—those indisputably in the private realm." Some individual control over intimate and personal secrets is necessary to protect self-identity, plans and actions, and possessions. "With no control over secrecy and openness, human beings could not remain either sane or free." Admittedly even in private relationships, secrecy as a habit or in a specific case can harm both the keeper and the excluded. An ability to exercise *discretion* is vital for judging the ethicality of secrecy. Discretion is the ability to "discern what is and is not intrusive and injurious," to cope with "the moral questions about what is fair or unfair, truthful or deceptive, helpful or harmful," and to know "when to hold back in order not to bruise" and "when to reach out."[75]

The relationship between secrecy and power occupies a central place in Bok's analysis.[76] Power may be exercised by a person in authority or by one who exercises unscrupulous means; power may be collective in groups or institutions. "When power is joined to secrecy, therefore, and when the practices are of long duration, the danger of spread and abuse and deterioration increases." Concerning personal matters there is a "presumption in favor of individual control over secrecy and openness" and "the burden of proof is on those who would deny them such control." In the cases of collective and institutional power joined with secrecy, the presumption reverses. When those who exercise such power "claim control over secrecy and openness, it is up to them to show why giving them such control is necessary and what kinds of safeguards they propose." For example, there "should be a strong presumption against governmental control over secrecy because of the abuses it can conceal, the power governments exercise, and their special obligations of accountability." The test of public debate and justification applies here to secrecy as it did in *Lying* to practices of institutions. A proposed or actual policy of secrecy should, in principle at least, be capable of public deliberation by reasonable persons, including those who oppose the practice and those who are directly affected by it. You may wish to review the section on lying earlier in this chapter, where the justification procedures Bok proposes are explained.

Ethical Responsibilities of Receivers

What are our ethical responsibilities as receivers or respondents in communication? An answer to this question may stem in part from the image we hold of the communication process. Receivers would seem to bear little, if any, responsibility if they are viewed as inert, passive, defenseless receptacles, as mindless blotters uncritically accepting arguments and ideas. If receivers actually behave as viewed by the communicator, then they have little or no responsibility to understand accurately and evaluate critically. In this view, they have minimal power of choice and almost automatically must agree with the communicator's ideas. In contrast, communication can be viewed as a transaction where both senders and receivers bear mutual responsibility to participate actively in the process. This shared responsibility may vary proportionally according to roles. This image of receivers as active participants might suggest a number of responsibilities. Here we will suggest two major responsibilities that perhaps are best captured by the phrases "reasoned skepticism" and "appropriate feedback."[77]

Reasoned skepticism includes a number of elements. It represents a balanced position between the undesirable extremes of being too open-minded, too gullible, on the one hand and being too closed-minded, too dogmatic, on the other. We are not simply unthinking blotters "soaking up" ideas and argument. Rather we should exercise our capacities actively to search for meaning, to analyze and synthesize, to interpret significance, and to judge soundness and worth. We do something to and with the information we receive; we process, interpret, and evaluate it. Also, we should inform ourselves about issues being discussed. We should tolerate, even seek out, divergent and controversial viewpoints to better assess what is being presented. We should not be so dogmatic, ego-involved, and defensive about our own views that we are unwilling to take into account (understand, evaluate, and perhaps even accept) the views and data presented by others.

As receivers, we must realize that accurate understanding of a communicator's message may be hindered by our attempt to impose prematurely our own ethical standards on him or her. Our immediate "gut-level" ethical judgments may cause us to distort the intended meaning. Only after reaching an accurate understanding of the sender's ideas can we reasonably evaluate the ethics of his or her communication strategies or purposes.

In this era of public distrust of the truthfulness of public communication, reasoned skepticism also requires that we combat the automatic assumption that most public communication always is untrustworthy. Just because a communication is of a certain type or comes from a certain source (government, political candidate, news media, advertiser), it must not automatically, without evaluation, be rejected as tainted or untruthful. Clearly, we must always exercise caution in acceptance and care in evaluation, as emphasized throughout this book. Using the best evidence available to us, we may arrive at our best judgment. However, to condemn a message as untruthful or unethical solely because it stems from a suspect source and before directly assessing it is to exhibit decision-making behavior detrimental to our political, social, and economic system. Rejection of the message, if such be the judgment, must come after, not before, our evaluation of it. As with a defendant in the courtroom, public communication must be presumed ethically innocent until we, or experts we acknowledge, have proved it guilty.

As active participants in the communication process, the feedback we provide to senders needs to be appropriate in a number of senses. Our response, in most situations, should be an honest and accurate reflection of our true comprehension, belief, feeling, or judgment. Otherwise communicators are denied the relevant and accurate information they need to make decisions. If we are participating in communication primarily for purposes other than seriously trying to understand and assess the information and arguments (perhaps to make friends, have fun, be socially congenial), we should reveal our intent to the other participants. It would seem ethically dubious to pretend acceptance of an argument with the actual intent of later condemning it on a more opportune occasion. Likewise it seems ethically dubious to lack understanding of an argument but to pretend to agree with it in order to mask our lack of comprehension. Our feedback might be verbal or nonverbal, oral or written, immediate or delayed. A response of puzzlement or understanding or of disagreement or agreement could be reflected through our facial expression, gestures, posture, inquiries, statements during a question-and-answer period, or letters to editors or advertisers. In some cases, because of our special expertise on a subject, we even may have the obligation to respond while other receivers remain silent. We need to decide whether the degree and type of our feedback are appropriate for the subject, audience, and occasion. For instance, to interrupt with questions, or even to heckle, might be appropriate in a few situations but irresponsible in many others.

A European scholar of media ethics, Cees Hamelink, proposes "Ten Commandments for Media Consumers." His ethics for us as evaluators of and responders to the media reflect the receiver responsibilities of reasoned skepticism and appropriate feedback that we have just discussed.[78] We should: (1) "be an alert and discriminating media consumer"; (2) "fight all forms of censorship"; (3) "not unduly interfere with editorial independence"; (4) "fight all forms of racist and sexist stereotyping in the media"; (5) "seek alternative sources of information"; (6) "demand a pluralist supply of information"; (7) "protect thy own privacy"; (8) "be a reliable source of information"; (9) "not participate in chequebook journalism"; and (10) "demand accountability from media producers."

Postmodernism and the Self as an Ethical Agent

Postmodernism is a collective term that covers a number of attacks on the principles and assumptions of modern or traditional science, philosophy, and ethics. There is no single generally accepted theory of postmodernism.[79] However, the spirit of the postmodern critique can be captured in a cluster of questions.[80] For example, what would be the result for communication ethics: If truth/reality is contextual, contingent, and constructed in discourse rather than universal, absolute, and discovered? If there is no individual moral agent—no autonomous, unencumbered, individual "self" deciding ethical questions impersonally about abstract others apart from the social, economic, and institutional contexts in which the self is imbedded and constructed? If there are no personal "speakers" in communication with attendant ethical responsibilities for choice but only interchangeable "role" players whose communication is dictated by the discourse "rules" of a dominant culture? If there are no grand master narratives or absolute universal values that warrant general allegiance across groups or cultures? If probing the nature of "human nature" is but a delusion or an exercise in political power? If the alternative to absolutism and universalism is nothing but fragmentation and alienation? If there can no longer be ethics as we have known it?

One attempt to grapple with such questions is Zygmunt Bauman's book, *Postmodern Ethics.* The human ethical impulse is inevitable because we always already are obligated to respond to the "call" or "voice" of the Other. Bauman argues that my obligation to respond to the other does not depend on whether or how the Other responds to me. He grounds much of his view in the works of contemporary philosopher Emmanuel Levinas who sees the bedrock of ethics as the direct or indirect encounter "I" have with the Other. Levinas believes that "my" ethical obligation is to hear and respond to (but not necessarily agree with) the call addressed to "me" (overtly or in silence) by the Other, especially the Other who is marginalized by society or otherwise in need. Bauman concludes his book on the optimistic note that "the moral conscience—that ultimate prompt of moral impulse and root of moral responsibility—has only been anesthetized, not amputated. It is still there, dormant perhaps, often stunned, . . . but capable of being awoken."[81]

Another attempt is Martha Cooper's essay, "Decentering Judgment: Toward a Postmodern Communication Ethic."[82] Cooper grounds her view in the inherent human moral impulse variously termed *obligation* or *conscience.* We have a sense of obligation or call to conscience when we encounter the Other and must respond to the call of the Other. In Cooper's view, there are three alternative responses that are available, as appropriate, in a well-rounded postmodern communication ethic: (1) a *discourse ethic* (adapted from Jürgen Habermas) that involves the practice of questioning through argument, deliberation, and judgment; (2) an *ethic of care* (rooted in feminist theories) that involves the practice of responding through narrative, empathy, and identification; and (3) an *ethic of resistance* (adapted from Michel Foucault and Nancy Fraser) that involves the practice of the Other affirming himself or herself through ritual celebration, detachment/connection, and tolerance/empowerment. Cooper carefully explains each of these key concepts, examines the ways that each of the three alternatives may be carried to unethical extremes, and notes ways in which each may offset or compensate for potential defects of the other alternatives. Finally, at length Cooper presents an illuminating example of what she sees as an instance of sexual harassment and describes how each of the three alternatives might be used by her in response to the call of the Other.

Can we develop a viable concept of the self as an ethical agent in communication? Or must we go all the way with some extreme postmodernists to a self that is completely fragmented, alienated, impotent, and determined—indeed to the death of the self? Steven Best and Douglas Kellner, two scholars of postmodernism, contend that "postmodern theory lacks an adequate theory of agency, of an active, creative self, mediated by social institutions and other people."[83] Some feminist scholars and some communitarian scholars envision a situated or contextualized self imbedded in a web of personal, economic and power relationships and responsibilities; this self makes decisions about and responds to concrete, particular persons.[84] Note, too, that the Confucian ethical tradition in China stresses a relational or process view of self as moral agent.[85]

Scholars of communication have explored conceptions of the self as a responsible moral agent. In their book, *The Organizational Self and Ethical Conduct*, James Anderson and Elaine Englehardt present a clearly postmodern perspective on communication ethics in organizations. A significant element in their stance is a relational view of the self as an ethical agent: "No longer is it possible to claim an independent autonomous individual as that agent. That agent is necessarily a constitution of some sort in which self and others participate."[86] Julia Wood describes an "interdependent sense of self" and endorses a concept of "dynamic autonomy" as an "awareness of both one's own plans, motives, and viewpoints and those of others, as being comfortable thinking and acting independently and thinking and acting cooperatively in relationship with others."[87]

Lynn O'Brien Hallstein presents a revisioned view for a feminist ethic of care from a postmodern perspective.[88] She terms the view of moral agency that she endorses as "constrained agency." "*Constrained agency* simultaneously grants women agency *and* recognizes that agency occurs within constraints. Constrained agency, then, also refuses the binary logic that either denies agency by viewing subjects as fully oppressed or denies oppression by viewing the subject as fully free." The fact that persons are constructed and constituted through discourses of class, race, and gender does not "mean that they are fully determined by those discourses." In addition, because persons are not completely constrained, they can be held morally accountable for the range of choices open to them.

Clifford Christians urges a "revitalized notion of human agency as we face the demise of the ethical and the transition to a new era beyond duty." He also contends that the "idea of institutions as moral agents" needs further exploration. Christians, with John Ferré and Mark Fackler, assume a "dialogic self"—a "self-in-relation" as opposed to a completely autonomous self. They agree with Martin Buber's view that our sense of self or personhood develops only in and through a range of I-Thou and I-It relationships.[89] Kenneth Cissna and Rob Anderson build a conception of a socially constructed interdependent self. But they also voice an important reservation: "Just as we reject an entirely monadic and individual conception of the self, we cannot accept an entirely social model in its place. Human beings . . . are not some variety of sponge, soaking up whatever self-definitions might spill our way. And, although the self is a social construction, one in which other people— and hence our society, our culture—are completely involved, we also know that the self is unique, individual."[90]

Internet Ethics

As new technologies are introduced and spread, they bring with them ethical issues both old and new. Some new technologies seem simply to follow the so-called "technological imperative." In other words, if we have the technological capacity to do something, we should go ahead and do it. Little thought is given to the purposes the new technology ought to serve or to the means that ought to be used to achieve those purposes. Some new technologies seem simply to follow the imperative of efficiency. If the new technology is more efficient (less costly, faster, more accurate, easier to use) than older technologies, then it should be used regardless of other concerns such as honesty, humaneness, and fairness.

Thomas Cooper describes "forty leading ethical issues" relevant to new communication technologies of the past several decades. Some of these issues are directly relevant to Internet ethics—to ethical issues and standards for the realm of the World Wide Web, listservs, news groups, Web sites, blogs, chat rooms, and e-mail:[91]

- *Dehumanization* is one concern. "The open and decentralized nature of the Internet has permitted many hate sites, gender biased chat groups, Holocaust denial locales, and so forth." Because message senders can be anonymous, their communication might be more self-disclosive and honest than in face-to-face interaction. But that anonymity also can facilitate racist slurs, sexual harassment, obscene e-mails, and a general lack of concern for the feelings of others.

- *Deception* concerns such behaviors as masking the message sender's identity, impersonating someone else, plagiarism, providing erroneous sources for data, lying, and digitally manipulating images to create a false impression.

- *Personal privacy* is both an ethical and legal matter. How can we prevent the irresponsible sending of unwanted messages to us? Even if it is legal, how ethical is it for employers to use computer technology to monitor employee behavior? How can we protect personal information about ourselves from being spread on the Internet?

- *Fair and equal opportunity* to utilize Internet resources is both an individual and societal issue. How can we avoid the development of what Tom Cooper terms an "information underclass"? To what degree is full utilization of Internet resources being hindered by a person's economic status, gender, or ethnicity? To what degree should there be some sort of general "public" access to Internet resources through such mechanisms as public libraries or financial subsidies? Some scholars argue, for example, that dominant metaphors currently used to describe the realm of cyberspace and the Internet (new world, frontier, anarchy, democracy, community) actually function to hinder Internet use by persons who already are marginalized, neglected, and devalued by society.[92]

There are some "characteristics of computer information technologies that may promote" what Richard Rubin terms "moral distancing." These characteristics allow an individual to create a moral distance between the person's act and the moral responsibility for that act. The person "is able to rationalize, remove oneself from, or ignore ethical considerations." Rubin calls these characteristics the "Seven Temptations."[93] *Temptation 1: Speed.* An unethical act can be committed in micro-seconds and the probability of being caught is not very high. Also speed diverts our focus from *what* we are doing to *how fast* we are doing it. *Temptation 2: Privacy and Anonymity.* We may feel invulnerable because we believe (perhaps erroneously) that we are not being observed. In addition, "when the perpetrator is stealing information at a remote source from an equally remote location, it does not 'feel' the same as if one is breaking into another person's home or office." *Temptation 3: Nature of the Medium.* A person can steal information without actually removing it and thus we are tempted to "believe that nothing is stolen, no one will know, and the owner has not been harmed, because his or her property remains." *Temptation 4: Aesthetic Attraction.* Hackers are tempted, in part, because success "requires creativity and artistry." *Temptation 5: Increased Availability of Potential Victims.* "In essence, the opportunity to behave unethically towards thousands of people with relatively little effort is well within our grasp." *Temptation 6: International Scope.* The power to influence on an international scope "distances us from the issue of whether many parts of the world are ready for such technologies or truly benefit from them." *Temptation 7: The Power to Destroy.* We can be tempted to use the power to destroy information through cleverly introducing such elements as viruses and worms into systems.

In *The Weblog Handbook*, Rebecca Blood contends that "the weblog's greatest strength—its uncensored, unmediated, uncontrolled voice—is also its greatest weakness." Also she laments that there "has been almost no talk about ethics in the weblog universe." Blood thus is aware of the tension between freedom and responsibility in this form of Internet communication. As several points in her book, she suggests principles to highlight ethical responsibilities for creators of and participants in blogs.[94] (1) "Publish as fact only that which you believe to be true. If your statement is speculation, say so." (2) "If material exists online, link to it when you reference it. . . . Online readers deserve, as much as possible, access to all of the facts." (3) "Publicly correct any misinformation." If you discover that one of your links was inaccurate or one of you statements was untrue, say so and correct it. (4) "Write each entry as if it could not be changed; add to, but do not rewrite or delete, any entry. . . . Changing or deleting destroys the integrity of the network." (5) Disclose any possible or actual conflict of interest so that audience trust is not undermined. (6) Clearly label biased or questionable sources, otherwise readers will lack necessary information to assess the merits of the source. (7) Respect other people's privacy. It is ethically questionable to repeat without permission someone's instant message, chat-room or real-life conversation, or e-mail. (8) Question someone's facts or arguments but don't personalize your attack by denouncing his or her stupidity or other personal characteristics. Ignore personal attacks on yourself; don't respond in kind. (9) Consider carefully the arguments and evidence presented by others and try to represent their positions fairly and accurately.

At the level of international Internet and cyberspace communication, Dutch media scholar Cees Hamelink supports the defense of human rights and human dignity as a widely agreed-to international grounding for ethical standards to guide digital communication, including the Internet.[95] One moral principle reflecting fundamental human rights is equality, which includes both the sense of "equal entitlement" and "nondiscrimination." A second moral principle is security, which involves protection against intentional psychological and physical harm to human integrity. A third moral principle is freedom, which involves noninterference with individual self-determination through communication and access to information. Finally, persons have the moral right to participate in decision making about technological developments that affect them.

Notes

[1] See, for example, Eugene Carson Blake, "Should Codes of Ethics in Public Life Be Absolute or Relative?" *Annals of the American Academy of Political and Social Science,* 363 (January 1961): 4–11.

[2] A helpful categorization of types of relativism is John H. Barnsley, *The Social Reality of Ethics: A Comparative Analysis of Moral Codes* (London: Routledge and Kegan Paul, 1972), ch. 9. Also see William B. Gudykunst and Young Yum Kim, *Communicating with Strangers: An Approach to Intercultural Communication*, 4th ed. (New York: McGraw-Hill, 2003).

[3] Jurgen Ruesch, "Ethical Issues in Communication," in *Communication: Ethical and Moral Issues*, Lee Thayer, ed. (New York: Gordon and Breach, 1973), pp. 16–17.

[4] Robert T. Oliver, *Culture and Communication* (Springfield, IL: Charles C. Thomas, 1962), p. 79.

[5] Thomas R. Nilsen, *Ethics of Speech Communication*, 2nd ed. (Indianapolis: Bobbs-Merrill, 1974), pp. 84–87.

[6] Thomas R. Nilsen, "Free Speech, Persuasion, and the Democratic Process," *Quarterly Journal of Speech*, 44 (October 1958): 235–243; Herbert W. Simons, *Persuasion in Society* (Thousand Oaks, CA: Sage, 2001); Edwin Black, *Rhetorical Criticism* (New York: Macmillan, 1965), p. 56.

[7] John E. Marston, *The Nature of Public Relations* (New York: McGraw-Hill, 1963), pp. 346–359.

[8] S. I. Hayakawa, *Language in Thought and Action*, 4th ed. (New York: Harcourt Brace Jovanovich, 1978), p. 257.

[9] B. J. Diggs, "Persuasion and Ethics," *Quarterly Journal of Speech*, 50 (December 1964): 366.

[10] Robert T. Oliver, *The Psychology of Persuasive Speech*, 2nd ed. (New York: Longmans, Green, 1957), p. 26.

[11] *New York Times*, December 7, 1962, p. 5. Also see Arthur Sylvester, "The Government Has the Right to Lie," *Saturday Evening Post*, 240 (November 18, 1967): 10ff.

[12] Winston L. Brembeck and William S. Howell, *Persuasion: A Means of Social Influence*, 2nd ed. (Englewood Cliffs, NJ: Prentice-Hall, 1976), p. 239.

[13] Warren G. Bovée, "The End Can Justify the Means—But Rarely," *Journal of Mass Media Ethics*, 6, no. 3 (1991): 135–145.

[14] Charles Fried, *Right and Wrong* (Cambridge: Harvard University Press, 1978), pp. 9–10, 29, 54–78; Carl Wellman, *Morals and Ethics*, 2nd ed. (Englewood Cliffs, NJ: Prentice-Hall, 1988), p. 41.

[15] George Yoos, "Rational Appeal and the Ethics of Advocacy," in *Essays on Classical Rhetoric and Modern Discourse*, Robert Connors et al., eds. (Carbondale: Southern Illinois University Press, 1984), pp. 82–97. For other explorations of definition, see Frederick Siegler, "Lying," *American Philosophical Quarterly*, 111 (April 1966): 128–136: Roderick M. Chisholm and Thomas D. Feehan, "The Intent to Deceive," *Journal of Philosophy*, 74 (March 1977): 143–159.

[16] David Corn, *The Lies of George W. Bush* (New York: Crown, 2003), pp. 1, 9.

[17] Sissela Bok, *Lying: Moral Choice in Public and Private Life* (New York: Vintage Books, 1979), ch. 1. For a much broader and more inclusive conception of lying that includes indirect, unconscious, and habitual lies, see Dwight Bolinger, "Truth Is a Linguistic Question," in *Language and Public Policy*, Hugh Rank, ed. (Urbana, IL: National Council of Teachers of English, 1974), pp. 161–175.

[18] Bok, *Lying*, ch. 2.

[19] Joseph Kupfer, "The Moral Presumption against Lying," *Review of Metaphysics*, 36 (September 1982): 103–126; also see Elizabeth Minnick, "Why Not Lie?" *Soundings*, 68 (Winter 1985): 493–509.

[20] Bok, *Lying*, ch. 6; J. Barton Bowyer, *Cheating* (New York: St. Martin's Press, 1982), p. 207.

[21] Bok, *Lying*, ch. 7.

[22] David Nyberg, *The Varnished Truth: Truth Telling and Deceiving in Ordinary Life* (Chicago: University of Chicago Press, 1993), pp. 1–5, 10–11, 25, 78, 114. Also see Arnold M. Ludwig, *The Importance of Lying* (Springfield, IL: Charles C. Thomas, 1965); and Robert L. Wolk and Arthur Henley, *The Right to Lie* (New York: Peter H. Wyden, 1970); George Serban, *Lying: Man's Second Nature* (Westport, CT: Praeger, 2001).

[23] See for example, Roger Hufford, "The Dimensions of an Idea: Ambiguity Defined," *Today's Speech*, 14 (April 1966): 4–8; William Empson, *Seven Types of Ambiguity*, 3rd ed. (Edinburgh: T. A. Constable, Ltd., 1947).

[24] Douglas Ehninger, *Influence, Belief and Argument: An Introduction to Responsible Persuasion* (Glenview, IL: Scott, Foresman, 1974), pp. 113–115; W. Ross Winterowd, *Rhetoric and Writing* (Boston: Allyn & Bacon, 1965), p. 277.

25 M. Lee Williams and Blaine Goss, "Equivocation: Character Insurance," *Human Communication Research*, 1 (Spring 1975): 265–270.

26 For discussions of contexts in which intentional ambiguity might be considered necessary, accepted as normal, or even ethical, see the following sources: Robert T. Oliver, *Culture and Communication* (Springfield, IL: Charles C. Thomas, 1962), pp. 65–69; I. A. Richards, *The Philosophy of Rhetoric* (New York: Oxford University Press Galaxy Book, 1965), p. 40; Raymond E. Anderson, "Kierkegaard's Theory of Communication," *Speech Monographs*, 30 (March 1963): 6–7; Fred C. Ikle, "Bargaining and Communication," in *Handbook of Communication*, Ithiel de Sola Pool et al., eds. (Chicago: Rand-McNally, 1973), pp. 837–840; B. Aubrey Fisher, "The Persuasive Campaign: A Pedagogy for the Contemporary First Course in Speech Communication," *Central States Speech Journal*, 20 (Winter 1969): 297–298; Murray Edelman, *The Symbolic Uses of Politics* (Urbana: University of Illinois Press, 1967), pp. 139, 141, 148; John C. Condon, *Semantics and Communication*, 2nd ed. (New York: Macmillan, 1975), pp. 114–115; Doris Graber, *Verbal Behavior and Politics* (Urbana: University of Illinois Press, 1976), p. 31.

27 For example, see Donald N. Levine, *The Flight from Ambiguity* (Chicago: University of Chicago Press, 1985); Eric M. Eisenberg, "Ambiguity as Strategy in Organizational Communication," *Communication Monographs*, 51 (September 1984): 227–242: William Kohlmann, "In Praise of Ambiguity," *Newsweek*, April 1, 1985, pp. 10–11; Chaim Perelman, "The Use and Abuse of Confused Notions," *ETC: A Review of General Semantics*, 36 (1979): 313–324; David Kaufer, "Metaphor and Its Ties to Ambiguity and Vagueness," *Rhetoric Society Quarterly*, 13 (Summer-Fall, 1983): 209–220.

28 Daniel Oran, *Law Dictionary for Non-Lawyers* (St. Paul, MN: West Publishing Co., 1975), pp. 330–331.

29 Craig R. Smith, *Orientations* to *Speech Criticism* (Chicago: Science Research Associates, 1976), p. 11; Tony Schwartz, *The Responsive Chord* (Garden City, NY: Anchor Books, 1974), pp. 96–97.

30 Lewis A. Froman, Jr., "A Realistic Approach to Campaign Strategies and Tactics," in *Electoral Process*, M. Kent Jennings and L. Harmon Zeigler, eds. (Englewood Cliffs, NJ: Prentice-Hall, 1966), p. 9.

31 This idea was suggested to Johannesen by Martha O'Grady in her graduate course research paper, "Ambiguity in the American Political and Legal Systems," Northern Illinois University, Department of Communication Studies, 1981.

32 Nilsen, *Ethics of Speech Communication*, pp. 75–76.

33 Black, *Rhetorical Criticism*, chs. 4 and 5.

34 Ivan L. Preston, "Theories of Behavior and the Concept of Rationality in Advertising," *Journal of Communication*, 17 (September 1967): 211–222; also see Preston, "Logic and Illogic in the Advertising Process," *Journalism Quarterly*, 44 (Summer 1967): 231–239.

35 Oliver, *Culture and Communication*, p. 155.

36 John C. Condon and Fathi Yousef, *An Introduction to Intercultural Communication* (Indianapolis: Bobbs-Merrill, 1975), ch. 10; also see D. Lawrence Kincaid, ed., *Communication Theory: Eastern* and *Western Perspectives* (San Diego, CA: Academic Press, 1987).

37 Interview with Marshall McLuhan in *McLuhan: Hot and* Cool, Gerald E. Stearn, ed. (New York: Dial, 1967), p. 270.

38 Fern L. Johnson, "A Reformulation of Rationality in Rhetoric," *Central States Speech Journal*, 24 (Winter 1973): 262–271.

39 Brembeck and Howell, *Persuasion*, ch. 8.

40 Stephen Toulmin et al., *An Introduction to Reasoning* (New York: Macmillan, 1979), espec. chs. 12–17; Richard D. Rieke and Malcolm O. Sillars, *Argumentation and the Decision Making Process*, 2nd ed. (Glenview, IL: Scott Foresman, 1984), chs. 4 and 5; Stephen Toulmin, *The Uses of Argument* (Cambridge, UK: Cambridge University Press paperback, 1964), pp. 14–15, 36, 175–176, 182–183, 248; Gidon Gottlieb, *The Logic of Choice* (New York: Macmillan, 1968); Richard E. Crable, *Argumentation as Communication* (Columbus, OH: Charles E. Merrill, 1976), ch. 7. George Yoos argues that ethical standards for advocacy differ between contexts of discourse, such as law, advertising, politics, and love. Yoos, "Rational Appeal and the Ethics of Advocacy," in *Essays on Classical Rhetoric and Modern Discourse*, Connors et al., eds., p. 111.

41 See, for example, Barnet Baskerville, "The Illusion of Proof," *Western Speech*, 25 (Fall 1961): 236–242. For emphasis on integrating and balancing the use of emotional and rational appeals, see Nilsen, *Ethics of Speech Communication*, pp. 57–59.

42 Such truth and rationality based standards are reflected throughout the American Association of Advertising Agencies' "Code of Ethics" and throughout the American Advertising Federation's "Advertising Code of American Business." (These codes are reprinted in chapter 10 of this book.) Also see Gunnar Andren, "The Rhetoric of Advertising," *Journal of Communication*, 30 (Autumn 1980): 74–80; Robert Spero, *The Duping of the American Voter* (New York: Lippincott and Crowell, 1980), pp. 5–6; Carl P Wrighter, *I Can Sell You Anything* (New York: Ballantine Books, 1972), ch. 3; Richard M. Weaver, *Life Without Prejudice and Other Essays* (Chicago: Regnery, 1965), pp. 121–128.

43 J. R. Carpenter, "Voice of the Advertiser," *Advertising Age*, 19 (April 1971): 57. Also see Ivan Preston, *The Great American Blow-Up: Puffery in Advertising and Selling* (Madison: University of Wisconsin Press, 1975); Neil Postman, *Amusing Ourselves to Death* (New York: Viking, 1984), pp. 127–128.

44 Lawrence W. Rosenfield et al., *The Communication Experience* (Boston: Allyn & Bacon, 1976), pp. 310–312, 324. Also see Richard DeGeorge, *Business Ethics,* 2nd ed. (New York: Macmillan, 1986), pp. 275–280; W Lance Hayes, "Of That Which We Cannot Write: Some Notes on the Phenomenology of Media," *Quarterly Journal of Speech*, 74 (February 1988): 1–17.

45 Rosenfield, *Communicative Experience*, pp. 254–283; Edward Spence and Brett Van Heereken, *Advertising Ethics* (Upper Saddle River, NJ: Pearson/Prentice Hall, 2005), pp. 41–53.

46 Theodore Levitt, "The Morality (7) of Advertising," *Harvard Business Review* (July-August, 1972): 84–92.

47 Tony Schwartz, *The Responsive Chord* (Garden City, NY: Anchor Books, 1974), pp. 18–22.

48 Also see Wayne Minnick, "A New Look at the Ethics of Persuasion," *Southern Speech Communication Journal*, 45 (Summer 1980): 352–362.

49 Schwartz, "Ethics in Political Media Communication," *Communication*, 6, no. 2 (1981): 213–224. A later book by Schwartz is *Media: The Second God* (New York: Random House, 1981).

50 Spence and Van Heereken, *Advertising Ethics*, pp. 54–69.

51 One early survey of over forty varied definitions is Frederick E. Lumley, *The Propaganda Menace* (New York: Century, 1933), ch. 2. Also see Erwin Fellows, "Propaganda: History of a Word," *American Speech*, 34 (October 1959): 182–189; Fellows, "Propaganda and Communication: A Study in Definitions," *Journalism Quarterly*, 34 (1957): 431–442; Garth Jowett and Victoria O'Donnell, *Propaganda and Persuasion,* 2nd ed. (Beverly Hills: Sage, 1992).

52 For example, see Terrence H. Qualter, *Propaganda and Psychological Warfare* (New York: Random House, 1962), ch. 1; Paul Kecskemeti, "Propaganda," in *Handbook of Communication*, Ithiel de Sola Pool et al., eds. (Chicago: Rand McNally, 1973), pp. 844–870; Nick Aaron Ford, ed., *Language in Uniform: A Reader on Propaganda* (Indianapolis: Odyssey Press, 1967), pp. vii–viii, 19–20; Thomas M. Garrett, quoted by Walter Taplin, "Morals," in *Speaking of Advertising*, John S. Wright and Daniel S. Warner, eds. (New York: McGraw-Hill, 1963), p. 336; Brembeck and Howell, *Persuasion*, p. 19.

53 For example see W. H. Werkmeister, *An Introduction to Critical Thinking,* rev. ed. (Lincoln, NE: Johnson, 1957), ch. 4; Stuart Chase, *Guides to Straight Thinking* (New York: Harper, 1956), chs. 20–21; Roy Paul Madsen, *The Impact of Film* (New York: Macmillan, 1973), pp. 441–444; Nilsen, *Ethics of Speech Communication*, pp. 81–82; Randal Marlin, *Propaganda and the Ethics of Persuasion* (Peterborough, Ontario: Broadview Press, 2002), pp. 22–23, 137–203.

54 Jacques Ellul, *Propaganda* (New York: Vintage Books paperback, 1973), pp. xv, xvii, 38, 61, 174–175, 180, 188, 217.

55 Jacques Ellul, "The Ethics of Propaganda: Propaganda, Innocence, and Amorality," *Communication*, 6, no. 2 (1981): 159–177.

56 Stanley B. Cunningham, *The Idea of Propaganda: A Reconstruction* (Westport, CT: Praeger, 2002), pp. 176–178.

57 For the list of propaganda devices as originally explained in 1937 by the Institute for Propaganda Analysis, see *Propaganda Analysis I* (October and November 1937): 1–8. The Institute

defined propaganda as "expression of opinion or action by individuals or groups deliberately designed to influence opinions or actions of other individuals or groups with reference to pre-determined ends." The original explanation of these devices is reprinted in Ford, ed., *Language in Uniform,* pp. 12–18.

58 Adapted from Stephan Lesher, "The New Image of George Wallace," *Chicago Tribune,* January 2, 1972, sec. 1A, p. 1.

59 The basic formulation from which these guidelines have been adapted was first suggested to Johannesen by Professor William Conboy of the University of Kansas. These five characteristics generally are compatible with standard scholarly attempts to define a demagogue. For instance, see Reinhard Luthin, *American Demagogues* (reprinted ed., Gloucester, MA: Peter Smith, 1959), pp. ix, 3, 302–319; Barnet Baskerville, "Joseph McCarthy: Briefcase Demagogue," reprinted in *The Rhetoric of the Speaker,* Haig A. Bosmajian, ed. (New York: D. C. Heath, 1967), p. 64; Charles W. Lomas, *The Agitator in American* Society (Englewood Cliffs, NJ: Prentice-Hall, 1968), pp. 18–19; Wayne C. Minnick, *The Art of Persuasion,* 2nd ed. (Boston: Houghton Mifflin, 1968), p. 6; G. M. Gilbert, "Dictators and Demagogues," *Journal of Social Issues,* 11, no. 3 (1955): 51–83.

60 Ludwig, *The Importance of Lying,* p. 5.

61 For one survey of research on silence, see Richard L. Johannesen, "The Functions of Silence," *Western Speech,* 38 (Winter 1974): 25–35. Also see Barry Brummett, "Towards a Theory of Silences as a Political Strategy," *Quarterly Journal of Speech,* 66 (October 1980): 289–303; Deborah Tannen and Muriel Saville-Troike, eds., *Perspectives on Silence* (Norwood, NJ: Ablex, 1985); Adam Jaworski, *The Power of Silence: Social and Pragmatic Perspectives* (Newbury Park, CA: Sage, 1993), ch. 4.

62 Several insights concerning ethical issues in nonverbal communication were suggested to Johannesen in a graduate course research paper by Deborah H. Lund, "Implications of Ethical Standards in Nonverbal Communication," (Northern Illinois University, Department of Speech Communication, 1973).

63 For additional nonverbal examples that raise ethical issues, see John L. Hulteng, *The Messenger's Motives: Ethical Problems of the News Media,* 2nd ed. (Englewood Cliffs, NJ: Prentice-Hall, 1985), ch. 9; E. S. Safford, "The Need for a Public Ethic in Mass Communication," in *Ethics, Morality, and the Mass Media,* Lee Thayer et al., eds. (New York: Hastings House, 1980), espec. pp. 143–144.

64 Jim Lewis, "Don't Believe What You See in the Papers: The Untrustworthiness of News Photography," *Slate Magazine* (August 10, 2006), http://www.slate.com/id/2147502

65 "Brady's Photographs: Pictures of the Dead at Antietam," *New York Times* (October 20, 1862), p. 5.

66 The issue has received voluminous coverage in the popular press and among academics. See, for example, David Carr, "Not to See the Fallen is No Favor," *New York Times* (May 28, 2007); Cynthia Kind and Paul Martin Lester, "Photographic Coverage during the Persian Gulf and Iraqi Wars in Three U.S. Newspapers," *Journalism and Mass Communication Quarterly,* 82. no. 3 (2005): 623–637; and John Taylor, "Iraqi Torture Photographs and Documentary Realism in the Press," *Journalism Studies,* 6, no. 1 (2005): 39–49.

67 Tom Junod, "The Falling Man," *Esquire Magazine* (September 1, 2003), http://www.esquire.com/feature/ESP0903-SEP_FALLINGMAN. See also J. B. Singer, "The Unforgiving Truth in the Unforgivable Photo," *Media Ethics,* 13 (2002): 30–31; and Martha Cooper, "Covering Tragedy: Media Ethics and TWA Flight 800," reprinted in the appendix of this book.

68 See Paul Martin Lester, "Faking Images in Photojournalism," *Media Development,* 1 (1988): 41–42; and Thomas Wheeler, *Phototruth or Photofiction? Ethics and Media Imagination in the Digital Age* (Mahwah, NJ: Erlbaum, 2002).

69 Larry Gross, John Stuart Katz, and Jay Ruby, eds., *Image Ethics: The Moral Rights of Subjects in Photographs, Film, and Television* (New York: Oxford University Press, 1988), pp. v, 32.

70 Larry Gross, John Stuart Katz, and Jay Ruby, eds., *Image Ethics in the Digital Age* (Minneapolis: University of Minnesota Press, 2003).

[71] Paul Martin Lester and Susan Ross, eds., *Images that Injure: Pictorial Stereotypes in the Media* (Westport, CT: Praeger, 2002). In addition, the entire issue of the *Journal of Mass Media Ethics*, 2 (Spring/Summer 1987) is devoted to photojournalism ethics. Other recommended readings are Paul Martin Lester, *Photojournalism: An Ethical Approach* (Hillsdale, NJ: Erlbaum, 1991); Paul Messaris, *Visual Persuasion: The Role of Imagery in Advertising* (Thousand Oaks, CA: Sage, 1997); and Paul Martin Lester, *Visual Communication: Images with Messages* (Belmont CA: Wadsworth, 2003).

[72] This section on ethics and ghostwriting is adapted from Richard L. Johannesen, "On Teaching the Social Responsibilities of a Speaker," in Jeffery Auer and Edward B. Jenkinson, eds., *Essays on Teaching Speech in the High School* (Bloomington: Indiana University Press, 1971), pp. 229–231. Also see Douglas Perret Starr, "A Practical View of the Ethics of Speech Ghostwriting," *Media Ethics*, 18 (Fall 2006): 10, 39–40.

[73] For some relevant sources, see the three essays on ghostwriting in *Communication Education,* 33 (1984): 301–307. Also see Kathleen Hall Jamieson, *Eloquence in an Electronic Age* (New York: Word University Press, 1988), pp. 201–237; Martin Medhurst, "Ghostwritten Speeches: Ethics Isn't the Only Lesson," *Communication Education,* 36 (July 1987): 241–249; Matthew Seeger, "Ghostbusting: Exorcising the Great Man Spirit from the Speechwriting Debate," *Communication Education,* 34 (October 1985): 353–358; Lois J. Einhorn, "The Ghosts Unmasked: A Review of the Literature on Speechwriting," *Communication Quarterly*, 30 (1981): 41–47.

[74] Sissela Bok, *Secrets: On the Ethics of Concealment and Revelation* (New York: Vintage Books, 1984), Intro. and ch. 1.

[75] Ibid., chs. 2 and 3.

[76] Ibid., chs. 8, 12, 13. Also see John M. Orman, *Presidential Secrecy and Deception: Beyond the Power to Persuade* (Westport, CT: Greenwood, 1980), pp. 4–7, 165–167; Edwin Black, *Rhetorical Questions: Studies of Public Discourse* (Chicago: University of Chicago Press, 1992), pp. 51–96.

[77] Some of the suggestions in this section derive from the following receiver-oriented sources: Crable, *Argumentation as Communication,* ch. 8; Nilsen, *Ethics of Speech Communication,* pp. 33–34, 74–75; Kenneth E. Andersen, *Persuasion,* 2nd ed. (Boston: Allyn & Bacon, 1978), chs. 15, 18; Mary John Smith, *Persuasion and Human Action* (Belmont, CA: Wadsworth, 1982), pp. 4–9, 76, 315; Lee Thayer, "Ethics, Morality, and the Media," in *Ethics, Morality and the Media,* Thayer et al., eds., pp. 14–17, 35–39; Gary L. Cronkhite, "Rhetoric, Communication, and Psycho-Epistemology," in *Rhetoric: A Tradition in Transition,* Walter R. Fisher, ed. (East Lansing: Michigan State University Press, 1974), pp. 261–278; William R. Rivers et al., *Responsibility in Mass Communication,* 3rd ed. (New York: Harper & Row, 1980), pp. 285–288.

[78] Cees J. Hamelink, "Ethics for Media Users," *European Journal of Communication*, 10 (1995): 497–511. Also see Rudiger Funiok, "Fundamental Questions of Audience Ethics," in *Media Ethics*, Bart Pattyn, ed. (Leuven, Belgium: Peeters, 2002), pp. 403–422.

[79] Zygmunt Bauman, *Postmodernity and Its Discontents* (Washington Square: New York University Press, 1997); Steven Best and Douglas Kellner, *Postmodern Theory: Critical Interrogations* (New York: Guilford, 1997), pp. ix, 16–29, 253–263; John D. Caputo, *Against Ethics* (Bloomington: Indiana University Press, 1993); Drucilla Cornell, "Toward a Modern/Postmodern Reconstruction of Ethics," *University of Pennsylvania Law Review,* 133 (1985): 291–380; Jean-Francois Lyotard, *The Postmodern Condition,* trans. G. Bennington and B. Massumi (Minneapolis: University of Minnesota Press, 1993). For a critical evaluation of some of the excesses of postmodernism, see Kenneth J. Gergen, "The Limits of Pure Critique," in *After Postmodernism: Reconstructing Ideology Critique,* Herbert W Simons and Michael Billig, eds. (Thousand Oaks, CA: Sage, 1994), pp. 58–78.

[80] Robert Audi, ed., *The Cambridge Dictionary of Philosophy* (Cambridge, UK: Cambridge University Press, 1995), pp. 634–635; Victor Taylor and Charles E. Winquist, eds., *Encyclopedia of Postmodernism* (London: Routledge, 2001), pp. 252–253.

[81] Zygmunt Bauman, *Postmodern Ethics* (Oxford, UK: Blackwell, 1993), pp. 50, 60, 84–86, 247–250; Zygmunt Bauman, *Life in Fragments: Essays in Postmodern Morality* (Oxford, UK: Blackwell), pp. 59–66; Zygmunt Bauman and Keith Tester, *Conversations with Zygmunt Bauman*

(Cambridge, UK: Polity, 2001), pp. 43–69; Emmanuel Levinas, *Ethics and Infinity*, trans. Richard Cohen (Pittsburgh, PA: Duquesne University Press, 1985), pp. 97–98; Emmanuel Levinas, *Otherwise than Being or Beyond Essence,* trans. Alphonso Lingis (Pittsburgh, PA: Duquesne University Press, 1998). Also see Amit Pinchevski, *By Way of Interruption: Levinas and the Ethics of Communication* (Pittsburgh, PA: Duquesne University Press, 2005); and Jeffrey W. Murray, *Face-to-Face in Dialogue: Emmanuel Levinas and (the) Communication (of) Ethics* (Lanham, MD: University Press of America, 2003).

82 Martha Cooper, "Decentering Judgment: Toward a Postmodern Communication Ethic," in *Judgment Calls: Rhetoric, Politics, and Indeterminacy,* John Sloop and James P. McDaniel, eds. (Boulder, CO: Westview Press, 1998), pp. 63–83. Also see Martha Cooper, "Ethical Dimensions of Political Advocacy from a Postmodern Perspective," in *Ethical Dimensions of Political Communication*, Robert E. Denton, Jr., ed. (New York: Praeger, 1991), pp. 23–47; and Martha Cooper and Carole Blair, "Foucault's Ethics," in *Moral Engagement in Public Life: Theorists for Contemporary Ethics,* Sharon Bracci and Clifford Christians, eds. (New York: Peter Lang, 2002), pp. 257–276.

83 Best and Kellner, *Postmodern Theory*, p. 283.

84 Seyla Benhabib, *Situating the Self: Gender, Community, and Postmodernism in Contemporary Ethics* (New York: Routledge, 1992), pp. 148–177, 215–216; Rita Manning, *Speaking from the Heart: A Feminist Perspective on Ethics* (Lanham, MD: Rowman and Littlefield, 1992), pp. 2–5, 28; Michael Sandel, *Liberalism and Its Critics* (New York: New York University Press, 1984), pp. 5–6. Also see Diana Tietjens Meyers, ed., *Feminists Rethink the Self* (Boulder, CO: Westview, 1997); Calvin O. Schrag, *The Self After Postmodernity* (New Haven, CT: Yale University Press, 1997), espec. pp. 8–9, 64–66, 107–109.

85 A. S. Cua, *Moral Vision and Tradition: Essays in Chinese Ethics* (Washington, DC: Catholic University of America Press, 1998), pp. 228–234.

86 James A. Anderson and Elaine E. Englehardt, *The Organizational Self and Ethical Conduct* (Fort Worth, TX: Harcourt, 2001), pp. viii, 2, 81–104, 131–148. Also see Susan Barnes, "Ethical Issues for a Virtual Self," in *Real Law @ Virtual Space*, Susan Drucker and Gary Gumpert, eds. (Cresskill, NJ: Hampton Press, 1999), pp. 371–398.

87 Julia T. Wood, *Who Cares: Women, Care, and Culture* (Carbondale: Southern Illinois University Press, 1994), pp. 108–110.

88 D. Lynn O'Brien Hallstein, "A Postmodern Caring: Feminist Standpoint Theories, Revisioned, Caring, and Communication Ethics," *Western Journal of Communication,* 63 (Winter 1999): 32–56.

89 Clifford G. Christians, "Review Essay: Current Trends in Media Ethics," *European Journal of Communication,* 10 (1995): 545–558; Clifford G. Christians, John P. Ferré, and P. Mark Fackler, *Good News: Social Ethics and the Press* (New York: Oxford University Press, 1993), pp. 13, 61–75. Also see Ronald C. Arnett, "A Dialogical Ethic 'Between' Buber and Levinas: A Responsive Ethical 'I,'" in *Dialogue: Theorizing Difference in Communication Studies*, Rob Anderson, Leslie A. Baxter, and Kenneth N. Cissna, eds. (Thousand Oaks, CA: Sage, 2004), pp. 75–90.

90 Kenneth N. Cissna and Rob Anderson, "Communication and the Ground of Dialogue," in *The Reach of Dialogue*, Rob Anderson, Kenneth N. Cissna, and Ronald C. Arnett, eds. (Cresskill, NJ: Hampton Press, 1994), p. 16. Also see Frank C. Richardson, Anthony Rogers, and Jennifer McCarroll, "Toward a Dialogical Self," *American Behavioral Scientist,* 41 (1998): 496–515.

91 Thomas W. Cooper, "New Technology Inventory: Forty Leading Ethical Issues," *Journal of Mass Media Ethics,* 13 (1998): 71–92. Also see Roger Clark, "Ethics and the Internet: The Cyberspace Behavior of People, Communities, and Organizations," *Business and Professional Ethics Journal*, 18 (Fall–Winter 1999): 153–167; Susan J. Drucker and Gary Gumpert, "Cybercrime and Punishment," *Critical Studies in Media Communication,* 17 (June 2000): 133–158, espec. 150–152; Cees J. Hamelink, *The Ethics of Cyberspace* (London: Sage, 2000), pp. x, 33–34, 37–38; Christopher J. Schroll, "Technology and Communication Ethics: An Evaluative Framework," *Technical Communication Quarterly,* 4 (Spring 1995): 147–164.

92 See, for example, Ann H. Gunkel and David J. Gunkel, "Virtual Geographies: The New Worlds of Cyberspace," *Critical Studies in Mass Communication,* 14 (1997): 123–137; David

Gunkel, *Hacking Cyberspace* (Boulder, CO: Westview, 2001); Hamelink, *The Ethics of Cyberspace*, pp. 79–106; Jana Kramer and Cheris Kramerae, "Gendered Ethics on the Internet," in *Communication Ethics in an Age of Diversity*, Josina M. Makau and Ronald C. Arnett, eds. (Urbana: University of Illinois Press, 1997), pp. 226–243; Alison Adam, *Gender, Ethics, and Information Technology* (New York: Palgrave Macmillan, 2005), pp. 69, 114, 132–136; Deborah G. Johnson, *Computer Ethics*, 3rd ed. (Upper Saddle River, NJ: Prentice-Hall, 2001), pp. 208–229.

[93] Richard Rubin, "Moral Distancing and the Use of Information Technologies: The Seven Temptations," in *Ethics in the Computer Age*, Joseph M. Kizza, ed. (New York: Association for Computer Machinery, 1994), pp. 151–155. For additional general discussions of cyberspace ethics, see Johnson, *Computer Ethics*, pp. 81–108; Robert I. Berkman and Christopher A. Shumway, *Digital Dilemmas: Ethical Issues for Online Media Professionals* (Ames, IA: Blackwell, 2003); Mark Wolf, ed., *Virtual Morality: Morals, Ethics, and the New Media* (New York: Peter Lang, 2003); Richard A. Spinello, *Cyberethics: Morality and Law in Cyberspace*, 3rd. ed. (Sudbury, MA: Jones and Bartlett, 2006); David J. Gunkel, *Thinking Otherwise: Philosophy, Communication, Technology* (West Lafayette, IN: Purdue University Press, 2007).

[94] Rebecca Blood, *The Weblog Handbook* (Cambridge, MA: Perseus, 2002), pp. 85–87, 114–121, 135–137. Also see Martin Kuhn, "Interactivity and Prioritizing the Human: A Code of Blogging Ethics," *Journal of Mass Media Ethics*, 14 (2007): 18–36.

[95] Hamelink, *The Ethics of Cyberspace*, pp. 55–63. Also see Robert M. Bird et al., eds., *Cyberethics: Social and Moral Issues in the Computer Age* (Amherst, NY: Prometheus Books, 2000); Richard A. Spinello, *Cyberethics: Morality and Law in Cyberspace* (Sudbury, MA: Jones and Bartlett, 2000).

Interpersonal Communication and Small Group Discussion

Interpersonal communication has become a label used to describe a number of different human communication processes.[1] Some simply designate it as one of several "levels" of human communication: intrapersonal (within a single person); interpersonal (between two people); small group (among three to nine people); public (one person to a formal audience); and mass media.

Dean Barnlund describes interpersonal communication as persons in face-to-face encounters in relatively informal social situations sustaining focused interaction through reciprocal exchange of verbal and nonverbal cues. Gerald Miller and his colleagues differentiate between noninterpersonal communication and interpersonal communication. In noninterpersonal communication, information known among participants about each other is primarily of a cultural or of a sociological (group affiliation) nature. In contrast, participants in interpersonal communication ground their perceptions and reactions in the unique psychological characteristics of each other's individual personalities. John Stewart sees the essence of interpersonal communication as centered in the quality of the communication among participants. Participants relate to each other as persons (unique, capable of choice, having feelings, being of inherent worth, and self-reflective) rather than as objects or things (interchangeable, measurable, responding automatically to stimuli, and lacking self-awareness).[2]

Julia T. Wood calls for a change in the way in which the culture of the United States addresses justice and morality in personal relationships.[3] She argues that the ways in which moral theorists and society at large have viewed personal relationships have resulted in cultural practices that do not adequately address unethical behavior in personal relationships. Citing theorists such as Aristotle, Rawls, and Unger, Wood notes that moral theorists have largely treated personal relationships as part of the private sphere that is outside the ethical norms of the public sphere. Wood suggests that moral theorists have viewed the public and private spheres as needing different standards for the regulation of behavior. Upon making this division, moral theorists have focused on the public sphere and identifying ways to regulate behavior "to ensure civil conduct among individuals not bound by love and affection."

Wood proposes that philosophers such as Hume, Rousseau, and Unger took the position "that the family is such a noble, intrinsically moral relation that it does not need and should not be subjected to 'mere' principles of justice." There has been an assumption that personal relationships are inherently moral, and as a result philosophers have not given attention to civility in personal relationships. However, as Wood notes, many personal relationships are not moral. She cites numerous examples of unethical behavior in personal relationships, including women severely battered by spouses, spousal emotional abuse, and male college students coercing or manipulating women into having sex when they don't want to, in order to illustrate the extent to which it is inadequate to presume that people develop personal ethics that lead them to engage in ethical behavior in their personal relationships.

In addition to critiquing moral theorists for their lack of attention to ethics in personal relationships, Wood notes that societal practices reinforce continued unethical behavior in personal relationships. She describes police officers' reluctance to intervene in domestic disputes because they are private matters, clergy encouraging people to return to abusive spouses, and the portrayal of relational violence in television programs and music videos as examples of the ways in which our society normalizes unethical practices in personal relationships.

Wood ends her critique with a call for change. She notes that authors of interpersonal textbooks need to find ways to make ethics a more prominent part of their texts and suggests that scholars might take more active roles in developing training programs for law enforcement and other institutions that deal with reports of unethical behavior in personal relationships. In addition, she proposes that communication scholars consider the ways in which communication practices that normalize unethical behavior in the private sphere might be changed. Finally, she advocates that more attention be given to the boundary between the private and public sphere. Recognizing the complexity of the issue of intervention, Wood indicates that we need to consider questions such as "when is social intervention into personal relationships justified" and how do we prevent abuse while respecting the "political and spiritual values that families teach to children"?

Some of the ethical stances we have examined previously in this book obviously can apply to interpersonal communication. The various dialogical perspectives described in chapter 4, although applicable in some degree to public communication, apply primarily to private, face-to-face communication and assume a particular quality or attitude among participants. Human nature and situational perspectives (chapters 3 and 5) would seem applicable both in interpersonal and public settings, and some religious and utilitarian approaches (chapter 6) would appear relevant.

What about the various sets of ethical guidelines that have been developed for public speaking, rhetoric, persuasion, argument, and mass communication? Are these ethical standards also applicable equally and uniformly to interpersonal communication? Or are ethical standards needed that apply uniquely and most appropriately solely to interpersonal communication? We now will survey some examples of criteria and guidelines that either have been offered as ethical standards for interpersonal communication or might be adapted to serve that purpose.

Condon's Interpersonal Ethic

John Condon explores a wide array of ethical issues that typically emerge in interpersonal communication settings: candor, social harmony, accuracy, deception, consistency of word and act, keeping confidences, and blocking communication. In discussing these ethical themes, Condon stresses that any particular theme may come into conflict with other themes and that we may have to choose one over the other in a given situation. Although Condon does not formulate specific ethical criteria, perhaps we can restate some of his views in the form of potential guidelines that we may want to consider.[4]

1. Be candid and frank in sharing personal beliefs and feelings. Ideally, "we would like no to mean no; we would like a person who does not understand to say so, and a person who disagrees to express that disagreement directly."

2. In groups or cultures where interdependence is valued over individualism, keeping social relationships harmonious may be more ethical than speaking our minds.

3. Information should be communicated accurately, with minimal loss or distortion of intended meaning.

4. Intentional deception generally is unethical.

5. Verbal and nonverbal cues, words and actions, should be consistent in the meanings they communicate.

6. Usually it is unethical to block intentionally the communication process, such as cutting off persons before they have made their point, changing the subject when the other person obviously has more to say, or nonverbally distracting others from the intended subject.

A Contextual Interpersonal Ethic

In developing what he labels as a "contextual approach" to interpersonal communication ethics, Ronald Arnett takes the position that while some concrete guidelines are necessary in ethical decisions, we simultaneously must remain flexible to the contextual demands of the moment.[5] Our ethical system is established, but it must be open to modification in the circumstances at hand. We should, he suggests, take neither an absolute, dogmatic stance nor an extremely relativistic, entirely situation-determined stance. From this vantage point, Arnett offers three propositions as ethical standards for interpersonal communication.

Proposition One: we must be open to information reflecting changing conceptions of self and others, but such openness does not imply agreement with those changes, only an attempt to understand the other's perceptual world. We also should be sensitive to our own and others' role responsibilities in concrete situations. *Proposition Two:* the self-actualization or self-fulfillment of participants should be fostered if at all possible; but the "good" decision may require sacrifice of something important to one or more participants. *Proposition Three:* we should take into account our own emotions and feelings, but emotions cannot be the sole guide for behavior. At times the "good" response or action requires doing what does not feel emotionally good. Arnett concludes by stressing that a "contextual ethic does not recognize 'self-actualization' and 'getting in touch with one's feelings' as the primary function of interpersonal communication."

An Ethic for Interpersonal Trust

Central to both public and interpersonal communication is a minimal level of trust among participants. Kim Giffin and Richard Barnes offer an ethic of interpersonal trust based on a particular view of human nature. They assume that while humans are essentially good by nature, there are realistic limits and constricting circumstances that most of the time limit achievement of ideal human potential.[6] An ethic that increases our trust in each other is desirable because our trust of others tends to stimulate their trust of us, because our own self-image can be improved, and because our psychological health is nurtured. They do recognize the dangers of trusting people. Others may use our trust to deceive us; continued exposure to broken trust breeds alienation from others and declining self-confidence.

Giffin and Barnes present three ethical guidelines for trust in interpersonal communication. First, we should actively attempt to extend our trust of those around us as widely as possible. This is desirable most of the time for most people. Second, "our trust of others should be tentative." Our trust should be offered a little at a time, and we should clarify to others "what we are risking, what we are counting on them to do or be, and what we expect to achieve." Third, trust should not only be given but it also should be earned. "An act of trust is unethical unless the trusted person is trustworthy—it takes two to trust one."

An Ethic for Everyday Conversation

Philosopher H. P. Grice views everyday conversation as one type of purposive, rational human behavior. He attempts to uncover some of the basic expectations that need to be fulfilled if conversation, whether to exchange information or to attempt influence, is to be adequate.[7] Grice assumes that contributions by participants should be appropriate for the purpose and for the particular stage of the conversation. Grice also outlines various maxims to guide adequate conversation. While he does not state them as ethical criteria, you may want to consider to what degree some or all of them could serve as ethical guidelines for most types of interpersonal communication. They are presented here in adapted and paraphrased form:

- *Quantity.* Contributions should present as much information, advice, or argument as is required by current purposes of the conversation but should not present more than is required.

- *Quality.* Try to make your contributions true; do not say what you believe is false and do not say anything lacking an adequate basis of evidence.

- *Relation.* Be relevant, taking account of the facts that participants may have different standards of relevance and that topics often shift during a conversation.

- *Manner.* Be clear, brief, and orderly; avoid intentional ambiguity and obscurity of expression.

Unfair Tactics in Verbal Conflict

Disagreement and conflict sometimes occur in intimate and informal interpersonal settings. In such situations, when at least one party may be emotionally vulnerable, individuals often affect each other in direct and powerful ways. When you as a receiver in such a situation decide to respond by expressing strong disagreement, there are some "unfair" tactics of verbal conflict you may want to avoid because they are ethically irresponsible.

The Intimate Enemy: How to Fight Fair in Love and Marriage is a provocative book by George Bach and Peter Wyden. Raymond Ross and Mark Ross have adapted some insights from this book to suggest unfair and unethical tactics of verbal conflict to be avoided.[8] Avoid monopolizing the talk with the intent of preventing others from expressing their own opinion. Avoid entrapment in which you lure someone into saying something that you intend to use later to embarrass or hurt him or her. Avoid verbally "hitting below the belt" by taking unfair advantage of what you know to be the other person's special psychological vulnerability. Avoid stockpiling or accumulating numerous grievances so that you can overwhelm the other person by dumping complaints on him or her all at once. Finally, avoid dragging in numerous irrelevant or trivial issues and arguments in order to pile up an advantage.

Individual Responsibility in Relational Communication

William K. Rawlins notes the tension between freedom and responsibility even for interpersonal and intimate communication: "For there to be *freedom* to converse intimately with another person, each party must take *responsibility* for communicative behavior." Rawlins also believes that "disclosing personal thoughts and feelings and speaking freely in a relationship are *rights*, not *obligations*. To allow viable associations to develop, intimates should acknowledge limits in their communication and respect each other's separateness." In part, contends Rawlins, "self-oriented communicative responsibility involves structuring messages that preserve personal privacy and shield self's vulnerabilities. Responsible other-directed communication fosters individuality by respecting others' privacy and protecting others' sensitivities."[9] In exploring an ethic of responsibility for interpersonal communication, Rawlins focuses on four topics: openness, privacy, protection, and deception.

Openness should not be without limits. There should be a "freedom to be open without the compulsion to be 'transparent.' . . . Truth-dumping and burdening another with personal affairs" may be harmful because they restrict the other's freedom "by thrusting emotional and cognitive work and/ or requirements of confidence on that person." Self-disclosure may restrict the other's choice by creating an expectation or duty to reciprocate. Unrestrained blanket honesty "evades personal responsibility for the effects of one's statements."

Privacy is essential in interpersonal relations and includes both the right to exclude other persons and a recognition of the other's right to privacy. The distinction between privacy and secrecy is an important one. Privacy usually protects behavior that is morally neutral or positively valued. In contrast, "secrecy usually hides something viewed negatively by self and others." Misevaluation of ethicality may occur if a legitimate right of privacy is asserted by a person but others perceive it as devious or deceptive secrecy.

"As intimates become aware of each other's" most private thoughts, feelings, and behaviors, they usually gain "knowledge of sensitive, hurtful issues." Thus, believes Rawlins, "protectiveness is essential for individuals to tolerate the vulnerability accompanying intimacy." The extremes of excessive protectiveness and total expressiveness of feelings both may be harmful to the relationship. "Thus, the tension between candor and restraint must be managed consciously in responsible relational communication."

While revealing personal information enables other to know self better, telling everything degrades self's privacy and makes self excessively vulnerable. Similarly, self must be candid in order for the other to trust in self's honesty; but self cannot be too blunt or other's privacy and/or feelings may be threatened, thereby diminishing other's trust in self's protection.

Rawlins draws a "basic distinction between duplicity" as a necessary element in social life and "deceit that is unethical or bad." With the "intentions motivating the behavior" as the crucial determinant, Rawlins finds that "benign or white sham is at times necessary to protect others and allow us to get along with them." But "black sham—exploitative and destructive fakery used to take advantage of others—undermines relationships."

In thinking about your own intimate interpersonal relationships, how adequate is the guidance provided by Rawlins's analysis? On what grounds would you rest your decisions about degree of ethical or responsible openness, privacy, protectiveness, and deception? With what aspects of Rawlins's analysis do you especially agree or disagree? Why?

Keeping the Conversation Going

In several of his works, Stanley Deetz develops a communication ethic of "keeping the conversation going." He starts with the assumption that the nature and character of humans are formed in communication interaction. Deetz builds upon the work of the German social critics Jürgen Habermas, Karl Otto Apel, and, especially, Hans-Georg Gadamer.[10] While Deetz believes that his view is applicable not only to interpersonal communication but also to public discourse, organizational communication, and mass communication, here we will suggest only its applications to interpersonal communication. Genuine conversation aims at "creating mutual understanding through open formation of experience" rather than at self-expression or at making one's view prevail. The focus is on mutual understanding of the subject matter of the conversation. Deetz proposes a guiding ethical principle "based on the very conditions of mutual understanding": "Every communicative act should have as its ethical condition the attempt to keep the conversation—the open development of experience—going." Genuine conversation should be "responsive to the subject matter of the conversation and at the same time help establish conditions for future unrestrained formation of experience"—future minimally constrained communication.

Genuine conversation, says Deetz, can be blocked or distorted, either occasionally or systematically, through a variety of unethical communication practices—practices often reinforced by unquestioned institutional and societal assumptions.

- *Freezing participants* involves using stereotypes, hardened categories, or frozen labels that shut down or constrict conversation by ignoring individual differences and potential for personal change. In Martin Buber's terminology, viewing a person as an It or an object strips the person of humanity and lessens the obligation to respect that person's rights and character. Or dismissing someone's view without examination simply by labeling the person as racist, sexist, homosexual, Pro-Life, or Pro-Choice constricts the possibility of genuine conversation.

- *Disqualification* centers on rules or norms that determine who has a right to speak on a subject. Societally formed ideas of "expertise, professional qualification, and specialization" often are used to dismiss a person's views or disqualify the person from speaking. To dismiss a person's idea automatically without examination simply by asserting that "you're no expert," or "you're merely an amateur," or asking "what right do you have . . . ?" may block genuine conversation.

- In *naturalization*, "one particular view of the subject matter" (from among multiple plausible ones) is "frozen as the way the thing is." Multiple viewpoints or potential for alternatives can be narrowed to one assertion or assumption about the way things or persons "naturally" are as fixed or unquestioned. Unchallenged statements, such as "that's just the way" that women, or blacks, or Jews "are," function to undermine genuine conversation.

- *Neutralization* "refers to the process by which value positions become hidden and value-laden activities are treated as if they were value free." Dismissal of a position as a "threat to progress" may be taken as a factual description without thought concerning the often competing values imbedded in differing notions of "progress."

- *Topical avoidance* centers on norms in the relationship or group that prohibit "the discussion of some events or feelings." Conversation is forced to "go around and leave out" taboo topics and thus valuable discussion of conflicts, emotions, priorities, and perceptions often are denied to participants.

- *Subjectification of experience* involves the dismissal or trivialization of another person's view as merely "a matter of opinion" and thus so subjective and individualized as not to be appropriate for discussion on an allegedly more factual or reasonable level.

- *Meaning denial* "happens when one possible interpretation of a statement is both present in the interaction and denied as meant." When you shout at another person during an interaction and yet proclaim that you are not angry, a "message is present and disclaimed; said and not said." The burden of creation of meaning unfairly is shifted entirely to the listener, and you retain "control without responsibility." You might assert irresponsibly that the person should have known you were angry despite what you said to the contrary.

- *Pacification* occurs when messages function to avoid valuable discussion of conflict, problems, and solutions by downplaying their seriousness or discounting the capacities of individuals to grapple with them. Issues are avoided by describing them as too trivial to warrant discussion or too monumental for us to do anything about them.

Ethical Responsibility and Interpersonal Influence

One form of communication in personal relationships that has the potential for unethical behavior is interpersonal influence. When we try to change our parents', friends', or significant other's behaviors or attitudes, we are engaging in interpersonal influence.[11] Steven Wilson suggests that some humanistic and feminist scholars, such as Rogers and Foss and Griffin have argued that influence is unethical in interpersonal relationships because it involves attempts to control others and to get them to agree or give in.[12] Wilson counters the argument that seeking compliance is in opposition to positive regard for another by arguing that seeking compliance and resisting compliance are inherent in the process of creating and sustaining close interpersonal relationships.

Wilson notes the complexities of ethics in influence in interpersonal contexts. He suggests that it is not always easy to know if being open and honest is an ethical approach when seeking to influence someone in an interpersonal relationship. Also, he notes that the line between influence and coercion can be blurred by the relationship. There are times that something is presented as a choice but the nature of the relationship leads one to believe that he or she is obligated. For example, a mother and daughter are shopping for the daughter's prom dress, and they have found two possible dresses. The mother says that she likes the blue one better than the red one, but tells her daughter that she should buy the one that the daughter likes best. On the surface it appears that the daughter has been given a choice. However, the daughter might feel obligated to pick the dress that her mother likes best, especially if the mother is paying for the dress. So, is the mother ethical in stating her preference? Is she really giving her daughter a choice? Is she coercing the daughter into getting the blue dress instead of the red one? What are ethical and unethical strategies for persuading those with whom we have interpersonal relationships? What guidelines should people use to engage in ethical compliance gaining?

Kathleen Verderber and Rudolf Verderber address several issues to which we can pay attention in order to engage in ethical influence.[13] First, we should provide reasons for the position we are advocating. Reasons allow the other person to see the basis for your position and to evaluate the reasoning in order to reach his or her own conclusion about the issue. When influence is based in reasoning the other person has the freedom to accept or reject your claims based on their merit. Second, since targets of influence evaluate the influence message based on the credibility of the persuader, we should recognize that people's perceptions of our credibility are influenced in part by our ethical or unethical behavior. Ethical persuaders operate within the "standards of moral conduct," and avoid trying to win at any cost (engaging in behaviors based on the belief that "the end justifies the means." Finally, we should strive to develop the characteristics that are the "essentials of ethical persuasion": telling the truth, resisting engaging in personal attacks on people who oppose our ideas, and disclosing all relevant information.

Stephen Littlejohn and David Jabusch develop a view in which ethical responsibility is a fundamental dimension of communication competence. Their ethical stance applies, they believe, to persuasion in interpersonal, organizational, and public communication. Littlejohn and Jabusch assume that communicators share the responsibility for the outcomes of the transaction and they center their view on the ethical principles of caring and openness. "*Caring* is concern for the well-being of self and others. It involves a feeling that what happens to others is as important as what happens to self. It is the spirit of good will. *Openness* is a willingness to share information with others and, conversely, an interest in the disclosures of other people. It is, in short, a spirit of honesty."[14]

Emerging from high and low degrees of interaction between the caring and openness orientations of a person are four positions judged as ethical to varying degrees.

- *Ethical Responsibility.* Communicators share responsibility for determining consequences. There is a high degree of completely and honestly shared information and a high degree of concern for the well-being of all participants.

- *Unshared Responsibility.* The communicator assumes total responsibility for consequences of the transaction by maintaining high concern for the well-being of others but withholding or distorting information for what he or she judges to be the best interest of others.

- *Abdicated Responsibility.* The communicator assumes no responsibility and leaves total responsibility for consequences to other participants. While the communicator may share information completely and honestly, he or she lacks concern for the effects of that honesty on others.

- *Irresponsibility.* The communicator not only refuses to assume responsibility but also denies others any opportunity to have control. The communicator not only withholds or distorts relevant information but also shows no concern for consequences and the well-being of others.

"Most of the time," contend Littlejohn and Jabusch, "you will probably have to choose between persuading with unshared responsibility and persuading with shared responsibility." On what grounds might you decide between these two orientations and decide their degree of ethicality? In what ways do you agree or disagree with their ethical viewpoint rooted in caring and openness? Try to think of four stereotypical communication situations that might clearly illustrate each of the four ethical positions.

Ross's Prima Facie Duties

British philosopher W. D. Ross intentionally avoids not only Kantian absolutes and categorical imperatives but also utilitarian consequentialism. Instead he develops a series of *prima facie* duties—duties that are reasonable and obvious without further proof as obligations if all other relevant factors are equal. But these duties are not absolute with no exceptions regardless of circumstances. Ross believes that these duties express a "moral order" that is "just as much a part of the fundamental nature of the universe . . . as is the spatial or numerical structure expressed in the axioms of geometry or arithmetic."[15]

For our purposes it is noteworthy that Ross grounds these duties in the nature of "morally significant" relationships that we may encounter every day, not in some abstract duty to humanity. Such a view, he believes, takes properly serious account of the "highly personal character of duty." These *prima facie* duties become "actual duties" only in light of the circumstances of morally significant relationships. The morally significant relationships he describes are those such as child–parent, spouse–spouse, friend–friend, neighbor–neighbor, promisor–promisee, creditor–debtor, and citizen–citizen. Note that most of these relationships are ones that we now comfortably would include in the categories of intimate or interpersonal communication.

Ross does not claim "completeness or finality" for the cluster of duties he presents. He realizes that two (or more) duties often come into conflict in a particular situation or relationship. In that case, there is no automatic or precise rule for choosing which has priority. Instead, persons must study all aspects of the situation and then reach a reflective judgment or "considered opinion" about which should take precedence, about which should be an actual duty. Ross suggests the following *prima facie* duties:

- *Fidelity* includes promise keeping and following the implicit promise "not to tell lies, which seems to be implied in the act of entering into a conversation."
- *Reparation* means compensation (not solely monetary) to others for wrongs we have done to them.
- *Gratitude* is shown in our actions for the good things or service others have done for us.
- *Justice* involves equitable distribution of pleasure and happiness according to merit.
- *Beneficence* obliges us to improve the conditions of others in the world (to improve their levels of education, happiness, and ethics).

- *Self-improvement* is the duty owed ourselves to improve our wisdom and ethics (not material comfort primarily).
- *Nonmaleficence* basically is the obligation not to harm or injure others and is more fundamental than the duty to do good for others.

Why and how might these duties apply in some concrete interpersonal communication situation you can think of? What are some interpersonal communication situations where you think they might not apply? What are some key terms in the statements of the duties that might require further clarification before they could be adequately applied? Which of these duties, if any, might you argue should not be used as ethical standards for interpersonal communication? Why?

Examples of Potential Ethical Problems in Interpersonal Communication

In the opening of this chapter, we noted that Julia Wood has called on communication scholars to pay more attention to ethics in interpersonal relationships. In this section, we identify some communication practices that can raise ethical problems in interpersonal relationships and that warrant more serious explanation as potential ethical issues.

Self-disclosure is an important feature in interpersonal communication because it helps us to develop and maintain interpersonal relationships.[16] Self-disclosure is also a complex topic because people in the United States value privacy and individualism. Several communication scholars have explored the intersection of disclosure, privacy, and secrecy, but little attention has been given to the ethical issues involved in balancing privacy and disclosure.[17] Self-disclosure involves purposefully sharing personal information with another person. While there are gradations in the degree of intentionality and level of personal information, all self-disclosure does involve the revealing of information that to some extent we view as private rather than public.[18] When engaging in disclosure people weigh their motivations for disclosing against the potential risks. In reviewing some of the motivations and risks, we point to some of the ethical issues that could be explored with regards to self-disclosure. Valerian Derlega and Janusz Grzelak have identified several *motivations* for disclosure, and four of these will be explored in terms of ethical issues.

One reason for self-disclosing is for catharsis or release.[19] The person who discloses might feel better after having shared the information because the sense of hiding something from the other person is removed. However, the person who hears the information may not have a positive reaction. The person might feel overwhelmed or burdened by the information. Is it ethical to overwhelm people with one's private information? How does one balance the need for release with the need to respect the boundaries of the other person? A second motivation for disclosure is for the purpose of social influence or persuading other people. Some of the issues previously discussed regarding influence in interpersonal relationships could be explored in terms of the ways in which people use self-disclosure as a means of seeking compliance from friends and family members. A third motivation for disclosure is manipulation. Is it ethical to share information for the purposes of getting people do things they would otherwise not do? Finally, people are motivated to disclose for the purpose of identity management; we share certain pieces of information in order to influence the ways in which people perceive us. To what extent is it ethical to withhold information so that people will not see us in a negative light? To what extent is it ethical to share positive information so that people will think good things about us? In considering people's motivations for disclosure we need to further explore the extent to which the motivations are ethical.

Ethical issues regarding disclosure may also be found in some of the *risks* associated with self-disclosure. One of the risks associated with self-disclosure is rejection or negative impression formation.[20] Kathryn Greene, Valerian Derlega, Gust Yep, and Sandra Petronio identify this risk as one of the factors leading people to fail to disclose HIV-positive status to friends, family members, sexual partners, and health care workers. However, this risk likely influences people's decisions to disclose other negative information as well (i.e., being fired from a job, receiving a failing grade at school, dropping out of school, having an addiction). In considering this risk from an ethical perspective several issues emerge. To what extent is it ethical to allow one's concerns about rejection or negative impressions to prevent one from disclosing personal information? Is it more unethical to withhold the information in some relationships than others? Is it more unethical to withhold some personal information than others? For instance, is withholding one's HIV status more unethical than withholding information about one's work or school performance? Another risk factor associated with disclosure is concern that the hearer will disapprove of the speaker. Greene, Derlega, Yep, and Petronio discuss this factor in terms of HIV-positive status noting that people's hesitancy about disclosing HIV status is because some are quick to conclude that the HIV-positive individual has engaged in socially disapproved behavior. To what extent is it ethical to judge another person based on the information being disclosed? Is it ethical to assume that a young woman was raped because she had dressed provocatively and drank heavily at a party? A third risk of disclosing is that the receiver might share that private information with a third party. In terms of ethics, it is important that we consider the extent to which we are obligated to maintain the confidentiality of the information we receive.

A second example of an area of interpersonal communication that could be further explored in terms of ethical issues is gossip and rumors. Gossip and rumors are forms of communication that raise ethical issues. Often people use gossip and rumors as means to develop relationships or to display status or power.[21] However, from an ethical perspective we need to realize that when we are gossiping we are usually making ethical judgments about someone else. In gossip, we have undertones that suggest another person's behavior was good or bad, right or wrong. Also, gossiping becomes unethical when it reveals information that is private and/or that is inaccurate. "If the gossip discloses information that is private or if it is inaccurate, the gossip may damage both the relationship in which it was exchanged and other relationships as well. Perhaps the most malicious kind of gossip is that which is engaged in for purposes of hurting or embarrassing the person who is not present."[22]

A third interpersonal communication issue is teasing. Communication scholars have studied the role of teasing in interpersonal relationships, identifying the ways it functions as a form of verbal play and intimate talk and the effects that teasing has on the target and the person doing the teasing.[23] Elizabeth Aronson and her colleagues studied teasing among college students and found prescriptive norms indicating that appearance, sexual orientation, ethnicity, religion, and race were not acceptable topics for teasing.[24] However, the researchers note that it is not clear if "these norms reflect underlying values, social desirability bias, or caution when interacting in a new environment." More attention needs to be given to the extent to which ethical guidelines influence prescriptive norms for teasing. Specifically, what ethical perspectives influence norms of teasing? Further, more attention needs to be given to ethical issues surrounding teasing in general. At minimum, we need to recognize that one's motivation for teasing (joking versus ridiculing or humiliating) affects the ethicality of this form of communication. When, if ever, is it ethical to tease someone? Is it ethical to tease one's romantic partner about his or her mismatched outfit? Is teasing ethical in all interpersonal relationships?

Another issue that could be further explored is the ethics of swearing in interpersonal communication. Aliana Winters and Steve Duck argue that in interpersonal communication swearing functions as a means of asserting self and exerting power.[25] They note that we commonly recognize that swearing can have negative associations: those who swear are often seen as uneducated, unattractive, and acting inappropriately. Further, swearing to exert power in an interpersonal relationship can be perceived as derogatory and abusive. Based on Julia Wood's arguments about ethics in interpersonal communication that we discussed above, derogatory and abusive swearing would be examples of unethical interpersonal communication. However, Winters and Duck's discussion of swearing makes it difficult to conclude that swearing in interpersonal communication is always unethical. They propose that an understudied aspect of swearing in interpersonal communication is swearing that functions "to signal bonding and acceptance." So, when is swearing ethical and unethical during interpersonal communication? Is swearing in order to bond with someone ethical? Does a virtuous person swear when engaging in interpersonal communication? To what extent do the ends justify swearing as a means? For example, is it ethical for one to engage in swearing in order to be accepted by a group of friends? Is it ethical to swear in order to convince a friend to not drive after drinking?

Finally, the area of technology use in interpersonal communication could be explored from an ethical point of view. Increasingly, we use technology (cell phones, e-mail, text messaging) to communicate interpersonally. Given the prevalence of technology in interpersonal communication, we should consider the extent to which technology might be affecting ethics in our interpersonal communication. Here we offer some issues to consider in terms of technology and interpersonal communication. A family is out for dinner at a restaurant and one parent talks on a cell phone with a friend through most of the dinner. Is talking on the cell phone instead of conversing with one's family an example of poor manners? To what extent does the way in which talking on the phone interferes with the building community within this family make this an ethical matter as well? A friend wishes another friend happy birthday through instant messaging. Is it simply inconsiderate to wish someone a happy birthday with a text message? Or is it unethical to wish someone happy birthday through text messaging? Does text-messaging result in communication that is more characteristic of what Buber termed an I-it relationship than an I-thou? A woman uses e-mail to break up with her boyfriend. Is her use of e-mail an unethical form of interpersonal communication? As you consider these questions and other issues you might raise regarding the use of technology in interpersonal communication, we would also like you to consider the ways in which and to what degree the approaches to interpersonal communication ethics discussed above apply to the use of technology for interpersonal communication.

We have tried to identify some areas of interpersonal communication that need more attention from an ethical perspective, but this is not an exhaustive list. We invite you to identify other areas and to further consider how we can address the ethics of the interpersonal communication issues while maintaining respect for the unique "political and spiritual values" that characterize people's interpersonal relationships.[26]

A Political Perspective for Small Group Discussion

Several writers suggest ethical standards for the type of small group communication that is task-oriented toward reaching a mutually agreeable decision or solving a problem. Ernest Bormann takes a political perspective based on the values central to U.S. representative democracy, especially on the "four moralities" developed by Karl Wallace and examined previously in chapter 2. In summarized and paraphrased form, here are the major ethical guidelines urged by Bormann in two of his writings:[27]

1. Participants should be allowed to make up their own minds without being coerced, duped, or manipulated.

2. Participants should be encouraged to grow and to develop their own potential.

3. Sound reasoning and relevant value judgments are to be encouraged.

4. Conflicts and disagreements that focus on participants as persons rather than on ideas or information should be avoided.

5. Participants who manipulate group members solely or primarily for their own selfish ends are unethical.

6. In the role of advisor, participants should present information honestly, fairly, and accurately. They should reveal their sources. They should allow others to scrutinize their evidence and arguments. Lying is unethical because it breaks the trust necessary for participants to assess information.

7. With respect to external groups or individuals, participants within the group should be committed to defending "true statements of fact, praiseworthy value statements, and sound advice."

8. Participants should communicate with each other as they would want others to communicate with them.

9. Communication practices in the group should be judged within a framework of all relevant values and ethical criteria, not solely or primarily by the worth of the end or goal to be reached. Gandhi's ethical touchstone is sound: "Evil means, even for a good end, produces evil results."

Respect for the Worth of Others

In his book, *Discussion, Conference, and Group Process*, Halbert Gulley supports a basic premise of Thomas Nilsen concerning the concept of The Good basic to our culture: communication that enhances and nurtures human personalities is good; communication that damages, degrades, or stifles human personalities is bad. Gulley identifies a number of guidelines for ethical communication in small group discussions.[28] They are presented below in partially paraphrased form:

1. A communicator has a responsibility for defending the policy decisions of groups in whose deliberations he or she participated. If the participant cannot, he or she should make the refusal of support clear at the time the decision is reached.

2. A communicator has a responsibility to be well informed and accurate. "To present a few facts as the whole story, tentative findings as firmly established conclusions, or partial understanding as authoritative is to mislead the group."

3. A communicator has a responsibility to encourage actively the comments of others and to seek out all viewpoints, including unpopular ones.

4. A communicator should openly reveal her or his own biases, and should identify her or his sources of information and any prejudices of such sources.

5. "Uninhibited lying, fabrication of evidence, inventing of sources, deliberate misquoting, and falsification of facts are obviously dishonest practices."

6. "The ethical group member does not attempt to manipulate the talk unfairly so that his selfish ends are served and the group wishes frustrated."

7. The ethical communicator avoids use of tactics to intentionally cloud analysis: name-calling, emotionally "loaded" language, guilt-by-association, hasty generalizations, shifting definitions, and oversimplified either-or alternatives.

Ethical Sensitivity

Dennis Gouran urges that "ethical sensitivity" is a leadership function that any small group discussion participant should be willing to perform.[29] "Groups are not always aware of the ethical implications of their decisions. Were a member to call this possibility to the attention of his or her own colleagues, in some instances they might arrive at a different decision." The ethically sensitive group participant seeks to avoid unintentionally unethical decisions and to promote exploration of issues from more than a purely pragmatic viewpoint. Rather than rendering rapid, dogmatic, either/or ethical judgments, the ethically sensitive discussant raises questions about the ethical justifiability of ideas and actions.

Gouran presents five considerations to guide assessment of the degree of ethical responsibility shown in a particular small group decision-making process. (1) Did we show proper concern for those who will be affected by our decision? (2) Did we explore the discussion question as responsibly as we were capable of doing? (3) Did we misrepresent any position or misuse any source of information? (4) Did we say or do anything that might have unnecessarily diminished any participant's sense of self-worth? (5) Was everyone in the group shown the respect due him or her?

A "Groupthink" Ethic

"Groupthink" is the collective label used by social psychologist Irving Janis to describe characteristics of small groups whose processes of problem solving and policy determination typically result in ineffectiveness, low quality decisions, and failure to attain objectives. Janis analyzed the historical records, observers' accounts of conversations, and participants' memoirs for a number of such actual disastrous decisions. He identifies eight main symptoms that characterize "groupthink." Janis simply describes these characteristic processes and does not intend them as ethical standards.[30] Nevertheless, it maybe fruitful for us to convert them to ethical guidelines for healthy, humane, reasonable, task-oriented small group discussions. How clear, appropriate, and applicable would you consider them to be as potential ethical guidelines?

1. Avoid the "illusion of invulnerability," which fosters "excessive optimism and encourages taking extreme risks."

2. Avoid rationalizations that hinder members from reassessing their basic assumptions before reaffirming commitment to previous decisions.

3. Avoid "an unquestioned belief in the group's inherent morality," a belief that inclines members to "ignore the ethical and moral consequences of their decisions."

4. Avoid stereotyping adversaries' views as "too evil to warrant genuine attempts to negotiate, or as too weak and stupid" to thwart your efforts against them.

5. Avoid pressure that makes members feel disloyal if they express "strong arguments against any of the group's stereotypes, illusions, or commitments."

6. Avoid individual self-censorship that minimizes for each person the importance of his or her own doubts or counterarguments.

7. Avoid a "shared illusion of unanimity concerning judgments conforming to the majority view." This illusion results both from "self-censorship of deviations" and from the "false assumption that silence means consent."

8. Avoid the emergence of "self-appointed mindguards." These are members "who protect the group from adverse information that might shatter their complacency about the effectiveness and morality of their decisions."

Notes

[1] See Joe Ayres, "Four Approaches to Interpersonal Communication," *Western Journal of Speech Communication*, 48 (Fall 1984): 408–440; Mark L. Knapp and John Daly, eds., *Handbook of Interpersonal Communication*, 3rd ed. (Thousand Oaks, CA: Sage, 2002).

[2] Dean Barnlund, *Interpersonal Communication: Survey and Studies* (Boston: Houghton Mifflin, 1968), pp. 8–10; Gerald R. Miller and Mark Steinberg, *Between People: A New Analysis of Interpersonal Communication* (Chicago: Science Research Associates, 1975), ch. 1; Gerald R. Miller and Michael J. Sunnafrank, "All for One But One Is Not for All: A Conceptual Perspective of Interpersonal Communication," in *Human Communication Theory: Comparative Essays*, Frank E. X. Dance, ed. (New York: Harper & Row, 1982), pp. 220–242: John Stewart, Karen E. Zediker and Saskia Witteborn, *Together: Communicating Interpersonally*, 6th ed. (New York: Oxford University Press, 2007; John Stewart, ed., *Bridges Not Walls*, 9th ed. (New York: McGraw-Hill, 2006).

[3] Julia T. Wood, "Ethics, Justice, and the 'Private Sphere,'" *Women's Studies in Communication*, 21 (1998): 127–149. See also John Hardwig, "In Search of an Ethics of Interpersonal Relationships," in *Person to Person*, George Graham and Hugh LaFollette, eds. (Philadelphia: Temple University Press, 1989), pp. 63–81.

4 John C. Condon, *Interpersonal Communication* (New York: Macmillan, 1977), ch. 8.

5 Ronald C. Arnett, "Ethics of Interpersonal Communication Revisited," paper presented at Speech Communication Association convention, Anaheim, CA, November 1981. Also see Arnett, *Communication and Community: Implications of Martin Buber's Dialogue* (Carbondale: Southern Illinois University Press, 1986), ch. 4; Arnett and Pat Arneson, *Dialogic Civility in a Cynical Age: Community, Hope, and Interpersonal Relationships* (Albany: State University of New York Press, 1999).

6 Kim Giffin and Richard E. Barnes, *Trusting Me, Trusting You* (Columbus, OH: Charles E. Merrill, 1976), ch. 7.

7 H. P. Grice, "Logic and Conversation," in *Understanding Arguments*, Robert J. Fogelin, ed. (New York: Harcourt Brace Jovanovich, 1978), pp. 329–343. For an analysis of Grice's maxims from a feminist theoretical perspective, see Gillian Michell, "Women and Lying: A Pragmatic and Semantic Analysis of 'Telling It Slant,'" *Women's Studies International Forum*, 7 (1983): 375–383.

8 Raymond S. Ross and Mark G. Ross, *Relating and Interacting* (Englewood Cliffs, NJ: Prentice-Hall, 1982), pp. 77, 138–141.

9 William K. Rawlins, "Individual Responsibility in Relational Communication," in *Communications in Transition*, Mary S. Mander, ed. (New York: Praeger, 1983): 152–167. Also see Rawlins, "Openness as Problematic in Ongoing Friendships: Two Conversational Dilemmas," *Communication Monographs*, 50 (March 1983): 1–13.

10 Stanley Deetz, "Reclaiming the Subject Matter as a Guide to Mutual Understanding: Effectiveness and Ethics in Interpersonal Interaction," *Communication Quarterly*, 38 (Summer 1990): 226–243; Deetz, "Keeping the Conversation Going: The Principle of Dialectic Ethics," *Communication*, 7, no. 7 (1983): 263–288; Deetz, *Democracy in an Age of Corporate Colonization: Developments in Communication and the Politics of Everyday Life* (Albany: State University of New York Press, 1992), pp. 145–198. Also see Frederick Bruce Bird, *The Muted Conscience* (Westport, CT: Quorum, 1996), ch. 7.

11 Kathleen S. Verderber and Rudolf F. Verderber, *Inter-Act: Interpersonal Communication Concepts, Skills, and Contexts*, 10th ed. (New York: Oxford University Press, 2004), p. 274.

12 Steven R. Wilson, *Seeking and Resisting Compliance: Why People Say What They Do When Trying to Influence Others* (Thousand Oaks, CA: Sage, 2002), pp. 8–13.

13 Verderber and Verderber, *Inter-Act*, p. 283.

14 Stephen W. Littlejohn and David M. Jabusch, *Persuasive Transactions* (Glenview, IL: Scott Foresman, 1987), pp. 12–22; Littlejohn and Jabusch, "Communication Competence: Model and Application," *Journal of Applied Communication Research*, 10 (Spring 1982): 29–37.

15 W. D. Ross, *The Right and the Good* (Oxford, UK: Clarendon Press, 1930), pp. 16–47. Also see David McNaughton, "An Unconnected Heap of Duties?" *Philosophical Quarterly*, 46 (1996): 433–447; Christopher Meyers, "Appreciating W. D. Ross: On Duties and Consequences," *Journal of Mass Media Ethics*, 18 (2003): 81–97.

16 Lawrence Rosenfeld, "Overview of the Ways Privacy, Secrecy, and Disclosure Are Balanced in Today's Society," in *Balancing the Secrets of Private Disclosures*, Sandra Petronio, ed. (Mahwah, NJ: Erlbaum, 2000) pp. 3–17.

17 See Petronio, ed., *Balancing the Secrets of Private Disclosures*.

18 Rosenfeld, "Overview," p. 6.

19 Valerian J. Derlega and Janusz Grzelak, "Appropriateness of Self-disclosure," in *Self-disclosure: Origins, Patterns, and Implications of Openness in Interpersonal Relationships*, Gordon J. Chelune, ed. (San Francisco: Jossey-Bass, 1979), pp. 151–176.

20 Rosenfeld, "Overview," p. 8; Kathryn Greene, Valerian J. Derlega, Gust A. Yep, and Sandra Petronio, *Privacy and Disclosure of HIV in Interpersonal Relationships: A Sourcebook for Researchers and Practitioners* (Mahwah, NJ: Erlbaum, 2003), pp. 36–83.

21 Ralph L. Rosnow, "Rumor and Gossip in Interpersonal Interaction and Beyond: A Social Exchange Perspective," in *Behaving Badly: Aversive Behaviors in Interpersonal Relationships*, Robin M. Kowalski, ed. (Washington, DC: American Psychological Association, 2001), pp. 203–232.

22 Verderber and Verderber, *Inter-Act*, p.72.

[23] Jess K. Alberts, Yvonne Kellar-Guenther, and Steven R. Corman, "That's Not Funny: Understanding Recipients' Responses to Teasing," *Western Journal of Communication,* 60 (1996): 337–357; Leslie Baxter, "Forms and Functions of Intimate Play in Personal Relationships," *Human Communication Research,* 18 (1992): 336–363; Robert Hopper, Mark L. Knapp, and Lorel Scott, "Couples' Personal Idioms: Exploring Intimate Talk," *Journal of Communication,* 31 (1981, Winter): 23–33; Robin M. Kowalski, Elise Howerton, and Michelle McKenzie, "Permitted Disrespect: Teasing in Interpersonal Interactions," in *Behaving Badly: Aversive Behaviors in Interpersonal Relationships,* Robin M. Kowalski, ed. (Washington, DC: American Psychological Association, 2001), pp. 177–202.

[24] Elizabeth Aronson et al., "Norms of Teasing among College Students," *Communication Research Reports,* 24 (2007): 169–176.

[25] Aliana M. Winters and Steve Duck, "You ****!: Swearing as an Aversive and a Relational Activity," in *Behaving Badly: Aversive Behaviors in Interpersonal Relationships,* Robin M. Kowalski, ed. (Washington, DC: American Psychological Association, 2001), pp. 59–77.

[26] Wood, "Ethics," p. 145.

[27] Ernest G. Bormann, "Ethical Standards for Interpersonal/Small Group Communication," *Communication,* 6, no. 2 (1981): 267–286; Bormann, *Small Group Communication: Theory and Practice,* 3rd ed. (New York: Harper & Row, 1990), ch. 11.

[28] Halbert E. Gulley, *Discussion, Conference, and Group Process,* 2nd ed. (New York: Holt, Rinehart and Winston, 1968), pp. 148–152.

[29] Dennis Gouran, *Making Decisions in Groups* (1982; reissue, Long Grove, IL: Waveland Press, 1990), pp. 166–167, 227. For Gouran's application of the ethical sensitivity approach, see his "The Watergate Cover-Up: Its Dynamics and Its Implications," *Communication Monographs,* 43 (August 1976): 176–186.

[30] Irving L. Janis, *Victims of Groupthink,* 2nd ed. (Boston: Houghton Mifflin, 1982), pp. 174–175. For a case study of groupthink and communication ethics, see Ronald R. Sims, *Ethics and Organizational Decision Making* (Westport, CT: Quorum, 1994), pp. 61–79. See also Philip Zimbardo, *The Lucifer Effect: Understanding How Good People Turn Evil* (New York: Random House, 2007).

Communication in Organizations

One role fulfilled by many persons in contemporary North American society is that of communicator within a formal organization, whether that be a large corporation, small business, governmental agency, health care organization, or educational institution. Formal organizations themselves communicate with their various publics, whether they be clients, consumers, other organizations, government regulatory agencies, or the public-at-large. Some versions of the ethical perspectives explored in earlier chapters could apply to organizational communication settings, as would some of the previously presented guidelines for ethical interpersonal and small group communication. However, the characteristics of formal organizations pose special constraints and influences on communication ethics.

Employee Perceptions of Workplace Ethics

The *2005 National Business Ethics Survey* of how employees perceive ethics at work provides some encouraging and some disturbing data. This was a random survey of 3,000 American workers from senior and middle managers to line employees and administrative personnel. Respondents were from non-profit, for-profit, and government organizations and there were relatively few differences of perceptions across these organizational types.[1] Ten percent reported feeling pressure to compromise organizational standards. The sources of pressure were top management (36%), middle management (39%), and coworkers (15%). One-third of the respondents indicated that they had encountered a situation that invited ethical misconduct, and 74 percent of those people reported observing one or more incidents of misconduct. The most frequently observed forms of misconduct were abusive or intimating behavior and lying.

Approximately half (55%) of those observing misconduct indicate that they report the behavior. Reasons people do not report misconduct include believing that no corrective action will take place, fear of retaliation, fear of losing anonymity, belief that someone else would report, and not knowing who to contact. Motivations for reporting included believing it was the right thing to do, feeling corrective action would be taken, having the support of management, and having the support of coworkers.

Assessing Ethical Responsibility

The complex, impersonal, hierarchical nature of modern organizations presents some difficulties for communication ethics. Indeed, Charles Redding summarizes the view of a number of critics that "there is something *inherently* present in any modern organization that facilitates unethical or immoral conduct."[2] Robert Jackall assumes that modern organizations are "vast systems of organized irresponsibility" that erode "internal and even external standards of morality."[3] What matters most in the organizational world, concludes Jackall:

> is not what a person is but how closely his [or her] many personae mesh with the organizational ideal; not his [or her] willingness to stand by his [or her] actions but his [or her] agility in avoiding blame; not what he [or she] believes or says but how well he [or she] has mastered the ideologies that serve his [or her] corporation; not what he [or she] stands for but whom he [or she] stands with in the labyrinths of his [or her] corporation.

How does a member of an organization, or an outsider, determine where responsibility and blame should rest for unethical communication? Does responsibility and accountability reside at the top with the president, corporate executive officer, or chair of the board? Does it reside with the immediate communicator? What ethical responsibilities should be borne by "relay" persons—who are in between the originator of a message and the receivers—in an organization? Such relay persons function to link parts of a system, to store information, to stretch and alter the message, and to exert control of information.[4] Is the responsibility to be shared equally—or to varying degrees—by every member of the organization? Would the responsibility most appropriately be placed on the organization or institution itself rather than on specific individuals? Is the responsibility a *negative* one in the sense of an obligation to avoid communication that harms others? Is it an *affirmative* responsibility to communicate actively to help others? On what basis is the responsibility being assigned? Does the person have the *capability* to influence the choice and either does or does not? Does the person's *formal role* specify certain obligations and functions?[5]

Assessing individual responsibility can be difficult. In *Political Ethics and Public Office*, Dennis Thompson argues for assessment of individual responsibility within an organizational context, whether the organization be a public service or private enterprise one. The sense of complexity and frustration he describes concerning governmental organizations applies equally well to corporations. "Because many different officials contribute in many different ways to decisions and policies . . . , it is difficult even in principle to identify who is morally responsible for . . . outcomes." It is difficult to locate a person who single-handedly made the policy or even one whose contribution "is significant enough to warrant credit or blame for it."[6] Matthew Seeger echoes this frustration, suggesting that problems with assigning responsibility are linked to the division of labor in organizations. As tasks become subdivided and people's work more specialized, it is harder to attribute responsibility to a single person.[7] Further, he argues that responsibility is communicatively and retrospectively constructed. After a wrongdoing has occurred, then people look back on the factors leading up to the event and construct a plausible explanation for who is responsible.

Organizations as Cultures

A significant scholarly perspective for studying a formal organization is to conceive of it as a "culture." Just as an anthropologist would study an ethnic or national culture, organizational researchers and consultants frequently describe an organization as a culture.[8] Central components of this culture are the organization's basic values, taken-for-granted assumptions, decision-making rules, managerial styles, organizational heroes and heroines, stories of success and failure, rituals and ceremonies, sense of tradition and loyalty, and accepted topics and methods of communication. Part of an organization's culture may include "a positive or negative approach to moral issues and moral actions," both by individuals and by the organization itself, when dealing with employees, customers, and other organizations.[9] David Shulman's investigation of deception in the workplace reveals that organizations have cultures that encourage and condone lying, and he argues that the cultural and structural features that contribute to deception might also encourage other unethical acts.[10] Robert Jackall also found that the pressure of getting ahead contributed to organizational cultures that preference success and efficiency rather than ethics.[11]

"The types of ethical climates existing in an organization or group influence what ethical conflicts are considered, the process by which such conflicts are resolved, and the characteristics of their resolution."[12] The *2005 National Business Ethics Survey* found the ethical culture of an organization influences people's perceptions and actions: ethical behaviors on the part of top management is associated with employees observing less misconduct; ethical actions by coworkers is associated with employees having an increased willingness to report misconduct; and employees' overall satisfaction increases when they perceive that organizational members are held accountable for their actions.[13] So, what can individuals and organizations do to develop strong ethical climates?

A number of elements have been identified that, taken together, would promote development of a healthy, vigorous ethical climate.[14] Top management must set a high ethical tone for the entire organization by demonstrating a firm and clear commitment to ethical behavior for all employees. The personal example of their own daily behavior is one way for top management to demonstrate such commitment. Also desirable is development of a formal code of ethics or set of written ethical expectations that explain in clear terms the ethical standards demanded by the organization. Ideally such a code of ethics, even if initially developed solely by top management, will evolve and modify over time through discussion by employees at a number of levels. The organization's ethical expectations must be reinforced not only through prompt, publicized, and appropriate punishment for violation but also through rewards and recognition for consistently or significantly upholding the ethical standards.

Commitment of resources also demonstrates an organization's concern for ethics. Companies can appoint an "ethics officer" or "ethics committee" whose functions are to make sure that ethical considerations are a routine part of major policy decisions and to provide interpretations of ethical guidelines for employees in doubt. An increasing number of organizations are hiring external ethics consultants to advise them on ways of improving the ethical climate. A major commitment of resources is represented by ongoing educational programs to sensitize supervisors and managers at various levels to the ethical dimensions of decisions or procedures and to train them in systematic ways of thinking about ethics. Another possibility suggested is a formal and periodic "ethics audit" of overall performance of the organization.[15]

The *2005 National Business Ethics Survey* suggests that formal ethics programs do make a difference.[16] Programs implementing more elements (written standards of conduct, training, mechanisms for obtaining advice, mechanisms for anonymously reporting misconduct, discipline for violators, and evaluation of employees based on ethical conduct) tended to be more effective in terms of reducing ethical misconduct, increasing reporting of ethical misconduct, and improving organizational members' satisfaction with the organization's response to reports of misconduct. Further, the effectiveness of formal programs is tied to organizational culture, with programs having more of an impact on outcomes in weak cultures.

Regardless of which means for promoting an ethical climate are used, it is essential that top management genuinely commits to the creation of an ethical climate. The daily business behavior of these top executives should embody the standards described in the organization's code of ethics. Unfortunately, this too often is not the case.

Consider the Enron Corporation scandal and collapse in the first years of the twenty-first century. In July 2000, Kenneth Lay, the founder, chairman, and CEO of Enron, sent all employees a 65-page code of ethics. Honesty, candor, and fairness were to mark the company's relations with its various stakeholders. Respect and integrity were basic values. Thus, "ruthlessness, callousness, and arrogance" were condemned, and open, honest, and sincere relationships were stressed. Kenneth Lay's signed introduction to the code emphasized that business must be conducted in a "moral and honest manner." He concluded by noting that "Enron's reputation finally depends on its people, on you and me." How ironic, then, that in May 2006 Kenneth Lay was convicted in federal court of various charges that involved lying and deception about Enron's profits and debts. (For a copy of the code of ethics, see: www.THESMOKINGGUN.com.)

In response to the corporate scandals that occurred at the beginning of the twenty-first century, the U.S. federal government responded by tightening the regulations pertaining to organizational ethics. The regulation most germane to this discussion is the 2004 U. S. Sentencing Commission's guidelines, which specify that organizations need to "promote an organizational culture that encourages ethical conduct and a commitment to compliance with the law."[17] According to the current regulations, organizations need more than "pro forma" programs; organizations need to develop means for embedding ethics in the daily lives of organizational members at all levels of the organization.[18]

A sense of ethics must be "institutionalized" into the organization.[19] Ethical concerns must be regarded as on a par with economic and pragmatic concerns in decision making. Procedures must be established so that ethical issues automatically are confronted as part of a decision. Opportunities and mechanisms should be established for employees to express their ethical concerns without fear of losing a promotion, being demoted or fired, or some other retribution. Employee "whistle-blowing" on ethical violations by the organization truly should become a rare and last resort.

> Organizations must consciously act to make ethics a legitimate topic of discussion, not only for those times of crisis when a personal value is challenged or painful competing claims are present, but also to allow employees to fully examine the range of options available, to anticipate pitfalls, and to explore creative ways of resolving their dilemmas.[20]

Character and Virtue Ethics

Ethical rules, principles, and codes can serve important functions as guides to ethical communication in organizations. But rules, principles, and codes are not enough. "Corporate culture and organizational policy are powerful forces that can mold the ethical spirit of an organization, but they are no substitute for the character of individual employees."[21]

Oliver Williams and Patrick Murphy explore the ethics of virtue as a moral theory for business.[22] They believe that ethical virtues can be shaped by our individual choices and encouraged by the "environments within which we live and work." In developing a proposed decision or policy, a theory of virtue prompts the developer to ask two key questions: What sort of person am I shaping? What sort of organization am I shaping? Moral vision and moral sensitivity—the abilities to "see" ethical implications of actions and communication where others do not—play central roles in virtue theory. However, Williams and Murphy also note that a "business organization can so shape people that they do not 'see' the ethical dimensions of the professional world." They argue: "Underpinned by a theory of virtue, an ethical corporate culture, through an ingrained set of habits and perspectives, trains all those in its purview to see things in a certain way and hence is likely to predispose them toward ethical behavior." In addition, role models have a vital function in a theory of virtue. We are educated and inspired by the behavior of moral role models we encounter directly or by examples of ethical behavior embodied in stories we hear about the organization.[23]

Several scholars suggest clusters of ethical virtues that they believe are especially appropriate for individuals in organizations. In his discussion of the virtues in a professional setting, William May advocates the relevance of virtues such as honesty, respect, benevolence, promise keeping, prudence, perseverance, courage, integrity, concern for the public good, compassion, justice, and humility.[24] In *Ethics and Excellence*, Robert Solomon develops an Aristotelian approach that stresses personal character and virtue in a business context.[25] He argues that his approach would encourage the "flourishing" of the individual, the business, and the society not just in the bottom-line sense of success but in the broader promotion of "excellence." At length Solomon discusses "the basic business virtues" of honesty, fairness, trust, and toughness and also the "virtues of the self" within a corporation of honor, loyalty, friendliness, and a sense of shame. Additionally important in his view are caring, compassion, and the "ultimate" virtue of justice. Matthew W. Seeger and Robert R. Ulmer examine two cases of organizational crisis using virtue ethics.[26] From their analysis of these two cases, they identify three virtues, immediacy of response, supportiveness of victims, and rebuilding and renewal, which are based in the values of corporate social responsibility and entrepreneurship.

A Model of Organizational Integrity

After extensive research with several thousand employees in almost a dozen organizations in the United States, Julie Belle White and Doug Wallace developed an organizational integrity audit from which they derived a Model of Organizational Integrity.[27] Their integrity audit identifies ethical standards characteristic of an ethical organizational climate. "The Model of Organizational Integrity describes organizational 'habits of the heart' which are akin to the personal virtues giving moral muscle to individuals of integrity. Through constant exercise of these habits the group develops the will and ability to handle ethical issues well." Six habits along with specific commitments and practices to implement them comprise the model. Here they are in paraphrased form.

Habit: Solving Ethical Problems Directly and Reflectively. The commitment to take an ethical stance involves taking an ethical viewpoint when discussing issues, being willing individually and collectively to tackle ethical problems, and striving to have the organization's ethical standards reflected in its actual priorities. The commitment to use responsive and responsible processes means seeking help when an ethical problem arises, persistently seeking to solve the ethical problem, considering the means used to solve the ethical problem to be as important as the goal sought, and willingness to accept consequences of ethical decisions (including negative ones). The commitment to dedicate and utilize resources involves spending necessary money, taking sufficient time, and securing necessary information to solve the ethical problem. The commitment to seek options requires the active search for options and the careful consideration of alternative courses of action.

Habit: Interacting Responsibly. The commitment to follow principles of justice and care requires that people be treated both fairly and with sensitivity. The commitment to interact with trust and respect involves showing respect for others' views and striving to trust and be trusted by individuals and groups. The commitment to communicate openly means being honest and open in relationships, freely sharing feelings and ideas, and communicating both good and bad news. The commitment to encourage dissent requires allowing dissent and allowing advocates of diverse ethical views to voice their positions.

Habit: Modeling Integrity. The commitment to have ethical role models throughout the organization demands that "the head of the organization publicly practices ethical values," that organizational leaders behave as good ethical models, and that "throughout the organization there are examples of individuals who act out their commitment to do the right thing." The commitment to assume responsibility for actions means that throughout the organization people feel free to admit their mistakes and people take responsibility for ethical decision making.

Habit: Sharing Organizational Purposes and Directions. The commitment to develop and implement an ethical organizational mission means that the organization clearly states and promotes its mission and ethical values and that the organization's ethical values are reflected in its mission and goals. The commitment to establish accountability requires communication and enforcement of organizational ground rules for ethical behavior, the holding of people accountable throughout the organization, the provision of an organizational structure that clearly indicates where ethical responsibility rests, the provision of a structure that facilitates adequate planning and participation, and organizational insistence on "compliance with laws and regulations."

Habit: Valuing Stakeholder Perspectives. The commitment to act as stewards means that the organization believes in "acting to protect the welfare of others"—in following the principle of stewardship. The commitment to consider and involve stakeholders requires that the viewpoints of all of those who have a stake in its decisions are considered by the organization, that "those affected by a decision are involved in the decision-making process," and that possible consequences of a decision are anticipated and prepared for.

Habit: Practicing Personal Integrity. The commitment to be consistent means that persons know the ethical thing to do and do it, that the values of individuals and the organization are consistent, and that members practice the organization's standards. At the same time, the commitment to act with courage demands that persons are "true to their own personal ethical values" and are willing to "pay the price" for acting ethically even if at odds with the organization.

A Typology for Analyzing Communication Ethics

Charles Redding suggests asking a nonexhaustive series of questions to understand how ethically suspect and unethical communication functions within an organization:[28] (1) "What messages or other communication events are perceived by which perceivers as unethical?" (2) Why? What ethical criteria are used to justify the ethical evaluations? (3) "In what respects do these criteria seem grounded in organizational (or other) cultures?" (4) "What are the consequences of unethical communication?" What are the impacts or effects of unethical communication, for example, on organizational policies or decisions, on evaluations of employee performance, or on development of trust in vertical, horizontal, and group relationships?

Redding also describes an exploratory typology, a tentative set of categories, of unethical "messages or message-related events as they frequently are observed in organizational life." Here is his set of categories in paraphrased and summary form: *Coercive* (intimidating, repressive, threatening) communication reflects abuses of power or authority involving unjustified invasions of an individual's autonomy. Coercive communication includes intolerance of dissent and restrictions on freedom of speech, refusal to listen, resorting to formal rules and regulations to stifle discussion or avoid complaints. *Destructive* (aggressive, abusive, insensitive) communication attacks others' self-esteem, reputation, or deeply held feelings; reflects unconcern or contempt for others' basic values. Destructive communication includes insults, derogatory innuendoes, negative labels, jokes (especially those based on gender, race, sex, religion, or ethnicity), put-downs, backstabbing, character assassination, using silence to avoid expected feedback to others, using "truth" as a weapon to launch hurtful personal attacks or to reveal information to unauthorized persons. *Deceptive* (dishonest, unfair, lying) communication intentionally distorts the truth in order to deceive or cheat. Deceptive communication includes evasive and deliberately misleading messages, intentional ambiguity to mislead, euphemisms to cover up defects or neutralize unpleasant facts. *Intrusive* communication violates "privacy" rights. Intrusive communication includes use of hidden cameras, use of computer technologies to monitor employee behavior, surveillance. *Secretive* communication includes hoarding information, using silence or unresponsiveness to mislead, sweeping information under the rug that, if revealed, would expose wrongdoing or incompetence. *Manipulative-exploitative* communication satisfies personal gain or shows unconcern for others by exploiting their fears, prejudices, or lack of knowledge. Manipulative-exploitative communication includes that which reflects a patronizing or condescending attitude toward others.

For our purposes, Redding's questions and categories can alert potential and actual members of an organization to possible unethical or ethically dubious communication. Consider now your reactions to his categories and examples. Are there other categories of unethical communication that you believe should be included? If so, why? To what extent do you agree with him that intentional ambiguity, as he describes it, is unethical? Later in this chapter this topic will be addressed more fully, and it already has been explored earlier in chapter 7, "Some Basic Issues." When might use of euphemistic language be considered ethical and acceptable?[29] How unethical is it for employers to monitor employee computer use to stop use for personal rather than organizational business? Redding intends his questions and typology to be used by researchers to study unethical communication within an organization. One application of his framework (along with a feminist perspective on ethics) is the study by Marifran Mattson and Patrice Buzzanell of the communication ethics involved in an actual case of job loss in an organization.[30]

Ethical Standards for Communication in Organizations

We now turn to additional sets of ethical criteria that specifically have been suggested for promoting ethical communication in organizations. In several writings, George Cheney and Phillip Tompkins have drawn upon Kenneth Burke's concept of "identification" as central to persuasion and explored its functioning in organizational communication settings.[31] Humans identify with other humans, groups, objects, institutions, and symbols to the degree that there are perceived to be substantial commonalities of values, beliefs, attitudes, goals, language, nonverbal symbols, images, and even common enemies. Identifications can have both powerful positive potentials and potent negative pitfalls, not only for individuals but also for organizations.

Cheney and Tompkins turn to Henry W. Johnstone, Jr., for the ethical standards they advocate to guide organizational communication. Here you may want to reread the earlier discussion of Johnstone's view of humans as persuaders in chapter 3. They believe that Johnstone's ethical stance harmonizes with Burke's view of rhetoric and offers a sound set of ethical principles for organizational communication. They accept Johnstone's premise that a defining characteristic of human nature is the capacity to persuade and to be persuaded. Also, they accept Johnstone's Basic Imperative: "So act in each instance to encourage, rather than suppress, the capacity to persuade and to be persuaded, whether the capacity in question is yours or another's." Johnstone's four ethical duties of resoluteness, openness, gentleness, and compassion are modified by Cheney and Tompkins for application in organizational communication contexts and become guardedness, accessibility, nonviolence, and empathy.

Guardedness. Communicators in organizations should use their own persuasive abilities to assess thoroughly overt and subtle messages from the organization and should avoid automatically and unthinkingly accepting the conventional "way things are" viewpoint. The often subtle use of the assumed "we" in organizational messages may or may not accurately reflect the degree of identification an employee really feels toward an idea, policy, or organization. Inappropriate self-identification may occur, for example, when an employee confuses his or her power or status with the power or status of the company.

Accessibility. Communicators in organizations should be open to the possibility of being changed by messages of others—of being persuaded. Our dogmatically held beliefs or narrowly focused viewpoints that blind us to useful information, a different view of a problem, or alternative solutions need to be offset or minimized. Guardedness and accessibility are ethical duties of organization members toward themselves. Ethical duties of members toward others are nonviolence and empathy.

Nonviolence. Certainly coercion, overt or subtle, of others is ethically undesirable. What are some subtle forms of coercion that may occur in an organizational context? Also, members should avoid using a persuasive stance that advocates one position as the one-and-only reasonable position. Such a "one best way" norm often guides an organization's policies and procedures.

Empathy. The empathic communicator genuinely listens to the arguments, opinions, values, and assumptions of others, is open to differing viewpoints, sets aside stereotypes triggered by labels or nonverbal cues, and respects the rights of all persons as persons to hold diverse views. In the organizational setting, notes Cheney, empathy involves the balancing of individual and organizational interests. Cheney and Tompkins believe that the ethic for organizational communication that they advocate facilitates celebration of individual values within the organizational context and minimizes "mindlessness" in performance of duties by forcing members to ask, "What are we doing?" The ethic promotes a sense of "community" that stresses cooperation, dignity, equality, and local involvement. Finally, the ethic encourages consideration of "purpose" so that overemphasis on means and techniques is minimized.

In chapter 2, Karl Wallace's "Four Moralities" approach was summarized in some detail. You are encouraged to review that discussion. Pamela

Shockley-Zalabak believes that Wallace's approach provides appropriate ethical guidelines for evaluating communication in organizational situations.[32] After summarizing Wallace's *Habit of Search, Habit of Justice, Habit of Preferring Public to Private Motivation,* and *Habit of Respect for Dissent*, she overtly applies them to organizational communication:

> When applied to the organizational setting, these guidelines suggest that individuals and groups are engaging in ethical communication behaviors when they thoughtfully analyze problems and issues, are open to diverse types and sources of information, conduct their deliberations openly without hidden agendas, and not only respect differing viewpoints but encourage disagreement and dissent in order to produce superior ideas and solutions. From this perspective, unethical organizational communication behavior suppresses examining issues, withholds relevant information in order to pursue personal interests or motivations, and uses dissent to press for personal rather than organizational advantage.

Moral Silence, Deafness, and Blindness

In his book, *The Muted Conscience: Moral Silence and the Practice of Ethics in Business,* Frederick Bird explores ways in which an organization member's "muted conscience" ("moral muteness") is manifested in the usually unethical practices that he describes as moral silence, moral deafness, and moral blindness.[33] The contributing factors that cause moral silence, deafness, and blindness are cultural, individual, and organizational in nature.

Cultural contributing factors include a dominant economic philosophy of rational self-interest, beliefs about the degree to which change is possible, beliefs about the degree to which laws should direct human behavior, and belief in tolerance of virtually all individual expression. The *individual* factors contributing to a weak or tepid moral conscience include fear of additional interactions in which we are vulnerable or lack control; a sense of futility or resignation that whatever we do is either trivial or is not perfect enough; fear that speaking up might involve us or implicate us in a questionable act; our claim that we are preoccupied with numerous, much more pressing and significant problems; and a feeling of being unable to state our concerns clearly and precisely. *Organizational* contributing factors (structures, policies, norms) include the discouraging or penalizing of dissent, questioning, or ethical criticism; the pattern of top-down accountability in which persons at upper levels in the organization hold those below accountable, but those at lower levels are not allowed to hold those above them accountable; an ineffective pattern of horizontal communication in which group rivalries and avoidance of openly discussing conflicts are hindrances; and the retarding of organizational learning because complacency or overconfidence undermines belief in the need for more knowledge.[34]

Moral silence includes avoiding whistle-blowing on abuses, misconduct, or violations whether legal or ethical; not voicing objection to policies or agreements that are ethically questionable; and not discussing aspects of decisions that actually are ethically debatable. Also, moral silence includes not advocating ideals and not arguing strongly enough for policies that would, among other outcomes, foster achievement of morally valued objectives. And moral silence also may be holding others insufficiently accountable through our own lack of adequate feedback to them in either supervisory or peer relationships. While Bird believes it usually is ethically wrong to be morally silent, he contends that there may be a few exceptional or temporary circumstances when it is morally justified. Such exceptions would include bargainers in negotiations not disclosing what their final positions would be; publicly withholding moral truths about someone to avoid public ridicule of that person or feeding malicious gossip—the ethical concerns could be raised in appropriate private settings; not revealing confidences to others who have no legitimate claims to the information.[35]

Moral deafness includes inattentiveness by not being willing to listen; not striving to make sense of what is being said; not focusing sufficiently to discern what is really important; and not making an effort to take interest in the message. "Attending to others," says Bird, "calls for us to take what others say seriously enough so that in our responses we attempt to reply to the particular concerns and issues they raise, even if in the process we reach quite different conclusions." Moral deafness also encompasses not being willing to hear bad news; not seeking out bad news that might be crucial; not comprehending messages because of an unresolved misunderstanding or our clinging to stereotypes or inappropriate presumptions; and unwillingness to consider seriously the accounts of others. As with moral silence, there may be rare temporary circumstances where moral deafness is justified ethically.[36]

Moral blindness includes not perceiving well by losing sight of issues, problems, or standards; failing to foresee consequences of actions; and not recognizing moral dimensions of organizational life such as obligations, promises, agreements, ethical principles, and ethical expectations. Moral blindness also includes misinterpreting or misunderstanding problems and issues because of ideological bias, stereotyping, and self-deception. And moral blindness includes seeing that lacks motivated vision, such as seeing that lacks scope, passion, concern, and awareness of opportunity. Again, while moral blindness generally is unethical, Bird argues it might temporarily and on occasion be justified ethically. One circumstance might be the avoidance of looking at one set of things in order to focus on another more important set of items. Another circumstance might involve overlooking minor ethical lapses in self or others in order to continue cooperative efforts and organizational commitments.[37]

Finally, Bird notes some of the undesirable consequences of moral silence, deafness, and blindness: ethical issues and unethical behavior are not addressed; problems of accountability and responsibility are aggravated or clouded; moral stress on and in organization members is intensified; available moral resources such as ideals, values, vision, imagination, and concern are neglected; and the role of ethics in the organization is confused, ignored, trivialized, or made superficial.[38]

Confronting Ethical Transgressions

When organizational members observe ethical misconduct, they face the difficulty of deciding how to respond. Michael E. Roloff and Gaylen D. Paulson note that not all instances of observed misconduct are addressed, and they propose using the social confrontation framework as a means for understanding why some people choose inaction after observing ethical transgressions.[39] Newell and Stutman developed the social confrontation framework to study the ways in which people confront someone for relational transgressions.[40] However, Roloff and Paulson argue that the framework can also be used to better understand people's responses to ethical breaches.

Roloff and Paulson discuss three stages of social confrontation. The first stage, preconfrontation, addresses the actions that occur prior to the observer initiating interaction with the transgressor. Many people do not confront a transgressor immediately and the preconfrontation stage may help to explain why this is the case. During the preconfrontation stage, sensemaking and action formation occur. Sensemaking involves processes that enable the witness to assure that the observed behavior was indeed a transgression. The processes may include assessing the accurateness of one's interpretation, monitoring the transgressor's behaviors for additional information about the observed behavior, and talking with others about the event to verify perceptions of misconduct.

Once one is relatively confident that an ethical transgression has occurred then action formation occurs. Newell and Stutman identified seven situational features influencing people's decision to confront transgressors.[41] First, does the action require urgent action? Will it cause serious harm? Has this happened frequently? Second, what is the relationship between the witness and the transgressor? Who has more power? How close are they? Third, to what extent does the witness perceive confrontation to be his or her responsibility? Fourth, what will be the transgressor's reaction to the confrontation? The more negative the anticipated reaction, the less likely the observer is to confront. Fifth, how many personal resources (time, emotional, physical, psychological, and financial) will the observer need to invest in the confrontation? Sixth, is this the appropriate time and place to confront the transgressor? Seventh, what are the costs and rewards of confronting? Is it likely that confrontation will lead to an end to the rule violation? How will the confrontation affect the relationship between confronter and transgressor? The assessment of the situation could lead to a decision not to confront, which may seem to be the easy and passive choice. Roloff and Paulson point out, however, that inaction may mean learning to cope with the stress of continued objectionable behavior. If the assessment of the situation leads to a decision to confront, then the witness needs to choose how to confront the transgressor. People attempt to accomplish three goals in confronting: presenting all arguments relevant to the wrongdoing, developing a clear and organized presentation, and engaging in behaviors that will prevent counterattacks from the transgressor.

The second stage of social confrontation, initial confrontation, begins when the witness tells the transgressor that his or her behavior violated a rule or norm. The way in which the initial confrontation is phrased sets the tone for the confrontation episode. Newell and Stutman indicate that initial confrontations vary in focus and explicitness. Some people focus on the behaviors of the transgressor while others focus on their own emotional reactions to the transgression. Some people are concerned about making the transgressor defensive, so they present their complaints in a more indirect manner. Other people are more direct in identifying the rule violation. After the interaction about the complaint, the sequence may be ended by remedying the problem, creating rules to prevent future transgressions, or no action.

The final stage in the social confrontation framework is postconfrontation. Closure of the initial confrontation episode does not mean the issue is settled and that there is no need for future confrontations. Even when confrontations end with some sort of remedy, it is possible that the remedy will not work and the need for confrontation will re-emerge. Two interaction patterns emerge in ongoing confrontations. One pattern is a scripted approach in which responses becomes predictable. Another pattern involves the confrontation becoming increasingly coercive. Either pattern can result in the observer giving up on the process or turning to others for support and perhaps blowing the whistle.

Whistle-Blowing

Employees in organizations sometimes face the complex and painful issue of whether to become a "whistle-blower"—to go outside normal internal communication and appeal channels in order to expose publicly a serious problem of safety, legality, or ethics not being adequately faced by the organization. Depending on a person's perspective or vested interests, people in our culture may view the whistle-blower either as a hero/heroine or as a traitor. On the one hand, whistle-blowers may be seen as patriots or, in the words of Myron and Penina Glazer in their book, *The Whistleblowers*, as "ethical resisters." On the other hand, our culture also enforces strong negative sentiment against the informer, squealer, fink, snitch, or tattler.

What guidelines might we use, for ourselves or in assessing actions of others, to separate responsible from irresponsible whistle-blowing? "Ethical

Tension Points in Whistleblowing" are explored at length by J. Vernon Jensen, and his judicious analysis merits reading in its entirety.[42] Jensen's two concluding paragraphs capture the complexity of both the procedural and substantive tension points to be resolved by the responsible whistle-blower:

> In summary, a conscientious whistleblower struggles with a number of ethical tension points. Many reside in procedural decisions which the whistle-blower has to make. (1) Am I fairly and accurately depicting the seriousness of the problem? (2) Have I secured the information properly, analyzed it appropriately, and presented it fairly? (3) Do my motives spring from serving a public need more than from serving a personal desire? (4) Have I tried fully enough to have the problem corrected within the organization? (5) Should I blow the whistle while still a member of the organization or after having left it? (6) Should I reveal my identity or keep it secret? (7) Have I made my claims with proper intensity and with appropriate frequency? (8) How ethical have I been in selecting my audience? (9) How ethical is it for me, a participant in the functioning of the group, to assume the role of a judge? (10) How ethical is it to set into motion an act which will likely be very costly to many people?
>
> In addition, in trying to balance loyalties in many directions, the sensitive whistleblower encounters a number of substantive ethical dilemmas. (1) How fully am I living up to my moral obligations to the well-being of my organization? (2) How fully am I living up to my moral obligations to my colleagues in the group? (3) Am I appropriately upholding the ethical standards of my profession? (4) How adversely will my action affect my family and other primary groups? (5) Am I being true to myself, to my own integrity and well-being? (6) How will my action affect the health of such basic values as freedom of expression, independent judgment, courage, fairness, cooperativeness, and loyalty?

The complexities experienced by whistle-blowers are illustrated in the 2002 *Time* "Persons of the Year" article (December 30, 2002/January 6, 2003, pp. 30–60), which describes the experiences of the three female whistle-blowers who brought attention to the practices of the FBI, Enron, and WorldCom.

Ethics for Communication Consulting and Training

Organizations often use communication experts, whether employed within the organization or hired as external consultants, to diagnose communication problems, propose appropriate solutions, or to train employees in improved communication skills. Labels such as training, organizational development, or human systems development frequently identify these functions for an organization. Communication experts may offer programs in public speaking, presentation of proposals or reports, argumentation, persuasion, interpersonal communication, nonsexist/nonracist communication, nonverbal communication, small group decision making, interviewing, listening, leadership, horizontal and vertical communication systems, and external organizational communication.

Charles Redding suggests five minimal yet challenging ethical guidelines that he believes all communication trainers should follow.[43] (1) Respect the integrity of the individual trainee. Individual dignity is fostered by deemphasizing rote learning of tasks and prescriptive drills and by capitalizing on the contributions and views of the trainee. (2) Provide the opportunity for self-actualization. To enhance each trainee's ability to achieve his or her true potential, deemphasize blind obedience to routine task and role specifications and to highly programmed ways of learning. Encourage creativity and autonomy in job performance and innovative and participative modes of learning. (3) Encourage the exercise of critical faculties. While not sowing seeds of discord or undermining motivation to carry out tasks, the trainer should encourage trainees to keep an "attitude of open-minded inquiry toward the directives, the mission, and the rhetoric of the organization." Rather than blind, "rah-rah" loyalty, stress should be on a realistic perception of the organizational system (including corporate politics) and on freedom to express doubts and to question what is being done. (4) Devote explicit attention to ethical problems and issues. A simple mind-set solely of results-orientation or ends-always-justify-the-means is replaced with an application of complexity in ethical judgment and of multiple relevant ethical criteria. (5) Demonstrate concern for long-term development of trainees. The trainer will devote attention not only to the trainees' skills for their immediate job but also to insights and techniques relevant to future career opportunities.

Daniel Montgomery, Daryl Wiesman, and Peter DeCaro offer a working proposal for an ethical code for communication consultants.[44] The first section focuses on the behavior of the communication consultant, emphasizing professional competence and courtesy, propriety, and integrity in communication. The second section focuses on "the communication consultants' ethical responsibility to clients." Those responsibilities include maintaining the client's interests as primary, protecting the client's autonomy and independent decision making, using validated and effective procedures, using peer consultation and review, maintaining client confidentiality and privacy, charging fees appropriate for the services performed, and disclosing the consultant's qualifications, training, and expertise in advertisements and public announcements. The third section addresses the communication consultant's responsibilities to third parties. Communication consultants should be committed to protecting noncontractual parties affected by their actions and avoiding intentional damage to the reputation of another professional. The final section focuses on the communication consultant's "responsibility to the profession, society, and continued professional development." These responsibilities include supporting and promoting the profession, servicing the community through pro bono activities, and remaining informed on research, innovations, and techniques so the consultant can provide up-to-date services.

Ethics in Public Relations

Public relations is a crucial communication function for most modern organizations, whether they be business, union, military, governmental, educational, religious, or social service organizations. This important function may be performed by a single person or a staff, by employees within the organization or an external public relations consultant. Increasingly the function may exist under such labels as public affairs, public information, or corporate communications. Audiences addressed through public relations include internal ones, such as line employees, supervisors, managers, or volunteers, and external ones, such as customers, stockholders, news media, government agencies, donors, critics, competitors, and the public-at-large.

Today public relations encompasses not only the transmission of information to the public but also the advocacy of corporate positions on public issues. Public relations is included among a number of standard management functions typical in organizations. According to the Public Relations Society of America, the public relations management function encompasses numerous tasks.[45] Public attitudes and issues that might positively or negatively impact the organization's plans or operations are anticipated, analyzed, and interpreted to management. Management at all levels is counseled with regard to policy decisions, courses of action, and communication, while at the same time taking into account public ramifications and the organization's societal responsibilities. On a continuing basis, programs of action and communication to achieve public understanding necessary for the success of the organization's aims are researched, conducted, and evaluated. Such programs may include marketing, fund-raising, employee relations, and community or governmental relations. The organization's efforts to influence or change public policy are planned and implemented. The staff and facilities necessary to accomplish all of the above must be managed.

Consider for a moment your answer to some of the following troubling ethical questions that a public relations practitioner might face.[46] Would I lie to my boss or staff? Would I lie on behalf of a client or employer? Would I help to conceal a dangerous situation, hazardous condition, or illegal act? Would I use deception to gain information about another practitioner's client? Would I attempt to bribe reporters or government officials with a gift, travel, or information? Would I present information that represents only part of the truth? Would I present true but misleading information in an interview or news conference that will mask some unpleasant fact? Would I hide or destroy evidence? Would I break a trust or confidence?

Finally, how would you respond to the following example?[47] Assume that you are employed in the public relations department of a large corporation. Your supervisor assigns you the task of presenting a series of speeches to community groups in a city where your company has just built a new production facility. In the speech prepared by your supervisor, you will describe the services and advantages of the plant that will benefit the community. But during a visit to the plant to familiarize yourself with its operation, you discover that the plant cannot actually deliver most of the services and advantages promised in the speech. Should you go ahead and present the speech as your supervisor prepared it? Should you refuse to give it at all? What changes might you in good conscience make to the speech? With or without your supervisor's approval? What ethical standards might you use in making your decisions? Why? What additional ethical issues might confront you in this situation?

Examples of Ethical Problems

A survey of typical problematic situations in organizational communication ethics should sensitize us to complex and less-than-ideal circumstances, help us identify relevant ethical issues, and encourage us to consider several rather than only one ethical standard.[48] Pamela Shockley-Zalabak provides excellent illustrations of varied ethical dilemmas in organizational communication. We will summarize and adapt only a few of them.[49] Communication specialists "interview, conduct surveys, facilitate meetings, advise and counsel individuals, review documents, and in a variety of other ways generate data important to their jobs." During both data collection and dissemination activities, "ethical decisions are made concerning what should remain confidential, who has a need to know, how accurate the information is, and what the criteria of interpretation are."

Assume that you are being interviewed for a job and tell the interviewer that you have a skill that you really do not possess. You are highly motivated to do excellent work if hired. What ethical criteria should apply? Does your motivation make your deception acceptable? When being interviewed or submitting an employment résumé, is it more unethical to include untrue material than to omit relevant but negative true material? In what circumstances, if any, would you argue that falsification of a job résumé is ethically justifiable? In what way might the nature or amount of falsification influence your ethical assessment? In your view, what is the difference, if any, between unethical falsification and ethically acceptable exaggeration?

In your work group, do you keep information about your mistakes hidden from your supervisor in order to appear more competent than you are? Do you blame others for problems even though you legitimately share some of the responsibility? In a supervisory or managerial role, you must give feedback to others about their performance. Are you hesitant to give negative feedback to a problem employee and thus provide him or her with a false sense of security? Does this decision involve an ethical issue, or are you simply being realistic that the worker would be demoralized if criticized?

A member of the night shift's manufacturing group comes to you as her personnel contact and expresses concern about drug use on the production line. She avoids giving you specific details for fear that the persons involved might discover who exposed them. While she urges you to investigate immediately, she also asks you not to involve her in any way. Among your options are the following (you may think of others): you can ask the worker to provide more concrete information before you will take action; you could ask your supervisor for advice on your next step; you could attempt to investigate on your own; at a general staff meeting, you could mention (without names) the drug problems the plant is experiencing and observe the reactions of your peers; without further evidence, you could ignore the situation. What would you do? What should you do?

Although Pamela Lutgen-Sandvik's research on workplace bullying does not focus specifically on ethical issues, it does address another problematic interaction pattern that raises ethical concerns.[50] Workplace bullying is on the rise, and the United States lags behind other countries in identifying and addressing this workplace problem. Workplace bullying is defined as involving "situations in which employees are subjected to repeated, persistent negative acts that are intimidating, malicious, and stigmatizing."[51] Imagine having a boss who on a regular basis got so angry that he or she turned red in the face and screamed at you, pointed a finger at you and spit while talking and even threw office supplies around the room. How would you respond to this bullying? For example, should you file a formal grievance? Should you find allies who would help fight the bully? Should you retaliate by gossiping about the bully? To what extent is it the organization's responsibility to take action? What ethical standards should be used to address workplace bullying?

Linda Klebe Trevino provides an additional complex example.[52] As a middle-level manager, you express concern for public safety to your supervisor, who has asked you to falsify data on reports. The supervisor assures you that you are not responsible for any negative consequences of such falsification, since higher officials in the organization are aware of the situation and will take responsibility for the consequences. What are the ethical courses of action you might take? How ethical is the supervisor's response to you? Why?

In *Bureaucratic Propaganda*, David Altheide and John Johnson examine the nature of official reports.[53] In their view, bureaucratic propaganda is "any report produced by an organization for evaluation and other practical purposes that is targeted for individuals, committees, or publics who are unaware of its promotive character and the editing process that shaped the report." You are urged to examine the diverse examples and case studies presented in their book. For instance, what ethical issues and criteria might be relevant for assessing official reports that "promote organizational careers, assign responsibility for a particular act to an 'enemy,' and in general 'cover your ass' from revelation before a sanctioning body?"

Consider the examples and arguments of Eric Eisenberg, who contends that intentional (strategic) ambiguity often is a necessary and ethical technique in organizational communication.[54] Strategic ambiguity promotes "unified diversity" in an organization by fostering "agreement on abstractions without limiting specific interpretations." Intentional ambiguity may foster creativity and lessen "acceptance of one standard way of viewing organizational reality." Organizational goals must be expressed ambiguously to satisfy multiple constituencies and to allow flexibility in adjusting to future conditions. Within an organization in interpersonal relationships, strategic ambiguity may be an appropriate alternative to brutally frank honesty, on the one hand, or to secrecy or lying, on the other hand. However, Alan J. Zaremba has critiqued strategic ambiguity as being patently unethical because it is a form of deception.[55] You are urged to review earlier discussions of the ethics of intentional ambiguity and vagueness in chapter 7 as well as read Eisenberg's analysis and Zaremba's critique in their entirety in order to identify more clearly the issues and standards you believe are most relevant for assessing specific strategic uses of ambiguity by and in organizations.

Cynicism and Relevance

"Teaching ethics to business students cannot alter the facts of business practice. In a capitalistic system, greed is the main fuel that drives the engine. Ethics works against greed. Business practice is not inherently immoral, but it is amoral. For virtually all decisions, ethics are irrelevant." Although the author of this cynical assessment is Herbert Rotfeld, a professor of advertising, it sounds similar to the sentiments voiced by the wheeler-dealer, raider-trader character played by Michael Douglas in the Hollywood film, *Wall Street*.[56] The issues, approaches, and guidelines presented in this chapter have attempted to demonstrate the *relevance* of ethical concerns in corporate (and all organizational) decisions involving communication goals and techniques. Here, again, we see manifested the tension between *is* and *ought*—between what the situation is and what it ought to be.

"I am convinced that most of the unethical acts I have seen committed in business were performed by essentially honest people. But they were people who felt under great pressure to achieve. In their desire to make good—to 'win'—they compromised themselves." To what extent do you agree with this judgment from a consultant on human resources management, Gerald Ottoson?[57] One goal of this chapter has been to stress the formation of sound, ethical "character" in organization members individually, and in the ethical "culture" of the organization as a whole, so that such compromises in communication can be kept to a minimum or avoided.

Notes

[1] Ethics Resource Center, *National Business Ethics Survey 2005: How Employees View Ethics in Their Organizations 1994–2005* (Washington, DC: Ethics Resource Center, 2005).

[2] Charles Redding, "Professionalism in Training—Guidelines for a Code of Ethics," paper presented at meeting of the Speech Communication Association, Chicago, November 1984. For example, see William G. Scott and David K. Hart, *Organizational America* (Boston: Houghton

Mifflin, 1979); John Sabini and Maury Silver, *The Moralities of Everyday Life* (New York: Oxford University Press, 1982); Charles D. Pringle and Justin G. Longenecker, "The Ethics of MBO," *Academy of Management Review,* 7 (1982): 305–312.

3 Robert Jackall, "Moral Mazes: Bureaucracy and Managerial Work," *Harvard Business Review,* 61 (1983): 118–130; also see Jackall, *Moral Mazes: The World of Corporate Managers* (New York: Oxford University Press, 1988).

4 Alfred G. Smith, "The Ethic of the Relay Man," in *Communication: Ethical and Moral Issues,* Lee Thayer, ed. (New York; Gordon and Breach, 1973), pp. 313–324.

5 See, for example, Richard T. DeGeorge, *Business Ethics,* 2nd ed. (New York: Macmillan, 1986), pp. 82–100; Barbara Toffler, *Tough Choices: Managers Talk Ethics* (New York: Wiley, 1986), pp. 35–38.

6 Dennis F. Thompson, *Political Ethics and Public Office* (Cambridge: Harvard University Press, 1987), pp. 40–65.

7 Matthew Seeger, "Ethics and Communication in Organizational Contexts: Moving from the Fringe to the Center," *American Communication Journal,* 5 (2001): 1–10. http://acjournal.org/holdings/vol5/special/seeger/seeger.htm

8 Terrence E. Deal and Allen A. Kennedy, *Corporate Cultures: The Rites and Rituals of Corporate Life* (Reading, MA: Addison-Wesley, 1982); Michael E. Pacanowsky and Nick O'Donnell-Trujillo, "Communication and Organizational Cultures," *Western Journal of Speech Communication,* 46 (1982): 115–130. Also see Gerald L. Pepper, *Communicating in Organizations: A Cultural Approach* (New York: McGraw-Hill, 1995).

9 DeGeorge, *Business Ethics,* pp. 96–97; also see Pamela Shockley-Zalabak, *Fundamentals of Organizational Communication,* 4th ed. (New York: Longman, 1999), pp. 425–434; Kathryn C. Rents and Mary Beth Debs, "Language and Corporate Values: Teaching Ethics in Business Ethics Writing Courses," *Journal of Business Communication,* 24 (Summer 1987): 37–48.

10 David Shulman, *The Role of Deception in the Workplace* (Ithaca, NY: Cornell University Press, 2007), pp. 144–155.

11 Jackall, *Moral Mazes,* pp. 191–204.

12 Bart Victor and John B. Cullen, "The Organizational Bases of Ethical Work Climates," *Administrative Science Quarterly,* 33 (1988): 101–125.

13 Ethics Resource Center, *National Business Ethics Survey 2005,* p. v.

14 Gerald Ottoson, "Essentials of an Ethical Corporate Climate," in *Doing Ethics in Business,* Donald G. Jones, ed. (Cambridge, MA: Oelgeschlager, Gunn & Hain, 1982), pp. 155–164; Michael R. Rion, "Training for Ethical Management at Cummins Engine," in *Doing Ethics in Business,* pp. 27–44; Toffler, *Tough Choices,* pp. 328–346; M. Cash Mathews, *Strategic Intervention in Organizations: Resolving Ethical Dilemmas* (Newbury Park, CA: Sage, 1988); Stanley A. Deetz, Sarah J. Tracy, and Jennifer Lynn Simpson, *Leading Organizations through Transition: Communication and Cultural Change* (Thousand Oaks, CA: Sage, 2000), ch. 6; Charlotte McDaniel, *Organizational Ethics: Research and Ethical Environments* (Burlington, VT: Ashgate, 2004), chs. 2, 6–8.

15 DeGeorge, *Business Ethics,* pp. 169–170; Douglas Sturm, "Assessing the Sun Company's Ethical Condition," in Jones, ed., *Doing Ethics in Business,* p. 110; Philip Meyer, *Ethical Journalism* (New York: Longman, 1987), pp. 189–200; Deetz, Tracy, and Simpson, *Leading Organizations through Transition,* pp. 138–141.

16 Ethics Resource Center, *National Business Ethics Survey 2005,* pp. v, 47–58. See also Linda K. Trevino and Gary R. Weaver, "Organizational Justice and Ethics Program 'Follow-Through': Influences on Employees' Harmful and Helpful Behavior," *Business Ethics Quarterly,* 11 (2001): 651–671.

17 United States Sentencing Commission, Chapter 8, *2004 Federal Sentencing Guidelines.* Retrieved May 21, 2007, from http://www.ussc.gov/2004guid/CHAP8.htm

18 Steven May, "Ethical Perspectives and Practices," in *Case Studies in Organizational Communication: Ethical Perspectives and Practices,* Steven May, ed. (Thousand Oaks, CA: Sage, 2006), pp. 35–38; Daniel Terris, *Ethics at Work: Creating Virtue in American Corporation* (Lebanon, NH: Brandeis University Press, 2005) pp. 6–9.

[19] Redding, "Professionalism in Training"; J. Weber, "Institutionalizing Ethics into the Corporation," *MSU Business Topics*, 29 (1981): 47–52.

[20] Toffler, *Tough Choices*, pp. 337–338. Also see Ronald R. Sims, *Ethics and Organizational Decision Making* (Westport, CT: Quorum, 1994), pp. 189–211; Spoma Jovanovic and Roy V. Wood, "Communication Ethics and Ethical Culture: A Study of the Ethics Initiative in Denver City Government," *Journal of Applied Communication Research*, 34 (November 2006): 386–405.

[21] Philip G. Clampitt, *Communicating for Managerial Effectiveness*, 2nd ed. (Thousand Oaks, CA: Sage, 2001), p. 254.

[22] Oliver F. Williams and Patrick Murphy, "The Ethics of Virtue: A Moral Theory for Business," in *A Virtuous Life in Business*, Oliver F. Williams and John W. Houck, eds. (Lanham, MD: Rowman and Littlefield, 1992), pp. 9–27; Patrick E. Murphy, "Character and Virtue Ethics in International Marketing," *Journal of Business Ethics*, 18 (January 1999): 101–124.

[23] See, for example, Terry L. Cooper and N. Dale Wright, eds., *Exemplary Public Administrators: Character and Leadership in Government* (San Francisco: Jossey-Bass, 1992).

[24] William F. May, "The Virtues in a Professional Setting," *Soundings: An Interdisciplinary Journal*, 67 (Fall 1984): 245–266.

[25] Robert C. Solomon, *Ethics and Excellence: Cooperation and Integrity in Business* (New York: Oxford University Press, 1992). Also see Solomon, *Ethics: A Short Introduction* (Dubuque, IA: Brown Benchmark, 1993), pp. 95–163.

[26] Matthew W. Seeger and Robert R. Ulmer, "Virtuous Responses to Organizational Crisis: Aaron Feuerstein and Milt Cole," *Journal of Business Ethics*, 31 (2001): 369–376.

[27] Julie Belle White, "Model of Organizational Integrity: Habits, Commitments, and Practices Indicative of an Organization's Ethical Climate," in *Proceedings of the Second National Communication Ethics Conference*, James A. Jaksa, ed. (Annandale, VA: Speech Communication Association, 1992), pp. 64–81. For a related but different view of what an ethical organization is, see May, "Ethical Perspectives and Practices," pp. 19–48.

[28] W. Charles Redding, "Ethics and the Study of Organizational Communication: When Will We Wake Up?," in *Responsible Communication: Ethical Issues in Business, Industry, and the Professions*, James A. Jaksa and Michael S. Pritchard, eds. (Cresskill, NJ: Hampton Press, 1996), pp. 17–40.

[29] For example, see Jackall, *Moral Mazes*, pp. 134–137.

[30] Marifran Mattson and Patrice M. Buzzanell, "Traditional and Feminist Organizational Communication: Ethical Analyses of Messages and Issues Surrounding an Actual Job Loss Case," *Journal of Applied Communication Research*, 27 (February 1999): 49–72.

[31] George Cheney, "Coping with Bureaucracy: Ethics and Organizational Relationships," presented at the Speech Communication Association Conference, Chicago, November 1986; George Cheney and Philip K. Tompkins, "Toward an Ethic of Identification," presented at the Burke Conference, Temple University, March 1984; George Cheney, "The Rhetoric of Identification and the Study of Organizational Communication," *Quarterly Journal of Speech*, 69 (1983): 143–158; George Cheney and Philip K. Tompkins, "Coming to Terms with Organizational Identification and Commitment," *Central States Speech Journal*, 38 (Spring 1987): 1–15.

[32] Shockley-Zalabak, *Fundamentals of Organizational Communication*, pp. 329–330.

[33] Frederick Bruce Bird, *The Muted Conscience: Moral Silence and the Practice of Ethics in Business* (Westport, CT: Quorum, 1996), pp. 1–26.

[34] Ibid., pp. 143–189.

[35] Ibid., pp. 27–53.

[36] Ibid., pp. 55–84.

[37] Ibid., pp. 85–121.

[38] Ibid., pp. 123–141.

[39] Michael J. Roloff and Gaylen D. Paulson, "Confronting Organizational Transgressions," in *Social Influences on Ethical Behavior in Organizations*, John M. Darley, David M. Messick, and Tom R. Taylor, eds. (Mahwah, NJ: Erlbaum, 2001), pp. 53–68.

[40] Sara E. Newell and Randall K. Stutman, "The Episodic Nature of Social Confrontation," *Communication Yearbook* 14, James A. Anderson, ed. (Newbury Park, CA: Sage, 1991), pp.

359–413; Sara E. Newell and Randall K. Stutman, "The Social Confrontation Episode," *Communication Monographs*, 55 (1988): 266–285.

[41] Newell and Stutman, "The Episodic Nature of Social Confrontation," pp. 382–384; also see Roloff and Gaylen, "Confronting Organizational Transgressions," pp. 58–59.

[42] J. Vernon Jensen, "Ethical Tension Points in Whistleblowing," *Journal of Business Ethics* (May, 1987): 321–328; Jensen, *Ethical Issues in the Communication Process* (Mahwah, NJ: Erlbaum, 1997), pp. 73–85. Also see Richard T. DeGeorge, *Business Ethics*, 3rd ed. (New York: Macmillan, 1990), pp. 200–216; Michael David, "Some Paradoxes of Whistleblowing," *Business and Professional Ethics Journal*, 15 (Spring 1996): 3–19.

[43] Redding, "Professionalism in Training"; also summarized in Gerald M. Goldhaber, *Organizational Communication*, 6th ed. (Dubuque, IA: Wm. C. Brown, 1993), pp. 340–344.

[44] Daniel Montgomery, Daryl W. Wiesman, and Peter DeCaro, "Toward a Code of Ethics for Organizational Communication Consultants: A Working Proposal," *American Communication Journal*, 5 (Fall 2001). http://www.acjournal.org/holdings/vol5/iss1/special/stewart.htm

[45] Official Statement on Public Relations adopted by the Public Relations Society of America Assembly, November 6, 1982, and reprinted in Otis Baskin and Craig Aronoff, *Public Relations: The Profession and the Practice*, 2nd ed. (Dubuque, IA: Wm. C. Brown, 1988), pp. 2–22. Also see Thomas H. Bivins, "Applying Ethical Theory to Public Relations," *Journal of Business Ethics*, 6 (April 1987): 195–200.

[46] Adapted from Don Bates, "The Role of the Public Relations Practitioner in Ethical Organizational Behavior," presented at Northern Illinois University, September 22, 1988, and from Baskin and Aronoff, *Public Relations*, pp. 85–86.

[47] Adapted from Donald B. McCammond, "Critical Incidents: The Practical Sides of Ethics," in *Public Relations: The Profession and the Practice*, 5th ed., D. Lattimore et al., eds. (New York: McGraw-Hill, 2004), pp. 84–85.

[48] Thompson, *Political Ethics and Public Office*, p. 9.

[49] Shockley-Zalabak, *Fundamentals of Organizational Communication*, pp. 442–451.

[50] Pamela Lutgen-Sandvik, "Take this Job and . . . Quitting and Other Forms of Resistance to Workplace Bullying," *Communication Monographs*, 73 (2006): 406–433; Lutgen-Sandvik, "The Communicative Cycle of Employee Emotional Abuse," *Management Communication Quarterly*, 16 (2003): 471–501. See also Gina Vega and Debra R. Comer, "Sticks and Stones May Break Your Bones, but Words Can Break Your Spirit: Bullying in the Workplace," *Journal of Business Ethics*, 58 (2005): 101–109; David Worman, "A Descriptive Investigation of Morality and Victimization at Work," *Journal of Business Ethics*, 45 (2003): 29–40.

[51] Sarah J. Tracy, Pamela Lutgen-Sandvik, and Jess K. Alberts, "Nightmares, Demons, and Slaves: Exploring the Painful Metaphors of Workplace Bullying," *Management Communication Quarterly*, 20 (2006): 148–185.

[52] Adapted from Linda Klebe Trevino, "Ethical Decision Making in Organizations: A Person-Situation Interactionist Model," *Academy of Management Review*, 11 (1986): 601–617.

[53] David L. Altheide and John M. Johnson, *Bureaucratic Propaganda* (Boston: Allyn & Bacon, 1980), pp. 1–43.

[54] Eric M. Eisenberg, "Ambiguity as Strategy in Organizational Communication," *Communication Monographs*, 51 (September 1984): 227–242.

[55] Alan Jay Zaremba, "A Critique of the Seminal Article Used to Support Strategic Ambiguity," paper presented at the Association for Business Communication Meeting (2003), Albuquerque, New Mexico. See also, Jim Paul and Christy A. Strbiak, "The Ethics of Strategic Ambiguity," *Journal of Business Communication*, 34 (1997): 149–159. For a case study demonstrating the questionable ethics of strategic ambiguity see, Robert R. Ulmer and Timothy L. Sellnow, "Consistent Questions of Ambiguity in Organizational Crisis Communication: Jack in the Box as a Case Study," *Journal of Business Ethics*, 25 (2000): 143–155.

[56] Herbert Rotfeld, "Ethics Training or not, Business Will Still Be Business," *Chicago Tribune*, February 29, 1988, sec. 1, p. 11.

[57] Ottoson, "Essentials of an Ethical Corporate Climate," p. 159.

10

Formal Codes of Ethics

Formal codes of ethics have been adopted or proposed by various communication-oriented professional associations, business organizations, and citizen-action groups in such fields as commercial advertising, public relations, technical writing, organizational consulting, print and broadcast journalism, and political campaigning. For some people, formal codes are a necessary mark of a true profession. For others, codes are worthless exercises in vagueness, irrelevance, and slick public relations.

Controversies surrounding computer communication on the Internet illustrate not only the tension between freedom and responsibility but also pressures for legalistic approaches to ethics and for the formation of formal codes of ethics. Should you be free to say or depict anything you want, without restriction, on the Internet—in an e-mail, in a chat room, or on a Web site? The freedom/responsibility tension is underscored by Frank Connolly, a professor of computer science at American University (*Washington Post National Weekly Edition*, Oct. 30–Nov. 5, 1995, p. 36): "With the Internet, we are in the situation where there are no controls, no cyber-cops, no speed limits. The other side of these freedoms is that individuals have to exercise responsibility for their actions." But there are pressures for controls and for formal rules of responsibility.

University officials, perhaps on your campus, have debated whether to apply to the surfing, e-mail, blogging, and downloading Internet activities of students existing campus speech codes that prohibit hate speech, pornography, and harassment, or whether to formulate specific codes of computer ethics to govern student use. On your campus, what official policies (set how and by whom?) govern ethically responsible student communication on the Internet? How adequately and appropriately do these policies speak to specific issues of communication ethics? In what ways do these policies actually seem to address matters of legality more than ethicality?

The early sections of this chapter are adopted (with permission of the editor) from Richard L. Johannesen, "What Should We Teach About Formal Codes of Communication Ethics?" *Journal of Mass Media Ethics*, 3, no. 1 (1988): 59–64.

We need to understand the range and complexity of pro and con arguments surrounding formal codes. We will summarize the major criticisms levied against codes. Then, standards for a sound ethical code will be presented. Finally, a number of positive functions of codes will be examined, with special emphasis on two: the argumentative function and the character-depiction function.

Objections to Formal Codes

What are some typical objections to or weaknesses of formal codes of ethics?[1] First, frequently they are filled with meaningless language, "semantically foggy clichés," and thus are too abstract, vague, and ambiguous to be usefully applied. For example, outsiders may interpret the unclear terms broadly as involving stringent standards while persons governed by the code may interpret them narrowly as allowing lesser standards.[2]

Second, their existence in the mass media, corporations, and political campaigning seems not to have promoted a significant improvement in ethicality of communication. Third, there is the danger that a code will be viewed as static, as settling matters once and for all. Fourth, standards in a code may appear universal when they are not. Contrary to face-value assumptions, the standards may not easily apply to cross-cultural communication or be flexibly applied in unique situations. Fifth, especially within journalism, some object that a formal code would inappropriately restrict the journalist's constitutional rights of free speech and free press. Sixth, many codes are castigated because they lack effective enforcement procedures to punish violators; they have no "teeth." Seventh, many codes are dismissed as mere public relations ploys aimed just at enhancing the group's image of responsibility with the public. Eighth, a code could be written cynically and manipulatively to provide approval of existing ethically suspect practices or policies by ignoring mention of them or by labeling them something other than what they actually are. Finally, members of an organization may come to believe that the code represents "all there is" to being ethical. As long as what they do or say is not specifically prohibited by the code, they may feel that they never need to raise additional ethical issues or consider additional ethical standards (such as their own personal ones or the ones of the larger society). In other words, organization members may take a very "legalistic" perspective on ethics (as discussed previously in chapter 6).

Developing a Sound Formal Code

Many of these objections might be lessened or removed. Drawing on suggestions made by Richard DeGeorge, John Kultgen, and others, we can describe guidelines for developing a sound formal code of ethics. First, the code should make clear which of its statements are *ideal goals* to be striven for but often not fully attained and which statements are *minimum conditions* that must be met to be considered ethical and to avoid punishment.[3] Second, under ordinary circumstances the code should not require heroic virtue, extreme sacrifice, or doing right no matter what the obstacles. Rather it should be aimed at persons of ordinary conscientiousness and persons willing to follow it on the condition that others do likewise.[4]

Third, language in the code should be clear and specific. Vagueness and ambiguity should be minimized. Key terms in code provisions, especially abstract value-laden terms, could be clarified through further explanation and concrete illustration. Among such terms might be distort, falsify, misrepresent, mislead, deceive, rational, reasonable, and public interest. Fourth, code provisions should be logically coherent. That is, relationships among provisions should be clear as to sequence, precedence, and scope.[5] For example, there could be some indication of the precedence among obligations to the client, the employer, the public, and the profession.

As a fifth guideline, the code should protect the general public interest and the interests of persons served by the group. The code should not be self-serving; it should not protect interests of the group at the expense of the public.[6] Sixth, code provisions should go beyond general admonitions against lying and cheating to focus on those facets of the group's functions "that pose particular and specialized temptations to its members."[7] Seventh, a code should stimulate continued discussion and reflection leading to possible modification or revision.[8] Eighth, a code for a profession or a business should provide ethical guidance for that profession as a whole, not just for individual members. For example, what action should be taken and by whom when the group as a whole, as an institution, acts unethically?[9]

As a ninth guideline, the code should make clear the general moral principles on which it is founded, the basic ethical values from which its provisions flow, such as justice, fairness, respecting rights of others, and weighing the consequences of an act for all those affected by it. DeGeorge illustrates the point: "The injunction, found in one code, to act in such a way that you would not be ashamed to have your actions exposed to the public—for instance in the headlines of a local newspaper—is a step in the right direction."[10] It is important to know not only *what* is the ethical thing to do but also *why* it is right. Tenth, provisions in a code for a specific organization should be developed through participation of a wide range of members of that organization. This means substantial participation by both management and labor, employers and employees, corporations and unions, higher- and lower-level professionals.[11]

A final and obvious guideline is that the code should be enforceable and enforced. There should be procedures and mechanisms for bringing charges and applying penalties. An enforcement system would provide mechanisms for interpreting what a code means and what it requires. A committee, board, or high-level executive officer, supported by necessary funds and staff, should administer fair procedures for reporting violations, investigating allegations, and reaching decisions.[12] Possible punishment options might include an informal warning, a request to cease a practice, a formal reprimand that becomes part of a record, suspension without pay, and expulsion or firing, possibly with a public explanation that justifies the action and names names.[13]

Useful Functions

We want to focus now on some of the useful functions of precisely worded ethical codes.[14] First, codes can educate new persons in a profession or business by acquainting them with guidelines for ethical responsibility based on the experience of predecessors and by sensitizing them to ethical problems specific to their field. Second, codes can narrow the problematic areas with which a person has to struggle; of course the more complex or unusual ethical problems still remain for deliberation. Third, the very process of developing the formal code can be a healthy one that forces participants to reflect on their goals, on means allowable to achieve those goals, and on their obligations to peers, to clients or customers, to employees, and to the public at large. A fourth function, openly urged in some organizations, is that an appropriate and effective voluntary code may minimize the need for cumbersome and intrusive governmental regulations. We move now to two additional functions of codes that we believe merit serious consideration, an argumentative function and a character-depiction function.

Argumentative Function

By an argumentative function we mean that it can serve as a starting point to stimulate professional and public scrutiny of major ethical quandaries in a field.[15] It could be the basis from which to launch a public debate over a specific communication practice. Or the standards in a code could provide focus as a corporation, profession, or other organization debates the ethicality of a communication policy *prior* to adoption or approval of that policy. As another argumentative application, provisions in a code could be cited by a communicator as justification for saying "no" to a communication practice requested of him or her by peers or employers.[16]

Richard Crable believes that formal ethical codes provide a visible and impersonal standard to which both critics and defenders of a communication practice can appeal in arguing their judgment.[17] The codes provide a "comparative standard by which to examine and justify behavior." By synthesizing and adapting the separate analyses of Richard Crable and of Peter Brown, we can sketch a range of argumentative claims that critics or defenders of a communication practice might use to assess ethicality in light of a code.[18] It could be argued that a particular practice (1) clearly is contrary to a precise, relevant, well-justified code; (2) is ethically suspect even though it falls outside the boundaries of any established code; (3) is ethical because the code invoked is irrelevant or inappropriate; (4) is unethical because, while the strict "letter" of the code was honored, the "spirit" of the code was violated; (5) is ethical because key terms of the code are too vague and ambiguous for precise or meaningful application; (6) is ethically justified because one applicable code is superseded by another relevant code, or because "higher" values take precedence over the formal code; (7) is ethical because the facts of the situation, including intent and context, are unclear; and (8) should be judged primarily by legal statutes rather than by an ethical code.

Character-Depiction Function

In her book, *Professional Ethics*, Karen Lebacqz suggests that formal ethical codes, especially in the professions, should be seen as having a function quite different from the typical one, namely, as rules for specific behavior or as admonitions concerning specific instances.[19] In her view, we must look beyond the action-oriented language of most codes ("do this," "avoid that") to the "overall picture of the type of person who is to *embody* those actions." As reconceptualized by Lebacqz, a code embodies a picture of the moral "character" to be expected of a professional in a given field; it would depict an ethical communicator's "being" collectively and over time. She contends that "codes do not give specific guidance for action as much as they say something about the character traits necessary for someone to be a professional." "In short," she says, "codes are geared primarily toward establishing expectations for character." In this view, codes are "guideposts to understand where stresses and tensions have been felt within a profession and what image of the good professional is held up to assist professionals through those stresses and tensions."

According to Lebacqz a wide range of professional codes reflect a core of central character traits, ethical principles, or obvious duties: "Justice, beneficence, non-maleficence, honesty, and fidelity." Often these are manifested in code provisions that collectively represent the ethical professional as fair, competent, honest, oriented toward the good of clients and society, and avoiding taking advantage of others by abusing knowledge or power.

Lebacqz believes that a "professional is called not simply to *do* something but to *be* something." At a fundamental level, codes depict a professional as "bound by certain ethical principles and as incorporating those principles *into his or her very character*." Ideally a code depicts the professional as "a person of integrity who not only does the 'right' thing, but is an *honorable person*." For example, a trustworthy person not only keeps a confidence but is "thoughtful about the impact" of decisions on others and is "sensitive to their needs and claims." An honest person "tries to avoid any kind of deception, not just explicit lies." Indeed, believes Lebacqz, "when we act, we not only do something, we also shape our own character. . . . And so each choice about what to do is also a choice about whom to *be*—or, more accurately, whom to become." This function of codes as embodying desirable character traits more than specific rules for specific actions is, we urge, a function overlooked and one that merits serious consideration.

Advertising Association Codes

The American Association of Advertising Agencies (AAAA) code of ethics was last revised in 1990. As you read the following standards, consider their degree of adequacy and the extent to which they presently are followed by advertisers. Association members agree to avoid intentionally producing advertising that contains:

1. False or misleading statements or exaggerations, visual or verbal
2. Testimonials that do not reflect the real choice of the individual(s) involved
3. Price claims that are misleading
4. Claims insufficiently supported or that distort the true meaning or practicable application of statements made by professional or scientific authority
5. Statements, suggestions, or pictures offensive to public decency or to minority segments of the population

While AAAA members acknowledge that there may be genuine differences of interpretation, they discourage advertising that is in questionable taste or that is intentionally irritating in sight and sound. And members agree that comparative ads with competing goods or services are governed by the same ethical standards as other types of ads.

The American Advertising Federation in 1984 adopted the following Advertising Ethics and Principles.

1. Advertising shall tell the truth, and shall reveal significant facts, the omission of which would mislead the public.
2. Advertising claims shall be substantiated by evidence in possession of the advertiser and advertising agency, prior to making such claims.
3. Advertising shall refrain from making false, misleading, or unsubstantiated statements or claims about a competitor or his products or services.
4. Advertising shall not offer products or services for sale unless such offer constitutes a bona fide effort to sell the advertised products or services and is not a device to switch consumers to other goods or services, usually higher priced.
5. Advertising of guarantees and warranties shall be explicit, with sufficient information to apprise consumers of their principal terms and limitations, or, when space or time restrictions preclude such disclo-

sures, the advertisement should clearly reveal where the full text of the guarantee or warranty can be examined before purchase.

6. Advertising shall avoid price claims which are false or misleading, or savings claims which do not offer provable savings.

7. Advertising containing testimonials shall be limited to those of competent witnesses who are reflecting a real and honest opinion or experience.

8. Advertising shall be free of statements, illustrations, or implications which are offensive to good taste or public decency.

The Code of Advertising issued by the Better Business Bureau in 1994 is a guide for advertisers, advertising agencies, and advertising media. It is very comprehensive and detailed in its coverage and much too lengthy to reproduce here (see: www.bbb.org/membership/codeofad.asp). Its guidelines encompass comparative pricing, claims of savings, credit offers, "bait and switch" offers, warranties and guarantees, layout and illustrations, comparative quality claims, contests, and results claims. Words and labels that frequently are abused get specific discussion: irregulars, seconds, factory to you, up to, sale, free, easy credit, as is, used, rebuilt, and discontinued. Superlative claims (the best, the most, etc.) are divided into objective (tangible quality and performance, subject to measurement against accepted standards or tests) and subjective (puffery—expressions of opinion or personal evaluation of intangible qualities). Puffery that misleads should be avoided. Misleading or confusing testimonials and endorsements include those that do not represent the current opinion of the endorser; that are quoted out of context, thus altering the meaning; that are literally true but create deceptive implications; and where the endorser is not competent or qualified to express a judgment of quality about the product or service. There are three basic principles that support the detailed ethical guidelines:

1. The primary responsibility for truthful and nondeceptive advertising rests with the advertiser. Advertisers should be prepared to substantiate any claims or offers before publication or broadcast and, upon request, present such substantiation promptly to the advertising medium or the Better Business Bureau.

2. Advertisements that are untrue, misleading, deceptive, fraudulent, falsely disparaging of competitors, or insincere offers to sell, shall not be used.

3. An advertisement as a whole may be misleading although every sentence separately considered is literally true. Misrepresentation may result not only from direct statements but by omitting or obscuring a material fact.

International Association of Business Communicators

The Code of Ethics of the International Association of Business Communicators (as revised in 1995) provides guidelines for IABC members and other communication professionals. The code covers communication and information dissemination, standards of conduct, confidentiality and disclosure, and professionalism.

1. Professional communicators uphold the credibility and dignity of their profession by practicing honest, candid and timely communication and by fostering the free flow of essential information in accord with the public interest.

2. Professional communicators disseminate accurate information and promptly correct any erroneous communication for which they may be responsible.

3. Professional communicators understand and support the principles of free speech, freedom of assembly, and access to an open marketplace of ideas; and, act accordingly.

4. Professional communicators are sensitive to cultural values and beliefs and engage in fair and balanced communication activities that foster and encourage mutual understanding.

5. Professional communicators refrain from taking part in any undertaking which the communicator considers to be unethical.

6. Professional communicators obey laws and public policies governing their professional activities and are sensitive to the spirit of all laws and regulations and, should any law or public policy be violated, for whatever reason, act promptly to correct the situation.

7. Professional communicators give credit for unique expressions borrowed from others and identify the sources and purposes of all information affecting the welfare of others.

8. Professional communicators protect confidential information and, at the same time, comply with all legal requirements for the disclosure of information affecting the welfare of others.

9. Professional communicators do not use confidential information gained as a result of professional activities for personal benefit and do not represent conflicting or competing interests without written consent of those involved.

10. Professional communicators do not accept undisclosed gifts or payments for professional services from anyone other than a client or employer.

11. Professional communicators do not guarantee results that are beyond the power of the practitioner to deliver.

12. Professional communicators are honest, not only with others but also, and most importantly, with themselves as individuals; for a professional communicator seeks the truth and speaks that truth first to the self.

Public Relations Society of America Code

In 2000 the Public Relations Society of America (PRSA) adopted a significantly revised Member Code of Ethics. A number of features of this code are noteworthy. Past PRSA ethics codes included enforcement powers and procedures residing in the Board of Ethics and Professional Standards and in regional judicial panels. This enforcement mechanism now is eliminated and the focus of the Board of Ethics is shifted to education and training programs. Nevertheless, the PRSA Board of Directors retains the power to deny membership or expel a member for unethical or illegal behavior. Added to the revised code is a commitment provision in the form of a Code of Ethics Pledge to be signed by PRSA members. The pledge commits members to the goals of truth, accuracy, fairness, and responsibility and to the provisions of the new code. A member signing the pledge also acknowledges that there are serious consequences for unethical or illegal misconduct "up to and including" membership denial or revocation.

The code now focuses on "universal values that inspire ethical behavior and performance." The tone of the code reflects what earlier in this chapter we discussed as the "character depiction" function of a code. The values, provisions, principles, and guidelines in the code all combine to depict the kind of formed ethical character expected of a public relations professional. The code also seems designed to serve what we discussed previously in this chapter as an "argumentative function" of a code. The core principles and specific guidelines for each principle serve as starting points for professional and public scrutiny of ethical issues in public relations. The code provides a visible standard to which both critics and defenders can appeal in judging the ethicality of a specific public relations practice. The code is meant to stimulate thinking and debate among public relations professionals as they seek guidance and clarification concerning ethics. Actual examples (scenarios) of improper conduct are given to illustrate the meaning of principles and guidelines. These factual examples are to function as precedents against which alleged unethical behavior can be judged for similarities and differences. Finally, a public relations practitioner could use the code as a justification for saying "no" to an ethically dubious practice or client, "such as declining representation of clients or organizations that urge or require actions contrary to this Code."

PRSA Member Statement of Professional Values

This statement presents the core values of PRSA members and, more broadly, of the public relations profession. These values provide the foundation for the Member Code of Ethics and set the industry standard for the professional practice of public relations. These values are the fundamental beliefs that guide our behaviors and decision-making process. We believe our professional values are vital to the integrity of the profession as a whole.

Advocacy

- We serve the public interest by acting as responsible advocates for those we represent.
- We provide a voice in the marketplace of ideas, facts, and viewpoints to aid informed public debate.

Honesty

- We adhere to the highest standards of accuracy and truth in advancing the interests of those we represent and in communicating with the public.

Expertise

- We acquire and responsibly use specialized knowledge and experience.
- We advance the profession through continued professional development, research, and education.
- We build mutual understanding, credibility, and relationships among a wide array of institutions and audiences

Independence

- We provide objective counsel to those we represent.
- We are accountable for our actions.

Loyalty

- We are faithful to those we represent, while honoring our obligation to serve the public interest.

Fairness

- We deal fairly with clients, employers, competitors, peers, vendors, the media, and the general public.
- We respect all opinions and support the right of free expression.

PRSA Code Provisions

Free Flow of Information
Core Principle

Protecting and advancing the free flow of accurate and truthful information is essential to serving the public interest and contributing to informed decision making in a democratic society.

Intent

- To maintain the integrity of relationships with the media, government officials, and the public.
- To aid informed decision making.

Guidelines—A member shall:

- Preserve the integrity of the process of communication.
- Be honest and accurate in all communications.
- Act promptly to correct erroneous communications for which the practitioner is responsible.
- Preserve the free flow of unprejudiced information when giving or receiving gifts by ensuring that gifts are nominal, legal, and infrequent.

Examples of Improper Conduct Under This Provision:

- A member representing a ski manufacturer gives a pair of expensive racing skis to a sports magazine columnist, to influence the columnist to write favorable articles about the product.
- A member entertains a government official beyond legal limits and/or in violation of government reporting requirements.

Competition
Core Principle

Promoting healthy and fair competition among professionals preserves an ethical climate while fostering a robust business environment.

Intent

- To promote respect and fair competition among public relations professionals
- To serve the public interest by providing the widest choice of practitioner options

Guidelines—A member shall:

- Follow ethical hiring practices designed to respect free and open competition without deliberately undermining a competitor.
- Preserve intellectual property rights in the marketplace.

Examples of Improper Conduct Under This Provision:

- A member employed by a "client organization" shares helpful information with a counseling firm that is competing with others for the organization's business.
- A member spreads malicious and unfounded rumors about a competitor in order to alienate the competitor's clients and employees in a ploy to recruit people and business.

Disclosure of Information

Core Principle

Open communication fosters informed decision making in a democratic society.

Intent

- To build trust with the public by revealing all information needed for responsible decision making

Guidelines—A member shall:

- Be honest and accurate in all communications.
- Act promptly to correct erroneous communications for which the member is responsible.
- Investigate the truthfulness and accuracy of information released on behalf of those represented.
- Reveal the sponsors for causes and interests represented.
- Disclose financial interest (such as stock ownership) in a client's organization.
- Avoid deceptive practices.

Examples of Improper Conduct Under This Provision:

- Front groups: A member implements "grass roots" campaigns or letter-writing campaigns to legislators on behalf of undisclosed interest groups.
- Lying by omission: A practitioner for a corporation knowingly fails to release financial information, giving a misleading impression of the corporation's performance.
- A member discovers inaccurate information disseminated via a Web site or media kit and does not correct the information.
- A member deceives the public by employing people to pose as volunteers to speak at public hearings and participate in "grass roots" campaigns.

Safeguarding Confidences

Core Principle

Client trust requires appropriate protection of confidential and private information.

Intent

- To protect the privacy rights of clients, organizations, and individuals by safeguarding confidential information

Guidelines—A member shall:

- Safeguard the confidences and privacy rights of present, former, and prospective clients and employees.
- Protect privileged, confidential, or insider information gained from a client or organization.

- Immediately advise an appropriate authority if a member discovers that confidential information is being divulged by an employee of a client company or organization.

Examples of Improper Conduct Under This Provision:

- A member changes jobs, takes confidential information, and uses that information in the new position to the detriment of the former employer.
- A member intentionally leaks proprietary information to the detriment of some other party.

Conflicts of Interest
Core Principle

Avoiding real, potential or perceived conflicts of interest builds the trust of clients, employers, and the publics.

Intent

- To earn trust and mutual respect with clients or employers
- To build trust with the public by avoiding or ending situations that put one's personal or professional interests in conflict with society's interests

Guidelines—A member shall:

- Act in the best interests of the client or employer, even subordinating the member's personal interests.
- Avoid actions and circumstances that may appear to compromise good business judgment or create a conflict between personal and professional interests.
- Disclose promptly any existing or potential conflict of interest to affected clients or organizations.
- Encourage clients and customers to determine if a conflict exists after notifying all affected parties.

Examples of Improper Conduct Under This Provision

- The member fails to disclose that he or she has a strong financial interest in a client's chief competitor.
- The member represents a "competitor company" or a "conflicting interest" without informing a prospective client.

Enhancing the Profession
Core Principle

Public relations professionals work constantly to strengthen the public's trust in the profession.

Intent

- To build respect and credibility with the public for the profession of public relations
- To improve, adapt and expand professional practices

Guidelines—A member shall:

- Acknowledge that there is an obligation to protect and enhance the profession.
- Keep informed and educated about practices in the profession to ensure ethical conduct.
- Actively pursue personal professional development.
- Decline representation of clients or organizations that urge or require actions contrary to this Code.
- Accurately define what public relations activities can accomplish.
- Counsel subordinates in proper ethical decision making.
- Require that subordinates adhere to the ethical requirements of the Code.
- Report ethical violations, whether committed by PRSA members or not, to the appropriate authority.

Examples of Improper Conduct under This Provision:

- A PRSA member declares publicly that a product the client sells is safe, without disclosing evidence to the contrary.
- A member initially assigns some questionable client work to a non-member practitioner to avoid the ethical obligation of PRSA membership.

In further evaluating the adequacy of the PRSA code, we will address several issues. First, how are the important concerns of lying and deception treated? Sometimes related but undefined phrases are used, such as "honest and accurate" and "truthfulness and accuracy." Partial clarification of these phrases is achieved by including "lying by omission" as unethical behavior. Several factual examples clarify what it means to "avoid deceptive practices" in disclosure of information. And the guidelines to "accurately define what public relations can accomplish" for clients illustrate practitioners' commitment to truthfulness.

Second, matters of vagueness and ambiguity of several key terms are apparent. The concept of "public interest" is used but undefined in two core values (advocacy and loyalty) and in one core principle (free flow of information). In the guidelines on Safeguarding Confidences and on Enhancing the Profession, the "appropriate authority" to whom members should report violations of ethics is not defined or illustrated.

Third, the internal coherence of standards is a potential issue. To what degree might there be an inconsistency between, on the one hand, "safeguarding the confidences and privacy rights of present, former, and prospective clients" and, on the other hand, the requirement to "reveal the sponsors for causes and interests represented"? Fourth, the code is intended to evolve and change over time. It is meant to be "a living, growing body of knowledge, precedent, and experience." For instance, more scenarios of actual misconduct will be "added as experience with the Code occurs."

The Center for Media and Democracy has a Web site that investigates public relations "spin" by both political and corporate sources. Evaluate the ethics of some of the examples on the Web site (http://www.prwatch.org).

Codes for Political Campaign Communication

For a presidential campaign, Common Cause, a national citizen lobbying organization, proposed a set of standards that still might aid voters in assessing the ethics of any political candidate's campaign. According to their criteria, an ethical candidate exhibits the following communication behavior:

- Engages in unrehearsed communication with voters, including participation in open hearings and forums with other candidates on the same platform, where the public is given opportunities to express their concerns, ask questions, and follow up on their questions

- Holds press conferences at least monthly throughout the campaign, and in every state where contesting a primary, at which reporters and broadcasters are freely permitted to ask questions and follow-up questions

- Discusses issues which are high on the list of the people's concerns, as evidenced, for example, by national public opinion polls; clarifies alternatives and trade-offs in a way that sets forth the real choices involved for the nation; and makes clear to the American people what choices he or she would make if elected to office

- Makes public all information relating to a given poll if releasing or leaking any part of a campaign poll (including when and where the poll was conducted, by whom, a description of the sample of the population polled, as well as all questions and responses)

- Allows interviews by a broad spectrum of TV, radio and newspaper reporters, including single interviewer formats which provide maximum opportunity for in-depth questions

- Takes full public responsibility for all aspects of his or her campaign, including responsibility for campaign finance activities, campaign practices of staff, and campaign statements of principal spokespersons

- Makes public a statement of personal financial holdings

- Does not use taxpayer-supported services of any public office now held—such as staff, transportation or free mailing privileges—for campaign purposes, except as required for personal security reasons

- Uses only advertising which stresses the record and viewpoint on issues of the candidates

Politicians as officeholders or engaged in election campaigns typically employ political consultants who provide advice on management of issues and arguments, advertising strategies and appeals, and relations with news media. Following is the Code of Professional Ethics that members of the American Association of Political Consultants pledge to uphold (http://www.theaapc.org/content/aboutus/codeofethics.asp).

- I will not indulge in any activity which would corrupt or degrade the practice of political consulting.
- I will treat my colleagues and clients with respect and never intentionally injure their professional or personal reputations.
- I will respect the confidence of my clients and not reveal confidential or privileged information obtained during our professional relationship.
- I will use no appeal to voters which is based on racism, sexism, religious intolerance or any form of unlawful discrimination and will condemn those who use such practices. In turn, I will work for equal voting rights and privileges for all citizens.
- I will refrain from false or misleading attacks on an opponent or member of his or her family and will do everything in my power to prevent others from using such tactics.
- I will document accurately and fully any criticism of an opponent or his or her record.
- I will be honest in my relationship with the news media and candidly answer questions when I have the authority to do so.
- I will use any funds I receive from my clients, or on behalf of my clients, only for those purposes invoiced in writing.
- I will not support any individual or organization which resorts to practices forbidden by this code.

In 2002, a survey was conducted of over 200 active political campaign consultants who advised both Republican and Democratic candidates.[20] A majority of the respondents felt that there should be a code of ethics for such consultants, and two-thirds favored some kind of censure for violations of the code. However, of the 150 familiar with the existing AAPC code (which lacks enforcement) only 10 percent believed it has any real impact on consultants' behavior. While consultants overwhelmingly agreed that making factually untrue statements is unethical, they considered the following practices as only questionable but not clearly unethical: making factually true statements out of context; focusing more on an opponent's negative personal characteristics than on the issues; suppressing voter turnout through negative advertising. What is your evaluation of the AAPC code? What is your view of the ethicality of the practices that consultants considered only questionable?

The Committee on Decent Unbiased Campaign Tactics (CONDUCT) is a nonpartisan citizen watchdog group in Chicago. This organization believes that some campaign tactics are "morally wrong, undermine the community peace and subvert the political process." CONDUCT provides a forum for all candidates and political parties to present complaints. If a complaint is substantiated and the offensive remark, statement, or action is not publicly repudiated by the offender, CONDUCT will publicize both the refusal and its findings on the complaint.[21] CONDUCT urges candidates to pledge themselves to observe the following Code of Fair Campaign Practice. Candidates:

- should not suggest directly or indirectly, through speeches or campaign literature, that their opponents ought to be defeated because of their race, religion, national origin or gender;
- should campaign among all the voters in the community they seek to represent or serve, being careful not to systematically exclude neighborhoods or groups other than their own;
- should not appeal to negative stereotypes or hostilities based on race, religion, ethnicity, gender or other irrelevant group identification;
- should not seek to gain support by arousing or exploiting the fears of one group toward other, different groups;
- should not use pamphlets, flyers, code words or advertising which appeal to bigotry or fear;
- should publicly condemn bigoted literature, statements or actions in support of their candidacy or in opposition to their opponent;
- should be accountable for the actions of their campaign staffs relative to this code.

A Journalism Code

Professional societies of print and electronic journalists often develop codes of ethics for their members. Such codes exist, for example, for the American Society of Newspaper Editors and for the Radio/Television News Directors Association. In addition, many newspaper chains, such as Scripps and Gannett, national news services, such as the Associated Press, national television network news organizations, and individual newspapers and television stations (large and small) have developed codes of ethics to guide employees.

One of the most prestigious associations for journalists is the Society of Professional Journalists (SPJ). Its code of ethics, adopted in 1996, endorses four fundamental values: seek truth and report it, minimize harm, act independently, and be accountable. Each value is elaborated as a statement of principle and each principle is followed by numerous specific guidelines that journalists should practice in carrying out the values and principles.

Note that the principles and standards of practice reflect the ongoing tension between freedom and responsibility we discussed in chapter 1. The code sensitizes journalists both to the freedom to report the truth and act independently on the one hand and their responsibilities to avoid harm to innocent others and to be publicly accountable on the other hand.

Tanni Haas, a journalism ethics scholar, analyzes such tensions and provides a further significant insight.[22] He pinpoints two ways of viewing the relationship of the four principles to their standards of practice. "First, the standards of practice could be seen to specify the means by which journalists would be able to honor the four principles. Second, the four principles could be seen to delineate ideals of ethical behavior to strive for, whereas the standards of practice could be seen to represent minimum expectations for professional conduct." Here is the code (http://www.spj.org/ethicscode.asp):

SPJ Code of Ethics

Preamble

Members of the Society of Professional Journalists believe that public enlightenment is the forerunner of justice and the foundation of democracy. The duty of the journalist is to further those ends by seeking truth and providing a fair and comprehensive account of events and issues. Conscientious journalists from all media and specialties strive to serve the public with thoroughness and honesty. Professional integrity is the cornerstone of a journalist's credibility. Members of the Society share a dedication to ethical behavior and adopt this code to declare the Society's principles and standards of practice.

Seek Truth and Report It

Journalists should be honest, fair and courageous in gathering, reporting and interpreting information.

Journalists should:

- Test the accuracy of information from all sources and exercise care to avoid inadvertent error. Deliberate distortion is never permissible.

- Diligently seek out subjects of news stories to give them the opportunity to respond to allegations of wrongdoing.

- Identify sources whenever feasible. The public is entitled to as much information as possible on sources' reliability.

- Always question sources' motives before promising anonymity. Clarify conditions attached to any promise made in exchange for information. Keep promises.

- Make certain that headlines, news teases and promotional material, photos, video, audio, graphics, sound bites and quotations do not misrepresent. They should not oversimplify or highlight incidents out of context.

- Never distort the content of news photos or video. Image enhancement for technical clarity is always permissible. Label montages and photo illustrations.

- Avoid misleading re-enactments or staged news events. If re-enactment is necessary to tell a story, label it.

- Avoid undercover or other surreptitious methods of gathering information except when traditional open methods will not yield information vital to the public. Use of such methods should be explained as part of the story.

- Never plagiarize.
- Tell the story of the diversity and magnitude of the human experience boldly, even when it is unpopular to do so.
- Examine their own cultural values and avoid imposing those values on others.
- Avoid stereotyping by race, gender, age, religion, ethnicity, geography, sexual orientation, disability, physical appearance or social status.
- Support the open exchange of views, even views they find repugnant.
- Give voice to the voiceless; official and unofficial sources of information can be equally valid.
- Distinguish between advocacy and news reporting. Analysis and commentary should be labeled and not misrepresent fact or context.
- Distinguish news from advertising and shun hybrids that blur the lines between the two.
- Recognize a special obligation to ensure that the public's business is conducted in the open and that government records are open to inspection.

Minimize Harm

Ethical journalists treat sources, subjects and colleagues as human beings deserving of respect.

Journalists should:

- Show compassion for those who may be affected adversely by news coverage. Use special sensitivity when dealing with children and inexperienced sources or subjects.
- Be sensitive when seeking or using interviews or photographs of those affected by tragedy or grief.
- Recognize that gathering and reporting information may cause harm or discomfort. Pursuit of the news is not a license for arrogance.
- Recognize that private people have a greater right to control information about themselves than do public officials and others who seek power, influence or attention. Only an overriding public need can justify intrusion into anyone's privacy.
- Show good taste. Avoid pandering to lurid curiosity.
- Be cautious about identifying juvenile suspects or victims of sex crimes.
- Be judicious about naming criminal suspects before the formal filing of charges.
- Balance a criminal suspect's fair trial rights with the public's right to be informed.

Act Independently

Journalists should be free of obligation to any interest other than the public's right to know.

Journalists should:

- Avoid conflicts of interest, real or perceived.
- Remain free of associations and activities that may compromise integrity or damage credibility.
- Refuse gifts, favors, fees, free travel and special treatment, and shun secondary employment, political involvement, public office and service in community organizations if they compromise journalistic integrity.
- Disclose unavoidable conflicts.
- Be vigilant and courageous about holding those with power accountable.
- Deny favored treatment to advertisers and special interests and resist their pressure to influence news coverage.
- Be wary of sources offering information for favors or money; avoid bidding for news.

Be Accountable

Journalists are accountable to their readers, listeners, viewers and each other.

Journalists should:

- Clarify and explain news coverage and invite dialogue with the public over journalistic conduct.
- Encourage the public to voice grievances against the news media.
- Admit mistakes and correct them promptly.
- Expose unethical practices of journalists and the news media.
- Abide by the same high standards to which they hold others.

National Communication Association

The National Communication Association (NCA) is a nonprofit professional organization of over 7,000 educators, practitioners, and students. It is the oldest and largest national organization to promote communication scholarship and education. The purpose is to promote study, criticism, research, teaching, and application of the artistic, humanistic, and scientific principles of communication. NCA has a Code of Professional Responsibilities to guide the conduct of members in their teaching, research, publication, professional relationships, and public service. In 1999 NCA adopted a Credo for Communication Ethics. Unlike the Code of Professional Responsibilities, this credo speaks more broadly both to members and to others in their *communication roles as citizens*. In developing the credo, input was solicited from the organization's Communication Ethics Commission, participants in a summer conference on crafting the credo, and from all association members. The NCA Credo differs from typical codes of ethics in several ways. It is a statement of beliefs and aspirations more than of rules and regulations, and there is no expectation that a credo will have an enforcement mechanism. As you read the preamble and principles of the National Communication Association Credo for Ethical Communication, think critically about its possible strengths and weaknesses.

NCA Credo for Ethical Communication

Questions of right and wrong arise whenever people communicate. Ethical communication is fundamental to responsible thinking, decision making, and the development of relationships and communities within and across contexts, cultures, channels and media. Moreover, ethical communication enhances human worth and dignity by fostering truthfulness, fairness, responsibility, personal integrity, and respect for self and others. We believe that unethical communication threatens the quality of all communication and consequently the well-being of individuals and the society in which we live. Therefore we, the members of the National Communication Association, endorse and are committed to practicing the following principles of ethical communication.

- We advocate truthfulness, accuracy, honesty, and reason as essential to the integrity of communication.
- We endorse freedom of expression, diversity of perspective, and tolerance of dissent to achieve the informed and responsible decision making fundamental to a civil society.
- We strive to understand and respect other communicators before evaluating and responding to their messages.
- We promote access to communication resources and opportunities as necessary to fulfill human potential and contribute to the well-being of families, communities and society.
- We promote communication climates of caring and mutual understanding that respect the unique needs and characteristics of individual communicators.
- We condemn communication that degrades individuals and humanity through distortion, intimidation, coercion, and violence and through the expression of intolerance and hatred.
- We are committed to the courageous expression of personal convictions in pursuit of fairness and justice.
- We advocate sharing information, opinions, and feelings when facing significant choices while also respecting privacy and confidentiality.
- We accept responsibility for the short- and long-term consequences for our own communication and expect the same of others.

Notes

1 See Jay Black and Ralph Barney, "The Case Against Media Codes of Ethics," *Journal of Mass Media Ethics*, 1 (Fall/Winter 1985–1986): 27–36; Clifford Christians, "Enforcing Media Codes of Ethics," *Journal of Mass Media Ethics*, 1 (Fall/Winter 1985–1986): 14–21; John C. Merrill, *Existential Journalism* (New York: Hastings House, 1977), pp. 129–138; Merrill, "Professionalization: Danger to Press Freedom and Pluralism," *Journal of Mass Media Ethics*, 1 (Spring/Summer 1986): 56–60; M. Cash Mathews, *Strategic Intervention in Organizations: Resolving Ethical Dilemmas* (Newbury Park, CA: Sage, 1988), pp. 51–82; William S. Howell, *The Empathic Communicator* (1982; reissue, Long Grove, IL: Waveland Press, 1986), pp. 188, 197; John L. Hulteng, *The Messenger's Motives: Ethical Problems of the News Media*, 2nd ed. (Englewood Cliffs, NJ: Prentice-Hall, 1985). pp. 205–207; Dan Nimmo, "Ethical Issues in Political Communication," *Communication*, 6, no. 2 (1981): 193–212.

2 John Kultgen, "Evaluating Professional Codes of Ethics," in *Profits and Professions: Essays on Business and Professional Ethics*, Wade L. Robison et al., eds. (Clifton, NJ: Humana, 1983), pp. 225–264.

3 Richard DeGeorge, *Business Ethics*, 2nd ed. (New York: Macmillan, 1986), pp. 341–342; Deni Elliott-Boyle, "A Conceptual Analysis of Ethical Codes," *Journal of Mass Media Ethics*, 1 (Fall/Winter 1985–1986): 22–26.

4 Kultgen, "Evaluating Professional Codes of Ethics," p. 251.

5 Ibid., pp. 232–235; Philip Meyer, *Ethical Journalism* (New York: Longman, 1987), p. 22.

6 DeGeorge, *Business Ethics*, p. 342.

7 Ibid., p. 342.

8 Ibid., p. 346; Kultgen, "Evaluating," p. 239.

9 DeGeorge, *Business Ethics*, pp. 343–344; Michael D. Bayles, *Professional Ethics* (Belmont, CA: Wadsworth, 1981), p. 24.

10 DeGeorge, *Business Ethics*, p. 345.

11 Lucinda D. Davenport and Ralph S. Izard, "Restrictive Policies of the Mass Media," *Journal of Mass Media Ethics*, 1 (Fall/Winter 1985–1986): 4–9; Kultgen, "Evaluating," pp. 247–250; Christians, "Enforcing Media Codes of Ethics," p. 19.

12 DeGeorge, *Business Ethics*, p. 342; Kultgen, "Evaluating" pp. 250–253; Bayles, *Professional Ethics*, 139–143; Norman E. Bowie, "Business Codes of Ethics: Window Dressing or Legitimate Alternative to Government Regulation?" in *Ethical Theory and Business*, Tom L. Beauchamp and Norman E. Bowie, eds. (Englewood Cliffs, NJ: Prentice-Hall, 1979), pp. 236–238.

13 Davenport and Izard, "Restrictive Policies of the Mass Media," p. 8; DeGeorge, *Business Ethics*, p. 347; Marvin N. Olasky, "Ministers or Panderers: Issues Raised by the Public Relations Society Code of Standards," *Journal of Mass Media Ethics*, 1 (Fall/Winter 1985–1986): 46.

14 Sissela Bok, *Lying: Moral Choice in Public and Private Life* (New York: Vintage, 1979), p. 260; Thomas M. Garrett, *Ethics in Business* (New York: Sheed and Ward, 1963), pp. 166–168; Earl W. Kintner and Robert W. Green, "Opportunities for Self-Enforcement Codes of Conduct," in *Ethics, Free Enterprise, and Public Policy*, Richard T. DeGeorge and Joseph A. Pichler, eds. (New York: Oxford University Press, 1978), pp. 249–250; DeGeorge, *Business Ethics*, pp. 345–346; Christians, "Enforcing Media Codes of Ethics," p. 25; Meyer, *Ethical Journalism*, p. 20; Huub Evers, "Codes of Ethics," in *Media Ethics*, Bart Pattyn, ed. (Leuven, Belgium: Peeters, 2000), pp. 255–281.

15 Meyer, *Ethical Journalism*, pp. 23–24.

16 DeGeorge, *Business Ethics*, p. 346.

17 Richard E. Crable, "Ethical Codes, Accountability, and Argumentation," *Quarterly Journal of Speech*, 64 (February 1978): 23–32.

18 Peter Brown, "Assessing Public Officials," in *Public Duties*, Joel Fleishman et al., eds. (Cambridge: Harvard University Press, 1981), pp. 291–294.

19 Karen Lebacqz, *Professional Ethics: Power and Paradox* (Nashville: Abingdon, 1985), pp. 63–91.

20 Harris Interactive, *Political Campaign Consultants*, prepared for The Center of Congressional and Presidential Studies at American University (Washington, D.C.), January 2003. Retrieved from www.american.edu/ccps/publications.php.

21 For example, see the *Chicago Tribune*, February 25, 1989, pp. A1, A6; also see W. J. Michael Cody and Richardson R. Lynn, *Honest Government: An Ethics Guide for Public Service* (Westport, CT: Praeger, 1992.)

22 Tanni Haas, "Reporters or Peeping Toms? Journalism Codes of Ethics and News Coverage of the Clinton-Lewinsky Scandal," in *Desperately Seeking Ethics: A Guide to Media Conduct*, Howard Good, ed. (Lanham, MD: Scarecrow Press, 2003), pp. 21–43.

11

Feminist Contributions

Feminism is not a concept with a single, universally accepted definition. For our purposes, elements of definitions provided by Barbara Bate and by Julia Wood are helpful.[1] Feminism holds that both women and men are complete and important human beings and that societal barriers (typically constructed through language processes) have prevented women from being perceived and treated as valued persons of equal worth with men. Feminism involves commitment to equality and respect for life. Feminism rejects oppression and domination as desirable values and believes that difference need not be equated with inferiority or undesirability. The feminist movement is not a monolithic, unitary social movement. Indeed, Wood describes a number of branches of the feminist movement: radical feminism, middle-class liberal feminism, separatism, structural feminists, lesbian feminists, and womanists.[2]

So, too, with feminist ethics. Alison Jaggar concludes her survey of issues in feminist ethics by noting that "feminist ethics, far from being a rigid orthodoxy, instead is a ferment of ideas and controversy. . . ."[3] In general, however, feminist ethicists offer critiques of male-dominated ethical traditions with special focus on ways in which traditional ethics have functioned to subordinate or trivialize women's ethical experience; rather, the moral experiences of women are worthy of equal respect. Among other things, feminist ethicists question the privileging of rationality over emotion, of universality and detachment over particularity and engagement, of the public sphere of discourse over the private sphere, and of individualism over relationships. Feminist scholars argue the case against sexist language, and some argue for the necessity to slant the truth in order to survive in a male-dominated world.[4]

Feminist ethicists, along with postmodern social critics and some other contemporary ethicists, challenge the standard image of the moral agent in traditional masculine-dominated Western philosophy—the autonomous, unencumbered, individual self impartially deciding ethical questions about abstract others apart from the social, economic, and institutional contexts in which that self is embedded and constructed. Rather, feminist ethicists envision a situated or contextualized self embedded in a web of relationships, roles, and responsibilities, making decisions about concrete, particular persons.[5] Some feminists remind us that gender is only one of a number of important, interrelated, situational variables, such as ethnicity/race, economic/social class, age, marital status, and sexual orientation, that must be considered in building adequate ethical theory and making sensitive ethical decisions.[6]

Traditional male-oriented European-American ethical theories generally have ignored a significant realm of ethical activity—the realm of interpersonal ethics. Traditional ethics has paid scant attention to the moral significance of family and friendship relationships and of emotions such as sympathy, compassion, care, and concern for individual others. Manning reminds us that these are "issues that arise in what is called the private sphere, a sphere that has been seen, in the Western tradition, as the province of women. Men were identified with the public sphere." And Jaggar argues that a key requirement for an adequate feminist ethic is that "it should be equipped to handle moral issues in both the so-called public and private domains."[7]

An Ethic of Care

While acknowledging the diversity and ferment within contemporary feminist ethics, feminist philosopher Virginia Held contends in her 2006 book, *The Ethics of Care: Personal, Political, and Global:* "The ethics of care now has a central, though not exclusive, place in feminist moral theorizing, and it has drawn increasing interest from moral philosophers of all kinds." She argues: "In the past few decades, the ethics of care has developed as a promising alternative to the dominant moral theories that have been invoked during the previous two centuries. . . . It is changing the ways moral problems are often interpreted and changing what many think the recommended approaches to moral issues out to be." Held concludes that "the ethics of care offers hope for rethinking in more fruitful ways how we ought to guide our lives."[8] We will examine now some of the different versions of the ethics of care that feminists have developed and touch on some of the issues raised by such conceptions.

The first version to be developed, and the one that generated considerable scholarly response, is by developmental psychologist Carol Gilligan. In her book, *In a Different Voice*, Gilligan critiques the work of others and presents her own research on the sequence or stages of individual human moral development. Gilligan contends that many studies of human moral development, such as the work of Lawrence Kohlberg, generalized the experiences and views of men as adequate to describe moral development for both men and women. With male standards taken as universal, moral judgments made by women frequently are viewed as deficient. In contrast, Gilligan argues that in contemporary North American culture there are two different but valuable and potentially complementary moral "voices" of full adulthood. These male and female voices, while typically manifested in men and women respectively, are modes of thought and themes that could be found either in men or women.[9]

The traditional *ethic of justice*, according to Gilligan, characterizes the male moral voice. It is rooted in the primacy of individual autonomy and independence. The ethic of justice judges competing rights and embodies a logic of equality and fairness. Reciprocal noninterference with rights describes an individual's obligation. Abstract, universalizable, impartial principles and rules concerning rights and justice are applied to a specific case. An *ethic of care*, says Gilligan, characterizes the female moral voice. It is rooted in the primacy of actual relationships and the interdependence of self and others. Compassion, empathy, and nurturance help resolve conflicting ethical responsibilities to all concerned, including the self. The ethic of care considers the needs of both self and others, not just the survival of one's self and not just the avoidance of hurting others. Focus is primarily on the concrete circumstances of particular relational situations to guide moral deliberation rather than solely on abstract rules and principles.[10]

In the intervening years, a number of issues relevant to Gilligan's assumptions, research methods, and implications have been debated by feminist and nonfeminist scholars from diverse disciplines. Treatments that support, attack, modify, or suggest new avenues are found in books, in anthologies on the topic, and in journal articles.[11] We will examine shortly books by three feminist scholars; each presents her own more or less complete version of an ethic of care.

What are some of the issues that have been and continue to be debated concerning versions of an ethic of care? Here are clusters of some major issues. (1) What grounding or basic assumptions are offered to undergird a care ethic? How is an ethic of care rooted in "natural" capacities common to all humans? To what degree is an ethic of care rooted in biology, maternal experience, cultural construction, or all of these? (2) Must an ethic of justice be essentialized only to men and a care ethic only to women? To what degree can or should the ethics of justice and care be available to both men and women? (3) How do such factors as race/ethnicity, economic/social class, and sexual orientation affect the development and functioning of an ethic of care? Is an ethic of care mostly reflective of the experiences of white, middle-class women? (4) What are some of the central dimensions or characteristics of an ethic of care that might help clarify or implement it? (5) What view of the "self" as moral agent is embedded in the care ethic? (6) What roles should rules or principles play, if any, in an ethic of care? (7) Are an ethic of care and an ethic of justice best seen as complementary, antagonistic, interdependent, or mutually exclusive? If both are valuable and applicable, does one uniformly take precedence over the other, or might it depend on the situation? Is care best seen as supplementary to justice or justice as supplementary to care? (8) Do an ethic of justice and an ethic of care, if both are broadly conceived, adequately cover the entire domain of moral decision making? How adequately can Kantian universalism, Rawlsian impartial justice, Ross's *prima facie* duties, versions of utilitarianism, and the virtue ethics tradition be subsumed under one or the other label? Are there multiple moral "voices" rather than just two? (9) How might the norms of a care ethic actually function to perpetuate the cultural subordination of women as the "natural" caregiver (rather than men also), as confined to the private sphere of home, family, and close relationships (rather than also as worthy in the public sphere of politics, policy, and work) and as engaged in expected duty more than respected work? Is the focus of a care ethic on the maintenance of relationships as primary over all other concerns and at all costs to the caregiver? Or is the focus on maintaining relationships wherein the needs/interests of *both* caregiver and cared-for have serious recognition and protection? (10) How might an ethic of care apply to voluntary and involuntary relationships and to equal and unequal power relationships? (11) To what degree can an ethic of care apply both to the private and public spheres of life? How might an ethic of care effectively be embedded in the policies and practices of institutions?

In *Caring: A Feminine Approach to Ethics and Moral Education* Nel Noddings grounds her ethic of caring in a kind of human nature ethical perspective. Her bedrock assumption is that "relation"—human encounter and emotional response—is a "basic fact of human existence." Natural caring is a relation that humans innately long and strive for and recognize as desirable. We "respond as one-caring out of love or natural inclination." Natural caring motivates ethical caring. "We want to be *moral* in order to remain in the caring relation and to enhance the ideal of ourselves as one-caring."[12]

Although Noddings intentionally avoids formal definition of a care ethic, she does at various points underscore what clearly are central dimensions of a caring relation.[13] *Engrossment*, the one-caring being engrossed in the needs of the one cared-for, permeates to some degree all caring. The one-caring is fully disposed and attentive toward the cared-for, has regard for the other, desires the other's well-being, and is responsive and receptive to the other. Noddings echoes Buber's concept of "being present" in describing engrossment. Through *motivational displacement* the one-caring retains but moves beyond her or his own interests to an empathy for or "feeling with" the experiences and views of the cared-for. Noddings draws upon Martin Buber's concept of "inclusion" to describe motivational displacement. The one-caring accurately and nonselectively strives to understand, both emotionally and intellectually, the position of the cared-for. The one-caring accepts the motives, intentions, and freedom of choice of the cared-for as long as they do not require abandonment of the one-caring's own ethical ideal. *Reciprocity* is required by the cared-for in order to complete the caring relationship. Here, again, Noddings has employed Martin Buber's concepts to elaborate her view. Reciprocity is not a contractual arrangement, nor does it demand one-to-one exchange of equal contributions. In Noddings's words:

> The freedom, creativity, and spontaneous disclosure of the cared-for that manifest themselves under the nurture of the one-caring complete the relation. . . . What the cared-for gives to the relation either in direct

response to the one-caring or in personal delight or in happy growth before her eyes is genuine reciprocity.

Noddings rejects "principles and rules as the major guide to ethical behavior." They are, she believes, too "ambiguous and unstable" because they always imply exceptions and foster divisiveness and denigration toward persons who hold "different" principles. The one-caring should not depend entirely or even primarily on rules—upon "a prior determination of what is fair and equitable." The one-caring is suspicious of rules and principles, "formulates and holds them loosely, tentatively," and persists in focusing on particular concrete persons and relations. At the same time, the one-caring is willing to develop principles rooted in concrete experience. Noddings also rejects the traditional ethical requirement of universalizability—the requirement that an ethical rule or principle that applies to me in my circumstances must also apply equally and universally to all other persons in similar circumstances. But Noddings does describe aspects of her ethic of caring as having universality. "The caring attitude," she argues, "that attitude which expressed our earliest memories of being cared-for and our growing store of memories of both caring and being cared for, is universally accessible." Noddings contends that while caring stems most naturally from the experiences of women (childbirth and child-rearing), the ethic of caring is available universally to both women and men. She believes that we have a primary, ongoing, and universal "obligation to meet the other as one-caring."[14]

Although Noddings rejects the primacy of rules and principles in ethics, she does describe a guide for our conduct, namely, the "ethical ideal."[15] The ethical ideal is "our best picture of ourselves caring and being cared for." It is our remembered image of the way we have been in genuine caring relationships and situations both as one-caring and as cared-for. That image changes as our caring experiences multiply. It also may be influenced by our insights gained from a person who is superior to us in caring. "It is limited by what we already have done and by what we are capable of, and it does not idealize the impossible so that we may escape into ideal abstraction." As the three most significant means of nurturing the ethical ideal, Noddings describes processes of practice, dialogue, and confirmation. Again, the latter two reflect in part Buber's philosophy of dialogic communication.

In some of her later works, Noddings addresses applications of a care ethic to the public sphere of social policies and political issues.[16] In *Woman and Evil* she links her view of a care ethic to such topics as war, terrorism, torture, psychological abuse, and teaching about these topics. In *The Challenge to Care in Schools* she suggests themes of care as a focus for change in bureaucratic, teaching, and curricular structure. And in *Starting at Home: Caring and Social Policy* she uses a care viewpoint to examine social policies for abortion, homelessness, and social deviance.

Rita Manning presents her version of an ethic of care in her book, *Speaking from the Heart: A Feminist Perspective on Ethics*. On some points she holds views similar to Noddings, but on others she differs. Like Noddings, Manning grounds her ethic of care in a type of human nature perspective. Manning believes that "we need not reject conceptions of human nature as providing a foundation for morality" and that "an ethic of care requires a new conception of human nature" that involves "a picture of humans as essentially involved with relationships with other humans." The moral bedrock of the "obligation to care . . . rests on our human capacity for caring interaction." In addition, Manning sees the ethic of care as appropriate for all humans, both women and men, and does not link it to sex and gender. At some length Manning describes her version:[17]

> An ethic of care involves morality grounded in relationships and response. When we are committed to an ethic of care, we see ourselves as part of a network of care and our obligation as requiring a caring response to those who share those networks and to those whose need creates an obligation to respond. In responding we do not appeal to abstract principles though we may appeal to rules of thumb; rather, we pay attention to the concrete other in his or her real situation. We also pay attention to the effect of our response on the networks of care that sustain us both.

In the care ethic the "importance of intimacy and connection to others is assumed." No one is expendable or simply a vehicle for utility. "Ties of affection, trust, and loyalty matter." Compromise and accommodation are valued in the search for solutions that try to accommodate everyone. Manning argues that "one need not respond to every need." We must consider carefully how and when to respond, the seriousness of the other's need, the benefit of our response to the one needing care, our capacity to respond to a particular need, and the competing needs of others (including oneself) affected by responding to the need. With attention focused on particular persons in an ethic of care, there must be recognition of all relevant facts of a situation and sensitive understanding of potential outcomes. Further, we must be willing to relate to the other on an emotional level.[18]

There are situations and contexts where rules and rights and an ethic of justice are most appropriate, notes Manning, and other occasions where relationship and response and an ethic of care are most relevant. Manning does not agree with Noddings's rejection of rules as moral guides. There are situations, perhaps in guiding our actions toward strangers, where tentative moral rules of thumb and principles based on our experiences with intimates are appropriate guides. For Manning, rules and rights could serve three purposes: (1) to persuade others who only will see a situation in terms of rules and rights; (2) to set a minimum standard of morality and provide some protection for the marginalized and helpless; and (3) to be used in deliberating about the needs of those persons to be cared for with whom we are not in direct relationship. Although Manning does not discuss the point at great length, she does emphasize that an adequate care ethic must have relevance to both the public and private spheres. Caring persons must work for changes in institutions, organizations, policies, and programs that would facilitate a caring world where all persons are able to "respond to his/her demands of care for self and other."[19]

In her book, *Moral Boundaries: A Political Argument for an Ethic of Care*, Joan Tronto develops her care ethic primarily in the context of the public sphere of politics and power relationships. While an ethic of care clearly is relevant to private situations and intimate relationships, Tronto argues that such an ethic should have significant application in public political and social contexts. She examines how a care ethic could function both as a political ideal and as a political strategy to influence public decisions on social policies. She explores at length the ways in which care is valued and devalued, facilitated and undermined, as well as strengthened and weakened by cultural norms, institutional structures, political policies, and power imbalances. She contends that if we "look at questions of race, class, and gender, we notice that those who are least well off in society are disproportionately those who do the work of caring and that the best-off members of society often use their positions of superiority to pass off caring work to others." She believes that the "world will look different if we move care from its current peripheral location to a place near the center of human life."[20] Tronto also argues that an ethic of care and an ethic of justice both are needed to address the significant issues in current moral theory. She does not view the ethic of care as unique or limited to women and that of justice limited to men. She stresses that an ethic of care "is incomplete unless imbedded in a theory of justice," that "justice without a notion of care is incomplete," and that an "ethic of care remains incomplete without a political theory of care."[21]

In a very general sense, Tronto views caring as all activities that we do *"to maintain, continue, and repair our 'world' so that we can live in it as well as possible.* That world includes our bodies, ourselves, and our environment, all of which we seek to interweave in a complex, life-sustaining web." She suggests four phases of caring as an ongoing process. First, *caring about* involves recognition that a need exists, recognition that caring is necessary, and an understanding of the position of the person or group in need. Second, *taking care of* involves "assuming some responsibility for the identified need" and deciding concretely how to respond to it. Third, *caregiving* involves actually caring through direct contact and physical work. The giving of money is more properly categorized as taking care of rather than caregiving. Fourth, *care-receiving* involves the actual responses of the cared-for and allows assessment of the adequacy of our care efforts. From these four phases derive four "ethical elements of care." *Attentiveness*, in a sense, means "to suspend one's own goals, ambitions, plans of life, and concerns, in order to recognize and to be attentive to others." *Responsibility* differs, Tronto contends, from obligation. In matters of obligation we look to formal relationships, formal agreements, explicit promises, formal rules, and agreed-upon duties. Responsibility looks beyond obligation, for example, to what our direct and indirect role may have been in contributing to the circumstances that give rise to the need for care and to whether we are somehow uniquely the most capable of giving the needed care. *Competence* demands that the caring work is performed compe-tently thus demonstrating that one truly cares. Except when adequate resources are lacking, competence is a necessary "part of the moral quality of care." And in a broader context, those in authority who should provide ade-quate resources for the caregiver should be held accountable. *Responsiveness* of the care-receiver to the care is the fourth moral element in an ethic of care. Responsiveness as a moral precept should alert us to potential abuses that may arise from inequality or vulnerability of the care-receiver. We must exer-cise caution in presuming to know accurately the needs of the care-receiver. Rather than projecting ourself into the other's position as a way of under-standing the other's needs, we should "consider the other's position as the other expressed it." In sum, Tronto believes that an ethic of care in society necessitates "an assessment of needs in a social and political, as well as a per-sonal, context."[22]

"Telling It Slant": Women and Lying

"Telling it slant" is a phrase from a poem by Emily Dickinson that some feminists have adopted to describe a way of speaking that they believe is forced upon women by a male-dominated society. According to Shirley Ardener, public discourse has been encoded by men; women need to monitor or transform their meanings to conform to male requirements. Muted group theory explains that the language of a culture does not serve all its speakers equally. Women are "muted" because the words for speaking are not gener-ated from or descriptive of *women's* experiences; the language women use is derivative because it developed from a male perception of reality. There is a block between experience and the verbal expression of those feelings. Shirley Ardener refers to this block as a necessary indirectness rather than spontane-ity. Tillie Olsen refers to it as telling it slant. Gillian Michell defines this phrase as a "way of speaking that conveys a message by distorting the truth somehow, so that what is conveyed is not the whole truth." Such a statement distorts the truth or withholds it in some way without actually being com-pletely false.[23]

The concept can be illustrated through an example (paraphrased) pro-vided by Michell. A female faculty member makes an excuse for missing a committee meeting to the man who chairs that committee. The female fac-ulty member had suffered severe menstrual cramps, so at the time of the meeting she had been home in bed, trying to proofread a report for the col-lege dean that she had completed the day before. She says, "Sorry I missed the meeting—I had to finish that report for the dean," instead of the more accurate, "Sorry I missed the meeting—I had terrible cramps." In this exam-ple, why might the woman have decided to "tell it slant"? Another way to understand the concept is to visualize that instead of telling the direct truth *straight up* (vertical) or telling a *flat out* lie (horizontal), a woman chooses to tell the partial truth *slant* (diagonal). While telling it slant might be viewed as falling somewhere between being truthful and lying, Michell notes that usually it would be categorized as a lie according to Sissela Bok's conception in her book, *Lying*. You may want to review Bok's conception as summarized earlier in chapter 7, "Some Basic Issues." Usually, telling it slant would be an intentionally deceptive message meant to make others believe what we personally do not believe.

Earlier in the chapter entitled "Interpersonal Communication and Small Group Discussion" we explored a possible ethic for everyday conversation extended from the work of philosopher H. P. Grice. Recall that Grice assumes that contributions by participants will be appropriate for the purpose and stage of conversation. To guide adequate conversation, Grice presents the maxims of *quantity, quality, relation*, and *manner*. Gillian Michell argues that Grice's rules are applicable most probably for white, male, middle-class conversation. Michell contends that the constraints of a sexist society frequently require that women tell it slant, and thus they could be judged as violating one or more of Grice's rules.

Michell sees telling it slant as ethically excusable and justifiable. First, telling it slant often is the most effective way for a woman to exchange information in a sexist setting—the best way to get her point across in a workable manner. Constraints on women's rights and options in male-dominated conversations are so potent in our patriarchal society that women are forced to tell it slant in order to survive or be successful. Second, concern for not hurting her hearer often motivates a woman to tell it slant. Recall here the "ethic of care" earlier analyzed in this chapter as the characteristic moral voice of women. Michell speculates that women also may sometimes tell it slant to "protect" men from views of reality with which men could not cope. An unfortunate consequence of telling it slant is that women may "lose the habit of telling it straight, even with those who have no real power over us, such as our female peers." Telling it slant, believes Michell, denies to both women and men the adequate information about life's complexities that they may need for sound decisions. Carefully consider Michell's conclusion:

> We see women are faced with a dilemma. If we tell it straight, our truth is not communicated effectively; if we tell it slant, what is communicated effectively is not really our truth. This dilemma complicates moral choices about truth telling for women in the most ordinary circumstances. It may be that for a woman to tell the truth requires more courage and requires it more often than we had thought.

Now what is your own personal viewpoint on telling it slant? Is it most accurately labeled as lying or as something else? Is it morally justifiable? Why? In your own experience, is telling it slant more characteristic of women than men in contemporary American culture? To what extent do you agree with Gillian Michell's analysis?

Rhetoric, Persuasion, Communication, and Mass Communication

"My indictment of our discipline of rhetoric springs from my belief that any intent to persuade is an act of violence." Thus, Sally Miller Gearhart opens her attack on rhetoric-as-persuasion because it reflects a masculine-oriented, "conquest/conversion mentality."[24] Traditional views of rhetoric have assumed that "it is a proper and even a necessary function to attempt to change others." The conquest/conversion model for persuasion is subtle and insidious, says Gearhart, "because it gives the illusion of integrity. . . . In the conversion model we work very hard not simply to conquer but to give every assurance that our conquest of the victim is really giving her what she wants." Gearhart contends that the rational discourse of traditional rhetoric actually is a "subtle form of Might Makes Right." Teachers of rhetoric, she, argues, "have been training a competent breed of weapons specialists who are skilled in emotional maneuvers, experts in intellectual logistics."

Based on feminist assumptions, Gearhart offers a particular view of "communication" as a more desirable and ethical alternative. This view of communication involves "deliberate creation or co-creation of an atmosphere in which people and things, if and only if they have the internal basis for change, may change themselves; it can be a milieu in which those who are ready to be persuaded persuade themselves, may choose to hear or choose to learn." Participants entering into this kind of interaction would try to develop an atmosphere where change for all participants can take place, would recognize that participants may differ in knowledge of subject matter and in basic beliefs, would look beyond these differences to attempt to create a sense of equal power for all, would be committed to working hard to achieve communication, and would be willing at a fundamental level to "yield her/his position entirely to the other(s)." This view of communication, believes Gearhart, moves away from a male-dominated model that assumes that all power was in the speaker/conqueror. Instead, the "womanization of rhetoric" focuses on atmosphere, listening, receiving, and a "collective rather than a competitive mode."

You are urged to compare and contrast Gearhart's view with several views of rhetoric examined in earlier chapters. For example, do Henry W. Johnstone's view of "humans as persuaders" (in chapter 3) and suggestions "toward an ethic for rhetoric" (presented at the end of chapter 4) tend more toward the conquest/conversion, speaker-centered conception of persuasion or more toward the view of communication or "womanized" rhetoric presented by Gearhart?

While they accept much of Gearhart's critique of a speaker-centered rhetoric of conquest, conversion, domination, and control, Sonja Foss and Cindy Griffin believe that such persuasion should remain one among several rhetorics available to humans for selection in varying contexts. They do not want to characterize such a view of rhetoric as inaccurate or misguided. As one alternative, Foss and Griffin develop an "invitational rhetoric" rooted in the feminist assumptions that relationships of equality are usually more desirable than ones of domination and elitism, that every human being has value because she or he is unique and is an integral part of the pattern of the universe, and that individuals have a right to self-determination concerning the conditions of their lives (they are expert about their lives).[25]

"Invitational rhetoric," say Foss and Griffin, invites "the audience to enter the rhetor's world and to see it as the rhetor does." The invitational rhetor "does not judge or denigrate others' perspectives but is open to and tries to appreciate and validate those perspectives, even if they differ dramatically from the rhetor's own." The goal is to establish a "nonhierarchical, nonjudgmental, nonadversarial framework" for the interaction and to develop toward the audience "a relationship of equity, respect, and appreciation." Invitational rhetors make no assumption that their "experiences or perspectives are superior to those of audience members and refuse to impose their perspectives on them." While change is not the intent of invitational rhetoric, change may be a result. Change may occur in the "audience or rhetor or both as a result of new understandings and insights gained in the exchange of ideas."

In the process of invitational rhetoric, contend Foss and Griffin, the rhetoric "offers" perspectives without advocating their support or seeking their acceptance. In invitational rhetoric, individual perspectives are expressed "as carefully, completely, and passionately as possible" to invite their full consideration. In offering perspectives, "rhetors tell what they currently know or understand; they present their vision of the world and how it works for them." Rhetors in invitational rhetoric "communicate a willingness to call into question the beliefs they consider most inviolate and to relax a grip on these beliefs." Invitational rhetors strive to create the conditions of safety, value, and freedom in interaction with audience members. *Safety* involves "the creation of a feeling of security and freedom from danger for the audience." Participants do not "fear rebuttal of or retribution for their most fundamental beliefs." *Value* involves acknowledging the intrinsic worth of audience members as human beings. In interaction, attitudes that are "distancing, depersonalizing, or paternalistic" are avoided. In invitational rhetoric, "listeners do not interrupt, comfort, or insert anything of their own as others tell of their experiences." *Freedom* involves the power to choose or decide. Restrictions are not placed on the interaction. Participants may introduce for consideration any and all matters; "no subject matter is off limits, and all presuppositions can be challenged." Furthermore, in invitational rhetoric the "rhetor's ideas are not privileged over those of the audience."

In concluding their explication of an invitational rhetoric, Foss and Griffin suggest that this rhetoric requires "a new scheme of ethics to fit interactional goals other than inducement of others to adherence to the rhetor's own beliefs." What might be some appropriate ethical guidelines for invitational rhetoric? What ethical standards seem already implied by the dimensions or constituents of such rhetoric described by them?

From her stance as a feminist teacher and scholar of communication, Lana Rakow spoke to an audience of students and teachers of communication at The Ohio State University.[26] She employed the norms of "trust, mutuality, justice, and reciprocity" as touchstones for communication relationships. As a part of a wide-ranging address on the "mission" of the field of communication study, Rakow contends that we must develop a communication ethic to guide our "relations between individuals, between cultures, between organizations, between countries." She asks, "What kind of 'ground-rules' would work across multiple contexts to achieve relationships that are healthy and egalitarian, and respectful?" She suggests three:

1. *Inclusiveness* means openness to multiple perspectives on truth, an encouragement of them, and a willingness to listen. Persons are not dehumanized because of their gender, race, ethnicity, sexual orientation, country, or culture.

2. *Participation* means ensuring that all persons must have the "means and ability to participate, to be heard, to speak, to have voice, to have their opinions count in public decision making." All persons "have a right to participate in naming the world, to be part of the discussion in naming and speaking our truths."

3. *Reciprocity* assumes that participants be considered equal partners in a communication transaction. There should be a "reciprocity of speaking and listening, of knowing and being known as you wish to be known."

In her article, "Feminist Theorizing and Communication Ethics," Linda Steiner explores particular applications to mass communication.[27] She argues that an adequate feminist ethic should confront "questions of systematic imbalances, including those that are mass mediated. It should address questions about whose interests are regarded as worthy of debate, who gets to talk, and who is regarded as an effective communicator to whom others must listen." Feminist ethics, believes Steiner, allows wide variation in ethical theories as individuals and systems reflect differences in gender, race, class, and historical circumstances. Also it focuses on *degrees* of rightness and wrongness of human actions. Feminist ethics rejects the conception of "the moral agent as the rational, autonomous individual, and of moral actions as short-term, discrete acts unaffected by history." Instead, feminist ethics envisions "the moral self as embedded in a web of family and communal relationships" and regards "caring and empathy as morally significant and legitimate virtues." Steiner rejects a sharp dichotomy between care and justice orientations. She contends that virtues such as empathy, caring, and nurturance can function in conjunction with integrity, respect for others, and fairness.

A feminist ethic for mass communication, in Steiner's view, assumes the significance of "who the communicators are, who is allowed to communicate and who is excluded, in part because this controls what is communicated, how, and to whom." A feminist ethic would "require mass media institutions to redefine communication in terms of process, rather than commodity; and to invent means of extending and broadening who gets to communicate." "Feminism," argues Steiner, "calls into question the very definition of news, as well as of entertainment, assumed by the dominant mass media." Media institutions would be challenged to define as news "communications by, for, and about peoples who are ignored, suppressed, or oppressed." Views of those who are outside of or who resist conventional authority structures should actively be sought. Lower profits and alienation of those in power are risks that mass media institutions should take. News, Steiner urges, should serve some larger transformatory good rather than simply present information for and about people in authority and thus "legitimate and reinforce existing institutional structures and values."

Finally, according to Steiner, a feminist ethic challenges the treatment of mass media subjects as objects—challenges the objectification of both mass media sources as well as audiences. "The goal would be to respect others' dignity and integrity, to make the process more collaborative and egalitarian, less authoritarian and coercive." Journalists, for example, could allow sources to raise issues as they see them, to ask questions, or to redirect questions. Or journalists might "share information and/or interpretations with sources before publication" and thus secure the sources' sense of accuracy and completeness of a story.

In a more recent essay, Steiner infuses feminist ethical perspectives into her enlargement and extension (items 5 and 6) of the so-called Potter Box framework for ethical analysis: (1) definition of the situation; (2) relevant values and ideals; (3) relevant ethical principles; (4) loyalties; (5) options; and (6) harms. She provides a penetrating illustration of how she would employ her framework to decide, as a booking agent for a cable TV variety entertainment show, whether to book a "gangsta" rap group whose lyrics and visuals are sexist and demeaning.[28]

Sandra Davidson Scott proposes a feminist theory of ethics for journalists that goes "beyond reason." She contends that emotion and empathy must play a larger and more significant role in journalism ethics.[29] Scott offers four guidelines as aids to making journalistic decisions, such as whether to take or publish a particular photo:

1. "Listen to one's emotions. Maybe the situation will require that one listen more than once."

2. "Quit rationalizing." "If one's gut says 'don't,' then one should avoid looking to one's head to concoct some fancy reason to go ahead."

3. Use one's moral imagination through seeing situations from the viewpoint of victims, their families, and the reading/viewing audience.

4. "Last, trust the emotions. One should not be duped into believing that one has to go through fancy mental machinations to come up with the right ethical decision."

Scott here confronts an issue of importance not only for journalists but also for human communication in general. What should be the legitimate role in ethical decision making for rational, reflective judgment and for emotional insight and intuition? We must remember that just because emotion by definition is nonrational (different than rationality) does not mean that emotion always is irrational (counter to reason).

Additional Communication Issues

As we saw in chapter 3, there are some human nature perspectives in the Western male-dominated cultural tradition that privilege rationality as an ethical standard for communication. These perspectives often have a built-in bias that automatically casts suspicion on communication by women. In the Western tradition, women have been assumed to be, by nature (rather than culture), less capable of rationality and more inclined toward irrational emotionality than men. Marilyn Pearsall vividly depicts the circumstances.[30]

> Women's nature has been held to be not only different from men's but also lesser, especially in regard to rationality. Men's nature is taken to be the standard for human nature, and women, presumably, fall short of that standard. Women have been described as emotional rather than rational, intuitive rather than logical, passive rather than active, and so on. This view, in turn, justified the confinement of women to the private/domestic sphere. And because women were held to be unfit for the public (political) sphere, where rationality is supposedly required, they were denied literacy and education and were kept from participating in political, legal, economic, and religious institutions.

Nel Noddings emphatically reminds us:

> It is not the case that women cannot arrange principles hierarchically and derive conclusions logically. It is more likely that we see this process as peripheral to, or even alien to, many problems of moral action. . . . Moral decisions are, after all, made in real situations; they are qualitatively different from the solution of geometry problems. Women can and do give reasons for their acts, but the reasons often point to feelings, needs, impressions, and a sense of personal ideal rather than to universal principles and their application.[31]

Certainly pornography as a type of contemporary communication generates heated debates concerning exactly what it is, whether it should be allowed, on what grounds it might be condemned or defended, and how First Amendment protections of freedom of speech should (or should not) apply to it.[32] Feminist ethicists do pinpoint some ethical grounds for condemning pornography. Helen Longino defines immoral behavior as that which

> causes injury to or violation of another person or people. Such injury may be physical or psychological. To cause pain to another, to lie to

another, to hinder another in the exercise of his or her rights, to exploit another, to degrade another, to misrepresent and slander another are instances of immoral behavior.[33]

Beyond pornography's degrading and dehumanizing depiction of women, to accomplish its purposes pornography must lie about women. Longino contends that pornography lies by saying women's sexual life is or ought to be subordinate to that of men, that women are depraved, that women's pleasure consists of pleasure for men not themselves, and that women are appropriate victims for rape, torture, bondage, or murder. "Pornography lies explicitly about women's sexuality," stresses Longino, "and through such lies fosters more lies about our humanity, our dignity, and our personhood." Jacqueline MacGregor Davies takes a post-liberal feminist position that condemns pornography as both politically and ethically objectionable. The assault, coercion, exploitation, sexual objectification, and dehumanization fostered by pornography "threaten the consensual process of articulating what it is to be human." In pornography "women are no longer present as human subjects who can generate signs. . . . They are spoken through." Pornography, in Davies's view, functions to deny women their status as members "of the community of subjects."[34]

In chapter 7, "Some Basic Issues," the ethical implications of nonverbal communication were explored. Silence, it was stressed, may carry ethical implications. Feminist theory can aid us in considering ethical implications of the silence and the silencing of women.[35] In North American culture, in many situations, women are expected to bear the primary responsibility for keeping talk going while men (by nature?) are not expected to be talkative. In these situations silence on the part of women is open to generally negative interpretations. In other situations, because they are viewed as inferior to men by nature, women must keep silent and let the men do the talking. Because the public sphere of politics and business has, until recently, been seen as the realm of male expertise and action, women effectively have been silenced by exclusion. Women are silenced when certain topics, communication roles, media of communication, and arenas of deliberation are assumed to be "off-limits" to them. In interpersonal communication, women are silenced when men feel quite free routinely to interrupt them but feel they have the right not to be interrupted. On the one hand, women may be silenced (denied their own personal voice) when routinely they are expected to communicate "like a man" in order to be taken seriously and to be successful. On the other hand, women may be silenced when routinely they are expected to communicate "like a woman" in certain stereotyped ways.

Finally, Adrienne Rich vividly probes the matters of lying and trust in personal relationships between women.[36] Rich describes a woman as feeling "a little crazy" when she discovers that another woman has lied to her. "We take so much of the universe on trust," Rich believes, so that when that bond of trust is broken we are "forced to reexamine the universe, to question the whole instinct and concept of trust." In Rich's imagery: "For awhile, we are thrust back onto some bleak, jutting ledge, in a dark pierced by sheets of fire, swept by sheets of rain, in a world before kinship, or naming, or tenderness exist; we are brought close to formlessness." In addition, Rich argues that "women have been forced to lie, for survival, to men"—to lovers, bosses, and any men who have power over them. With what effects? Lying to others (men or women) involves a woman in lying to herself by denying the truth or significance of something; thus, she removes a part of her life and lessens her confidence in her own life. Furthermore, when women lie so routinely that they forget they are lying or when they routinely use lying as a weapon of power, they run the great risk that lying will "carry over into relationships with people who do not have power over us," such as close friends and lovers.

Robert Solomon provides a fitting summary for our exploration of feminist contributions to communication ethics:[37]

> Feminist ethics has become one of the most important influences in ethics today. . . . The feminist argument reminds us of the important role of the moral sentiments and close and intimate relationships in happiness and the good life. It suggests that dispassionate reason . . . need not be seen as the highest virtue and insists that an admirable person will also be a passionate person who is concerned with other people and cares deeply about his or her family and loved ones.
>
> What makes us moral, first of all, is our personal concern for those closest to us. Secondarily we learn to have similar concerns, even if based on principles rather than personal attachments, for the many people we never have met and for humanity in general.

Notes

[1] Barbara Bate and Judy Bowker, *Communication and the Sexes*, 2nd ed. (Long Grove, IL: Waveland Press, 1997); Julia T. Wood, *Gendered Lives: Communication, Gender, and Culture*, 6th ed. (Belmont, CA: Wadsworth, 2005).

[2] Wood, *Gendered Lives*.

[3] Alison Jaggar, "Feminist Ethics: Some Issues for the Nineties," *Journal of Social Philosophy*, 20 (Spring/Fall 1988): 91–107.

[4] For example, see Rita C. Manning, *Speaking from the Heart: A Feminist Perspective on Ethics* (Lanham, MD: Rowman & Littlefield, 1992), pp. 15, 28–29; Mary C. Raugust, "Feminist Ethics and Workplace Ethics," in *Explorations in Feminist Ethics*, Eve Browning Cole and Susan Coultrap-McQuin, eds. (Bloomington: Indiana University Press, 1992), pp. 127–128. For an analysis that questions the view that traditional philosophy has a pervasive male-dominated viewpoint, see Iddo Landau, *Is Philosophy Androcentric?* (University Park: Pennsylvania State University Press, 2006).

[5] Manning, *Speaking from the Heart*, pp. 2–5; Michael Sandel, *Liberalism and Its Critics* (New York: New York University Press, 1984), pp. 5–6; Seyla Benhabib, *Situating the Self: Gender, Community and Postmodernism in Contemporary Ethics* (New York: Routledge, 1992), pp. 148–177. Also see Catriona MacKenzie and Natalie Slotjar, eds., *Relational Autonomy: Feminist Perspectives on Autonomy, Agency, and the Social Self* (New York: Oxford University Press, 2000).

[6] Jaggar, "Feminist Ethics," p. 94; Eve Browning Cole and Susan Coultrap-McQuin, "Toward a Feminist Conception of Moral Life," in Cole and Coultrap-McQuin, eds., *Explorations in Feminist Ethics*, p. 9. Also see Elisabeth Porter, *Feminist Perspectives on Ethics* (London: Longman, 1999), pp. 1–26.

[7] Manning, *Speaking from the Heart*, p. 14; Jaggar, "Feminist Ethics," p. 92; Virginia Held, *Feminist Morality: Transforming Culture, Society, and Politics* (Chicago: University of Chicago Press, 1993), pp. 57, 73.

8 Virginia Held, *The Ethics of Care: Personal, Political, and Global* (New York: Oxford University Press, 2006), pp. 3–5, 28. But also see Samantha Brennan, "Recent Work in Feminist Ethics," *Ethics*, 109 (July 1999): 858–893.

9 Carol Gilligan, *In a Different Voice: Psychological Theory and Women's Development* (Cambridge: Harvard University Press, 1982), pp. 2, 14, 18, 155–156, 173–174. Also see Lawrence Kohlberg, *The Psychology of Moral Development: The Nature and Validity of Moral Stages* (San Francisco: Harper and Row, 1984). For a partial critique of Gilligan and presentation of her own version of a care ethic, see Julia T. Wood, *Who Cares: Women, Care and Culture* (Carbondale: Southern Illinois University Press, 1994).

10 Gilligan, *In a Different Voice*, pp. 19, 63, 69, 73–74, 127, 143, 156–165, 174. Also see Carol Gilligan, Jamie Victoria Ward, and Jill McLean Taylor, *Mapping the Moral Domain* (Cambridge, MA: Harvard University Graduate School of Education, 1988); Gilligan, "Hearing the Difference: Theorizing Connection," *Hypatia*, 10 (Spring 1995): 120–127; Gilligan, "Letter to My Readers, 1993," in Gilligan, *In a Different Voice* (Cambridge, MA: Harvard University Press, 1993), pp. ix–xxvii.

11 For example see Peta Bowden, *Caring: Gender-Sensitive Ethics* (London: Routledge, 1997); Mary M. Brabeck, ed., *Who Cares? Theory, Research, and Educational Implications of the Ethic of Care* (New York: Praeger, 1989); Alisa L. Carse and Hilde Lindemann Nelson, "Rehabilitating Care," *Kennedy Institute of Ethics Journal*, 6 (1996): 19–35; Grace Clement, *Care, Autonomy, and Justice* (Boulder, CO: Westview, 1996); D. Lynn O'Brien Hallstein, "A Postmodern Caring: Feminist Standpoint Theories, Revisioned Caring, and Communication Ethics," *Western Journal of Communication*, 63 (Winter 1999): 32–56; Susan J. Hekman, *Moral Voices, Moral Selves: Carol Gilligan and Feminist Moral Theory* (University Park: Pennsylvania State University Press, 1995); Virginia Held, ed., *Justice and Care: Essential Readings in Feminist Ethics* (Boulder, CO: Westview, 1995); Daryl Koehn, *Rethinking Feminist Ethics: Care, Trust, and Empathy* (London: Routledge, 1998); Mary Jeanne Larrabee, ed. *An Ethic of Care: Feminist and Interdisciplinary Perspectives* (New York: Routledge, 1993); Sarah Clark Miller, "A Kantian Ethic of Care?" in *Feminist Interventions in Ethics and Politics*, Barbara S. Andrew, Jean Keller, and Lisa H. Schwartzman, eds. (Lanham, MD: Rowman and Littlefield, 2005), pp. 111–127; Linda Kerber et al., "On *In a Different Voice*: An Interdisciplinary Forum," *Signs*, 11 (1986): 304–333; Fiona Robinson, *Globalizing Care: Ethics, Feminist Theory, and International Relations* (Boulder, CO: Westview, 1999); Kathryn Tanner, "The Care that Does Justice: Recent Writings in Feminist Ethics and Theology," *Journal of Religious Ethics*, 24 (Spring 1996): 171–191; Rosemarie Tong, *Feminine and Feminist Ethics* (Belmont, CA: Wadsworth, 1993).

12 Nel Noddings, *Caring: A Feminine Approach to Ethics and Moral Education* (Berkeley: University of California Press, 1984), pp. 4–5, 27–28, 49, 83, 130, 175. Also see Noddings, "Feminist Fears in Ethics," *Journal of Social Philosophy I*, 21 (Fall/Winter, 1990): 25–33; Noddings, "A Response," *Hypatia*, 5 (Spring, 1990): 120–126; Noddings, "Ethics from the Standpoint of Women," in *Theoretical Perspectives on Sexual Difference*, Deborah L. Rhode, ed. (New Haven, CT: Yale University Press, 1990), pp. 160–173.

13 Noddings, *Caring*, pp. 17–19, 33, 69–75, 170, 176–177, 182–197. Also see Richard L. Johannesen, "Nel Noddings's Uses of Martin Buber's Philosophy of Dialogue" *Southern Communication Journal*, 65 (Winter/Spring 2000): 151–160; James W. Walter, *Martin Buber and Feminist Ethics: The Priority of the Personal* (Syracuse, NY: Syracuse University Press, 2003).

14 On rules, principles, universalizability, and universality, see Noddings, *Caring*, pp. 5, 13, 17, 55, 85. For her recent modified view on the relation of justice and care, see Noddings, "Introduction," in *Justice and Caring: The Search for Common Ground in Education*, Michael S. Katz, Nel Noddings, and Kenneth A. Strike, eds. (New York: Teachers College Press, 1999), pp. 1–4.

15 Noddings, *Caring*, pp. 49, 80, 104–131, 182–197.

16 Nel Noddings, *Women and Evil* (Berkeley: University of California Press, 1989); Noddings, *The Challenge to Care in the Schools: An Alternative Approach to Education* (New York: Teachers College Press, 1992), pp. 172–180; Noddings, *Starting at Home: Caring and Social Policy* (Berkeley: University of California Press, 2002), pp. 230–282. Also see Gary Pech and Rhona Leibel, "Writing in Solidarity: Steps Toward an Ethic of Care in Journalism," *Journal of Mass Media Ethics*, 21 (2006): 141–155.

17 Manning, *Speaking*, pp. 49, 56, 65–69, 139, 152.

18 Ibid., pp. xiv, 48, 64, 149, 161.

[19] Ibid., pp. 29, 62, 69, 73–82, 147–149, 156, 160.

[20] Joan C. Tronto, *Moral Boundaries: A Political Argument for an Ethics of Care* (New York: Routledge, 1993), pp. 13, 102–180. Also see Tronto, "Care as a Basis for Radical Political Judgments," *Hypatia*, 10 (1995): 141–149; Tronto, "Vicious Circles of Privatizing Care," in *Socializing Care: Feminist Ethics and Public Issues*, Maurice Hamington and Dorothy C. Miller, eds. (Lanham, MD: Rowman and Littlefield, 2006), pp. 3–25.

[21] Tronto, *Moral Boundaries*, pp. 61–97, 151–169.

[22] Ibid., pp. 102–108, 126–137.

[23] Gillian Michell, "Women and Lying: A Pragmatic and Semantic Analysis of 'Telling it Slant,'" *Women's Studies International Forum*, 7 (1984): 375–383. Also See Shirley Ardener, ed., *Perceiving Women* (Malaby Press, 1975), pp. xi–xii, 20–22; Cheris Kramarae, *Women and Men Speaking* (Newbury House Publishers, 1981); Tillie Olsen, *Silences* (New York: Delacorte, 1978); Adrienne Rich, *Lies, Secrets and Silence* (Norton, 1979); Dale Spender, *Man Made Language* (Routledge & Kegan Paul, 1980).

[24] Sally Miller Gearhart, "The Womanization of Rhetoric," *Women's Studies International Quarterly*, 2 (1979): 195–201.

[25] Sonja K. Foss and Cindy L. Griffin, "Beyond Persuasion: A Proposal for an Invitational Rhetoric," *Communication Monographs*, 62 (March 1995): 2–18. Also see Sonja K. Foss and Karen A. Foss, *Inviting Transformation: Presentational Speaking for a Changing World*, 2nd ed. (Long Grove, IL: Waveland Press, 2003); Josina M. Makau and Debian Marty, *Cooperative Argumentation: A Model for Deliberative Community* (Long Grove, IL: Waveland Press, 2001); Kathleen J. Ryan and Elizabeth J. Natalle, "Fusing Horizons: Standpoint Hermeneutics and Invitational Rhetoric," *Rhetoric Society Quarterly*, 31 (Spring 2001): 69–90.

[26] Lana Rakow, "The Future of the Field: Finding Our Mission," address presented at The Ohio State University, May 13, 1994.

[27] Linda Steiner, "Feminist Theorizing and Communication Ethics," *Communication*, 12 (1989): 157–173. Also see Linda Steiner and Chad M. Okrusch, "Care as a Virtue for Journalists," *Journal of Mass Media Ethics*, 21 (2006): 102–122.

[28] Linda Steiner, "A Feminist Schema for Analysis of Ethical Dilemmas," in *Ethics in Intercultural and International Communication*, Fred L. Casmir, ed. (Mahwah, NJ: Erlbaum, 1997), pp. 59–88. For an application, see Marifran Mattson and Patrice M. Buzzanell, "Traditional and Feminist Organizational Communication Ethical Analyses of Messages and Issues Surrounding an Actual Job Loss Case," *Journal of Applied Communication Research*, 27 (February 1999): 49–72. A detailed explanation of the Potter Box framework for ethical analysis is Clifford G. Christians et al., *Media Ethics: Cases and Moral Reasoning*, 7th ed. (Boston: Pearson/Allyn & Bacon, 2005), pp. 3–9, 22–24.

[29] Sandra Davidson Scott, "Beyond Reason: A Feminist Theory of Ethics for Journalists," *Feminist Issues*, 13 (1993): 23–40.

[30] Marilyn Pearsall, ed., *Women and Values: Readings in Recent Feminist Philosophy* (Belmont: CA: Wadsworth, 1986), p. 33.

[31] Noddings, *Caring*, pp. 2–3, 96.

[32] For a survey of the controversy, see Daniel Linz and Neil Malamuth, *Pornography* (Newbury Park, CA: Sage, 1993).

[33] Helen E. Longino, "Pornography, Oppression, and Freedom: A Closer Look," in Pearsall, ed., *Women and Values*, espec. pp. 168–172.

[34] Jacqueline MacGregor Davies, "Pornographic Harms," in *Feminist Perspectives: Philosophical Essays on Method and Morals*, Lorraine Code, Sheila Mullett, and Christine Overall, eds. (Toronto: University of Toronto Press, 1988), espec. pp. 137–138, 142–143.

[35] Many of the following points are raised in Adam Jaworski, *The Power of Silence: Social and Pragmatic Perspectives* (Newbury Park, CA: Sage, 1993), pp. 118–122; Tillie Olsen, *Silences*. Also see Marsha Houston and Cheris Kramarae, "Speaking from Silence: Methods of Silencing and Resistance," *Discourse and Society*, 24 (1991): 387–399. Also see Audre Lorde, *Sister Outsider* (Freedom, CA: Crossing Press, 1984), pp. 40–44.

[36] Adrienne Rich, *On Lies, Secrets, and Silence* (New York: Norton, 1979), pp. 185–194.

[37] Robert C. Solomon, *Ethics: A Short Introduction* (Dubuque, IA: Brown & Benchmark, 1993), pp. 132–133.

Intercultural and Multicultural Communication

"North Americans . . . too often assume that people elsewhere hold comparable values, or would, at least if they were given the opportunity." Thus John Condon underscores the fact that standards for ethical communication rooted in a North American value system, such as the political perspectives discussed in chapter 2, are not widely shared throughout the world. Criteria of linear logic, empirical observation, and objective truth are not used to assess communication ethicality in various other cultures, religions, and political systems.[1]

Intercultural communication and multicultural communication are concepts used in various ways and thus warrant definition here. In this chapter, *intercultural* communication refers to communication across national borders and between citizens of different nations (national cultures). We could, for example, explore ethical issues for communication between Chinese and Americans, Canadians and Mexicans, Brazilians and British, or Nigerians and Egyptians. *Multicultural* communication refers to communication *within* a particular nation, among residents of that nation from different racial, ethnic, religious, or cultural heritages. Within the United States, for example, we could explore ethical issues for communication between African Americans and European Americans, Latino Americans and Asian Americans, Native Americans and Japanese Americans, Jews and Christians, and, in a broad sense of differing "cultures," between men and women and between heterosexuals and homosexuals. For both intercultural and multicultural communication, our concern should be not only for the ethicality of communication between different groups but also for the ethics of how we communicate *about* groups that are different from our own.

Elements of a culture are "common sense" views, explicit or implicit, about "the way things are" and "the way things should be." Cultural elements pervade all aspects of life and, consciously or unconsciously, influence how we talk, think, and act. Cultural elements are communicated from generation to generation through varied learning processes. These cultural beliefs, norms, attitudes, and behaviors include: fundamental values and ethical standards; taken-for-granted assumptions about nature, human nature, and religion; accepted modes of evidence and argument; cultural heroes and heroines; stories of group accomplishment and defeat; rituals and ceremonies to foster a sense of tradition and loyalty; conceptions of the ideal; and accepted topics, places, and methods of communication. Because shared cultural elements are felt deeply and often held unconsciously, they exert powerful pressure toward unity, cohesion, and community. In the extreme, this pressure leads to the belief that one's culture is the best, better than other cultures, or even that other cultures must be marginalized, subordinated, or eliminated.

The Search for Transcultural Ethics

Some scholars advocate development of an overarching, transcendent, transcultural ethic to guide communication between people of different national cultures or of different cocultures within a nation. Can we legitimately search for some minimum transcultural ethical standards for communication? If these transcultural values are to be considered universal, in what sense should we mean universal? In his book, *Through the Moral Maze: Searching for Absolute Values in a Pluralistic World*, Robert Kane offers several relevant insights. Universal does not have to mean that we are absolutely certain about the values or that we have a right to impose them on others through fanaticism or authoritarianism. Universal simply means that we believe these values are valid for all persons, times, or viewpoints. "The real issue," says Kane, "is whether we can have good reasons for believing in (at least some) universal values and truths despite not being certain." Kane also argues that we need not require "that the ethically relevant human traits we are seeking be completely universal traits and provably so, rather than merely *common* human traits." It is enough, he contends, "to know that human beings commonly need certain things. For we can reason that *since we are human, there is high probability that we need these things as well for a fulfilling human life.*"[2]

We will examine now some books that attempt to uncover universal, transcultural values to guide our ethical choices. *Shared Values for a Troubled World: Conversations with Men and Women of Conscience* reflects Rushworth Kidder's interviews with twenty-four "ethical thought leaders" from diverse positions in diverse world cultures. Kidder is founder of the Institute for Global Ethics. He discerned in the interviews a transcultural ethical code rooted in the widely shared values of love, truthfulness, fairness, freedom, unity, tolerance, responsibility, and respect for life. In another study, conducted by Kidder and William Loges, 272 participants in an international meeting on global ethics were administered a "global values survey." These persons represented 40 countries and 50 different religious communities. Their average age was 51, and 57 percent were male. From a list of fifteen suggested values, the clearly predominant ones were truth, compassion, responsibility, freedom, respect for life, and fairness. Note the considerable overlap of values between the two studies.[3]

Philosopher and ethicist Sissela Bok, in her book, *Common Values*, presents her argument for a "minimalist" starting point for the search, one that "seeks out the values that are in fact broadly shared, without requiring either absolute guarantees for them or unanimity regarding them." Such minimalist values can serve as a basis for communication and cooperation across cultures and for discussion of how they might be applied or extended in scope. In addition, such common values "provide criteria and a broadly comprehensible language for critique of existing practices" both within a particular society or culture and also across societal boundaries.[4] Bok identifies a small cluster of minimalist moral values that are held in common by most human beings and that have had to be worked out by all human societies: positive duties of mutual support, care, loyalty, and reciprocity; negative duties to refrain from the hurtful actions of deceit, betrayal, and violence; and the standards for "rudimentary fairness and procedural justice" when conflicts arise. Bok's effort embodies her own warning to take seriously the doubts raised against simplistic views of human nature and universal values "without relying so uncritically on those doubts as to reject all study of what human beings have in common."[5]

The Dalai Lama is the Buddhist religious leader-in-exile of Tibet. In his book, *Ethics for the New Millennium*, he seeks a transcultural ethics "based on universal rather than religious principles." Humans, he believes, can live an ethical life "without recourse to religious faith." However, although religious faith is not a necessary precondition to behaving ethically, the world's religions can have a valuable role to play in ethics.[6] The Dalai Lama starts with a basic assumption about human nature—that all humans desire to be happy and avoid suffering. He then seeks a set of principles that are universally binding but not absolute moral laws in the sense of no interpretation or exceptions. He rejects the Kantian idea that some behaviors are right or wrong in themselves. Instead he would apply basic ethical principles by evaluating an act's promotion of happiness or suffering, the context of the act, the motivation and intent of the act, and the person's degree of freedom in choosing the act.[7] The transcultural ethical virtues, or essential "qualities of the human spirit," proposed by the Dalai Lama include: "love and compassion, patience, tolerance, forgiveness, contentment, a sense of responsibility, a sense of harmony." Such principles would caution communicators against telling lies, expressing hatred or racism, or having malicious intent.[8]

Clifford Christians and Michael Traber, scholars of communication ethics, philosophy, and religion, edited an anthology of original essays, *Communication Ethics and Universal Values*. In their own introductory and concluding essays, Christians and Traber search for universal values rooted not solely in anthropological sameness, although some relevant commonalities exist, but rooted in philosophical assumptions about human nature. The ethical values they identify are not foundational, assumed certainties; they are commitments open to reexamination. "The universality of these values," they believe, "is beyond culture. It is rooted ontologically in the nature of human beings. It is by virtue of what it means to be human that these values are universal."[9] Furthermore, no matter the cultural differences that focus either on individualism or on community, there "is a growing consensus that certain universal standards for the social accordance of human dignity must be upheld, regardless of cultural differences." As the protonorm or foundational value underlying most cultures and at the heart of what it means to be human is the sacredness of life, the "irrevocable status" of respecting human life.[10] Christians and Traber identify the following universal ethical principles rooted in the protonorm as guides for our uniquely human capacity to use language: truth-telling, human dignity, no harm to the innocent, unconditional acceptance of the other as a person, and solidarity with the weak and vulnerable.[11]

Christians and Traber argue for a "worldview pluralism" in which ethical beliefs are held in good faith and debated openly and in which "a commitment to universals does not eliminate all differences" of viewpoint. "The only question," for them, "is whether our worldviews and community formations contribute in the long run to truth-telling, human dignity, and nonmaleficence." Sissela Bok agrees: "Cultural diversity can and should be honored, but only within the context of respect for common values. Any claim to diversity that violates minimalist values . . . can be critiqued on cross-cultural grounds involving basic respect due all human beings."[12]

The Golden Rule

"Do unto others as you would have them do unto you." Most of us probably are familiar with this statement of ethical principle that we have come to know as the Golden Rule. Persons familiar with the Christian religious tradition may think that the Golden Rule is unique to that religion. In the New Testament we find: "And as ye would that men should do to you, do ye also to them likewise" (Luke 6:31; also see Matthew 7:12). However some version of the Golden Rule is found in the sacred literature of the major world religions.[13] *Judaism:* "What is hateful to you, do not to your fellow men. This is the entire law: all the rest is commentary." *Islam:* "No one of you is a believer until he desires for his brother that which he desires for himself." *Buddhism:* "Hurt not others in ways that you yourself would find hurtful." *Hinduism:* "This is the sum of duty: Do naught unto others which would cause you pain if done to you." *Confucianism:* "Surely it is a maxim of loving kindness: Do not unto others that you would not have them do unto you." *Taoism:* "Regard your neighbor's gain as your own gain and your neighbor's loss as your own loss."

Zoroastrianism: "That nature alone is good which refrains from doing unto another whatsoever is not good for itself." *Jainism:* "In happiness and suffering, in joy and grief, we should regard all creatures as we regard our own self."

One interpretation of the Golden Rule would be that we should only do *specific actions* to others if we would allow them to do the same specific actions to us. Another interpretation would not require mutually specific actions but would require that the *ethical principles* or *standards* that we follow in relating to others are the same ethical principles or standards we would expect others to follow in relating to us.[14] Marcus G. Singer, a contemporary philosopher, concludes:[15]

> The golden rule, in one version or another, has a prominent place in all the major world religions and most minor ones; it has been enunciated by pagan philosophers both before and after Christ. . . . The nearly universal acceptance of the golden rule and its promulgation by persons of considerable intelligence, though otherwise divergent outlooks, would therefore seem to provide some evidence for the claim that it is a fundamental ethical truth.

In the context of intercultural and multicultural communication, however, Milton Bennett argues that the Golden Rule best applies *within* a culture that has wide consensus on fundamental values, goals, institutions, and customs. In other words, the Golden Rule assumes that other people *want* to be treated like we do. But such an assumption is not applicable automatically in intercultural and multicultural communication. Often we may focus primarily or solely on our own standards or desires to the exclusion of standards or desires of others that may differ from ours. As an alternative to the Golden Rule, Bennett offers the Platinum Rule: "Do unto others as they themselves would have done unto them."[16] Certainly the Platinum Rule forces us to take into account seriously the standards and desires of others, perhaps through empathy for or imagining of their experiences and worldview. But we need to be careful that we do not interpret the Platinum Rule as requiring us automatically and unquestioningly, in Singer's words, to "always do what anyone else wants you to do." In fact, Singer would combine the logic of both the Golden Rule and the Platinum Rule (a combination that he terms the Inversion of the Golden Rule): "What the Golden Rule requires is that everyone ought to act in his relations with others on the same standards or principles that he would want to have them apply in their treatment of him, taking account of and respecting, but not necessarily acceding to, their wishes and desires."[17]

Chen and Starosta's Reciprocity Ethic

In their book, *Foundations of Intercultural Communication*, Guo-Ming Chen and William Starosta attempt to "integrate both universal and relative perspectives" in proposing an ethic for intercultural and multicultural communication. They believe that while some different ethical standards for different cultures may be necessary because of divergent value assumptions, a set of "universal principles of intercultural communication ethics can be generated." They start with *reciprocity* as the fundamental universal principle of interpersonal communication. They accept a variation of the Golden Rule: "Communicate unto others as you wish them to communicate unto you." This general principle is to be applied through four other principles. Through *mutuality* "both parties must actively search for a mutual symbolic ground that allows the fullest and clearest possible exchange of ideas." Through *nonjudgmentalism* information flows freely and we willingly "recognize, appreciate, and accept different views and ideas." Through *honesty* we assume that "information is true as the sender understands it." Through *respect* we "preserve the dignity of our partner as a human being" and we avoid deception.[18]

These basic ethical principles lead Chen and Starosta to offer five specific ethical guidelines: (1) promote voluntary participation in the interaction; (2) seek individual focus prior to cultural focus in order to avoid stereotypes; (3) maintain the right to freedom from harm—physical, social, or psychological; (4) maintain the right of others to privacy of thought and action; and (5) avoid imposing personal biases and especially avoid using those biases to mislead or deceive. Finally, they propose for further reflection and discussion twelve "propositions" for ethical intercultural communication. The ethical communicator:

1. Perceives people to be equal, even when their beliefs differ
2. Actively seeks out and interacts with persons of diverse ethnicity and national origin
3. Listens carefully and nonjudgmentally
4. Questions patiently to ascertain intended meaning
5. Is slow to reach closure and recognizes that misunderstanding often arises from out-of-awareness cultural differences
6. Solicits and provides feedback to ensure that messages were received as intended
7. Seeks to learn the culture and language of the Other in considerable detail
8. Works from the belief that the Other is rational when understood in cultural context
9. Places a positive value on cooperation and conflict resolution
10. Seeks synergy in dealings with the Other, with the understanding that no one language, religion, or gender orientation among the diverse ones in a nation should be taken as speaking for or representative of the whole nation
11. Seeks to include all voices in the interaction
12. Sets only those conditions for the Other that will be honored equally by the Self

Now consider what difficulties there might be in interpreting or applying the principles, guidelines, and propositions suggested by Chen and Starosta. Consider the word "respect." As used by them, does it primarily seem to mean agreement/approval, or tolerance, or being considerate, or holding in esteem? At several points they urge nonjudgmentalism in order to promote free flow of information and careful understanding and appreciation of ideas. Does this seem to imply that we also automatically must "accept" the other person's behavior or ideas and that, in intercultural communication, we never should criticize the ethics of the other person's ideas or methods? What advantages or disadvantages do you see in their proposal?

Kale's Human Nature Ethic

The grounding of David Kale's proposed ethic for intercultural communication is his view of human nature. While acknowledging that different cultures develop different value systems and "thus must have different ethical codes," he also assumes that all people "share a human spirit that is the same regardless of cultural background."[19] This fundamental human spirit generates our capacities to hold values and make value judgments, to make ethical decisions about degrees of right and wrong, and to envision dimensions of a worthwhile life. Kale believes that "the guiding principle of any universal code of intercultural communication should be to protect the worth and dignity of the human spirit." Kale also grounds his ethic, not in freedom of choice as a fundamental human value, but rather in world cultures living at peace with each other. Such a goal represents a continuum ranging from minimal peace (absence of conflict) through moderate peace ("conflicting parties are willing to compromise on goals they want to achieve") to optimal peace ("parties consider each others' goals as seriously as they do their own").

Based on these groundings, Kale proposes four principles as a universal code of ethics for intercultural communication. *Principle 1:* "Ethical communicators address people of other cultures with the same respect that they would like to receive themselves." In light of this principle, verbal or nonverbal communication that demeans or belittles others' cultural identity is unethical. *Principle 2:* "Ethical communicators seek to describe the world as they perceive it as accurately as possible." Because deception undermines the ability of people of different cultures to trust each other, ethical communicators avoid intentionally deceiving or misleading. *Principle 3:* "Ethical communicators encourage people of other cultures to express themselves in their uniqueness." No matter the degree of popularity or unpopularity of their political or social views, it is both ethnocentric and unethical to grant peoples of other cultures equal status in international debate and dialogue "only if they choose to express themselves in the same way we do." *Principle 4:* "Ethical communicators strive for identification with people of other cultures."

The goal is mutual understanding and unity of spirit while allowing for uniqueness of cultural identities. Communication that stirs racial hatred or heightens ethnic divisions is ethically suspect because it probably will promote conflict rather than peace.

Multicultural Communication

As indicated at the beginning of this chapter, multicultural communication is a concept much discussed today and often defined in quite varied ways. For the purposes of this chapter, the definition offered by Lawrence Blum provides insight.[20]

> Multiculturalism involves an understanding, appreciation, and valuing of one's own culture, and an informed respect and curiosity about the ethnic cultures of others. It involves a valuing of other cultures, not in the sense of approving all aspects of those cultures, but of attempting to see how a given culture can express value to its own members.

As used in this chapter, multicultural communication includes communication between subcultural groups within the larger U.S. national culture and between members of subcultural groups and the dominant white heterosexual male culture. Instead of multicultural communication, Marquita Byrd employs the term "intracultural communication" for communication "among people who are citizens of the same geopolitical system, and also hold membership in one or more tributary groups." Tributary groups are "distinguishable from the power dominant/general population on the basis of racial characteristics, ethnic heritage, religious beliefs, gender identification, sexual orientation, socioeconomic level, age, and/or ableness." As examples of intracultural (multicultural) communication, Byrd mentions women with men, disabled with abled, homosexuals with heterosexuals, blacks with whites, and Hispanic Americans with Asian Americans.[21] We need to remember that multiculturalism may apply to an individual. "For many people . . . not one but several cultures contribute to a single identity. . . . Not only societies, but people are multicultural."[22] Bear in mind that some of the issues and principles discussed in the first half of the this chapter also may apply here.

Ethnic Ethics

In his book, *Ethnic Ethics: The Restructuring of Moral Theory*, Anthony Cortese argues at length that "morality must be bound to a particular cultural or sociocultural context."[23] "Morality," he contends, "contains no intrinsic laws of development. Its validity has no ultimate basis. Instead, moral systems prosper or fail within specific cultural and historical settings." From Cortese's perspective, traditional "moral principles that are allegedly universal are viewed as the highest good." But he takes the position "that people are more important than principles, that relationships are more crucial than conceptions of justice, and that subcultural moral systems are more relevant than universal standards of ethics."

"The key to morality is in social relations," argues Cortese, "not in abstract rational principles. . . . Ethnic background, gender, role demands, and socioeconomic status" are key factors. And yet "the structures of moral reasoning used by Western middle-to-upper-middle-class white males appear to be taken to be everyone's ideal type by many researchers. Similarly the norms of the dominant culture are taken as the model for the entire society." Cortese takes seriously "the possibility that ethnic groups have different moral structures, each adequate to the reproduction of the social life-world found in each ethnic group." He believes, "One must also consider the possibility that the 'scientific findings' on moral development are more appropriately viewed as ideology that sets the Western European social life-world as the model for all people in all places."

Modified Universalism

The moral pluralism view developed by Cortese need not necessarily lead to a radical cultural or ethical relativism wherein whatever ethical standards "work" for an ethnic group or culture uniformly ought to be acceptable. Rather what Emmet terms "soft" moral relativism, what Gutmann calls "deliberative universalism," and what Benhabib labels "interactive universalism" open up for examination the possibility that cultural variation in certain moral principles between cultures or within a culture does not preclude moral judgments of better or worse between or within those cultures.[24] Lack of commitment solely to a complete set of invariable or universalizable principles does not mean impossibility of a minimum set of ethical norms that are or should be transcultural. And while a minimum set of ethical standards should apply universally in principle to everyone everywhere, those minimum standards need not apply in every case. Occasional special circumstances may allow for an exception in a particular case. An occasional exception does not invalidate universal applicability. We would suggest for consideration such potential transcultural ethical standards as humaneness, truthfulness, trust, promise keeping, nonviolence, and caring relationships. Consider again the transcultural values discussed in the first section of this chapter. Other ethical standards within a culture or subculture properly may be more relative to specific cultural, ethnic, class, or gender factors; some of these more relativistic standards might be critiqued in light of the transcultural norms. The Josephson Institute of Ethics, for instance, proposes six "core consensus ethical values that transcend cultural, ethnic, and socioeconomic differences": trustworthiness, respect, responsibility, justice and fairness, caring, and civic virtue and citizenship. Yet, the institute also recognizes that there are additional ethical values that properly vary among cultures, ethnic groups, religions, and political philosophies.[25]

Moral Exclusion

Moral exclusion, in Susan Opotow's description, "occurs when individuals or groups are perceived as *outside the boundary in which moral values, rules, and considerations of fairness* apply. Those who are morally excluded are perceived as nonentities, expendable, or undeserving; consequently, harming them appears acceptable, appropriate, or just." Persons morally excluded are denied their rights, dignity, and autonomy.[26]

Opotow isolates for analysis and discussion over two dozen symptoms or manifestations of moral exclusion. For our purposes a noteworthy fact is that many of them directly involve communication behavior. While all of the symptoms she presents are significant for a full understanding of the mind-set that characterizes a person who engages in moral exclusion, here we will paraphrase only those that clearly involve communication.

1. Showing the superiority of you or your group by making unflattering comparisons to others or another group

2. Denigrating and disparaging others by characterizing them as lower life forms (vermin) or inferior beings (barbarians, aliens)

3. Denying that others possess humanity, dignity, ability to feel, or the right to compassion

4. Redefining as an increasingly larger category the category of "legitimate victims"

5. Blaming the victim; placing the blame for any harm on the victim not the doer

6. Justifying harmful acts by claiming that the morally condemnable acts committed by the adversary are significantly worse

7. Misrepresenting cruelty and harm by masking, sanitizing, and conferring respectability on them through use of neutral, positive, technical, or euphemistic terms to describe them

8. Justifying harmful behavior by claiming it is widely accepted (everyone is doing it) or that it was isolated and uncharacteristic behavior (just this once)

An example may clarify how language choices function to achieve moral exclusion. The category of "vermin" (mentioned in item 2) includes such parasitic insects as fleas, lice, mosquitoes, bedbugs, and ticks, which can infest human bodies. In World War II Nazi Germany, Adolf Hitler's speeches and writings often referred to Jews as some type of parasite infesting the pure Aryan race (non-Jewish Caucasians of Nordic heritage) or as some type of disease, such as cancer, attacking the German national body. The depiction of Jews as parasites or a disease placed Jews outside the moral boundary where ethical standards apply to human treatment of humans. Jews were classified or categorized as nonhumans. As parasites they should be exterminated or as a cancerous disease be cut out of the national body.[27] Nazi ideology also saw the so-called "Jewish problem" as best solved through the "final solution," a more or less neutral phrase (see item 7) that masked or sanitized the horror of the holocaust program of attempting to exterminate the Jewish race.

Another example of moral exclusion is the genocide (attempted extermination of an entire ethnic group) that occurred in the African nation of Rwanda in 1994. In about 100 days, some 800,000 people were slaughtered, most by being hacked to death with machetes. The ethnic Hutus in power organized soldiers and ordinary citizens to murder ethnic Tutsis (men, women, and children), many of whom had been friends and neighbors. While there are multiple causes or influences that led to the massacre, clearly the language of moral exclusion was a contributing factor. A lengthy government propaganda campaign using radio programs fostered in the minds of the Hutus a view of Tutsis as less than human, as the prey of "hunting expeditions," and as "cockroaches" to be squashed. For horrifying yet routine examples of this process, we urge you to read Jean Hatzfeld, *Machete Season: The Killers in Rwanda Speak* (2005). To experience the atmosphere at that time, rent the fact-based film *Beyond the Gates* (2005).

Even headlines we read daily in newspapers, magazines, and Internet blogs may reflect (perhaps unconsciously) the process of moral exclusion. Consider this headline that appeared in the Tempo section of the *Chicago Tribune* (May 29, 2000): "An Eskimo Encounters Civilization—and Mankind." In what two ways do words in the headline reflect moral exclusion? How do these words place people outside the categories (boundaries) where human ethics normally apply?

In the following section we will see how moral exclusion functions through racist and sexist language and through "hate speech" on college campuses.

Racist/Sexist Language and Hate Speech

In *The Language of Oppression*, Haig Bosmajian demonstrates how names, labels, definitions, and stereotypes have been employed to degrade, dehumanize, and suppress Jews, blacks, Native Americans, and women. His goal is to expose the "decadence in our language, the inhumane uses of language," that have been used "to justify the unjustifiable, to make palatable the unpalatable, to make reasonable the unreasonable, to make decent the indecent."

Bosmajian reminds us: "Our identities, who and what we are, how others see us, are greatly affected by the names we are called and the words with which we are labeled. The names, labels, and phrases employed to 'identify' a people may in the end determine their survival."[28]

"Every language reflects the prejudices of the society in which it evolved. Since English, through most of its history, evolved in a white, Anglo-Saxon, patriarchal society, no one should be surprised that its vocabulary and grammar frequently reflect attitudes that exclude or demean minorities and women." Such is the fundamental position of Casey Miller and Kate Swift, authors of *The Handbook of Nonsexist Writing*. Conventional English usage, they believe, "often obscures the actions, the contributions, and sometimes the very presence of women." Because such language usage is misleading and inaccurate, they see ethical implication in it. "In this respect, continuing to use English in ways that have become misleading is no different from misusing data, whether the misuse is inadvertent or planned."[29]

To what degree is use of racist/sexist language unethical and by what standards? At the least, racist/sexist terms place people in artificial and irrelevant categories. At worst, such terms intentionally demean and "put down" other people through embodying unfair negative value judgments concerning traits, capacities, and accomplishments. What are the ethical implications, for instance, of calling a Jewish person a "kike," a black person a "nigger" or "boy," an Italian person a "wop," an Asiatic person a "gook" or "slant-eye," or a thirty-year-old woman a "girl" or "chick"? Here is one possible answer:

> In the war in Southeast Asia, our military fostered a linguistic environment in which Vietnamese people were called such names as *slope, dink, slant, gook*, and *zip*; those names made it much easier to despise, to fear, and to kill them. When we call women in our society by such names as *gash, slut, dyke, bitch*, or *girl*, we—men and women alike—have put ourselves in a position to demean and abuse them.[30]

Note how the term *zip*, slang for zero or nothing, or *bitch*, the name for a female dog, literally categorize others as worthless or nonhuman. Persons labeled with such terms thus are morally excluded from the arena in which human ethical standards apply.

The issue of "hate speech" on college and university campuses illustrates the tension between the right of freedom of speech and ethically responsible exercise of that right.[31] For our purposes in this section, however, the focus will be on ethical issues and standards. Hate speech is a very broad label that has come to designate verbal attacks (spoken or written) on persons because of their race, religion, ethnicity, sex, or sexual orientation.

Examples of hate speech on college campuses typify the kinds of communication at issue.[32] Eight Asian-American students on their way to a dance at the University of Connecticut were harassed for almost an hour by a group of football players who called them "Oriental faggots," sat on them, and challenged them to a fight. At the University of Arizona at Tempe, a fight broke out and police were called to restore order after some white fraternity members harassed a black student by chanting "coon," "nigger," and "porch monkey." A fraternity at the University of Wisconsin held a mock slave auction. Two white freshmen at Stanford put obviously Negroid features on a picture of Beethoven and posted it in a black studies dormitory. "African Nigger do you want some bananas? Go back to the jungle" was the message that an African woman at Smith College found under her dormitory door. "A mind is a terrible thing to waste—especially on a nigger" was written anonymously on a blackboard at the University of Michigan.

By 1992 over 100 American colleges and universities had instituted speech codes to prohibit such hateful and offensive messages. Among the varied forms of expression punishable under these speech codes are: use of derogatory names, inappropriately directed laughter, inconsiderate jokes, and conspicuous exclusion of another person from conversation; language that stigmatizes or victimizes individuals or that creates an intimidating or offensive environment; face-to-face use of epithets, obscenities, and other forms of expression that by accepted community standards degrade, victimize, stigmatize, or pejoratively depict persons based on their personal, intellectual, or cultural diversity; extensive or outrageous acts or communications intended to harass, intimidate, or humiliate a student on the basis of race, color, or national origin thus reasonably causing him or her severe emotional distress.[33] When the constitutionality of some of the campus speech codes has been tested in court, typically the codes have been ruled unconstitutional as violations of First Amendment protections of freedom of speech.

Several scholars of the First Amendment rest their cases for control of hate speech through law or codes primarily on ethical grounds. R. George Wright advocates the adoption of tort laws or criminal laws both because of the psychological harms he believes stem from hate speech and, more important, because of community agreement that the "use of racial epithets involves a clear and fundamental moral wrong." Wright rests his view firmly on the "sheer moral disvalue of racist speech." Hate speech fundamentally is a "deontic moral wrong."[34] In other words, hate speech is, in his view, by its very nature unethical; it is unethical in and of itself, it never is ethically justifiable. Wright seeks use of legal enforcement of a primarily ethical judgment.

Andrew Altman favors narrowly worded regulations against hate speech because it is a type of illocutionary "speech act" that by its very utterance treats someone as a moral subordinate—as having inferior moral status. "Treating persons as moral subordinates," argues Altman, "means treating them in a way that takes their interests to be intrinsically less important, and their lives inherently less valuable," than those of others. Epithets such as "kike," "faggot," "spic," or "nigger" are "verbal instruments of subordination" and degradation that not only express hatred and contempt for persons but also "put them in their place" as having inferior moral standing. Note here that Altman is describing the process of moral exclusion through language that places people or groups in a subhuman category that puts them in their "place" as having inferior moral standing. Altman roots his ethical judgment in a version of a political perspective—the belief that "wrongs of subordination based on such characteristics as race, gender, and sexual preference . . . are among the principle wrongs that have prevented—and continue to prevent—Western liberal democracies from living up to their ideals and principles."[35]

Hate speech also could be condemned as unethical because it violates versions of Immanuel Kant's Categorical Imperative (see our discussion of Kant in chapter 3 on human nature perspectives).[36] First, a person's use of hate speech is not universalizable in that the person probably would not want others to use the type of hate speech against him or her that the person is using against others. The principle the person is using to justify hate speech against others is not a principle he or she would allow others to use in reverse. Second, Kant believed: "Always act so that you treat humanity, whether in your own person or another, as an end, and never merely as a means." The language of hate speech does not respect targets as beings deserving of at least minimal respect as humans, and such language sees targets as subhuman means to be used or abused for the hater's purposes. First Amendment scholar Timothy Shiell contends that hate speakers "simply aim to silence their targets, to hurt them, to use them as mere objects upon which to vent their hostility, aggression, frustration, and rage, to reduce rational human beings to subhuman status."[37] Here, again, we see the process of moral exclusion functioning by categorizing others as objects or as subhuman and thus outside the moral boundaries where human ethical standards apply.

Regardless how issues of First Amendment constitutionality are decided concerning campus hate speech, clearly such communication, and racist/sexist language generally, should be condemned on ethical grounds that we have discussed previously as representative democracy political perspectives, human nature perspectives, dialogical perspectives, and feminist viewpoints. Hate speech in the form of racist, sexist, and homophobic communication dehumanizes—makes a person less than human—by demeaning other people through embodying unfair negative value judgments concerning traits, capacities, or accomplishments. Communication that dehumanizes reinforces stereotypes, conveys inaccurate depictions of people, dismisses taking serious account of people, dismisses people as citizens worthy of participating in public discourse on public issues, and even makes people invisible for purposes of decision or policy. Communication that dehumanizes undermines the human capacities for symbol-use and reasonableness. Communication that dehumanizes reflects a superior, exploitative, inhumane attitude of one person toward another, thus hindering equal opportunity for self-fulfillment. Communication that dehumanizes views others, not as persons inherently worthy of minimal respect as humans, but as things or objects to be manipulated for the communicator's pleasure or selfish gain.

We call your attention to two Web sites that provide reliable information about hate groups that foster hate speech. Check the Hate Groups Map on the Southern Poverty Law Center Web site and surf its various links to see the extent and nature of such groups (www.splcenter.org/intel/map/hate.jsp). On the Anti-Defamation League Web site (www.adl.org) type in the search window: poisoning the web. Then click on the table of contents to surf the various listings of topics.

Communicating about Ethics Across Cultural Differences

How can we communicate in productive and ethically responsible ways across cultural differences of ethics and values? Of course the standards and concepts already discussed in this chapter can guide us in our communication. The standards and attitudes presented in chapter 3 on human nature perspectives, chapter 4 on dialogical perspectives, and chapter 8 on interpersonal communication also can apply. And communication "virtues" that facilitate conversations across intercultural and multicultural differences on ethics are relevant:

> These virtues include tolerance, patience, respect for differences, a willingness to listen, the willingness to admit that we may be mistaken, the ability to reinterpret or translate one's own concerns in a way that makes them comprehensible to others, the self-imposition of restraint in order that others may "have a turn" to speak, and the disposition to express one's self honestly and sincerely.[38]

Ethicist Deni Elliott offers five practical principles to facilitate communication across cultural differences on ethics.[39] We summarize and paraphrase them here. *First,* recognize needs and interests held in common, such as avoiding harm or preserving the environment. *Second,* "begin agreement by recognizing what both groups consider to be intolerable." Rather than starting by discussing what is ideal, start with agreements on what is ethically prohibited by both parties (groups or individuals). *Third,* "value diversity over assimilation." Generally assimilation demands only one right way to which all people should conform. Diversity promotes more inclusive standards for success and recognizes that synthesis of both viewpoints may result from openness to alternative approaches. *Fourth,* "listen to and value the nondominant culture." Neither the dominant culture nor the nondominant culture "is always right or all wrong." But those in the dominant culture may expect, for example, that communication be rationally linear and fact-based and thus miss the relevant information a nondominant group member presents in a "narrative or stream-of-consciousness approach to thinking about issues." *Fifth,* "in those instances where everyone's needs cannot be met, favor the vulnerable." Favoring the most vulnerable, usually the nondominant group, compensates for past harms and recognizes that there may be other ways in which the needs and interests of the dominant group can be met.

There is reason to hope that such intercultural and multicultural communication about ethics could occur. In his book, *Human Universals,* Donald Brown asks: "What do all people, all societies, all cultures, and all languages have in common?" His interpretation of relevant research leads him to describe what he terms Universal People who "distinguish right from wrong, and at least implicitly. . . recognize responsibility and intentionality. They recognize and employ promises. Reciprocity. . . is a key element in their morality. So, too, is the ability to empathize."[40]

Discarding Rigidity

As for the chapter on feminist contributions, Robert Solomon offers a fitting summary of many of the issues and themes discussed in this chapter on intercultural and multicultural communication ethics.[41]

> We try too hard, and impossibly, to be above any particular society and culture and so, in the name of universalism, find ourselves nowhere at all. . . . But ethics need not take the form of a rigid set of moral principles backed by an ironclad theory of justification. Rather it is a shared way of life in which certain practices and rules of morality play an accepted role but are flexible and always open to question. To question everything is to be left with nothing, but to refuse to question at all, or to insist on an ultimate justification, relegates morality to the realm of stubborn habits and condemns multicultural society to bitter political and endless battles.

Solomon advocates a new ethics of pluralism especially suited to contemporary American society rather than to ancient Greek society or to Kant's eighteenth-century Germany. The United States, he contends, is a society with values and one capable of making ethical judgments among better and worse actions. "But we are a society with a multiplicity of values, in which it therefore becomes all the more urgent for each of us to clarify, understand, and within modest limits, justify our values and our views." In his view, the complex ethos or national "character" that "constitutes American society is still in the making, and it is by doing ethics that we can assist in its formation."

Notes

[1] John Condon, "Values and Ethics in Communication across Cultures: Notes on the North American Case," *Communication*, 6, no. 2 (1981): 255–266; John Condon and Fathi Yousef, *An Introduction to Intercultural Communication* (Indianapolis: Bobbs-Merrill, 1975), chs. 4, 5, 10, 11.

[2] Robert Kane, *Through the Moral Maze: Searching for Absolute Values in a Pluralistic World* (New York: Paragon, 1994), pp. 9, 15–16, 51. Also see Don Browning, ed., *Universalism vs. Relativism: Making Moral Judgments in a Changing, Pluralistic, and Threatening World* (Lanham, MD: Rowman & Littlefield, 2006).

[3] Rushworth M. Kidder, *Shared Values for a Troubled World: Conversations with Men and Women of Conscience* (San Francisco: Jossey-Bass, 1994); William E. Loges and Rushworth M. Kidder,

Global Values, Moral Boundaries: A Pilot Study (Camden, ME: Institute for Global Ethics, 1997). Also see Kidder, *Moral Courage* (William Morrow, 2005), pp. 43–68.

4 Sissela Bok, *Common Values* (Columbia: University of Missouri Press, 1995).

5 Ibid., pp. 13–19, 26, 49, 57, 70, 78–79. Also see Bernard Gert, *Common Morality* (New York: Oxford University Press, 2004).

6 His Holiness The Dalai Lama, *Ethics for the New Millennium* (New York: Riverhead Books, 1999), pp. xii–xiii, 19–20, 219–231.

7 Ibid., pp. xii, 5, 27–33, 47, 147–150.

8 Ibid., pp. 22, 150, 223.

9 Clifford G. Christians and Michael Traber, eds., *Communication Ethics and Universal Values* (Thousand Oaks, CA: Sage, 1997), pp. viii–xv, 3–23, 327–343; esp. pp. 17, 341; for a view that doubts the possibility of a transcultural communication ethic, see Robert Shuter, "Ethics and Communication: An Intercultural Approach," in *Intercultural Communication: A Reader*, 10th ed., Larry A. Samovar and Richard E. Porter, eds. (Belmont, CA: Wadsworth/Thomson, 2003), pp. 449–455.

10 Christians and Traber, *Communication Ethics*, pp. x–xii, 6–7, 13, 17, 337. Thomas Cooper suggests that the sacredness of all life, both human and nonhuman, virtually is a universal ethical standard of indigenous or native cultures of the world. See Thomas W. Cooper, *A Time Before Deception: Truth in Communication, Culture, and Ethics* (Santa Fe, NM: Clear Light Press, 1998), pp. 92–94, 164, 187.

11 Christians and Traber, *Communication Ethics*, pp. x–xv, 13–15, 330, 334–336, 339–340.

12 Ibid., p. 18; Bok, *Common Values*, p. 24.

13 These versions from the sacred literature of world religions are cited in Kane, *Through the Moral Maze*, p. 34; also see Larry A. Samovar, Richard E. Porter and Edwin R. McDaniel, *Communication between Cultures*, 6th ed. (Belmont, CA: Wadsworth, 2007).

14 See Marcus G. Singer, "The Golden Rule," *Philosophy*, 38 (1963): 293–314.

15 Marcus G. Singer, "Golden Rule," in *Encyclopedia of Philosophy*, Vol. 3, Paul Edwards, ed. (New York: Macmillan and the Free Press, 1967), pp. 365–366.

16 Milton J. Bennett, "Overcoming the Golden Rule: Sympathy and Empathy," in *Communication Yearbook 3*, ed. Dan Nimmo (New Brunswick, NJ: Transaction Books, 1979), pp. 407–422.

17 Singer, "The Golden Rule," 313.

18 Guo-Ming Chen and William J. Starosta, *Foundations of Intercultural Communication* (Boston: Allyn & Bacon, 1998), pp. 284–292. For additional approaches, see Bradford "J" Hall, *Among Cultures: The Challenge of Communication* (Belmont, CA: Thomson/Wadsworth, 2005), ch. 11; Stella Ting-Toomey and Leeva C. Chung, *Understanding Intercultural Communication* (Los Angeles: Roxbury, 2005), ch. 13.

19 David W. Kale, "Peace as an Ethic for Intercultural Communication," in Samovar and Porter, eds., *Intercultural Communication*, pp. 466–470.

20 Lawrence Blum, cited in Larry and Shari Collins Sharratt, eds., *Applied Ethics: A Multicultural Approach* (Englewood Cliffs, NJ: Prentice Hall, 1994), p. 2. Also see Susan Miller Okin, "Feminism and Multiculturalism: Some Tensions," *Ethics*, 108 (July 1998): 61–84.

21 Marquita L. Byrd, *The Intracultural Communication Book* (New York: McGraw-Hill, 1993), pp. 1, 10.

22 Amy Gutmann, "The Challenge of Multiculturalism in Political Ethics," *Philosophy and Public Affairs*, 22 (Summer 1993): 171–206.

23 Anthony Cortese, *Ethnic Ethics: The Restructuring of Moral Theory* (Albany: State University of New York Press, 1990), pp. 1–6, 41, 91–94, 107. For one brief critique of Cortese's moral pluralism view, see Joan C. Tronto, *Moral Boundaries: A Political Argument for an Ethic of Care* (New York: Routledge, 1993), p. 94.

24 Dorothy Emmet, *Rules, Roles, and Relations* (London: Macmillan, 1966), pp. 89–109; Gutmann, "The Challenge of Multiculturalism in Political Ethics," pp. 171–206; Seyla Benhabib, *Situating the Self, Gender, Community and Postmodernism in Contemporary Society* (New York: Routledge, 1992), pp. 1–19, 153.

25 Michael Josephson, *Making Ethical Decisions*, 2nd ed. (Marina del Rey, CA: The Josephson Institute of Ethics, 1993), pp. 1–10.

26 Susan Opotow, "Moral Exclusion and Injustice: An Introduction," *Journal of Social Issues*, 46 (1990): 1–20 (italics in original).

27 For additional detail, see Steven Perry, "Rhetorical Functions of the Infestation Metaphor in Hitler's Rhetoric," *Central States Speech Journal*, 34 (Winter 1983): 229–235; Richard A. Koenigsberg, *Hitler's Ideology* (New York: Library of Social Science, 1975), pp. 16–25.

28 Haig Bosmajian, *The Language of Oppression* (Washington, DC: Public Affairs Press, 1974), pp. 1–10. Also see J. Dan Rothwell, *Telling It Like It Isn't* (Englewood Cliffs, NJ: Prentice-Hall, 1982), chs. 5 and 6.

29 Casey Miller and Kate Swift, *The Handbook of Nonsexist Writing* (New York: Barnes and Noble paperback, 1981), pp. 3–8. Second Edition, Lincoln, NE: iUniverse, 2001.

30 Richard W. Baily, "George Orwell and the English Language," in *The Future of Nineteen Eighty-Four*, Ejner J. Jensen, ed. (Ann Arbor: University of Michigan Press, 1984), pp. 42–43. Also see two essays in *Philosophy and Sex*, Robert Baker and Frederick Elliston, eds. (Buffalo, NY: Prometheus Books, 1975): Barbara Lawrence, "Four Letter Words Can Hurt You," pp. 31–33; and Robert Baker, "'Pricks' and 'Chicks': A Plea for 'Persons,'" pp. 45–64.

31 For extensive analysis of ethical issues and free speech issues in the areas of hate speech, pornography, and obscene rock and rap music lyrics, see Richard L. Johannesen, "Diversity, Freedom, and Responsibility in Tension," in *Communication Ethics in an Age of Diversity*, Josina M. Makau and Ronald C. Arnett, eds. (Champaign: University of Illinois Press, 1997), ch. 8. Also see Larry Williamson and Eric Pierson, "The Rhetoric of Hate on the Internet," *Journal of Mass Media Ethics*, 18 (2003): 250–267.

32 The following examples are cited in Thomas L. Tedford and Dale A. Herbeck, *Freedom of Speech in the United States*, 5th ed. (State College, PA: Strata, 2005), p. 183; Samuel Walker, *Hate Speech: The History of an American Controversy* (Lincoln: University of Nebraska Press, 1994), pp. 129–130.

33 Tedford and Herbeck, pp. 183–184; Walker, pp. 127–158.

34 R. George Wright, *The Future of Free Speech Law* (New York: Quorum, 1990), pp. 58–59, 69, 73–76.

35 Andrew Altman, "Liberalism and Campus Hate Speech: A Philosophical Examination," *Ethics*, 103 (January 1993): 302–317.

36 Timothy C. Shiell, *Campus Hate Speech on Trial* (Lawrence: University Press of Kansas, 1998), pp. 33–35.

37 Ibid., p. 35.

38 Nicholas C. Burbules and Suzanne Rice, "Dialogue across Differences: Continuing the Conversation," *Harvard Educational Review*, 61 (1991): 411.

39 Deni Elliott, *Ethics in the First Person: A Guide to Teaching and Learning Practical Ethics* (Lanham, MD: Rowman and Littlefield, 2007), pp. 116–117.

40 Donald E. Brown, *Human Universals* (Philadelphia: Temple University Press, 1991), pp. 131, 139.

41 Robert C. Solomon, *Ethics: A Short Introduction* (Dubuque, IA: Brown Benchmark, 1993), pp. 159–163.

Appendix
Case Studies of Theory and Practice

Each of the case studies reprinted in this Appendix reflects one or more of the ethical "perspectives" discussed in this book. Where ethical standards are applied to specific instances of communication, you are encouraged to render your own ethical judgments of the instances examined. Does the critic show that the standards he or she employs are reasonable and relevant for the techniques being evaluated? Does the critic indicate in what ways the techniques examined measure up or fail to measure up to clearly explained standards? To what extent, and why, do you agree or differ with the critic's ethical assessment?

In *The Abuse of Casuistry* (Berkeley: University of California Press, 1988), Albert Jonsen and Stephen Toulmin detail the historical development and potential current applications of casuistry [*kazh' ö i strë*] as a method of moral reasoning about paradigmatic ethical cases or "cases of conscience." They formally define casuistry as "the analysis of moral issues, using procedures of reasoning based on paradigms and analogies, leading to the formulation of expert opinion about the existence and stringency of particular moral obligations, framed in terms of rules or maxims that are general but not universal or invariable. . . ." (257). Keith Hearit, *Crisis Management by Apology* (Mahwah, NJ: Erlbaum, 2006) proposes a casuistical or paradigm case approach for judging the ethics of corporation responses to charges of wrongdoing (pp. 58–78, written with Sandra Borden). David Boeynik, "Casuistry: A Case Bound Method for Journalists," *Journal of Mass Media Ethics*, 7, no. 2 (1992): 107–20, modifies the casuistic method for application to situations involving journalistic ethics. Read these sources to determine in what ways casuistry might be used in doing case studies of communication ethics. Also see Richard B. Miller, *Casuistry and Modern Ethics: A Poetics of Practical Reasoning* (Chicago: University of Chicago Press, 1996); James M. Tallmon, "Casuistry and the Role of Rhetorical Reason in Ethical Inquiry," *Philosophy and Rhetoric*, 28 (1995): 377–87.

Preview to "A Role for Shame in Communication Ethics." What is the nature of the emotion we call shame? What does "to be ashamed" involve? Can feeling "ashamed of oneself" have both positive and negative consequences? Can shame promote ethical behavior in us and in others? Is it ethical to intentionally shame someone else privately? In a public setting? These are some of the issues explored in this essay. In *True To Our Feelings: What Our Emotions Are Really Telling Us* (Oxford University Press, 2007), philosopher Robert Solomon observes that shame is an emotion about responsibility, "including moral responsibility." He believes that "our society seems a bit overzealous about guilt but disturbingly short on shame." According to Solomon, shame "is or can be a most effective tool for moral cultivation" (pp. 90–100).

In her book, *Blush: The Faces of Shame* (University of Minnesota Press, 2005), gender studies scholar Elspeth Probyn recognizes that shame can be harmful but on the whole sees it as positive and productive. "Shame compels an involuntary and immediate reassessment of ourselves. . . . Shame in this way is positive in its self-evaluative role; it can even be self-transforming. . . . The things that make me ashamed have to do with a strong interest in being a good person. . . . Shame reminds me about the promises we keep to ourselves" (pp. xii–x). In *Hiding from Humanity: Disgust, Shame, and the Law* (Princeton University Press, 2004), philosopher Martha Nussbaum argues against use in the legal system of public shame-based punishments. Nevertheless, she also argues that "shame can at times be a morally valuable emotion, playing a constructive role in development and moral change. . . . The person who is utterly shame-free is not a good friend, lover, or citizen, and there are instances when the invitation to feel shame is a good thing—most often when the invitation is issued by the self, but at least sometimes when another person issues it" (pp. 211, 216).

A valuable exercise is to examine the ethical role of shame in another culture. For example, in the Confucian ethical tradition in China, there are legitimate roles for an ethical sense of shame. And to be shameless, without a sense of shame, would mark one as less than fully human. See the essay by Brian Van Norden in *Confucian Ethics: A Comparative Study of Self, Autonomy, and Community*, eds. Kwong-Loi Shun and David B. Wong (Cambridge University Press, 2004), pp. 148–182; also see the essay by Dong-Hyum Byum and Keshyeung Lee in *Moral Engagement in Public Life*, eds. Sharon L. Bracci and Clifford G. Christians (Peter Lang Publishers, 2002), pp. 72–96.

A Role for Shame in Communication Ethics*

Richard L. Johannesen

For shame! I feel so ashamed of myself! You ought to be ashamed of yourself! Shame on you! That's shameful! Have you no shame? You are absolutely

*Revised from Keynote Address for the Seventh National Communication Ethics Conference, Western Michigan University, May 31, 2002.

shameless! These phrases and feelings represent some of the typical roles that shame has played in the past in our culture. For the most part, such judgments seem to be downplayed in current culture. Jean Bethke Elshtain, Professor of Social and Political Ethics at the University of Chicago, describes a predominant cultural attitude toward shame (Elshtain, 1995, p. 69):

> My late friend Christopher Lasch was right to claim that much of what is disturbing in contemporary democratic life is the result of what he called "the triumph of therapeutic culture"—the idea that the wider culture exists only to minister to our individual needs and wants. . . . One of the promises of therapeutic culture is that shame can and should be banished. This is a mistake. I think that "the boundary of shame" has an important place in culture.

Elshtain supports the "accurate, honest, and authentic" presumption "that there are some things that are simply shameful, even if the *boundary* of shame is different for different cultures." Carl Schneider, a psychotherapist and theologian, notes that "popular magazines and journals regularly bring us new psychological theories urging that we realize our true humanity by divesting ourselves of guilt and shame." But he argues that "shame is not a 'disease'; as we shall see, it is a mark of our humanity" (1977, pp. xiii–xiv; also see Schneiderman, 1995, pp. 48–50).

Can some conception of shame be legitimate as a part of communication ethics? This is not a topic that has been much on the mind of scholars writing about communication ethics. As an index item, "shame" does not appear in the five general communication ethics textbooks that span three decades, including the first four editions of this text. Nor does shame appear in the index of the four organizational communication ethics textbooks, nor in the index of the numerous media and journalism ethics textbooks I have examined. There are a few isolated exceptions to this neglect. Although textbooks on interpersonal communication also seem not to treat shame as relevant, Harold Barrett's book, *Maintaining the Self in Communication*, describes a central positive role for shame in ethical development (1998, pp. 5–6, 56–58, 93–94, 181, 262). Molefi Asante, an African American communication scholar, not only laments the decline of civility in contemporary society, but also condemns the "trivialization of shame" (1995, pp. 12–15). A major exception to the general neglect of shame by communication scholars is a lengthy essay, "Messages of Shame and Guilt," published in 2000 in *Communication Yearbook 23* (Planalp et al., 2000).

Despite this downplaying of shame and neglect of a role for it by most communication scholars of ethics, articles spanning the '70s, '80s, and '90s in such diverse sources as the *New York Times*, *Harper's*, *The Nation*, *Newsweek*, and *National Review* urge the rehabilitation of shame as a legitimate ethical force in society. Consider the titles of these essays: "Long Live Shame! (Hoffer, 1974); "There's No More Shame" (Kaus, 1982); "For Shame" (Lasch, 1992); "In Praise of Shame" (Lapin, 1995); and "The Return of Shame" (Alter and Wingert, 1995).

The issue of shame does surface from time to time in the news. For example, two liberal critics condemned President Reagan for being "literally shameless when it came to the question of factuality" (Green and MacColl, 1987, p. 11). A syndicated political columnist condemned President Clinton for "routine and unending deceptions" on matters not only of personal behavior but also on public policy. The columnist concluded: "What inhibits most people from routine lies is a sense of shame. Clinton seems to lack this" (Samuelson, 1998). And Clinton belatedly did say in one of his speeches of public apology: "I am profoundly sorry for all I have done in words and deeds. . . . Quite simply, I gave in to my shame" (Clinton, 2000).

Shame as a Contested Concept

Shame as a human emotion is a contested and controversial concept in such fields as anthropology, psychology, psychiatry, and moral philosophy. Some of the major disagreements focus on definitional characteristics, on its differences from guilt, on whether it is a legitimate concept in ethics, and whether shame plays positive or negative roles (or both) in human moral development (Deigh, 1983; Gilbert and Andrews, 1998; Gilligan, 1976; Isenberg, 1949; Katz, 1997; Kekes, 1988; Kellenberger, 1995; Lamb, 1983; O'Hear, 1976–77; Planalp, et al., 2000; Scheff, 1995; Tangeny and Fischer, 1995). The current dominant negative focus in psychiatry and psychology is on shame as a corrosive, self-destroying pathology or as a threat to a person's fragile self-esteem (Broucek, 1991; Karen, 1992; Kass, H., 1998; Lansky and Morrison, 1997; Miller, 1996; Morrison, 1996; Nathanson, 1987; Nathanson, 1992; Nussbaum, 2001; Wurmser, 1981). For example, Andrew Morrison views shame as an unhealthy burden on the self. He emphasizes the relation of shame to such feelings as failure, inferiority, defectiveness, unworthiness, incompetence, passivity, despair, unlovability, and low self-esteem (1996, pp. x, 10, 22–57). Melvin Lansky and Andrew Morrison observe: "Often the hidden dimension, shame has been called the 'veiled accompaniment' of such clinical phenomena as widespread and divergent as narcissism, social phobia, envy, domestic violence, addiction, identity diffusion, post-traumatic stress disorder, dissociation, masochism, and depression" (1997, p. xv).

Normal or Situational Shame

In contrast to such negative pathological emphases, I urge consideration also of what some call normal or situational shame (Karen, 1992, pp. 42, 58, 62; Nussbaum, 2001, p. 218). I am thinking about the view of philosopher Gabriele Taylor who sees shame as an emotion with positive roles in moral self-assessment and self-protection (1985, pp. 53–84; also see Boonin, 1983; Haidt, 2003). Normal or situational shame includes the following dimensions. Shame is a feeling or emotion we experience when something we do or say (or fail to do or say) falls short of or violates our own basic moral character. We recognize that our behavior is less than expected by our own ideal moral self or image of our self at our best ethically. It is thus that the phrase, "I am ashamed of myself," takes on meaning. Of course our ideal moral self-image is constructed by us over time under the eyes of others in the context of group or cultural norms that we accept or reject. In shame we feel like hiding or avoiding. A normal or situational sense of shame is a kind of moral compass to help us monitor the ethics of our behavior. The feeling of shame need not be an all or nothing matter. We may experience degrees of shame. Because persons are not perfect and in order to be a healthy emotion, shame should not persist indefinitely or be universalized by us to make us ashamed of all our behavior. Shame as a moral concept can stimulate us to more closely approximate our ideals as long as they do not demand impossible perfection. A sense of shame can help us avoid ethically dubious behavior in the future (Morris, 1976, pp. 59–63; Piers and Singer, 1953, p. 11; Thrane, 1979a).

Shame as Central to Ethics

Let us consider some philosophers, psychologists, and psychiatrists who see shame as central to human ethics (for example, Gibbard, 1990, pp. 135–140, 145, 295–300; Greenspan, 1995; Hanson, 1997, pp. 165–168; Liszka, 1999, pp. 12–39). While recognizing the scholarly emphasis on the pathologies of shame, Schneider contends that such studies have traced such pathologies "without simultaneously bearing witness to the constructive role played by shame in moral development" (1987, p. 200). In his book on shame, Schneider emphasizes the worth of shame as an "integral dimension of human experience" and as a "resource in the journey toward individuation and maturity." For him, shame is not solely a problem to be solved or eliminated (1977, pp. ix–xviii). In the social ethics of Agnes Heller, shame is "the only inborn moral feeling in us," cannot be overcome or eliminated, and should not even if we could (1985, pp. 6, 53; Heller, 1988, pp. 99–100). Gary Thrane argues that not all "shame reactions are infantile or unhealthy" and that the human "liability to shame is now seen as an inevitable by-product of the loving construction of the self. Identity and individuation are protected by the fear of shame" (1979b, p. 339). "The liability to shame," contends Thrane, "is the price we pay for knowing what we are, for knowing what we admire, and for wishing the two to be one" (1979a, p. 161).

Peter French believes that to be without a sense of shame, to be shameless, is bad morally and that shame "is a virtue or very like a virtue. Having some shame seems to be morally obligatory" (1989, p. 343). Robert Solomon describes a complex web of emotions or moral sentiments that stimulate our sense of individual and social justice. He gives shame a significant role. To feel shame about not doing something we ought to do, or about something we did but ought not to have done, may contribute to our realization that an injustice must be rectified. To be shameless, Solomon believes, "is a profound vice, perhaps the worst of all vices" (1989, p. 367). Shame is not just an emotion "appropriate for earlier epochs"; it is essential to a sense of justice (Solomon, 1990, p. 296). Aaron Ben Ze'ev provides an excellent summary concerning a significant role for shame in ethics (2000, pp. 527–529):

> *Shame* is probably one of the most powerful emotions for moral behavior.... Its emergence indicates that some of our most profound values are violated. Shame prevents many people from behaving immorally and from losing their own self-respect.... [Shame] expresses the fact that we care about this norm and this caring is commendable from a moral point of view.... The presence of shame, which expresses our basic values, is helpful in maintaining human dignity and integrity.

Even among the psychiatrists and psychologists who focus their research on the pathologies of shame, some recognize a central role for normal shame in healthy human ethical growth (Gilbert and Andrews, 1998, pp. 78–79, 225, 228–229; Morrison, 1984, p. 86; Morrison, 1996, p. 15; Wurmser, 1981, pp. 64–67). Donald Nathanson, for example, believes that a developed sense of ethics implies a "healthy awareness of shame—not too much and not too little." If we choose to reflect on our shame, we can learn from it. We can "decide to use this particular moment of shame as a spur to personal change—an unexpected opportunity to make ourselves different" (1992, pp. 308, 327, 460). Nathanson reminds us (1987, pp. 194–195):

> Yet shame is not a disease. Rather it is a mark of our humanity. We are valuing animals, and shame plays an important role in our system of values, despite the fact that what is valued changes from generation to generation. The importance of shame cannot be overlooked. . . . It is shame that protects our privacy, just as the sense of shame can draw us more deeply into our own spaces to determine if our actions and attitudes are acceptable to our personal morality.

Feminist Perspectives

Of course we must bear in mind that unwarranted shame and pathological shame routinely work to the disadvantage and detriment of persons who (because of class, race, or gender) are marginalized, trivialized, demeaned, or ignored by society as inferior or defective (Planalp, et al., 2000, p. 47). Some feminists discuss the harmful effects of shame on women in our culture (Bartky, 1990, pp. 83–98; Jamieson, 1995, pp. 77–88; Starhawk, 1987, pp. 176–179). But several feminist scholars who stress the generally negative effects of shame on disempowered and marginalized women also argue for a legitimate role for shame in the moral life of privileged and empowered women (for example, see Fisher, 1984; Probyn, 2005, pp. 75–106). After examining the ways in which guilt and shame have functioned to subordinate women, Elizabeth Spelman (1991) argues that shame should remain a valuable element in feminist ethics. Her argument on this point warrants extended quotation (pp. 228–229):

> Feminist ethics, I have been insisting, must at least address the history of woman's inhumanity to woman. This part of the history is shameful. However, I am not proposing a daily regimen of shame-inducing exercises. Nor do I think that deep self-doubt that is part of shame can serve as the immediate ground of a vibrant feminist politics. . . . But I do not see how women who enjoy privileged status over other women (whether it is based on race, class, religion, age, sexual orientation, or physical mobility) can come to think it is desirable to lose that privilege (by force or consent) unless they see it not only as producing harm to other women but also as deeply disfiguring to themselves. . . . Seeing myself as deeply disfigured by privilege and desiring to do something about it may be impossible without my feeling of shame. The degree to which I am moved to undermine systems of privilege is closely tied to the degree to which I feel shame at that sort of person such privilege makes me or allows me to be.

Shame and Moral Conscience

The centrality of normal shame to ethics also has been argued by connecting a sense of shame with a sense of moral conscience (for example, Braithwaite, 1989, pp. 71–75; Langston, 2001, pp. 127–128; Miller, 1996, pp. 33–34; Seidler, 2000, p. 89). Few go as far as Virgil Aldrich who not only gives shame a central role in ethics but also *equates* shame with conscience and describes shame as the "voice of conscience" (1939, pp. 59–60). Some see shame as one important aspect or dimension of conscience. Communication scholar Michael Hyde introduces his book, *The Call of Conscience*, by saying: "Indeed people whose lives are uninformed by conscience are otherwise known as psychopaths. Such people cannot be trusted, for they lie without compunction, injure without remorse, and cheat with little fear of detection. . . . Forget about such things as guilt and shame, compassion and fairness, duty and justice" (2001, p. 1). Ben-Ze'ev contends that the "feeling of shame . . . can bear witness to an uncorrupted conscience; and such a person is better than one who is both wicked and shameless" (2000, p. 528). Gershen Kaufman concludes: "Shame is an innate universal affect which has inherently adaptive, and therefore distinctly positive, features. Shame is crucial to the development of identity, conscience, and a sense of dignity" (1992, p. xii). Several scholars make an even tighter linkage between shame and conscience. Although his research focuses on the pathologies of shame, Morrison states that because "the threat of shame can serve to maintain a moral level of behavior aimed at preserving a good image of the self, I believe that it can serve as an instrument of conscience" (1996, p. 14). In his overview introduction to a special issue on shame in the *American Behavioral Scientist*, Thomas Scheff concludes: "Shame signals serve not only to keep the right distance from others but also to establish a moral direction for our behavior. What is called 'conscience' is constituted not only by cognition but also by emotion." Feelings of shame in anticipation of our actions "serve as an automatic moral gyroscope somewhat independently of moral reasoning about consequences" (1995, p. 1057).

Public Shaming Arenas

Now I turn to various arenas in which intentional public shaming can occur and to some of the issues concerning public shaming. We should bear in mind at the outset the warning in the entry on "shame" in a recent encyclopedia of ethics: "The act of invoking shame is itself a moral question and should be approached with moral care. For example, while there may be good cause to say, 'You should be ashamed of yourself for stealing from your parents,' there may not be good cause to say, 'You should be ashamed of yourself for crying'" (Shame, 1999, p. 248).

First we turn to the arena of law and criminal justice where public shaming has resurfaced in recent years. In fact "judges have been reviving shame-based sentencing in pockets across the country, doling out alternative punishments designed to humiliate the criminal and send a stern message to the public" (Deardorff, 2000, p. 18; also see Schodolski, 2005, pp. 1, 28). Some judges have required offenders to display their crime using "scarlet-letter type signs, bumper stickers, or clothing." In lieu of jail time, in a North Carolina city a shoplifter stood outside the victimized store with a sign describing her crime. Some city governments place derogatory signs in front of slum buildings to shame the owners (Deardorff, 2000, p. 18). In an attempt to cope with prostitution, some cities have purchased space in local newspapers or created a Web site "wall of shame" to publish the names (and sometimes mug shots) not only of convicted prostitutes but also of clients caught seeking sex for money (Targeting, 1995, p. 24; Washburn and Sheehan, 2005, sec. 1, pp. 1, 28; also see Alter and Wingert, 1995, pp. 21–25). The state of Illinois created an Internet Web site that displayed the names, pictures, and last known addresses of "deadbeat" parents who owe more than $5,000 in past due child support. The state Child Support Enforcement Administrator said: "We think shame can be a powerful motivating force" (Shame's Force, 2003, p. 7).

On the one hand, proponents of shaming say it should not "be used on everyone but is worthwhile if it keeps people out of jail, acts as a deterrent, rehabilitates the perpetrator, and satisfies the victim." On the other hand, critics of shame-based punishment contend that it "causes psychological damage and that crime should be stigmatized, not the criminal" (Deardorff, 2000, p. 18). Two books provide thorough analyses of the pro and con arguments concerning use of public shaming as part of the legal system. Nussbaum (2004) generally opposes public shaming as punishment for breaking the law. In contrast, Braithwaite (1989) advocates use of "reintegrative shaming" that expresses community disapproval followed later by "gestures of reacceptance into the community of law abiding citizens." He condemns disintegrative shaming that stigmatizes by creating a permanent outcast (p. 55). He also describes how reintegrative shaming can apply to white-collar crime as well as diverse crime-in-the-streets.

Public shaming also surfaces in citizen letters to the editor of newspapers and in citizen opinion columns. One citizen condemned the comments by professional basketball player Dennis Rodman that attacked Mormons and their religion. This citizen argued that "public figures holding court in public places must meet some minimal standards of decency, or must be held to account for failing that basic test. . . . That is exactly what we should do now. The kind of bigotry that Dennis Rodman showed deserves public shaming now" (Lipson, 1997, p. 27). Another citizen chastised the television networks for the proliferation of reality-based shows, such as *Survivor*, that promote such survival skills as lying, cheating, backstabbing, exploitation of others, and survival of the fittest at all costs. Laments this citizen: "What a national shame" (Johnson, 2000, p. 11). A letter writer condemned the *Chicago Tribune* for publishing in the sports section a lengthy feature article describing how a father and son shot a leopard during an African safari. The writer judged: "Hiding in a blind waiting for an unsuspecting animal is an act of cowardice, something that should bring a feeling of shame, not pride" (Martineau, 2001, p. 18). After the September 11 terrorist attacks, a letter writer condemned Americans who turn hatred on others because of their religion or ethnicity and thus lower themselves to the level of the terrorists. The writer concluded: "Don't bring shame on America" (Downs, 2001, p. 16). Another letter writer took issue with a reporter's column that faulted President Bush's speech to the nation on the evening of the terrorist attacks for being awkwardly worded and delivered. The writer felt that these were trivial matters in light of the massive loss of life and the heroism of rescue workers. This writer opened her letter by stating simply: "Shame on James Warren for writing a column criticizing President Bush's speech" (Bogart, 2001, p. 22). "George Bush's use of American children to raise money for the children of Afghanistan is nothing but a shameless political ploy," asserted a letter writer (Taylor, 2001, p. 18) who questioned: "How many Afghan children have died as a result of our dropping bombs on them?"

Political columnists comment on shame. Concerning the detailed public exposure of Bill Clinton's sexual behaviors, Leonard Pitts, Jr., observed: "Who in history—Nixon included—has ever been so roundly and profoundly humiliated? . . . Who has ever been so thoroughly shamed?" (1998, p. 19). On the same day in the same paper, John Kass noted that while Clinton was on the telephone with a congressman, Monica Lewinsky testified that "Clinton unzipped himself and she did her duty." Kass concluded: "He is without shame" (1998, p. 3). In a lengthy article in *Harper's*, Robert Kaus condemned the corruption and unethicality of Washington influence peddlers. In the 1960s and 1970s, he believed, "there was something, less formal than law, that at least held corruption in check. This was a public morality and its disciplinary mechanism, shame." However, as of 1982, he noted sarcastically: "Breathe free, Washingtonians. There's no shame anymore" (1982, pp. 9, 11, 15).

Figures in the political lime-light also use shaming. In her moving speech to the 1992 Republican National Convention, Mary Fisher, an HIV-positive middle-class white wife and mother, tried to bolster the spirits of AIDS victims who found little support around them. "It is not you who should feel shame, it is we. We who tolerate ignorance and practice prejudice, we who have taught you to fear. We must lift our shroud of silence, making it safe for you to reach out for compassion" (2000, p. 170). In his 1995 presidential campaign speech attacking sex and violence in the entertainment media, Bob Dole warned: "But those who cultivate moral confusion for profit should understand this: we will name their names and shame them as they deserve to be shamed" (1997, p. 246). Republican House Majority Leader Richard Armey condemned President Clinton as a "shameless person" concerning Clinton's sexual behavior (Barbs fly, 1998, p. 3).

Of course corporations and other organizations utilize and are targets of public shaming. Planalp and her colleagues have examined at length both the positive and destructive ways in which organizations employ shame or are targets of it. I will not attempt to summarize their analysis, but I urge you to read their excellent treatment (Planalp, 2000, pp. 27–38). Here I will simply offer a few additional examples. Philosopher Peter French advocates the use of what he calls "The Hester Prynne Sanction" against the legal and ethical misdeeds of corporations. This would involve court-mandated and supervised adverse publicity and advertising describing the corporations' misdeeds and punishment. The adverse publicity would be financed out of the offending company's advertising budget, published and aired in appropriately visible outlets, and produced by an advertising agency not employed by the corporation. French believes that such a scarlet letter of shame is an appropriate threat to a corporation's prestige, image, and social acceptance. He contends: "[T]he imposition of the Hester Prynne Sanction on a corporation broadcasts a corporate offender's behavior, thus arousing (1) appropriate social contempt, (2) a recognition of failure to measure up, and (3) the kind of adjustments to operating procedures, policies, and practices that are required for the corporate offender to regain moral worth both in its own eyes and those of the community" (1985, p. 25; also see French, 1986). A month after the terrorist attacks of 9-11, an irate reader of the *Chicago Tribune* argued: "United Airlines Chairman and Chief Executive James E. Goodwin's announcement that UAL 'will perish' is nothing but shameless pandering in the wake of the September attack against our country. United's problems stem from long-term mismanagement of its core business, at the expense of quality employee relations and customer service" (Fournier, 2001, p. 18).

Media scholar Marvin Olasky (1985/1986) has urged public shaming of public relations practitioners for ethical lapses. If the Board of Directors of the Public Relations Society of America expels a member, Olasky believes that the board should publicly explain "the reasons for the expulsion, with names named. PRSA would thus bring shame into play." In addition, says Olasky, there is a need for individuals, organizations, and the media to monitor the ethicality of public relations practice and through exposure "help to restore a sense of shame" (pp. 45–46). Cees Hamelink (2000), an international media scholar, notes with approval: "Amnesty International cannot hand out prison sentences to those who violate human rights. However, its politics of shame and exposure is certainly effective and provides a good deal of protection for victims of human rights violations" (p. 192). "The moral power of groups like Amnesty International, Human Rights Watch, and Lawyers Committee for Human Rights is considerable. Fully engaged in the mobilization of shame, they are relentless, persuasive, and pervasive" (Drinan, 2001, p. 193).

The reasoning of those who advocate the use of public shaming for varied purposes perhaps is best captured by Alter and Wingert (1995):

> In other words, the restoring of a sense of shame is only partly about today's miscreants. It's more about tomorrow's—the ones who might grow up in a world where the moral boundaries are clearer. And it's ultimately about the law abiding as much as the law-breakers—the moral compass of a nation. . . . If the public believes that those who transgress will be called to account, its cynicism may ease a bit. That would make a little finger pointing more worthwhile. (p. 25)

Shaming in the Classroom

Whether it is termed public shaming or private interpersonal shaming, one of the most controversial uses of institutional shaming is in the classroom. To what degree is shaming focused on ethical issues an acceptable educational method? Although he uses the term guilt, in his book, *Educating for Character*, Thomas Lickona actually describes the role of situational, normal, or constructive shame as a moral feeling necessary for full development of a sense of conscience. Constructive shame, he believes, says "I didn't live up to my own standards. I feel bad about that, but I'm going to do better." In addition, Lickona argues that development of the capacity for constructive shame "helps us resist temptation" (1991, pp. 56–58). Now consider the personal example reported by legal scholar and social critic Stephen Carter in his book, (*integrity*). He reflects on a childhood chastisement he received for cheating.

I do remember that I was made to feel terribly ashamed; and it is good that I was made to feel that way, for I had something to be ashamed of. The moral opprobrium that accompanied that shame was sufficiently intense that it has stayed with me ever since, which is exactly how shame is supposed to work. As I grew older, whenever I was tempted to cheat . . . I would remember . . . the humiliation of sitting before my classmates, revealed as a cheater. (1996, pp. 3–4; for a hypothetical but similar experience, see Schneiderman, 1995, p. 246)

In her 1992 address to the Second National Communication Ethics Conference, Josina Makau condemned the use of shaming as a classroom teaching technique because it undermines a student's development of critical or liberatory consciousness. Her conclusion warrants quotation at length.

Inherently unloving and authoritarian, shame inhibits the achievement of authentic self-awareness, growth, and nurturant connectedness. Used primarily to control, shame reinforces external, often arbitrary standards of judgment, inhibiting the likelihood of achieving authenticity. Shame jeopardizes the development of a natural spiritual sense of connection, caring, and empathy. As a result, shame inhibits the development of perhaps the most essential elements of critical consciousness, critical and empathetic understanding. (pp. 7–8)

In 1996 in the pages of the journal, *Communication Studies*, Makau disagreed with Lawrence Frey, Lee Artz, and their colleagues at Loyola University of Chicago about the relationship of a sense of shame, a sense of justice, and classroom shaming (Frey, et al., 1996). She objected to privileging justice "over other virtues such as love, compassion, care, sensitivity, and connection." She recognized that shame has been utilized by educators to "explore prejudice, unreflective acceptance of privilege, or other modes of belief and conduct often associated with societal patterns of injustice and inequality." She contended, however, that although "shame has been associated with developing a social justice sensibility, it is arguably an anathema to cultivation of an ethic of love and care." Makau asked the Loyola scholars, would they "condemn shame as an 'appropriate emotion' to be cultivated in communication classrooms?" (Makau, 1996, pp. 135–136). The Loyola scholars replied that they agreed that cultivation of shame "is an inappropriate goal in our classrooms." Nevertheless, they argued that "recognition by students and teachers of their own complicity in creating and perpetuating social injustice may invoke a feeling of shame." And certainly if "shame *is* evoked in classroom situations, it is incumbent on all involved to move beyond such a feeling toward constructive activity that might alleviate the shame and its sources" (Pollock, et al., 1996, pp. 147–148).

In her 1998 keynote address to the Fifth National Communication Ethics Conference, Makau contended that while "there may well be an appropriate role for shame in the broader study and understanding of communication ethics, there is no appropriate role or use for shame in the classroom." She argued that classroom shaming "has great potential to undermine our efforts to inculcate an ethic of love and care, of respect, and of compassion for all, and little prospect for contributing to the fulfillment of these outcomes" (p. 6). However, discussions by

Makau with some of the participants during the course of the conference led her to conclude: "As a result of these dialogues, I am less confident that my unequivocal and unqualified view on this issue is warranted, and I look forward to future opportunities for exploration" (Makau, 1998, p. 6, note #2). Here I would extend Makau's call and urge further examination of situational or normal shame as an outcome of classroom shaming (for example, see Ryan, 2002, p. 5; Tombs, 1995).

Ethical Guidelines for Shaming

Planalp, Hafen, and Adkins (2000) suggest five ethical guidelines for using messages of shame and guilt. I adapt them for our further consideration of the ethical use of shaming in public and in the classroom. *First*, what *grounds* for shame should we encourage or discourage through such messages? Some grounds for shame may be accepted generally, such as lying, cheating, stealing, physically hurting others, or neglecting close relationships. Other grounds for shame appear less important or actually harmful, such as "not owning certain consumer products, wearing socially inappropriate clothing, having less-than-ideal body shape or size, being of a devalued race or ethnicity, being a survivor of a disaster or downsizing, being a victim of a crime, being poor, or being disabled." But some grounds may be more uncertain or controversial, such as "performing inadequately at work, failing to repay a loan, gender bending, gossiping, being on welfare, the sins of our forebears" (pp. 52–53). *Second*, to be most constructive and least damaging, where appropriate shame should be *acknowledged* privately and publicly. Acknowledgment of shame promotes reflection about its grounds and consequences, minimizes its "conversion into self-protective or other-blaming rage," minimizes perpetuation of shame in the guise of "blaming, insulting, or demeaning others," and promotes (especially through apology) the "psychological and spiritual healing" of both the transgressor and the victim (p. 53).

Third, in terms of enhancing or damaging *self-esteem* in the long run, shame messages should be rooted in standards that are realistic (not set too high or too low) and that are clearly explained considering the level of understanding involved (pp. 53–54). *Fourth*, to what degree does the person or group being shamed actually have *control* over the grounds of the shame? To be ashamed for ones sex, race, or disability hardly seems ethical. Also determine when shaming seems to serve a person's selfish goals through controlling others rather than the nurturing of collective values. For example, do "I shame my class for not doing reading because I want them to try harder to learn or because I am irritated about having to lecture?" (p. 54). *Fifth* and finally, messages of shame should promote rather than undermine the *connections and relationships* "among people and between people and the larger society." For groups and society to cohere, shame must "coexist with honor, pride, and loyalty." Compassion and caring must be integrated with "just and responsible shaming" (pp. 54–55).

Conclusion

Philosopher Bernard Williams (1993) reminds us of the essential role of normal or situational shame in our lives. "By giving through the emotions a sense of who one is and of what one hopes to be, it mediates between act, character, and consequence, and also between ethical demands and the rest of life" (p. 102). As I conclude my examination of a role for shame in communication ethics, let us consider Aristotle's discussion of shame and shamelessness. In the context of Aristotle's theory of virtue ethics, or character ethics, shamelessness is always bad. To be without the capacity for shame, to be without a sense of shame, is undesirable. Shame can act as an ethical restraint on wrong actions. Both always feeling ashamed of everything and never feeling ashamed of anything are states of character to be avoided (Aristotle, 1941, pp. 959, 961, 1001–1002, 1392 [1107a, 10–14; 1108a, 30–34; 1128b, 10–34; 1383b, 12–21]; also see Palmour, 1986, pp. 284–299; Sokolon, 2006, pp. 109–125).

In light of Aristotle's discussion, we can understand better the urging of Stuart Schneiderman (1995) that our search should be for a "reasonable mean, one that avoids suggesting that we need never to feel shame and that we need always feel it" (p. 55). In a somewhat similar vein, Planalp and her colleagues warn of the "danger of two extremes: ignoring the value of shame and (re)acting against shame unwisely" (Planalp, Hafen, and Adkins, 2000, p. 55). The issue of whether there should be a legitimate role for shame in communication ethics is captured in a final question I pose: Is there literally nothing anymore that persons could speak, write, or depict for which they justifiably should feel a sense of shame?

References

Aldrich, V. C. (1939). An ethics of shame. *Ethics, 50,* 57–77.

Alter, J., and Wingert, P. (1995, October 6). The return of shame. *Newsweek*, pp. 21–25.

Aristotle. (1941). *The basic works of Aristotle.* Richard McKeon (Ed.). New York: Random House.

Asante, M. K. (1995). Unraveling the edges of free speech. *National Forum, 75,* 12–15.

Barbs fly over whether Clinton should quit. (1998, April 8). *Chicago Tribune,* sec. 1, p. 3.

Barrett, H. (1998). *Maintaining the self in communication.* Incline Village, NV: Alpha and Omega Book Publishers.

Bartky, S. L. (1990). *Femininity and domination: Studies in the phenomenology of oppression.* New York: Routledge.

Ben-Ze'ev, A. (2000). *The subtlety of emotions.* Cambridge, MA: MIT Press.

Bogart, M. (2001, September 16). Trivial points. *Chicago Tribune,* sec. 1, p. 22.

Boonin, L. (1983). Guilt, shame, and morality. *Journal of Value Inquiry, 17,* 295–304.

Braithwaite, J. (1989). *Crime, shame, and reintegration.* Cambridge, UK: Cambridge University Press.

Broucek, F. J. (1991). *Shame and the self.* New York: Guilford.

Carter, S. L. (1996). *(integrity).* New York: Basic Books.

Clinton, B. (2000). Statement by the President. In R. L. Johannesen, R. R. Allen, W. A. Linkugel, and F. J. Bryan (Eds.), *Contemporary American Speeches* (9th ed., pp. 131–132). Dubuque, IA: Kendall-Hunt.

Deardorff, J. (2000, April 12). Shame returns as punishment. *Chicago Tribune,* sec. 1, p. 18.

Deigh, J. (1983). Shame and self-esteem: A critique. *Ethics, 93,* 225–245.

Dole, B. (1997). Sex and violence in the media. In R. L. Johannesen, R. R. Allen, W. A. Linkugel, and F. J. Bryan (Eds.), *Contemporary American Speeches* (8th ed., pp. 242–247). Dubuque, IA: Kendall-Hunt.

Downs, R. J. (2001, September 17). America's shame. *Chicago Tribune,* sec. 1, p. 16.

Drinan, R. F. (2001). *The mobilization of shame: A world view of human rights.* New Haven: Yale University Press.

Elshtain, J. B. (1995, November-December). Turn down the volume. *Utne Reader, 72*, 67–73.

Fisher, B. (1984). Guilt and shame in the women's movement: The radical ideal of action and its meaning for feminist intellectuals. *Feminist Studies, 10*, 185–212.

Fisher, M. (2000). Address on AIDS to the 1992 Republican convention. In R. L. Johannesen, R. R. Allen, W. A. Linkugel, and F. J. Bryan (Eds.), *Contemporary American Speeches* (9th ed., pp. 168–171). Dubuque, IA: Kendall-Hunt.

Fournier, T. (2001, October 21). United's woes. *Chicago Tribune*, sec. 1, p. 18.

French, P. (1985, Winter). The Hester Prynne sanction. *Business and Professional Ethics Journal, 4*, 19–32.

French, P. (1986). Principles of responsibility, shame, and the corporation. In Hugh Curtler, (Ed.), *Shame, responsibility, and the corporation* (pp. 17–55). New York: Haven.

French, P. (1989). It's a damn shame. In C. Penden and J. P. Sterba (Eds.), *Freedom, equality, and social change* (pp. 337–347). Lewiston, NY: Edwin Mellen Press.

Frey, L. R., Pearce, W. B., Pollock, M. A., Artz, L., and Murphy, B. A. O. (1996). Looking for justice in all the wrong places: On a communication approach to social justice. *Communication Studies, 47*, 110–117.

Gibbard, A. (1990). *Wise choices, apt feelings: A theory of normative judgment*. Cambridge, MA: Harvard University Press.

Gilbert, P. and Andrews, B. (Eds.). (1998). *Shame: Interpersonal behavior, psychopathology, and culture*. New York: Oxford University Press.

Gilligan, J. (1976). Beyond morality: Psychoanalytic reflections on shame, guilt, and love. In T. Lickona (Ed.), *Moral development and behavior* (pp. 144–170). New York: Holt, Rinehart, and Winston.

Green, M. and MacColl, G. (1987). *Reagan's reign of error*. Rev. Ed. New York: Pantheon.

Greenspan, P. S. (1995). *Practical guilt: Moral dilemmas, emotions, and social norms*. New York: Oxford University Press.

Haidt, J. (2003). The moral emotions. In R. J. Davidson, Scherer, K. R., and Goldsmith, H. H. (Eds.), *Handbook of affective sciences* (pp. 852–870). New York: Oxford University Press.

Hamelink, C. J. (2000). *The ethics of cyberspace*. London: Sage.

Hanson, K. (1997). Reasons for shame, shame against reason. In M. R. Lansky and A. P. Morrison (Eds.), *The widening scope of shame* (pp. 155–179). Hillsdale, NJ: Analytic Press.

Heller, A. (1985). *The power of shame: A rational perspective*. Boston: Routledge & K. Paul.

Heller, A. (1988). *General ethics*. Oxford, UK: Blackwell.

Hoffer, E. (1974, October 18). Long live shame! *New York Times*, p. 41.

Hyde, M. (2001). *The call of conscience: Heidegger and Levinas, rhetoric and the euthanasia debate*. Columbia, SC: University of South Carolina Press.

Isenberg, A. (1949). Natural pride and natural shame. *Philosophy and Phenomenological Research, 10*, 1–24.

Jamieson, K. H. (1995). *Beyond the double bind*. New York: Oxford University Press.

Johnson, W. D. (2000, August 28). An exercise in bad form. *Chicago Tribune*, sec. 1, p. 11.

Karen, R. (1992, February). Shame. *Atlantic Monthly*, 40–70.

Kass, H. D. (1998). Series editor's introduction. In G. B. Adams, and D. L. Balfour, *Unmasking administrative evil* (pp. ix–x). Thousand Oaks, CA: Sage.

Kass, J. (1998, September 15). Sure Clinton's tryst is a private matter—just like war is. *Chicago Tribune*, sec. 1, p. 3.

Katz, J. (1997). The elements of shame. In M. R. Lansky and A. P. Morrison (Eds.), *The widening scope of shame* (pp. 231–260). Hillsdale, NJ: Analytic Press.

Kaufman, G. (1992). *Shame, the power of caring*. 3rd Rev. Ed. Rochester, VT: Schenkman.

Kaus, R. (1982, August). There's no shame anymore. *Harper's*, pp. 8–15.

Kekes, J. (1988). Shame and moral progress. *Midwest Studies in Philosophy, 13*, 282–296.

Kellenberger, J. (1995). *Relationship morality*. University Park: Pennsylvania State University Press.

Lamb, R. E. (1983). Guilt, shame, and morality. *Philosophy and Phenomenological Research*, *43*, 329–346.

Langston, D. C. (2001). *Conscience and other virtues*. University Park: Pennsylvania State University Press.

Lansky, M. R. and Morrison, A. P. (Eds.). (1997). *The widening scope of shame*. Hillsdale, NJ: Analytic Press.

Lapin, D. (1995, September 25). In praise of shame. *National Review*, pp. 87–89.

Lasch, C. (1992, August 10). For shame. *The New Republic*, pp. 29–34.

Lickona, T. (1991). *Educating for character*. New York: Bantam Books.

Lipson, C. (1997, June 12). Rodman's shameful spews. *Chicago Tribune*, sec. 1, p. 27.

Liszka, J. J. (1999). *Moral competence: An integrated approach to the study of ethics*. Upper Saddle River, NJ: Prentice-Hall.

Makau, J. M. (1992). Raising consciousness in the classroom. In J. A. Jaksa (Ed.), *Proceedings of the second national communication ethics conference* (pp. 1–17). Annandale, VA: Speech Communication Association.

Makau, J. M. (1996). Notes on communication education and social justice. *Communication Studies*, *47*, 135–141.

Makau, J. B. (1998, May). An outcome-based approach to ethical communication education. Transcript of Keynote Address at the Fifth National Communication Ethics Conference. Gull Lake, MI.

Martineau, J. (2001, November 27). Shameful safari. *Chicago Tribune*, sec. 1, p. 18.

Miller, S. B. (1996). *Shame in context*. Hillsdale, NJ: Analytic Press.

Morris, H. (1976). *On guilt and innocence*. Berkeley: University of California Press.

Morrison, A. P. (1984). Shame and the psychology of the self. In P. E. Stepansky and A. Goldberg (Eds.), *Kohut's legacy: Contributions to self psychology* (pp. 71–90). Hillsdale, NJ: Analytic Press.

Morrison, A. P. (1996). *The culture of shame*. New York: Ballantine Books.

Nathanson, D. L. (Ed.). (1987). *The many faces of shame*. New York: Guilford.

Nathanson, D. L. (1992). *Shame and pride: Affect, sex, and the birth of the self*. New York: W. W. Norton.

Nussbaum, M. C. (2001). *Upheavals of thought: The intelligence of emotions*. Cambridge, UK: Cambridge University Press.

Nussbaum, M. C. (2004). *Hiding from humanity: Disgust, shame, and the law*. Princeton, NJ: Princeton University Press.

Olasky, M. N. (1985/86). Ministers or panderers: Issues raised by the Public Relations Society Code of Standards. *Journal of Mass Media Ethics*, *1*, 43–49.

O'Hear, A. (1976–77). Guilt and shame as moral concepts. *Proceedings of the Aristotelian Society*, *77*, 73–86.

Palmour, J. (1986). *On moral character: A practical guide to Aristotle's virtues and vices*. Washington, DC: Archon Institute of Leadership Development.

Piers, G. and Singer, M. B. (1953). *Shame and guilt: A psychoanalytic and cultural study*. Springfield, IL: Charles C. Thomas.

Pitts, Jr., L. (1998, September 15). Advice for the "comeback kid": It's time to go. *Chicago Tribune*, sec. 1, p. 19.

Planalp, S., Hafen, S., and Adkins, A. D. (2000). Messages of shame and guilt. In Michael Roloff (Ed.), *Communication Yearbook 23* (pp. 1–65). Thousand Oaks, CA: Sage.

Pollock, M. A., Artz, L., Frey, L. R., Pearce, W. B., and Murphy, B. A. O. (1996). Navigating between Scylla and Charybdis: Continuing the dialogue on communication and social justice. *Communication Studies*, *47*, 142–151.

Probyn, E. (2005). *Blush: The face of shame*. Minneapolis: University of Minnesota Press.

Ryan, K. (2002). The six Es of character education. *Issues in Ethics*, *13*, 2–5.

Samuelson, R. (1998, January 30). Clinton's problem with the other "L" word. *Chicago Tribune*, sec. 1, p. 17.

Scheff, T. J. (1995). Shame and related emotions: An overview. *American Behavioral Scientist, 38,* 1053–1059.

Schneider, C. D. (1977). *Shame, exposure, and privacy.* Boston: Beacon Press.

Schneider, C. D. (1987). A mature sense of shame. In D. L. Nathanson (Ed.), *The many faces of shame* (pp. 194–213). New York: Guilford.

Schneiderman, S. (1995). *Saving face: America and the politics of shame.* New York: Knopf.

Schodolski, V. J. (2005, December 29). When jail time won't do, the judge may opt to humiliate you. *Chicago Tribune,* sec. 1, pp. 1, 28.

Seidler, G. (2000). *In other's eyes: An analysis of shame.* Trans. Andrew Jenkins. Madison, CT: International Universities Press.

Shame. (1999). In S. N. Terkel and R. S. Duval (Eds.), *Encyclopedia of ethics.* New York: Facts on File.

Shame's force. (2003, November 25). Associated Press Report. Northern Illinois University *Northern Star,* p. 7.

Sokolon, M. K. (2006). *Political Emotions: Aristotle and the Symphony of Reason and Emotion.* DeKalb: Northern Illinois University Press.

Solomon, R. C. (1989). The emotions of justice. *Social Justice Research, 3,* 345–374.

Solomon, R. C. (1990). *A passion for justice.* Reading, MA: Addison-Wesley.

Spelman, E. V. (1991). The virtue of feeling and the feeling of virtue. In C. Card (Ed.), *Feminist ethics* (pp. 213–232). Lawrence: University Press of Kansas.

Starhawk. (1987). *Truth or dare: Encounters with power, authority, and mystery.* San Francisco: Harper and Row.

Tangeny, J. P. and Fischer, K. W. (Eds.). (1995). *Self-Conscious emotions: The psychology of shame, guilt, embarrassment, and pride.* New York: Guilford.

Targeting sex-for-cash. (1995, February 6). *Newsweek,* p. 24.

Taylor, G. (1985). *Pride, shame, and guilt: Emotions of self-assessment.* Oxford, UK: Clarendon Press.

Taylor, S. P. (2001, October 21). Hurting children. *Chicago Tribune,* sec. 1, p. 18.

Thrane, G. (1979a). Shame. *Journal of the Theory of Social Behavior, 9,* 139–166.

Thrane, G. (1979b). Shame and the construction of the self. *The Annual of Psychoanalysis, 7,* 321–341.

Tombs, D. (1995). "Shame" as a neglected value in schooling. *Journal of Philosophy of Education, 29,* 23–32.

Washburn, G., and Sheehan, C. (2005, June 22). Web site puts "johns" on the spot. *Chicago Tribune,* sec. 1, pp. 1, 28.

Williams, B. (1993). *Shame and necessity.* Berkeley: University of California Press.

Wurmser, L. (1981). *The mask of shame.* Baltimore, MD: Johns Hopkins University Press.

Preview to "A Rational World Ethic versus a Narrative Ethic for Political Communication." One way to view the "narrative paradigm" of communication is to see it as a version of the human nature perspective on communication ethics. In other words, the narrative paradigm identifies the human capacity for narration—for storytelling—as the characteristic that gives humans their humanness. Note that in the opening of this essay, philosopher Alasdair MacIntyre is quoted as contending that "man is in his actions and practices... essentially a story-telling animal...." In his book, *Human Communication as Narration* (pp. 62–63), Walter

Fisher argues that "the essential nature of human beings" is best captured by the root metaphor of homo narrans—"human beings as storytellers."

This essay suggests that a critic's choice of ethical perspective or selection of specific ethical standards to assess a communication event constrains the ethical judgments possible or appropriate. Different initial ethical assumptions or frameworks may lead to quite different ethical judgments of the communication. Consider how adequately the essay illustrates the claim that "our judgments of ethicality for any particular communication might be rather different depending upon whether we employed a rational world paradigm or a narrative paradigm."

This essay also summarizes two attacks on the adequacy of Fisher's conception of the narrative paradigm—those by Barbara Warnick and by Robert Rowland. Rowland has attempted to sharpen his criticisms in a journal article, "On Limiting the Narrative Paradigm," and Fisher has offered an indirect reply to his critics by "Clarifying the Narrative Paradigm" (both in *Communication Monographs*, 6, March 1989, pp. 39–58). You are urged to read both of these articles. Also see Alan Bush and Victoria Davies Bush, "The Narrative Paradigm as a Perspective for Improving Ethical Evaluations of Advertisements," *Journal of Advertising*, 23 (1994): 31–41; David M. Ryfe, "The Principles of Public Discourse: What is Good Public Discourse?" in *Public Discourse in America*, eds. Judith Rodin and Stephen P. Steinberg (Philadelphia: University of Pennsylvania Press, 2003), pp. 163–177.

A Rational World Ethic versus a Narrative Ethic for Political Communication*

Richard L. Johannesen

In their essay, "Toward a New Political Narrative," Lance Bennett and Murray Edelman argue: "Stories are among the most universal means of representing human events. In addition to suggesting an interpretation for a social happening, a well-crafted narrative can motivate the belief and action of outsiders toward the actors and events caught up in its plot" (1985, p. 156). A central thesis presented by philosopher Alasdair MacIntyre in *After Virtue* (1984, p. 216) is that, in our actions and practices, we are essentially a storytelling animal: "A teller of stories that aspire to truth. . . . I can only answer the question 'What am I to do?' if I can answer the prior question 'Of what story do I find myself a part?'"

Scholars in such disciplines as anthropology, sociology, law, history, literary criticism, and rhetoric are exploring the centrality of narrative to human belief and action. Some specifically are suggesting standards for assessing the rationality and/or ethicality of narrative in public discourse. Political communication would seem one obvious arena on which to focus such exploration. By political communication I mean not just the communication of presidents, politicians,

*This essay originally was presented at the annual national conference of the Speech Communication Association, Boston, November 6, 1987.

political campaigns, or a particular party. I would include communication by appointed governmental officials. I would include any public communication by citizens on public issues and policy broadly defined, whether military, economic, social, or governmental, whether national, state, or local.

My intent is to compare what Walter Fisher describes as the "rational world paradigm" for the rhetoric of public issues with what he proposes as the "narrative paradigm." First, I will explore the premises, values, procedures, and ethical standards that seem basic to this rational, or traditional, paradigm as those norms typically are espoused for American political communication. Second, I will examine the standards for an ethic of narrative in political communication suggested by Fisher. Third, using Ronald Reagan's rhetoric as an illustrative case, I show how rather different ethical judgments can be reached depending upon which paradigm is employed. Finally, I note some of the modifications and criticisms that have been made of Fisher's view.

For almost a decade in articles and essays, and synthesized in his 1987 book, *Human Communication as Narration*, Walter Fisher has developed his view of the traditional "rational world paradigm" for sound and ethical rhetoric as contrasted with the more encompassing and adequate "narrative paradigm." In a public lecture in 1986 at Marquette University on "Ethics, Rationality, and Narrativity," Fisher declared that "conceptions of rationality are intertwined with ethics" (1986, p. 3; also see Fisher, 1987a).

According to Fisher, the fundamental presuppositions of the rational world paradigm are (1987b, pp. 59–60):

> (1) humans are essentially rational beings; (2) the paradigmatic mode of human decision making and communications is argument—discourse that features clear-cut inferential and implicative structures; (3) the conduct of argument is ruled by the dictates of situations—legal, scientific, legislative, public, and so on; (4) rationality is determined by subject-matter knowledge, argumentative ability, and skill in employing the rules of advocacy in given fields; and (5) the world is a set of logical puzzles that can be solved through appropriate analysis and application of reason conceived as an argumentative construct. In short, argument as product and process is the means of being human, the agency of all that humans can know and realize in achieving their *telos*.

The logicality of reasons is judged by the traditional tests of sound evidence and reasoning (Fisher, 1987b, pp. 108–109; 1986, pp. 13–14). First, determine whether the statements in a message that purport to be "facts" are actually facts, "that is, are confirmed by consensus or reliable, competent witnesses." Second, "determine whether relevant facts have been omitted or misrepresented." Third, "using mainly the standards from informal logic," assess the soundness of patterns of reasoning, such as sign, cause, classification, analogy, and example. Fourth, assess the individual arguments for relevance, distortion, and omission. Fifth, "determine whether the key issues have been addressed: the questions on which the matter should turn." Fisher believes that Douglas Ehninger and Wayne Brockriede's *Decision by Debate* (1st ed. 1963; 2d ed. 1979) "is the best representative available" of the rational world paradigm (1987b, pp. 46–47).

Within our culture I would contend that the rational world paradigm typically is reflected in values and procedures central to the health and growth of our system of governing, namely, representative democracy. These values guide ethical scrutiny of political communication within our system. Scholars have identified a number of such fundamental values and procedures (Burke, 1986, 64, 67, 235; Margolis, 1981; Moore, 1981; Nilsen, 1958; Nilsen, 1974, chs. 1–4; Redford, 1969, 6–9; Wallace, 1955; Warwick, 1981, 115–124). Among them are: the intrinsic dignity and worth of all persons; equal opportunity for fulfillment of individual potential; enhancement of citizen capacity to reach rational decisions; access to channels of public communication; access to relevant and accurate information on public issues; maximization of freedom of choice; toleration of dissent; honesty and clarity in presenting values relevant to problems and policies; honesty in presenting motivations and consequences; thoroughness, accuracy, and fairness in presenting evidence and alternatives; and recognition that the societal worth of an end seldom should be the sole justification of the ethics of the means to achieve that end.

Typical textbook discussions of the ethics of communication, persuasion, and argument often include lists of ethical standards. Such criteria frequently are rooted, implicitly if not explicitly, in the values and procedures central to American representative democracy. I have attempted to synthesize a number of such traditional lists.

1. Do not use false, fabricated, misrepresented, distorted, or irrelevant evidence to support arguments or claims.

2. Do not intentionally use unsupported, misleading, or illogical reasoning.

3. Do not represent yourself as informed or as an "expert" on a subject when you are not.

4. Do not use irrelevant appeals to divert attention or scrutiny from the issue at hand. Among the appeals that commonly serve such a purpose are: "Smear" attacks on an opponent's character; appeals to hatred and bigotry; derogatory insinuations—innuendos; God and Devil terms that cause intense but unreflective positive or negative reactions.

5. Do not ask your audience to link your idea or proposal to emotion-laden values, motives, or goals to which it actually is not related.

6. Do not deceive your audience by concealing your real purpose, by concealing self-interest, by concealing the group you represent, by concealing your position as an advocate of a viewpoint.

7. Do not distort, hide, or misrepresent the number, scope, intensity, or undesirable features of consequences or effects.

8. Do not use "emotional appeals" that lack a supporting basis of evidence or reasoning, or that would not be accepted if the audience had time and opportunity to examine the subject themselves.

9. Do not oversimplify complex, gradation-laden situations into simplistic, two-valued, either/or, polar views or choices.

10. Do not pretend certainty where tentativeness and degrees of probability would be more accurate.

11. Do not advocate something in which you do not believe yourself.

Now, I turn to Fisher's description of the narrative paradigm for rhetoric, which he believes overarches and subsumes the rational world paradigm (1987b, xi, pp. 64–65; 1986, pp. 8–9). (1) Humankind should be reconceptualized as story-tellers, as *homo narrans*. (2) The distinctive mode of human decision making and communication is "good reasons"—values or value-laden warrants for believing or acting. These vary in form among communication situations, genre, and media. (3) Presentation of good reasons is governed by history, culture, character, and the constraints of specific circumstances. (4) All humans have a natural capacity for narrative logic and naturally use the principles of probability/coherence and of fidelity for assessing narration. (5) The world is a set of stories from which we must choose if we are to live our lives in a continual process of re-creation.

As standards for narrative rationality and ethicality, Fisher suggests the dual touchstones of probability (coherence) and fidelity (truthfulness and reliability). *Probability*, whether a story "hangs together," is tested first by internal argumenta-tive and structural coherence; second by material coherence, by comparison and contrast with stories in other discourses; and third by characterological coher-ence, the harmony of character and action, the dependability of characters both as narrators and actors (1987b, p. 47; 1986, p. 12).

Fidelity addresses the "truth" qualities of the story, the truth both of reason-ing and of value judgment (1987b, pp. 47–48, 108–109; 1986, pp. 13–14). The logic of reasons within the story is assessed by the traditional standards for evi-dence and reasoning previously itemized. The values imbedded in the story are tested according to the standards of fact, relevance, consequence, consistency, and transcendental issues. "What are the explicit and implicit values? Are the val-ues appropriate to the nature of the decision that the message bears upon? What would be the effects of adhering to the values in regard to one's concept of one-self, to one's behavior, to one's relationship with others and society, and to the process of rhetorical transaction? Are the values confirmed or validated in one's personal experience, in the lives and statements of others whom one admires or respects, and/or in a conception of the best audience that one can conceive? And even if a *prima facie* case exists or a burden of proof has been established, are the values the message offers those that would constitute an ideal basis for human conduct?" (1986, p. 14; 1987b, p. 109).

We will now turn to the consideration that our judgments of ethicality for any particular political communication might be rather different depending upon whether we employed a rational world paradigm or a narrative paradigm. Depending on the paradigm used, for example, ethical assessments might vary of President Reagan's habitual use of stories and anecdotes and his identification with powerful narrative or mythic structures in American culture, such as the hero, the jeremiad tradition, or the American Dream.

I published a detailed evaluation of the ethics of President Reagan's rhetoric for the 1981–1982 period. I operated primarily from a rational worldview within the con-text of values and procedures central to American representative democracy. After examining representative news conferences, interviews, speeches, and informal com-ments, I concluded that President Reagan warranted ethical condemnation for rather routinely misstating facts, statistics, and situations and for misusing factual illustra-tions and anecdotes as proofs. I shall quote several of my conclusions at length.

This long-standing habit has been characterized satirically as Reagan's "anecdotage" problem. He likes to use vivid and dramatic real-life stories to prove this point or that. Unfortunately, these anecdotes, even if not misstated, frequently are found to be misleading or unrepresentative. In this regard, William Safire, a former speech writer for President Nixon, chastises Reagan for taking a "simplistic approach to complex matters." Syndicated political columnists Jack Germond and Jules Witcover describe Reagan's proclivity for "generalizing from the simplistic particular," for overgeneralizing individual abuses into proof of a major problem. A *Christian Century* editorial objects that Reagan's illustrations too often do not inform or provide evidence for an argument; rather they "exacerbate feelings" by arousing "latent hostility among true believers." James David Barber condemns Reagan for having "contempt for the facts" and issuing "spurious specifics with cavalier abandon." More precisely, Barber depicts Reagan as the "Aesop of the Oval Office, tossing off parables instead of arguments." Such stories are not easily judged by tests of evidence, notes Barber, and he urges that we must "rely on public discourse in which the proposals meet facts in a test clear enough for reason to grasp." (p. 233)

Should Reagan's sincere belief in what he says, even if what he says is inaccurate, misleading, or unrepresentative, soften our ethical judgment of his rhetoric? David Gergen, White House director of communications, would seem to believe so. Gergen told reporters that what is important is not "making sure we have every single fact straight," but rather "whether the larger points are right." Gergen also defended Reagan's story-telling as a "folk art" wherein the anecdotes have a "parable-like quality to them" and are used simply to illustrate "how society works." However, as I urged earlier, sincerity of intent and ethicality of rhetorical techniques most appropriately should be judged separately. In Reagan's case, whether he is sincere or not, the ethicality of his rhetorical tactics must be independently assessed. . . . I believe he is ethically irresponsible in rather regularly employing erroneous, misleading, or atypical information. Reagan has a duty to present to citizens the relevant and accurate data they need to make reasonable decisions on public issues. Meg Greenfield, the *Newsweek* political columnist, contends that Reagan is obliged in justifying his policies to use "arguments and real evidence" rather than "episodes or isolated case studies." (p. 236)

In contrast we turn to William Lewis's narrative interpretation of Reagan's rhetoric. He contends that Reagan's primary vehicle for communication is the story, both individual anecdotes and a larger tapestry of mythic structures that are potent in American culture. Lewis modifies Fisher's standards for narrative rationality. Lewis excludes the traditional tests for soundness of evidence and reasoning. He proposes scrutinizing the internal coherence and consistency of the rhetorical narrative, examining the implicit and explicit morals and values promoted, and assessing consistency with "common sense," the knowledge shared by the community as opposed to elitist, technical, or scientific knowledge.

Even from the narrative viewpoint, Lewis does fault Reagan for overextending the applicability of a "single, unquestioned narrative structure" and for assuming that this dominant narrative is permanent and insulated from contrary events and criticism (1987, pp. 295–296). Nevertheless, the tone of Lewis's interpretation is much more generous and less hostile than mine. In part Lewis argues (pp. 288–290):

> If the story is not true, it must be true-to-life; if it did not actually happen, it must be evident that it could happen or that, given the way things are, it should have happened. When narrative dominates, epistemological standards move away from empiricism. . . . Events become meaningful in stories and meaning depends upon the significance of the events within the context of the story. As a consequence, the perception of truth depends upon the story as a whole rather than upon the accuracy of its independent statements.

> Because his story is so dominant, so explicit, and so consistent, political claims are likely to be measured against the standard of Reagan's mythic American history rather than against other possible standards such as technical competence or ideological dogma. In this way, the story's dominance has diminished the significance of claims about factual inaccuracies. . . . Those most successful in confronting Reagan, such as Mario Cuomo, have been those few politicians who offer alternative stories.

> Reagan's stories are not completely self-contained . . . but this is a special kind of reality. The basis for accepting the referential value of Reagan's stories is not empirical justification, but consistency with the moral standards and common sense of his audience.

In these extremely brief excerpts from my and Lewis's analyses, we glimpse the possibility of quite different ethical assessments of Reagan's rhetoric stemming from the rational mind and narrative paradigms. For similar contrasts, we could turn to Fisher's own evaluation of Reagan's rhetoric in his book (1987b, pp. 143–157), to the article by Dowling and Marraro, in the *Western Journal of Speech Communication* (1986), and to my own article on "Ronald Reagan's Economic Jeremiad" (1986).

Now I will discuss some of the reactions generated, directly or indirectly, by Fisher's work. Several scholars have offered alternative or supplementary tests for narrative rationality or ethicality. I already have mentioned Lewis's modifications. Within the context of conversation and rhetoric, Farrell offers a series of questions as a start toward an "ethic of narrative" (1985, pp. 124–125):

> What public character is implied by the course we have taken? What forms of social learning are yet available to us? What legacy of experience do we wish our story to yield to future generations? Which episodes in our unfinished and unbounded narrative of collective action are irretrievable or lost? Which need to be ended altogether, which prolonged, which begun anew? Which audiences, thus far neglected, need to have their own stories articulated?

Bennett and Edelman contrast undesirable "stock political narratives" with a desirable "new political narrative" that promotes creativity and critical insight. Evaluative criteria can be inferred from their analysis. The distortions and contradictions characteristic of stock political narratives should be avoided: (1) they rest "on claims of dubious historical standing" and "rationalize such claims in tautological fashion"; (2) they "will overlook features of a situation that would change the narrative if taken into account"; and (3) the "significance will be changed, often into an ideologically opposing view, when documenting details are moved from central to peripheral positions in the narrative structure" (1985, p. 170). A new political narrative would meet the tests of "descriptive adequacy, testability, and openness to change based on challenge and feedback." Such a narrative would introduce "new information in terms of unfamiliar dilemmas, puzzles, and contradictions of the sort that promote critical thought and a self-consciousness of problem-solving behavior" (pp. 162, 164, 168).

Lucaites and Condit argue that tests of narrative adequacy differ for its three pure functions, poetic (to delight), dialectical (to instruct), and rhetorical (to move). Rhetorical discourse, they contend, aims at the enactment of an interest or the wielding of power and the tests of rhetorical narrative flow from the demands of audience adaptation, context, and material gain. In their view a sound rhetorical narrative is internally consistent with itself as well as the larger discourse of which it is a part and is externally consistent with the audience's logical and sociological expectations. It is brief enough to avoid audience weariness and disinterest through digressions or unnecessary detail. It is univocal, having a unity of direction and purpose, thus reinforcing proof of a single interpretation of a fact, value, or policy claim. Finally, using an extended example of British Prime Minister Margaret Thatcher, they contend that a sound rhetorical narrative rests on credibility, on "inherent, formal unity of narrator, author, and speaker" (1985, pp. 101–102).

Other scholars have gone beyond modification to direct attack. It is important to note that the critics mentioned here did not have the benefit of Fisher's most recent version of his position as found in his book or in two published essays incorporated into it. Lewis rejects "Fisher's assertion of the moral superiority of the narrative paradigm" and his belief, along with Aristotle's, that "the 'people' have a natural tendency to prefer the true and the just" (Lewis, 1987, pp. 296–297). While Fisher sees the rational and narrative paradigms as different yet essentially compatible, Lewis contends that they "can be distinctive and incommensurable" (pp. 294–295, 297).

McGee and Nelson conceive of narration as the "*techne* of translation," with a function similar to the syllogism in scientific demonstration, and they believe that narrative rationality in public argument should be rooted in an "epistemology of myth," a move not developed by Fisher (McGee and Nelson, 1985, pp. 146, 149–152). They reject Fisher's claim that "experts" have dominated public discourse and decisions with technical reasoning, and they reject his dichotomy between technical/traditional rationality and narrative rationality (pp. 140, 144).

Warnick has mounted a massive attack, adding her own to the "small chorus of voices expressing reservations about the paradigm as originally articulated" (1987, p. 172). First, Fisher is unclear, across his various works, whether traditional rationality is less desirable than narrative rationality and whether it is compatible with but subsumed by narrative. Second, the "people" do not necessarily prefer the "true and just" view, and Fisher fails to demonstrate "how we can assume that the public will not choose bad stories based on self-delusion or ratio-nalization" (pp. 176–177, 181). Third, the concept of "good reasons" is circular, and Fisher is equivocal in wanting to include the standards of "the best audience one can conceive" and the "ideal basis for human conduct" while admitting that "values are context-dependent and particular to the rhetorical situation giving rise to discourse" (pp. 178–179, 181). Finally, without traditional rationality, the ideal audience, or audience judgment as reliable standards, we are left with the "arbitrary and personal" judgment of the critic, which "in the applications dem-onstrated by Fisher as critic, is unsupported by data on public values, the effects of value adoption, or rational analysis" (pp. 179–181). In sum, Warnick finds that the "narrative rationality concept in his paradigm itself lacks narrative probability or coherence" (pp. 181).

A second frontal assault on Fisher's position comes from Rowland. While preserving a major role for narrative argument in human decision making, Row-land questions the clarity and generalizability of the proposed narrative para-digm. He argues, first, "that the narrative has been defined so broadly that the term loses much of its explanatory power" (1987, pp. 265–268). Second, the nar-rative paradigm offers inadequate standards of rationality as an alternative to the informal logic tests of the rational world paradigm. Indeed Rowland believes that, as developed so far, the narrative tests of probability and fidelity are not sig-nificantly different from "traditional tests of evidence and reasoning" (pp. 268–271). Finally, Rowland contends that Fisher's fear of "elite domination of the public sphere" through technical reason is a fear overstated and a fear not ade-quately solved, to the degree it exists, through the narrative paradigm (pp. 271–273). Rowland concludes that, "despite its potential, narrative theory has not yet reached the point that it makes sense to treat narrative as a paradigm rather than a mode of discourse" (p. 274).

The conclusion reached by Lucaites and Condit in 1985 still seems true today: "if there is a unified narrative paradigm of human communication, or a universal narrative metacode, they have not yet been discovered." But they also believe that the search should continue and that, even if not productive of a para-digm or metacode, "it should at least illuminate the full range of practices in which narrative participates" (pp. 105–106). Clearly, political communication is a major arena of narrative practice. In *Tales of a New America*, Robert Reich notes that on the surface we take political discourse about public issues to be editorials, political candidates' programs, economists' analyses, Congressional committee hearings, television documentaries, and specialists' disagreements. "But in the background—disguised and unarticulated—are the myth-based morality tales that determine when we declare a fact to be a problem, how policy choices are characterized, how the debate is framed. These are the unchallenged subtexts of political discourse" (1987, p. 6).

References

Bennett, W. Lance, and Murray Edelman. "Toward a New Political Narrative." *Journal of Communication*, 35 (Autumn 1985): 156–171.

Burke, John P. *Bureaucratic Responsibility.* Baltimore. MD: Johns Hopkins University Press. 1986.

Dowling, Ralph E., and Gabrielle Marraro. "Grenada and the Great Communicator: A Study in Democratic Ethics." *Western Journal of Speech Communication*, 50 (Fall 1986): 350–367.

Farrell, Thomas B. "Narrative in Natural Discourse: On Conversation and Rhetoric." *Journal of Communication*, 35 (Autumn 1985): 109–127.

Fisher, Walter R. "Ethics, Rationality, and Narrativity." Unpublished lecture, Marquette University, Milwaukee, November 11, 1986.

Fisher, Walter R. "Technical Logic, Rhetorical Logic, and Narrative Rationality." *Argumentation*, 1 (1987a): 3–21.

Fisher, Walter R. *Human Communication as Narration: Toward a Philosophy of Reason, Value, and Action.* Columbia: University of South Carolina Press, 1987b.

Johannesen, Richard L. "An Ethical Assessment of the Reagan Rhetoric: 1981–1982." In *Political Communication Yearbook 1984,* Keith R. Sanders, Lynda Lee Kaid, and Dan Nimmo, eds. Carbondale: Southern Illinois University Press, 1985, pp. 226–241.

Johannesen, Richard L. "Ronald Reagan's Economic Jeremiad." *Central States Speech Journal*, 37 (Summer 1986): 79–89.

Lewis, William F. "Telling America's Story: Narrative Form and the Reagan Presidency." *Quarterly Journal of Speech*, 73 (August 1987): 280–302.

Lucaites, John Lewis, and Celeste Michelle Condit. "Reconstructing Narrative Theory: A Functional Perspective." *Journal of Communication*, 35 (Autumn 1985): 90–108.

MacIntyre, Alasdair. *After Virtue*, 2d ed. Notre Dame: University of Notre Dame Press, 1984.

Margolis, Joseph. "Democracy and the Responsibility to Inform the Public." In *Ethical Issues in Government*, Norman E. Bowie, ed. Philadelphia: Temple University Press, 1981, pp. 237–248.

McGee, Michael Calvin, and John S. Nelson. "Narrative Reason in Public Argument." *Journal of Communication*, 35 (Autumn 1985): 139–155.

Moore, Mark H. "Realms of Obligation and Virtue." In *Public Duties: The Moral Obligations of Government Officials*, Joel L. Fleishman, Lance Liebman, and Mark H. Moore, eds. Cambridge: Harvard University Press, 1981, pp. 3–31.

Nilsen, Thomas R. "Democratic Ethics and the Hidden Persuaders." *Quarterly Journal of Speech* XLIV (December 1958): 385–392.

Nilsen, Thomas R. *Ethics of Speech Communication*, 2d ed. Indianapolis: Bobbs-Merrill, 1974.

Redford, Emmette S. *Democracy in the Administrative State.* New York: Oxford University Press. 1969.

Reich, Robert B. *Tales of a New America.* New York: Times Books, 1987.

Rowland, Robert C. "Narrative: Mode of Discourse or Paradigm?" *Communication Monographs*, 54 (September 1987): 264–275.

Wallace, Karl R. "An Ethical Basis of Communication." *Speech Teacher*, IV (January 1955): 1–9.

Warnick, Barbara. "The Narrative Paradigm: Another Story." *Quarterly Journal of Speech*, 73 (May 1987): 172–182.

Warwick, Donald R. "The Ethics of Administrative Discretion." In *Public Duties: The Moral Obligations of Government Officials,* Joel L. Fleishman, Lance Liebman, and Mark H. Moore, eds. Cambridge: Harvard University Press, 1981, pp. 93–127.

Preview to "Virtue Ethics, Character, and Political Communication." This essay first explores the tradition of virtue ethics or character ethics as a complement to the current dominant deontological (duty-based) theories, such as Kant's Categorical Imperative, and to teleological (consequentialist) theories, such as utilitarianism. The essay probes the applications and implications of character ethics for the practice of political communication, whether by candidate or officeholder.

The ethical character of President George W. Bush came under scrutiny during his two terms. As Bush's first term drew to a close, journalist Ronald Kessler concluded his book, *A Matter of Character* (New York: Sentinel/Penguin Group, 2004), by praising Bush's character for "vision, courage, patience, optimism, integrity, focus, discipline, determination, decisiveness, and devotion to America" (p. 290). In contrast, about the same time philosopher Peter Singer published *The President of Good and Evil: The Ethics of George W. Bush* (New York: Dutton/Penguin Group, 2004), based on his evaluation of Bush's speeches, writings, other comments, and policy decisions. Although Singer took Bush's communication and actions at face value as sincere, he ends by condemning Bush's ethical character for dishonesty, inconsistency, weakness, and promise breaking. Also about that time, the editorial page editor of the *Atlanta Journal-Constitution*, Cynthia Tucker, noted that "Bush ran on his claims to be a man of strong character.... Yet, this administration has produced more dissembling and distortion, more fabrications and pseudo-facts, than any White House in recent memory—Richard Nixon's included. They lie brazenly and repeatedly.... The entire premise of the Bush presidency—that he is a man of principle, of honor, of candor—is crumbling" (DeKalb, IL, *Daily Chronicle*, April 12, 2004). Well into Bush's second term, a significant portion of citizens held serious doubts about his ethical character. A Gallup poll on personal characteristics of President Bush, taken April 26–30, 2006, found that 56 percent of respondents did not perceive him as honest and trustworthy (www.gallup.com). In what ways and why would you agree or disagree with these positive and negative assessments of Bush's ethical character?

For an interesting comparative culture perspective on a tradition of virtue ethics or character ethics in Asian Confucianism, see A. S. Cua, *Moral Vision and Tradition: Essays in Chinese Ethics* (Washington, DC: Catholic University Press of America, 1998), chs. 8, 12, and 13.

Virtue Ethics, Character, and Political Communication*

Richard L. Johannesen

The contemporary philosophy of ethics has been dominated by an emphasis on duties, obligations, rules, rights, principles, and the resolution of complex ethical dilemmas, quandaries, or borderline cases (Jonsen and Toulmin 1988; Kupperman 1988; Pincoffs 1986). This dominant emphasis has been true whether as variations

*Reprinted by permission of the publisher from Richard L. Johannesen, "Virtue Ethics, Character, and Political Communication," in *Ethical Dimensions of Political Communication*, Robert E. Denton, Jr., ed. (New York: Praeger, 1991), pp. 69–90. Praeger is an imprint of Greenwood Publishing Group, Inc., Westport, CT.

on Immanuel Kant's categorical imperative, on John Rawls's depersonalized veil of ignorance to determine justice, on statements of intrinsic ultimate goods, or on Jeremey Bentham's or John Stuart Mill's utilitarian/consequentialist views. The past several decades, however, have seen a growing interest among ethicists in a largely ignored tradition that goes back at least as far as Plato's and Aristotle's philosophies of ethics (Adler 1970, 235–65; Geatch 1977; MacIntyre 1984, 146–64; Mayo 1958, 200, 209–12; Palmour 1987; Rorty 1980, 106). This largely bypassed tradition typically is called virtue ethics or character ethics. Indeed, Alderman argues that "Aristotle's moral philosophy is *properly* to be construed as the first important virtue theory" (1982, 128).

Most ethicists of virtue or character see that stance as a crucial complement to the current dominant ethical theories (Becker 1975, 1986; Brandt 1981; Frankena 1970; Kupperman 1988, 123; Meilaender 1984, 4–5; Pincoffs, 1986, 5, 35; Sichel 1988, 82; Wallace 1978; Walton 1988, 7). A few elevate character ethics to the position of "primary moral category" and argue that "character is a more adequate final court of appeal in moral philosophy than either rights, goods, or rules" (Alderman 1982). But Hudson (1981) contends that a complete moral theory should encompass both rules and principles "which specify a person's moral obligations and duties" and the significant role of the virtues of character in guiding moral action. The strengths and weaknesses of a character or virtue ethics approach are explored in an anthology edited by French, Uehling, and Wettstein (1988).

Some philosophers draw distinctions between ethics and morals as concepts. Ethics denotes the general and systematic study of what ought to be the grounds and principles for right and wrong human behavior. Morals (or morality) denotes the practical, specific, generally agreed-upon, culturally transmitted standards of right and wrong. Other philosophers, however, use the terms ethics and morals more or less interchangeably, as will be the case here.

The Nature of Ethical Character

In *After Virtue*, MacIntyre views moral character as "the arena of the virtues and vices" (1984, 168). Ethicists describe virtues variously as deep-rooted dispositions, habits, skills, or traits of character that incline us to see, feel, and act in ethically right and sensitive ways. Virtues also are described variously as learned, acquired, cultivated, reinforced, capable of modification, capable of conflicting, and ideally coalesced into a harmonious cluster (see Hauerwas 1981a, 115; Hauerwas 1981b, 49; MacIntyre 1984, 149, 154, 205, 219; Mayo 1958, 101–2, 214; Meilaender 1984, 6–11; Pinckaers 1962; Pincoffs 1986, 73–100; Sichel 1988, 75, 83; Slote 1983).

Consider the nature of moral character as described at some length by three ethicists and a theorist of rhetoric. According to Richard DeGeorge,

> As human beings develop, they tend to adopt patterns of actions, and dispositions to act in certain ways. These dispositions, when viewed collectively, are sometimes called character. A person who habitually tends to act as he morally should has a good character. If he resists strong temptation, he has a strong character. If he habitually acts immorally, he has a morally bad character. If despite good intentions he frequently succumbs

to temptation, he has a weak character. Because character is formed by conscious actions, in general people are morally responsible for their characters as well as for their individual actions. (1986, 89)

Karen Lebacqz believes that

indeed, when we act, we not only *do* something, we also shape our own character. Our choices about what to do are also choices about whom to be. A single lie does not necessarily make us a liar; but a series of lies may. And so each choice about what to do is also a choice about whom to *be*—or, more accurately, whom to become. (1985, 83)

In line with this view, Joseph Kupfer (1982; also see Michell 1984; Minnick 1985) contends that the "moral presumption against lying" rests on two lines of argument that demonstrate ultimate negative effects on the "character" *of the liar.* First, lying causes immediate restriction of the freedom of the deceived. Lying inclines the liar toward a general disrespect for persons—toward abuse of the uniquely human capacity for language as necessary for understanding and reflective choice. Second, lying involves the self-contradiction of "repudiating in speech what we believe." Liars disguise their "real self" from others by contradicting their real beliefs and, thus, who they really are. This self-opposition threatens the integration or coherence of the liar's personality. By disguising the self, the liar rejects the opportunity for self-knowledge; reactions of others useful for self-definition are possible only in response to truthful self-disclosure of beliefs.

Both of the negative effects on the liar—an attitude of disrespect for persons and threat to coherence of personality—weaken his or her moral character. Walter Fisher considers character to be an "organized set of actional tendencies" (1987, 47) and observes: "If these tendencies contradict one another, change significantly, or alter in 'strange' ways, the result is a questioning of character. . . . Without this kind of predictability, there is no trust, no community, no rational human order" (1987, 147–48).

Significant in many discussions of character ethics is the concept of "vision" (Birkhead 1989; Palmour 1987, 20–22). Moral character involves a spectrum of moral excellences or a range of reasons for our actions that provide moral vision (Hauerwas 1981b, 59; Sichel 1988, 256–58). To live morally, believes Hauerwas, "we must not only adhere to public and generalizable rules but also see and interpret the nature of the world in a moral way. The moral life is as much a matter of vision as it is a matter of doing" (1981b, 66). Meilaender describes "*vision* as a central theme of any ethic of virtue" (1984, ix). "Our virtues do not simply fit us for life; they help shape life. They shape not only our character but the world we see and inhabit" (1984, 5). He concludes: "*Being* not *doing* takes center stage; for what we ought to do may depend on the sort of person we are. What duties we perceive may depend upon what virtues shape our vision of the world" (1984, 10).

Some Functions of Ethical Character

In living the ethical life, what functions may be served by the virtues of character? Our formed ethical character does influence our choices and actions (Adler, 1970, 162, 253; Adler 1988, 247, 253–55, 266; Cunningham 1970; Hauerwas 1981b, 62). "Character surrounds action" and often is "a set of limitations restraining or shaping actions in certain ways. . . . Action occurs within the context of character" (Wilbur 1984, 176). In urging us to take virtues seriously, Hudson maintains that "an ethic of virtues can require both that we be of a certain character and that we perform certain kinds of acts. Human good *consists* (in part) both in virtuous action and in being a person of a certain character" (1981, 198–99). He explains that while a coward occasionally may do a courageous thing, this "does not make him a courageous" person, for the courageous person acts courageously as a matter of course or "second nature." Mayo says that according to character ethics, "there is another way of answering the fundamental question 'What ought I to do?' Instead of quoting a rule, we quote a quality of character, a virtue: we say 'Be brave,' or 'Be patient' or 'Be lenient'" (1958, 213). Sommers explains that the virtue-based theorist, by "concentrating attention on character rather than action, tacitly assumes that a virtuous person's actions generally fall within the range of what is right and fair" (1985, xii–xiii).

Our ethical character sensitizes us to ethically difficult or problematic situations, motivates our concern so that the situation matters to us, and undergirds our commitment—our long-term loyalty—to necessary values and actions (Kupperman 1988, 115–21). Hauerwas believes that only "if we have a morally significant character can we be relied upon to face morally serious questions rather than simply trying to avoid them" (1981b, 64). Also, however, as Meilaender argues, in redressing the overemphasis in current ethical theory on "troubling moral dilemmas" and on "borderline cases":

> An ethic of virtue seeks to focus not only on such moments of great anxiety and uncertainty in life but also on the continuities, the habits of behavior which make us the persons we are. Not whether we should frame one innocent man to save five—but on the virtue of justice, with its steady, habitual determination to make space in life for the needs and claims of others. Not whether to lie to the secret police—but on that steady regard for others which uses language truthfully and thereby makes a common life possible. (1984, 5)

Ethical character influences what *roles* we play in life and how we play them. The roles that we choose should be appropriate to and reflective of our character, not supplant that character (Cochran 1982, 17–21). The ethical virtues and commitments that comprise our moral character "control which roles can be accepted" and "influence how any role is actually lived" (Sichel 1988, 229–30; also see MacIntyre, 1984, 204–8). Ethical character also is related to the *rules* and abstract principles specified by various ethical theories. MacIntyre (1984, 150, 232–35, 257, 268) traces some of these relationships throughout the history of ethical theory. But particularly important is the way in which ethical character can humanize the application of abstract rules and principles. According to Sichel, the virtues of character "interject concern for concrete persons and foster more humane and sensitive feelings, compassion and sympathy, concern for moral ideals and qualities that abstract principles often seem to ignore" (1988, 266; see also Williams 1981, 1–19).

Ethical Character and Communication

A virtue is not a "habit" in the sense of dictating a "weary repetition of identical acts" (Cunningham 1970, 98) or in the sense of automatic, mechanistic repetition (Simon 1986). Rather, Pinckaers (1962) argues at length that moral virtues are formed by the repeated exercise of "interior acts" of practical reason and will that "insure their mastery" over exterior actions. Varied exterior acts in various circumstances may reflect the same internal disposition of virtue. Moral virtues reflect creativity and inventiveness in both their formation and their application, and they dispose a person to produce the maximum of what he or she "is able to do on a moral plane." Although a virtue does not involve "a series of identical material acts tirelessly reproduced," it is characteristic of a moral virtue "to permit an action to be performed without further need for lengthy reflection, without hesitation, and without interior conflict" (Pinckaers 1962, 65, 81).

Ethical communication is not simply a series of careful and reflective decisions, instance by instance, to communicate in ethically responsible ways (Cochran 1982, 32–33; Hauerwas 1977, 20, 29; Klaidman and Beauchamp 1987, 17–20; Lebacqz 1985, 77–91; Sichel 1988, 26, 33–37). Deliberate application of ethical rules sometimes is not possible. Pressure may be so great or a deadline so near for a decision that there is not adequate time for careful deliberation. We may be unsure what ethical criteria are relevant or how they apply. The situation may seem unique, and thus applicable criteria do not readily come to mind. In such times of crisis or uncertainty, our decision concerning ethical communication stems less from deliberation than from our "character." Furthermore, our ethical character influences the terms with which we describe a situation and whether we believe the situation contains ethical implications.

In Judeo-Christian or Western cultures, good moral character usually is associated with the habitual embodiment of such virtues as courage, temperance, prudence (or practical wisdom), justice, fairness, generosity, patience, truthfulness, and trustworthiness. Contemporary feminist scholars would interject additional vital virtues: caring for self and others, compassion, nurturance of relationships, responsiveness to growth and appreciation for change, resilient good humor and clear-sighted cheerfulness, attentive and realistic love, and a humble "sense of the limits of one's actions and of the unpredictability of the consequences of one's work" (Ruddick 1980; Gilligan 1982; Gilligan et al. 1988; Noddings 1984). Martin Buber's dimensions of true dialogue could be viewed as virtues of ethical character: authenticity, inclusion, confirmation, and presentness (Johannesen 1990, 57–77). Other cultures may praise additional or different virtues that they believe constitute good ethical character. Instilled in us as habitual dispositions to feel, see, and act, such virtues guide the ethics of our communication when careful or clear deliberation is not possible.

Codes of Ethics and the Character-Depiction Function

We turn to the possible connection between formal codes of ethics and the concept of character ethics. Formal codes of ethics have been proposed by various communication-oriented professional associations, corporations, and citizen-action groups in such fields as commercial advertising, public relations, technical writing, organizational consulting, print and broadcast journalism, and political communication. While varied objections have been raised concerning the usefulness of formal codes, and while a number of significant functions for formal codes of ethics have been identified (Johannesen 1990, 169–91), I will concentrate on one important and largely ignored function of such codes.

In her book, *Professional Ethics* (1985, 63–91), Karen Lebacqz suggests that formal ethical codes, especially in the professions, should be seen as having a function quite different from the typical one, namely, as rules for specific behavior or as admonitions concerning specific instances. In her view, we must look beyond the action-oriented language of most codes ("do this," "avoid that") to the "overall picture of the type of person who is to *embody* those actions." As reconceptualized by Lebacqz, a code embodies a picture of the moral "character" to be expected of a professional in a given field; it would depict, for example, an ethical communicator's "being" collectively and over time. She contends that "codes do not give specific guidance for action as much as they say something about the character traits necessary for someone to be a professional." "In short," she says, "codes are geared primarily toward establishing expectations for character." On this view, codes are "guideposts to understand where stresses and tensions have been felt within a profession and what image of the good professional is held up to assist professionals through those stresses and tensions."

According to Lebacqz, a wide range of professional codes reflect a core of central character traits, ethical principles, or obvious duties: "Justice, beneficence, non-maleficence, honesty, and fidelity." She believes that a "professional is called not simply to *do* something but to *be* something." At a fundamental level codes depict a professional as "bound by certain ethical principles *and* as incorporating those principles *into his or her very character*." Ideally a code depicts the professional as "a person of integrity who not only does the 'right' thing, but is an *honorable person*." As illustration Lebacqz says that a trustworthy person not only keeps a confidence but is "thoughtful about the impact" of decisions on others and is "sensitive to their needs and claims." An honest person "tries to avoid any kind of deception, not just explicit lies." As noted earlier, Lebacqz contends that "when we act, we not only *do* something, we also shape our own character. . . . And so each choice about what to *do* is also a choice about whom to *be*—or, more accurately, whom to become."

This function of ethical codes as depicting desirable virtues of character more than (or at least as much as) specific rules for specific actions is exemplified by a code urged by the Josephson Institute for the Advancement of Ethics. The institute is a nonprofit organization established to "advance ethical awareness, commitment and behavior in both the public and private sectors of society." In its journal, *Ethics: Easier Said Than Done*, the Josephson Institute published a code of "Ethical Values and Principles in Public Service" (Spring/Summer 1988, 153). The institute believes that these are the "characteristics and values that most people associate with ethical behavior." Although the code does not specifically focus on communication ethics, many of its elements appropriately could be adapted for communication. Each of the eleven values presented in the Josephson code might be viewed as a character virtue for persons in public service—whether elected public official, political campaigner, or appointed bureaucrat: honesty, integrity, promise keeping, fidelity, fairness, caring, respect, good citizenship, excellence, accountability, and public trust (Johannesen 1990, 182–84). Each of the values or virtues is briefly explained in the code by describing obligations stemming from it. For example, promise keeping: "Persons worthy of trust keep promises, fulfill commitments, abide by the spirit as well as the letter of an agreement; they do not interpret agreements in an unreasonably technical or legalistic manner in order to rationalize noncompliance or create justifications for escaping commitments." Or consider caring: "Concern for the well-being of others manifests itself in compassion, giving, kindness and serving; it requires one to attempt to help those in need and to avoid harming others." The Josephson code does, I believe, serve a character-depiction function.

Ethical Character and Political Communication

A social/institutional ethic for assessing political communication can be rooted in the values and procedures central to the health and growth of our system of governing, representative democracy. Among them are the intrinsic dignity and worth of all persons; equal opportunity for fulfillment of individual potential; enhancement of citizen capacity to reach rational decisions; access to channels of public communication; access to relevant and accurate information on public issues; maximization of freedom of choice; toleration of dissent; honesty and clarity in presenting values relevant to problems and policies; honesty in presenting motivations and consequences; thoroughness, accuracy, and fairness in presenting evidence and alternatives; and recognition that the societal worth of an end seldom should be the sole justification of the ethics of the means to achieve that end (Johannesen 1990, 21–37, 236–37, 255). Often informal standards and formal codes of ethics for various types of political communication are founded implicitly or explicitly on such fundamental values (Johannesen 1990, 31–34, 184–91).

In contrast, a number of scholars are suggesting that virtue ethics or character must have a significant place in political ethics. Such books as *Character, Community, and Politics* (Cochran 1982) and *Character: An Individualistic Theory of Politics* (Homer 1983) represent attempts to situate character ethics at the center of the philosophy of political ethics. In ancient Greece, according to MacIntyre (1984, 135, 138, 219), whether the ethical views of the older sophists, Plato, or Aristotle are considered, all took "it for granted that the milieu in which the virtues are to be exercised and in terms of which they are to be defined is the *polis*." Today ethical character is no less important for politics and public service.

> Today's leaders have neglected the whole issue of moral character in both theory and practice and no longer encourage informed public reflection on the kind of people we are becoming and on our responsibilities to one another now and in the future. . . . The reality of moral character is unavoidable . . . in the so-called "character" issue of the public's trust in politicians. (Palmour 1987, 14–15)

If the concept of ethical character were given a preeminent place in political philosophy, contends Homer, the result would be "a profound change in the way we think about politics. . . . Character would force us to reexamine the way we bring up our children to think about politics, the way we should know political institutions, and the way we should act in the world." Emphasis on character would "refocus the debate in political theory on the enduring question of how to live well in the proximity of others" (1986, 166–67). Lilla laments the overemphasis in the education of students preparing for public service on ethical rules for application and on the study of ethical dilemmas and catastrophic cases. The moral life of the public official primarily consists, Lilla believes, of "a set of virtues which the official has acquired through his education and it reveals itself in the attitudes and habits he displays to the political process and the public in his day-to-day work" (1981, 5). And what Gilligan (1982; et al. 1988) describes as the male moral voice of rights, rules, justice, and fairness and the female moral voice of care, compassion, relationships, and responsiveness both must be legitimized as encompassing virtues necessary for the moral conduct of politics broadly defined (Ruddick 1980, 345, 361; Sichel 1988, 218–24).

Cynical Views

Humbuggery and Manipulation is F. G. Bailey's analysis of the art of leadership— primarily political leadership. One of his main arguments is that "no leader can survive as a leader without deceiving others (followers no less than opponents) and without deliberately doing to others what he would prefer not having done to himself" (1988, ix). Bailey summarizes his view:

> Leaders are not the virtuous people they claim to be: they put politics before statesmanship; they distort facts and oversimplify issues; they promise what no one can deliver; and they are liars. But I have also insisted that leaders, if they are to be effective, have no choice in the matter. They could not be virtuous (in the sense of morally excellent) and be leaders at the same time. I do not mean that a leader should necessarily behave immorally. . . . I mean only that he must have the imagination (and—a paradox—the moral courage) to set himself above and beyond established values and beliefs if it is necessary to do so to attain his ends. (1988, 174–75)

To what degree should we accept Bailey's viewpoint? Does he believe that leaders must lie and deceive routinely or only occasionally? Do political leaders really have no "choice," as he argues? From his perspective, Bailey seems to describe not only what *is* the case but also what *ought to be* the case. I would contend that while we might agree with the former, we should reject the latter view.

Although scholars continue to debate the meaning of Niccolo Machiavelli's conception of virtue (Garver 1987; Hannaford 1972; Plamenatz 1972; Wood 1967), arguably Machiavelli saw prudence and practical wisdom as intellectual virtues more than as moral virtues; described other traditional moral virtues, such as honesty and courage, simply as means to be used strategically (even violated) to preserve the state; and urged that a leader must exercise the practical virtue of self-control. Machiavelli also believed that private moral virtues were inappropriate and ineffective for public political life and that at best a leader need only pretend to possess these moralities (Hariman 1989; O'Leary 1989).

During his presidential campaign and his administration, Jimmy Carter "offered a vision of authority based entirely on character" and "argued that virtue was the sole criterion for leadership" (O'Leary 1989, 123). Carter explicitly offered the virtues of honesty, efficiency, competence, compassion, and love. He assumed that essentially private virtues also appropriately operate in the conduct of public duties. In the long run, however, Carter was unable to translate these virtues into effective public policies and into sufficient public support. Indeed, contends O'Leary, Carter's reliance on a classical conception of virtue was "ultimately bound to fail in a world that has accepted the assumptions of the Machiavellian ethic" (1989, 123). Furthermore, he argues, "To a public that has accepted the assumption that it is not only permissible, but necessary, for a politician to lie in the performance of his duties, Carter's promise of honesty (to the extent that it was believed) could only serve as direct evidence of his incompetence" (1989, 126).

Presidents Johnson and Reagan

In her book, *Character*, Gail Sheehy describes the "habit of deceit" that had developed throughout Lyndon Johnson's lifetime; it was the "aspect of his character most deeply engraved and evident as a pattern throughout his youth and adulthood" (1988, 16). His public duplicity on the Vietnam War as candidate and as president "played a crucial role in the disillusionment of a political generation." The legacy of the "credibility gap" and a "long-term mistrust of the president . . . can be laid directly at the door of one man's character" (1988, 17).

Throughout his two terms as president, Ronald Reagan continued a long-standing habit of playing fast and loose with the facts (Barber 1985, 491–96; Green and MacColl 1987; Johannesen 1990, 235–52; Sheehy 1988, 257–303). In his news conferences, informal comments, and speeches, Reagan routinely misstated facts, statistics, and situations. Another aspect of playing fast and loose with the facts was Reagan's misuse of factual illustrations and stories for proof, characterized satirically by the press as his "anecdotage" problem. Reagan frequently used vivid and dramatic real-life stories to prove this point or that. Unfortunately, these anecdotes, even when not misstated, often were found to be misleading or unrepresentative. Reagan's misstatements of facts and misuse of anecdotes were not rare, occasional, or on minor matters. Rather, they were routine, sometimes repeated even after exposure, and often on matters of important public policy. The standard is not perfect accuracy. Occasional slips on minor details may be expected. The obligation is not to ultimate truth in some absolute and invariable sense. But given the major resources at his or her command for verifying information, a president does have an obligation regularly to present highly probable conclusions and data that are as accurate and fair as possible.

Is what James David Barber terms Reagan's attitude of "contempt for the facts" an ethical character flaw, a vice? Reagan was "literally shameless when it came to the question of factuality" (Barber 1985, 493; Green and MacColl 1987, 11). His unconcern for accuracy was, in view of Green and MacColl, "a habit he apparently cannot unlearn." Indeed, they characterize Reagan as "incorrigible" on this matter. "He is simply incapable of entertaining information that conflicts with his ideology. When facts differ from his beliefs, he changes the facts, not his beliefs. He has sunk to a point where he can't make a major statement without making a major misstatement" (Green and MacColl 1987, 18).

The 1988 Presidential Candidates

During 1987 and 1988 intense news media scrutiny of presidential primary candidates focused on the "character issue" and the search for significant "character flaws." Democratic candidate Gary Hart temporarily withdrew from the race after allegations of a pattern of sexual indiscretion in his private life. If nothing else, the virtues of temperance, fidelity, and prudence were at issue. Republican television evangelist Marion "Pat" Robertson denied any pattern of deception in the numerous exaggerated, misleading, or erroneous statements about himself in his résumé, speeches, and books (see Alter 1987b; Reid 1987; Wills 1987).

The withdrawal of Senator Joseph Biden from the Democratic presidential primary race clearly illustrates the relation of moral character and communication ethics. A pattern of plagiarism was a major issue of communication ethics in Biden's case. *Plagiarism* stems from the Latin word for kidnapper. It involves a communicator who steals another person's words and ideas without properly acknowledging their source and who presents those words or ideas as his or her own. Plagiarism may take such varied forms as repeating almost word for word another's sentences, "repeating someone else's particularly apt phrase without appropriate acknowledgment, paraphrasing another persons argument as your own, and presenting another's line of thinking in the development of an idea as though it were your own" (Gibaldi and Achtert 1988, 21).

Previously the press had characterized Biden positively as the most eloquent of the Democratic contenders or negatively as glib and shallow-minded. Now the press revealed that in campaign speeches Biden often presented as his own, without acknowledgment, various phrases, sentences, and long passages from speeches by John F. Kennedy, Robert Kennedy, and Hubert Humphrey. On two occasions Biden plagiarized a lengthy segment from a speech by British Labour Party leader Neil Kinnock. In this case, however, Biden also inaccurately presented parts of Kinnock's life history as his own. Biden falsely claimed that his ancestors were coal miners and that he was the first in his family to attend college. In addition, evidence surfaced that while a first-year law student, Biden had plagiarized, word for word, five pages from a law journal article. Although not a matter of plagiarism, a final element in Biden's flawed character emphasized by the news media involved his false claims in an informal interview with a small group of New Hampshire voters. Biden claimed that he graduated with three degrees and was given an award as the outstanding political science student. Further, he claimed that he attended law school on a full academic scholarship and won an international moot court competition. In fact, none of these claims were true ("Biden's Borrowings" 1987; "Biden Was Eloquent" 1987; Kaus 1987; Margolis 1987a, 1987c).

What defenses and excuses were offered by Biden and his staff? Staff members pointed out that on some occasions Biden had credited Kinnock and Robert Kennedy as sources. Biden contended that the episodes of plagiarism stemmed from ignorance, stupidity, or inattention to detail rather than from intentional deceptiveness. Concerning the plagiarism from Kinnock's speech by Biden at the Iowa State Fair, an aide explained: "He's under a huge amount of pressure. He didn't even know what he said. He was just on automatic pilot" (Coffey 1987; Margolis 1987b).

To what degree, if at all, should any of these defenses justify Biden's communication or soften our ethical judgment? In what ways should inattention to detail or lack of conscious intent to deceive influence our ethical assessment (Johannesen 1990, 10–11)? Biden's case illustrates patterns or habits of communication that the news media interpreted as serious character flaws. Lack of judgment to restrain impulses, falsification of facts, and inflation of his intellectual and communication abilities became the elements of Biden's doubtful character. At issue were such ethical virtues as humility, prudence, temperance, fairness, truthfulness, and trustworthiness (Broder 1987; Kaus 1987).

Character, Image, and Issues in Campaigns

Praise of an issue-oriented campaign as responsible and condemnation of an image-oriented campaign as superficial, even as unethical, has become a conventional judgment in political commentary (Bennett 1989). However, some political and rhetorical scholars do not share this automatic preference for issues over image in political campaigns. These scholars argue that issues and stands on issues are too transitory and too complex for voters to make dependable judgments. For example, an issue vital today often soon fades, to be replaced by one unforeseen during the campaign. Or issues may have to be created if none loom large in the public mind at the inflexible time when the campaign must occur. Instead, suggest some scholars, the basic dimensions of a candidate's image, largely defined as character, are as important as, if not more important than, particular stands on particular issues for citizen evaluation of political candidates during campaigns (Sheehy 1988, 21). One view describes images and issues as inextricably intertwined through the values espoused and contested by a candidate (Fish 1989; Weiss 1981; Werling 1987).

Granted, image stereotypically is viewed as intentionally deceptive and misleading—as largely unrelated to the candidate's actual nature. But image also may be conceived of as a composite audience perception of the candidate's actual personal qualities and abilities as reflected in her or his record of choices. With image defined in this manner, the key questions in the long run become the following: Does the candidate's past record demonstrate strength of moral character, decisiveness of action, openness to relevant information and alternative viewpoints, thoroughness in studying a problem, respect for the intelligence of other persons, and ability to lead through public and private communication (Barber 1985, 1–11; Gonchar and Hahn 1973; Hahn and Gonchar 1972).

Rhetorician Lloyd Bitzer contends that "the stuff of ordinary campaigns consists of arguments, position statements, testimonials, commercials, and other materials relating to the prudence, good character, and right intentions of the candidate—to the image" (1981, 242–43). He argues

> The public forms fairly reliable judgments about the candidates by observing their mistakes—especially their flaws in reasoning, character, and prudence. Most voters are not well educated about details of issues and legislation, although they should be; consequently, most are not good judges of a candidate's pronouncements on complicated issues. But most voters do have sound views on the constituents of logical reasoning, good character, and prudence. Thus when a candidate makes a mistake of reasoning, or of practical wisdom, or a mistake resulting from a flaw in character, the public is quick to recognize and, by and large, competent to judge it. (1981, 242)

Michael McGee, from the viewpoint of a rhetorician, argues that the conventional wisdom of preferring "issues" over "images" actually may be "ultimately unjustifiable and dangerous." Citizens generally

> do not have the necessary information to judge measures; such information could not be communicated to them in the context of an election campaign because the decisions to be made are too complicated for the limited time available; and, finally, the information needed for decision seems so technical and esoteric that most of "the people" could not judge it properly if it were available. (1978, 53)

Indeed, contends McGee, the only "issue" that the citizen is competent to judge is "the general character and trustworthiness displayed by candidates for office." Even when we believe that our choice stems from our evaluation of "the issues, we are in fact judging the character and the general trustworthiness of those who tell us what 'the issues' are" (1978, 154).

In her book, *Eloquence in an Electronic Age*, Kathleen Jamieson describes the current era as one in which

> voters are searching behind the promises for clues about whether a candidate is honest, knowledgeable, high principled, and temperamentally suited to lead the nation. In voter decisions, the candidate's character is now more central than his or her stands on issues and party identification. (1988, vii–viii)

However, in contrast with eras with fewer filters of communication mediation interposed between candidate and citizen, Jamieson views the present era as a time in which assessment of ethos—of practical wisdom, goodwill, and worthy moral character—is increasingly difficult. She concludes:

> With the advent of an electorate of millions and a country spanning oceans, direct experience of the character of a speaker is unattainable for most called on to judge public discourse. When we see a potential leader through the filter provided by pseudo-events, news bites, or nuggetized ads and then can know for certain only that most politicians do not speak their own words, ethos is a less reliable anchor for belief. (1988, 240)

In a synthesis of political theory and empirical survey research, Miller, Wattenberg, and Malanchuk argue that

> evaluating candidates on the basis of personal qualities has for years been regarded as emotional, irrational, and lacking in political relevance. . . .

The evidence now suggests that a reinterpretation is clearly needed. Rather than representing a concern with appearance, previously labeled "personality," the candidate assessments actually concentrate on the manner in which a candidate would conduct the affairs of office. (1985, 210)

Such assessments indeed may be "reasonable and intelligible performance evaluations." Miller et al. (1985) believe that voters primarily assess candidates along four dimensions of personal qualities: (1) competence—political experience and statesmanship, comprehension of political issues, realism, and intelligence; (2) integrity—trustworthiness, honesty, and sincerity; (3) reliability—dependable, strong, hardworking, decisive, and aggressive; and (4) charisma—leadership, dignity, humbleness, patriotism, and ability to communicate with people and inspire them.

"Of course issues are important. . . . But can any issue be more important in a presidential election than character?" Marshall Manley, chief executive officer of an insurance company, elaborates this position in a "My Turn" citizen editorial in *Newsweek*. He contends that

no matter how much we know about a candidate's views on specific issues, we can't really predict how he, or she, will react to the shifting demands and crises of an actual term in office. . . . Most voters wisely look beyond a candidate's stand on the issues to something more important: qualities of mind and character. (1988, 8)

Manley suggests five qualities of character essential for a president: (1) trustworthiness and integrity; (2) toughness in the sense of courage, stamina, and determination; (3) gregariousness, including ability to build coalitions, shape consensus, and work with peers; (4) a grasp of the lessons of history, both problems and solutions; and (5) a capacity for "love of country, love of family, and love of the rough and tumble of politics" (1988, 8).

As guidelines for assessing the character of a political candidate, we can reflect on the adequacy of the four dimensions described by Miller et al. and the five qualities suggested by Manley. Are there additional dimensions or qualities that should be significant for evaluating a candidate's character? Which of the dimensions or qualities seem to focus primarily on ethical characteristics? For example, to what degree should competence, determination, a grasp of the lessons of history, or love of the rough and tumble of politics be viewed as matters of ethics generally or more specifically as ethical virtues?

Conclusions

Political columnist Stephen Chapman (1987) offers three reasons why media scrutiny of character was so intense on the 1988 presidential candidates. First, voters are imposing increasingly higher ethical standards. Second,

personal integrity is one of the few matters that lend themselves to first-hand judgments by the voters. Most voters may feel unable to judge whether a politician is right about the defense appropriations bill. But they are able to consider evidence about a politician's ethics and reach a verdict, since they make similar evaluations about people every day. (1987, 3)

Third, voters "tend to vote for general themes, trusting candidates to apply them in specific cases. A politician who creates doubt about his personal honesty . . . creates doubt that his concrete policies will match his applause lines" (1987, 3).

In greater depth, Gail Sheehy probes three reasons why it is essential that "we examine the character of those who ask us to put our country in their hands" (1988, 20). Primarily, "it is to protect ourselves from electing a person whose character flaws, once subjected to the pressures of leading a superpower through the nuclear age, can weaken or endanger the course of our future" (1988, 21). With issues a less sure guide than we once thought, we "are left to search out those we can believe in as strong and sincere, fair and compassionate: real leaders to whom we can leave the responsibility to use good judgment when crises catch us unaware" (1988, 29).

Second, "We need the cold slap of insight to wake us up from the smoothly contrived images projected by highly paid professional media experts who market the candidates like perfumed soap" (1988, 29). Of course, candidates and their managers can exploit the "character issue" to their own advantage. But reporters, editorialists, commentators, and investigative journalists could assist citizens in major ways by providing information about a candidate's character development—about past and present relevant virtues and vice—about significant contexts and influences through which the moral character was formed, so that the manufactured pseudo character can be penetrated to judge character more realistically. "In judging character," Sheehy reminds us, "one can never be sure the judgment is 100 percent accurate." But to that reminder I would add that it is crucial that we continue to make the most informed judgment that we can.

A final reason that we should examine the moral character of our leaders and potential leaders is to learn about ourselves. In Sheehy's view, the case histories of the characters of political leaders

> instruct us in how, and how not, to conduct ourselves to win at life. We can use these characters as mirrors of our own character reflecting both our flaws and strengths. Seeing how their various attempts to change and adapt have played out from earliest childhood through public life can be a catalyst for taking steps to change ourselves. (1988, 29)

In *The Virtuous Journalist*, Klaidman and Beauchamp argue that citizens "should expect good character in our national leaders, and the same expectations are justified for anyone in whom we regularly place trust" (1987, 17). The *Wall Street Journal* ("Oliver North" 1987) surveyed dozens of top executives of American companies to see if they would hire Lt. Col. Oliver North (of the Iran-Contra scandal) if he applied for a job. Many executives enthusiastically said they would hire him, but some would restrict his responsibilities. Among those who would refuse to hire him, one especially pinpointed the matter of character, saying, "It is a real character flaw when someone is willing to lie, cheat, and steal to accomplish the end of his superiors. That flaw will ultimately hurt the company. It's a character flaw that I would find unacceptable despite the strengths of his loyalty. The integrity flaw outweighs any other" ("Oliver North" 1987, 35). Here we see the virtue of fidelity in conflict with the virtues of truthfulness and trustworthiness. An emphasis on virtue ethics or character ethics as a viable approach to ethics in organizations, both business and governmental, is reflected in such essays and books as Des Jardins' "Virtues and Corporate Responsibility" (1984); Kolenda's *Organizations and Ethical Individualism* (1988); Scott and Mitchell's "The Problem or Mystery of Evil and Virtue in Organizations" (1988); Walton's *The Moral Manager* (1988); and Wilbur's "Corporate Character" (1984).

Admittedly, the news media (or anyone) may at times be overzealous and focus on trivial or irrelevant character traits. But in general the emphasis on moral character in evaluating presidential candidates is central "to what the electorate seems to value most in its presidents—authenticity and honesty" (Taylor 1987, 23; Broder 1987, 7). To aid in assessing the ethical character of any person who is in a position of responsibility or who seeks a position of trust, we can modify guidelines suggested by journalists (Alter 1987a). Will the recent or current ethically suspect communication probably continue? Does it seem habitual? Even if a particular incident seems minor in itself, does it "fit into a familiar pattern that illuminates more serious shortcomings?" If the person does something inconsistent with his or her public image, "is it a small miscue or a sign of hypocrisy?"

"At this point in our political history," Sheehy emphasizes, "the concentration on character issues is unparalleled in its intensity" (1988, 11). The reason, she says, "is simple and stark." "By the time they become national leaders, the candidates' characters are sown. And if the character is destiny, the destiny they reap will be our own. . . . We must therefore know our would-be leaders in a deeper way than ever before" (1988, 21).

Communication ethics should encompass both individual ethics and social ethics. What are the ethical virtues of character and the central ethical standards that should guide individual choices? What are the ethical standards and responsibilities that should guide the communication practices of organizations and institutions—public and private, corporate, governmental, or professional? For an ethically suspect communication practice, where should individual and collective responsibility be placed? The study of communication ethics should suggest standards both for individual daily and context-bound communication choices and also for institutional/systemic policies and practices.

In her provocative essay, "Ethics Without Virtue," Christina Hoff Sommers (1984) warns that the present "system of moral education is silent about virtue." She condemns moral education as presented in most American universities today for addressing itself "not to the vices and virtues of individuals, but to the moral character of our nation's institutions." She argues:

> Inevitably the student forms the idea that applying ethics to modern life is mainly a question of learning how to be for or against social and institutional policies. . . . in that sort of ethical climate, a student soon loses sight of himself as a moral agent and begins to see himself as a moral spectator or protojurist. . . . The result of identifying normative ethics with public policy is justification for and reinforcement of moral passivity in the student. (1984, 388)

A curriculum of ethics without virtue, Sommers concludes, "is a cause for concern."

References

Adler, Mortimer J. 1970. *The time of our lives: The ethics of common sense.* New York: Holt, Rinehart and Winston.

———. 1988. *Reforming education: The opening of the American mind.* New York: Macmillan.

Alderman, Harold. 1982. By virtue of a virtue. *Review of Metaphysics* 36 (September): 127–53.

Alter, Jonathan. 1987a. The search for personal flaws. *Newsweek* 19 October, 79.

———. 1987b. A change of Hart. *Newsweek* 28 December, 12–16.

Bailey, F. G. 1988. *Humbuggery and manipulation: The art of leadership.* Ithaca, NY. Cornell University Press.

Barber, James David. 1985. *The presidential character: Predicting performance in the White House,* 3rd ed. Englewood Cliffs, NJ: Prentice-Hall.

Becker, Lawrence C. 1975. The neglect of virtue. *Ethics* 85 (January): 110–22.

———. 1986. *Reciprocity.* London: Routledge and Kegan Paul.

Bennett, W. Lance. 1989. Where have all the issues gone? Explaining the rhetorical limits in American elections. In *Spheres of argument,* ed. Bruce E. Gronbeck, 128–35. Annandale, VA: Speech Communication Association.

Biden was eloquent—if not original. 1987. *Chicago Tribune* 12 September, sec. 1, 1–2.

Biden's borrowings become an issue. 1987. *Chicago Tribune* 16 September, sec. 1,4.

Birkhead, Douglas. 1989. An ethics of vision for journalism. *Critical Studies in Mass Communication* 6 (September): 283–94.

Bitzer, Lloyd F. 1981. Political rhetoric. In *Handbook of political communication,* ed. Dan D. Nimmo and Keith R. Sanders, 225–48. Beverly Hills: Sage.

Brandt, R. B. 1981. W. K. Frankena and the ethics of virtue. *Monist* 64 (July): 271–92.

Broder, David S. 1987. The latest departed candidate. *Indianapolis News* 25 September, A-7.

Chapman, Stephen. 1987. How seriously has Joe Biden hurt his presidential effort? *Chicago Tribune* 20 September, sec. 4, 3.

Cochran, Clarke E. 1982. *Character, community, and politics.* University: University of Alabama Press.

Coffey, Raymond. 1987. Biden's borrowed eloquence beats the real thing. *Chicago Tribune* 18 September, sec. 1, 23.

Cunningham, Stanley B. 1970. Does "does moral philosophy rest upon a mistake?" make an even greater mistake? *Monist* 54 (January): 86–99.

DeGeorge, Richard T. 1986. *Business ethics,* 2d ed. New York: Macmillan.

Des Jardins, Joseph. 1984. Virtues and corporate responsibility. In *Corporate governance and institutionalizing ethics,* ed. W. Michael Hoffman, Jennifer Mills Moore, and David A. Fedo, 135–42. Lexington, MA: D. C. Heath.

Fish, Duane R. 1989. Image and issue in the second Bush-Dukakis debate: The mediating role of values. In *Spheres of argument,* ed. Bruce E. Gronbeck, 151–57. Annandale, VA: Speech Communication Association.

Fisher, Walter R. 1987. *Human communication as narration: Toward a philosophy of reason, value, and action.* Columbia: University of South Carolina Press.

Frankena, William K. 1970. Pritchard and the ethics of virtue. *Monist* 54 (January). 1–17.

French, Peter A., Theodore Uehling, Jr., and Howard K. Wettstein, eds. 1988. *Midwest studies in philosophy,* Vol. XIII, *Ethical theory—character and virtue.* Notre Dame, IN: University of Notre Dame Press.

Garver, Eugene. 1987. *Machiavelli and the history of prudence.* Madison: University of Wisconsin Press.

Geatch, Peter. 1977. *The virtues.* Cambridge: Cambridge University Press.

Gibaldi, Joseph, and Walter S. Achtert. 1988. *MLA handbook for writers of research papers,* 3rd ed. New York: Modern Language Association.

Gilligan, Carol. 1982. *In a different voice: Psychological theory and women's development*. Cambridge: Harvard University Press.

Gilligan, Carol et al. 1988. *Mapping the moral domain: A contribution of women's thinking to psychological theory and education*. Cambridge: Harvard University Graduate School of Education.

Gonchar, Ruth, and Dan Hahn. 1973. Rhetorical biography: A methodology for the citizen-critic. *Speech Teacher* 22 (January): 48–53.

Green, Mark, and Gail MacColl. 1987. *Reagan's reign of error*, Rev. and enl. ed. New York: Pantheon Books.

Hahn, Dan, and Ruth Gonchar. 1972. Political myth: The image and the issue. *Today's Speech* 20 (Summer): 57–65.

Hannaford, I. 1972. Machiavelli's concept of virtù in *The Prince* and *The Discourses* reconsidered. *Political Studies* 20 (June): 185–89.

Hariman, Robert. 1989. Before prudence: Strategy and the rhetorical tradition. In *Spheres of Argument*, ed. Bruce E. Gronbeck, 108–16. Annandale, VA: Speech Communication Association.

Hauerwas, Stanley. 1977. *Truthfulness and tragedy*. Notre Dame: University of Notre Dame Press.

———. 1981a. *A Community of character: Toward a constructive Christian social ethic*. Notre Dame: University of Notre Dame Press.

———. 1981b. *Vision and virtue*. Notre Dame: University of Notre Dame Press.

Homer, Frederic D. 1983. *Character: An individualistic theory of politics*. Lanham, MD: University Press of America.

Hudson, Stephen. 1981. Taking virtues seriously. *Australasian Journal of Philosophy* 59 (June): 189–202.

Jamieson, Kathleen Hall. 1988. *Eloquence in an electronic age: The transformation of political speechmaking*. New York: Oxford University Press.

Johannesen, Richard L. 1990. *Ethics in human communication*, 3rd ed. Long Grove, IL: Waveland Press.

Jonsen, Albert R., and Stephen Toulmin. 1988. *The abuse of casuistry: A history of moral reasoning*. Berkeley: University of California Press.

Josephson Institute. 1988. Ethical values and principles in public service. *Ethics: Easier Said Than Done* 1 (Spring/Summer): 153.

Kaus, Mickey. 1987. Biden's belly flop. *Newsweek* 28 September, 23–24.

Klaidman, Stephen, and Tom L. Beauchamp. 1987. *The virtuous journalist*. New York: Oxford University Press.

Kolenda, Konstantin, ed. 1988. *Organizations and ethical individualism*. New York: Praeger.

Kupfer, Joseph. 1982. The moral presumption against lying. *Review of Metaphysics* 36 (September): 103–26.

Kupperman, Joel. 1988. Character and ethical theory. *Midwest studies in philosophy*, Vol. XIII, *Ethical theory: Character and virtue*, ed. Peter A. French, Theodore E. Uehling, Jr., and Howard K. Wettstein, 115–25. Notre Dame: University of Notre Dame Press.

Lebacqz, Karen. 1985. *Professional ethics*. Nashville, TN: Abingdon Press.

Lilla, Mark T. 1981. Ethos, "ethics," and public service. *The Public Interest* 63 (Spring): 3–17.

MacIntyre, Alasdair. 1984. *After virtue*, 2d ed. Notre Dame: University of Notre Dame Press.

Manley, Marshall. 1988. Going beyond "the issues." *Newsweek* 18 January, 8.

Margolis, Jon. 1987a. Biden threatened by accusations of plagiarism in his speeches. *Chicago Tribune* 17 September, sec. 1, 3.

———. 1987b. Biden on quote furor: I've done some dumb things. *Chicago Tribune* 18 September, sec. 1, 3.

———. 1987c. For Biden, as for Hart, it's the stupidity that hurts. *Chicago Tribune* 22 September, sec. 1, 15.

Mayo, Bernard. 1958. *Ethics and the moral life.* London: Macmillan.

McGee, Michael. 1978. "Not men, but measures": The origins and import of an ideological principle. *Quarterly Journal of Speech* 64 (April): 141–54.

Meilaender, Gilbert C. 1984. *The theory and practice of virtue.* Notre Dame: University of Notre Dame Press.

Michell, Gillian. 1984. Women and lying: A pragmatic and semantic analysis of "telling it slant." *Women's Studies International Forum* 7: 375–83.

Miller, Arthur H., Martin P. Wattenberg, and Oksana Malanchuk. 1985. Cognitive representations of candidate assessments. *Political communication yearbook 1984*, ed. Keith R. Sanders, Lynda Lee Kaid, and Dan Nimmo, 183–210. Carbondale: Southern Illinois University Press.

Minnick, Elizabeth. 1985. Why not lie? *Soundings* 68 (Winter): 493–509.

Noddings, Nel. 1984. *Caring: A feminine approach to ethics and moral education.* Berkeley: University of California Press.

O'Leary, Stephen D. 1989. Machiavelli and the paradox of political hypocrisy: The fragmentation of virtue in the public and private spheres. In *Spheres of argument*, ed. Bruce E. Gronbeck, 117–27. Annandale, VA: Speech Communication Association.

Oliver North, businessman? Many bosses say that he's their kind of employee. 1987. *Wall Street Journal* eastern ed. 14 July, sec. 2, 35.

Palmour, Jody. 1987. *On moral character: A practical guide to Aristotle's virtues and vices.* Washington, DC: Archon Institute for Leadership Development.

Pinckaers, Servais. 1962. Virtue is not a habit. *Cross Currents* 12 (Winter): 65–81.

Pincoffs, Edmund L. 1986. *Quandaries and virtues: Against reductivism in ethics.* Lawrence: University of Kansas Press.

Plamenatz, John. 1972. In search of Machiavellian "virtù." In *The political calculus: Essays on Machiavelli's philosophy*, ed. Anthony Parel, 157–78. Toronto: University of Toronto Press.

Reid, T. R. 1987. Rewriting the book on Pat Robertson. *Washington Post National Weekly Edition* 15 October, 15.

Rorty, Amehe Oksenberg, ed. 1980. *Essays on Aristotle's ethics.* Berkeley: University of California Press.

Ruddick, Sara. 1980. Maternal thinking. *Feminist Studies* 6 (Summer): 342–67.

Scott, William G., and Terence R. Mitchell. 1988. The problem or mystery of evil and virtue in organizations. In *Organizations and ethical individualism*, ed. Konstantin Kolenda, 47–72. New York: Praeger.

Sheehy, Gail. 1988. *Character: America's search for leadership.* New York: William Morrow.

Sichel, Betty A. 1988. *Moral education: Character, community, and ideals.* Philadelphia: Temple University Press.

Simon, Yves R. 1986. *The definition of moral virtue.* New York: Fordham University Press.

Slote, Michael. 1983. *Goods and virtues.* New York: Oxford University Press.

Sommers, Christina Hoff. 1984. Ethics without virtue. *The American Scholar* 53 (Summer): 381–89.

———. ed. 1985. *Vice and virtue in everyday life.* New York: Harcourt Brace Jovanovich.

Taylor, Paul. 1987. Our people-magazined race for the presidency. *Washington Post National Weekly Edition* 2 November, 23.

Wallace, James D. 1978. *Virtues and vices.* Ithaca, NY: Cornell University Press.

Walton, Clarence C. 1988. *The moral manager.* Cambridge, MA: Ballinger.

Weiss, Robert. 1981. The presidential campaign debates in their political context: The image-issue interface in the 1980 campaign. *Speaker and Gavel* 18: 22–27.

Werling, David S. 1987. Presidential debates: Epideictic merger of images and issues in values. In *Argument and critical practices*, ed. Joseph W. Wenzel, 229–38. Annandale, VA: Speech Communication Association.

Wilbur, James B., III. 1984. Corporate character. In *Corporate governance and institutionalizing ethics*, ed. W. Michael Hoffman, Jennifer Mills Moore, and David A. Fedo, 173–84. Lexington, MA: D. C. Heath.

Williams, Bernard. 1981. *Moral luck.* Cambridge: Cambridge University Press.

Wills, Gary. 1987. Hart's guilt trick. *Newsweek* 28 December, 17–18.

Wood, Neal. 1967. Machiavelli's concept of virtù reconsidered. *Political Studies* 15 (June): 159–72.

Additional Sources not Referenced

Booth, Wayne C. 1988. *The company we keep: An ethics of fiction.* Berkeley: University of California Press.

Crisp, Roger, and Michael Slote, eds. 1997. *Virtue Ethics.* New York: Oxford University Press.

Foot, Phillipa. 1978. *Virtues and vices and other essays in moral philosophy.* Oxford: Basil Blackwell.

Hudson, Stephen. 1986. *Human Character and Morality.* Boston: Routledge.

Hursthouse, Rosalind. 1999. *On Virtue Ethics.* New York: Oxford University Press.

Kruschwitz, Robert B., and Robert C. Roberts, eds. 1987. *The Virtues: Contemporary Essays on Moral Character.* Belmont, CA: Wadsworth.

Kupperman, Joel. 1991. *Character.* New York: Oxford University Press.

Sherman, Nancy. 1989. *The Fabric of Character: Aristotle's Theory of Virtue.* New York: Oxford University Press.

Slote, Michael. 1992. *From Morality to Virtue.* New York: Oxford University Press.

Preview to "In Other's Words: Plagiarism as Deceptive Communication." Many people define plagiarism as "stealing" words or ideas that belong to others. From this perspective the primary moral victim of plagiarism is the original author—the person from whom the words or ideas were stolen. In this essay, Karen E. Whedbee proposes an alternative definition which allows for a more precise description of the moral harms of plagiarism. Rather than focusing on plagiarism as "theft," she defines it as a kind of "deceptive communication" and "fraud." A plagiarizer is one who deceives an audience by posing as the original author of words or ideas that were actually composed by someone else. The plagiarizer exploits the audience's expectation for original authorship in order to receive credit or reward which would not have been given if the audience had recognized the words or ideas as copies. Seen from this perspective, the original author is not the only victim of plagiarism. In fact, the primary victim of plagiarism is the audience who is deceived and convinced to do things that they would not have done had they known the truth. In addition, the act of plagiarism harms the reputation of those communities and organizations who have sponsored or otherwise associated themselves with the plagiarizer. Finally, plagiarizers may harm themselves because they are guilty of self-deception. By pretending to be something they are not (namely, proficient writers) they reinforce (rather than correct) their own failures of original thought and creative composition.

This revised description of plagiarism implies that an audience's expectations regarding original authorship are crucial to determining whether something is or is not plagiarism. Readers might consider how this definition would be applied in specific situations. Is the expectation for originality a categorical claim? In other words, do audiences have a right to expect speakers and writers to reveal their sources at all times, regardless of the situation or the cultural context? Alternatively, is the expectation for originality something that varies according to the setting and context? Do audiences have different expectations for originality depending on whether they are reading an academic paper or a business letter? How would this differ from an audience that listens to a political speech, a religious sermon, or a classroom lecture? In each of these situations, does it matter whether the speech or writing is an original composition or a copy? Would the audience treat the speaker or writer differently had they known the truth? Finally, what steps should ethically responsible writers and speakers take in order to avoid misleading audiences about issues of originality?

In Other's Words:
Plagiarism as Deceptive Communication*

Karen E. Whedbee

In 2006, the publisher Little, Brown and Company released a new "chick-lit novel" written by a promising young literary talent named Kaavya Viswanathan. The event was noteworthy because Viswanathan was so young—only nineteen years old. Two years earlier, when she was seventeen, she had submitted the manuscript, *How Opal Mehta Got Kissed, Got Wild, and Got a Life*, to the publisher. The editors were so impressed that they offered her a contract, which involved a substantial advance on book royalties. She also was able to sell the movie rights for the book to DreamWorks. These contracts and endorsements won the attention of Harvard University, which admitted Viswanathan as a student. Unfortunately, all the accolades turned out to have been too good to be true. *Opal Mehta* had hardly been off the presses when readers began to raise doubts about its originality. Investigation revealed that the plot and numerous passages duplicated the writing of a more established author, Megan McCafferty. Viswanathan was only posing as the originator of a literary work that was actually created by someone else. For a time, readers were deceived into giving her credit and profit for words and ideas that, in fact, did not "belong" to her. But once the deception was discovered, Viswanathan became the subject of unexpected and embarrassing publicity. Presented with substantial evidence of "literary theft," Little, Brown recalled some 50,000 unsold copies of the book and canceled all contracts with Viswanathan.[1]

This is only one recent, high profile example of plagiarism. Charges of plagiarism also have been raised, for example, against the historian Stephen E. Ambrose, Kennedy biographer Doris Kearns Goodwin, journalist Jayson Blair, Senator and presidential candidate Joseph Biden, and civil rights activist Martin Luther King, Jr.[2] In other cases which may or may not make the evening news, plagiarism has become a widespread problem for businesses and other profes-

*This essay was written especially for *Ethics in Human Communication*, 6th Edition.

sional organizations. Incidents of plagiarism are reported by those who work in many professions including journalism, science, computer science, mechanical engineering, nursing, marketing, and business.[3] And finally, while plagiarism is a growing problem among professionals, it is a special and long-standing problem for students, teachers, and researchers who work in academic settings.

In all of these situations, plagiarism is a serious accusation. Students who are found guilty of plagiarism receive failing grades on assignments and in courses. They may be suspended or dismissed from their school. Among professionals, those found guilty of plagiarism risk being fired from their jobs. In some professions, they risk losing access to government funding. Plagiarizers open themselves and their employers up to the possibility of expensive copyright infringement lawsuits. Ultimately, those who are accused of plagiarism carry a reputation for intellectual dishonesty that may follow them for the remainder of their careers.[4]

Given the prevalence of the problem and the seriousness of the consequences, academics and professionals have become increasingly sensitive to plagiarism as an issue of communication ethics. In this essay, I address the issue by, first, offering a working definition of plagiarism; second, examining some of the ways in which differing assumptions about "authorship" and the importance of "originality" may influence an audience's interpretation of plagiarism; and, third, identifying some of the major ethical harms that result from acts of plagiarism.

Defining Plagiarism

Plagiarism may be defined as a kind of deceptive communication in which a speaker or writer misleads his or her audience by pretending to be the original author of words or ideas that were actually composed by someone else. As a result of the deception, the speaker or writer receives credit or reward that would not otherwise have been given.[5]

The word "plagiarism" comes from the Latin *plagiarius*, which means "kidnapper" or "plunderer." Thus, plagiarism frequently is associated with "intellectual theft"—stealing words or ideas that "belong" to someone else.[6] Plagiarizers sometimes are described as "thought thieves" and "intellectual shoplifters."[7] Although this association with theft is common, it is also somewhat misleading. Theft of intellectual property frequently is involved in plagiarism (consider the case of Viswanathan's book described above). But theft is not an essential attribute of plagiarism. For example, one of the classic cases of plagiarism is that of the student who "buys" a term paper from a "research service." Technically, there is no *theft* involved because the original author gives permission to the student to copy the essay in exchange for monetary compensation. Since the student *bought* copies of the essay, the exchange cannot be described as *theft*. Even so, if the student now takes her copy and turns it in for academic credit in her history class, this act would still constitute a straightforward (and serious) case of plagiarism. The student has copied the work of someone else and then represented that copy *as if it were her own original composition*. What makes the action plagiarism is not *taking* (or copying) someone else's essay but the creation *of a false impression that the student was the originating author of the essay*.

As Richard A. Posner explains, although theft frequently is involved in plagiarism, it is the deception (not the theft) that is the essential characteristic of plagiarism. And furthermore, he explains that

> a judgment of plagiarism requires that the copying, besides being deceitful in the sense of misleading the intended readers, induce *reliance* by them. By this I mean that the reader does something because he thinks the plagiarizing work original that he would not have done had he known the truth.[8]

So, for example, neither Little, Brown and Company nor DreamWorks would have offered the Kaavya Viswanathan contracts for her book manuscript had they known it was not her manuscript to sell. Fans of chick-lit novels would have been less inclined to buy a book by Viswanathan had they known the book was substantially only a copy of something they had already read by Megan McCafferty. Viswanathan's deception induced readers to perform actions they would not have performed had they known the truth. Or again, consider the case of the student who buys a term paper. The history professor would not have awarded the student academic credit for having written the paper if he had known that the student *copied* it and did not actually *compose* it as required by the assignment. That the student copied the words composed by someone else is not (by itself) what makes the act plagiarism. Instead, the key feature in plagiarism is that the student has created in the mind of the professor a fraudulent impression that she should be given the credit as the original author of words or ideas that in fact were not original.

Covered under this general definition of plagiarism, there are various specific forms of plagiarism. These include the following:

(1) *Copying a whole work* (e.g., a book, a research paper, or a speech) that was written by someone else and misleading the audience by making them think that the work is one's own original composition. This type of plagiarism covers such practices as the student who buys a copy of a paper from a research service or essay bank (prewritten or specially written) and then passes the copy off for academic credit in a class as if it were an original composition. A student who turns in a copy of a paper that was originally written by a friend, a fraternity brother or sorority sister, or by a parent in order to receive academic credit in a class (with or without the original author's consent) would also be guilty of this type of plagiarism.

(2) *Copying portions of another author's work* (e.g., a key phrase, a sentence, a paragraph, or series of paragraphs) but leaving out quotations marks and a citation to the original work, thus giving the impression that the words are one's own rather than someone else's. This type of plagiarism is associated with the "cut and paste" essay that consists of sentences and paragraphs taken from Internet sources, magazines, or books and then spliced together in a "patchwork" composition. In fact, anytime one copies the words of another author without attribution, the possibility of being accused of plagiarism is high. In general, one must take great care to use quotation marks and to provide proper attribution whenever quoting phrases or passages from another author.

(3) *Paraphrasing ideas from other sources in a summary form without adding anything original of one's own* and then passing that paraphrase off as if it were an orig-

inal composition. The claim of "authorship" carries an obligation to offer the audience "something new" or "something original" that goes beyond just summary. In other words, it is the offering of "something new" that gives one the right to distinguish between being a "copier" of other people's ideas and being an "author" in one's own right. For example, imagine a newspaper editorialist who copies the structure and major arguments of someone else's editorial and then presents this paraphrased summary with his own name listed as the author. The copy may not be verbatim (word for word), but it is still only a restatement or paraphrase of someone else's composition. Among professional journalists, the presentation of a paraphrased copy as if it were an original would be condemned as plagiarism.[9] Furthermore, even if the original source were cited in the essay, the editorial writer has no right to claim "authorship" unless he has offered something that goes beyond merely paraphrasing the composition of someone else.

Ultimately, in all these various situations, the defining feature of plagiarism is that the plagiarizer deceives an audience by making them think that a copy of a text is not a copy but an original composition. As a consequence of this deception, the audience gives the plagiarizer credit or reward that would otherwise only be granted to the original author.

Authorship and the Expectation of Originality

In theory, plagiarism as defined above would appear to be relatively straightforward and easy to detect. In practice, however, we all know how complicated the subject can be. As C. Jan Swearingen explains, students are frequently given contradictory messages about plagiarism. On one hand, a teacher will warn students to "do their own work" or risk the charge of plagiarism. But in the next breath, the teacher explains that students will be required to participate in collaborative writing projects with their peers or they are advised to visit the school "writing lab" (where they receive help from tutors who sometimes make substantial contributions to their project without receiving any authorial credit).[10] Given these conflicting messages, the process of determining what plagiarism is and is not can be genuinely confusing. Some of the questions can be clarified, however, by examining more closely the relationship between "plagiarism" and "authorship."

As we have seen, plagiarism is a form of deception in which a speaker or writer misleads an audience by posing as the *original author* of words or ideas that were actually composed by someone else. Plagiarism occurs when an audience has an expectation for original authorship that is violated. But when a writer or speaker uses quotation marks and cites a source, this has the effect of informing the audience that "this isn't my idea" or "these aren't my words" and "person X deserves the credit for this, not I." So long as the speaker or writer openly gives credit where credit is due, plagiarism is not likely to arise as a problem.

We might wonder though, are speakers and writers always obliged to indicate direct quotations and source citations? The answer is more complicated than it might appear. For example, on February 10, 2007, the junior Senator from Illinois, Barack Obama, announced his candidacy for the presidency of the United States. Obama gave the announcement while speaking from one of the most important political locations in the state of Illinois, the Old State Capitol in Springfield. He explained to the media and to those audience members unfamiliar with Illinois history that this was the site at which his fellow Illinoisan and sixteenth president of the United States, Abraham Lincoln, delivered one of the most influential speeches in American history. Obama directly quoted the Biblical reference that inspired Lincoln's speech: "a house divided against itself cannot stand" (Matthew 12:25). This was the only formal citation of Lincoln's words in the speech. But Obama repeatedly "alluded" to Lincoln throughout his announcement. For example, in his introduction, Obama expressed the ideal of government as the pursuit of "that more perfect union." He did not explain to the audience that the phrase comes from the Preamble to the United States Constitution or that it was famously quoted by Lincoln in his First Inaugural in 1861. Later in the announcement, Obama said:

> Together, starting today, let us finish the work that needs to be done, and usher in a new birth of freedom on this Earth.

Obama did not explain to his audience that he was invoking the words Lincoln uttered at Gettysburg in 1863:

> . . . that this nation, under God, shall have a new birth of freedom—and that government of the people, by the people, for the people, shall not perish from the Earth.

Given the fact that Obama did not explicitly cite his source, we might wonder, should he be charged with plagiarism? For most people, considering the speech in its original context, the accusation of plagiarism would be misdirected and even silly. The criterion for plagiarism is not that the speaker fails to cite his sources explicitly, but that the speaker *misleads* his audience about the original source for the words or ideas. While it is not always as obvious as in this example, there is an important distinction to be made between "plagiarism" and "literary allusion." In plagiarism, the speaker takes credit for words not his own and *conceals* from his audience the original author. By contrast, in literary allusion, the speaker refers to famous words or ideas, assuming that the audience will be familiar with the original sources. In other words, although he did not say so explicitly, Obama was intentionally invoking Lincoln in his speech (explicitly through his words and implicitly through his choice of the location for the speech). Far from wanting to deceive his audience about his original source, Obama wanted to invoke for his audience the memory and spirit of Lincoln. It is a clear case of literary allusion, not of plagiarism.[11]

This distinction between allusion and plagiarism is helpful because it reminds us that there are situations in which audiences do not expect or require the speaker to cite sources. Technically, plagiarism can only occur if the audience is liable to be misled into believing that a copy of a text is actually an original. And further, the audience has to give the originating author credit or reward that wouldn't be due to a person who only copied a text. If the audience isn't misled—or if originality doesn't matter—then, by this definition, plagiarism would not arise as a relevant issue.

As Posner explains, the "reader has to *care* about being deceived about the authorial identity in order for the deceit to cross the line to fraud and thus constitute plagiarism."[12] He suggests that there are numerous professional and cultural settings in which originality and individual authorship are not especially important features of the communicative interaction. Posner cites an example of the legal profession where originality tends to be valued less than consistency and adherence to precedent. It is understood by members of the legal community that judges rarely write their own legal opinions for cases. Much of the writing is done by the judge's staff of law clerks. Since legal professionals know this, there is little question that they would be deceived about authorship. In this case, what matters to the audience is not whether the judge composed (*authored*) an opinion but whether the judge endorsed (*authorized*) the opinion. Posner asserts that to accuse a judge of plagiarizing from his law clerks would be seen by most legal professionals as beside the point. Since they already know that law clerks are responsible for much of the writing, they are not susceptible to deception.

In a similar situation, William Safire has argued that a reasonable audience member would understand that, given the demands of the office, the president of the United States does not have time to write his own speeches. It follows that there is no deception involved when the president employs speech writers. The president does not need to announce that he uses speech writers every time he speaks because the announcement would be redundant. Safire asserts that a speaker's use of a "ghost writer" becomes morally problematic only when audience members have an expectation for original authorship and the speaker violates that expectation.[13]

Finally, we should note that although originality and individual authorship are highly valued in many cultures today, this was not always the case historically. Through human history there have been many societies that considered the preservation of communal knowledge to be more important than the original discovery of new knowledge. In other words, to transmit the ideas of past generations through repetition and "copying" (usually without providing attribution to sources) would be seen by members of these communities as commendable in its own right apart from any claims to uniqueness or originality. This sort of attitude was famously expressed by the fourth century Christian, Augustine of Hippo. He maintained all genuine knowledge traces to the "Original Author": God. In so far as a mere human speaker or writer can become an instrument of the Divine Voice, the question of plagiarism is irrelevant. If preachers

> take something written by another, memorize it, and offer it to the people in the person of the author, they do not do wickedly. For those who steal take something from another, but the word of God is not another's to those who obey it; They make their own those things which they themselves could not compose.[14]

For members of a community that consider God to be the Author of all important words and ideas, placing emphasis on a human author (separate from the Divine) would be not only an error but also, technically, a blasphemy. Thus, the early Christian Church was an example of a community that considered knowledge and learning to be a collective accumulation that could be "claimed" equally by any individual member of the community.[15]

In summary, determining what is and what is not plagiarism can, in some situations, be very complex. In these controversial cases, the determination of plagiarism requires careful attention to the audience's expectations about authorship and originality.

The Moral Harms of Plagiarism

Setting aside these controversial cases, whenever a speaker or writer addresses an audience that *does* place value on originality and individual authorship the possibility for plagiarism becomes a live concern. The author must take care not to mislead the audience into thinking that copied words or ideas are original. Depending on the specific situation, this sort of deception would entail various kinds of moral harm.

As noted earlier, in some cases, the harm associated with plagiarism may consist of the "theft" of another person's "intellectual property." The issue here is that, in modern economic terms, the process of composing an original work requires a significant investment of talent, time, energy, and/or money. In particular, professional writers are dependent on the fact that they will receive credit and reward for their original investment. If a plagiarist is allowed to "steal" the composition and then "resell" it under her own name, the market value of the original author's work would be compromised. Thus, the plagiarist who copies a work "cheats" the original author out of compensation for her "investment." We should note as well that when the plagiarism involves appropriating another person's writing and then "reselling" it to an audience, the plagiarism frequently will extend beyond issues of ethics and enter into the realm of the law. Specifically, the purpose of copyright law is to protect authors and their publishers by assuring that their original work cannot be copied for profit without some sort of compensation to the holder of the copyright. Thus, to copy another person's work and then "resell" it under one's own name is to open oneself up not only to ethical condemnation but also (depending on the situation) to the possibility of a copyright infringement lawsuit.[16]

Suppose, however, that the plagiarism does not involve any "theft." Imagine, as is sometimes the case, the original author of a work grants permission (explicitly or implicitly) to copy her work. Or imagine that by copying the work, little or no harm is done to the original author. Even when "theft" is not an issue, there are still potential moral harms that would need to be taken into account. As Laurie Stearns explains:

> Copying from any source qualifies as plagiarism. . . . Even where no harm could possibly result to the original work (which may be long out of print) or to the original author (who may be long dead), the audience is still duped, and plagiarism is still viewed as a misuse of the creative process.[17]

The plagiarizer "dupes" an audience by representing a copy of something as if it were an original. This is an act of deception or fraud, and, as such, plagiarism entails the same sort of moral harm as any other act of deception. Imagine, for example, that students are enrolled in a public speaking class. The purpose of the class is that the students will learn how to write and present public speeches. Suppose that one student presents a speech in class that he did not actually write. This student misleads his audience (the instructor and the other students), giving them the impression that he was the original author of the speech when in fact the real author was, let us say, his mother. By delivering a speech written by his mother, the student is misrepresenting himself with the intent to gain credit (applause, respect, and academic credit) for work that he did not actually complete. By his actions, the student displays disrespect for the accomplishments of other students in the class who, with good or bad results, did compose their own original speeches. As well, the student displays disrespect for the teacher who, after listening to the speech, is in danger of making decisions (assigning grades and granting academic credit) based on inaccurate information. It is hardly surprising that the audience would interpret this kind of dishonesty as a personal insult.[18]

The deception associated with plagiarism affects not only the immediate audience but also larger communities to which the plagiarizer belongs. For example, the integrity and the fairness of the public speaking class are compromised when a student is given academic credit for work he did not in fact complete. If it were to become known that the university allows students to claim knowledge and skills that they have never actually demonstrated, the reputation of the university would be diminished. This is not as far-fetched as some might think. Consider that when the book by Kaavya Viswanathan was discovered to have been plagiarized, the bad publicity reflected not only on Viswanathan as an individual but also on all the communities to which she belonged. As John Taylor Williams, a literary agent and lawyer, explained in an interview with the *Boston Herald*, the publisher Little, Brown "is a famous imprint with a reputation for very well-edited books." The accusation of plagiarism against one of their authors "goes to the core of their reputation. They have put others in the line of fire—retailers, their sales force. All their reputations could have been tarnished."[19] Viswanathan's actions harmed the reputation of Little, Brown, and Company as well as the reputation of Harvard University, which had accepted her as a student in large part because of her supposed authorship of the book. Some observers wondered whether the failure to detect Viswanathan's plagiarism was symptomatic of lower standards at Harvard. Thus, her dishonesty cast a shadow over the accomplishments of all her classmates.

Finally, we should note that plagiarism has implications not only for the original author, the immediate audience, and the larger community, it also has implications for the plagiarizer herself. An individual is likely to engage in plagiarism in order to cover up for some limitation in her own writing. Frequently, this limitation consists of the basic problem that the plagiarizer does not have a capacity for original thought or expression. She resorts to plagiarism in order to compensate for this personal deficiency. By plagiarizing, she pretends to be something she is not: A good writer. Ironically, however, by covering over her personal deficiencies, the deficiencies are only likely to be reinforced. The attempt to maintain an illusion of competence is self-deluding. Because she is unable to recognize her own weaknesses, she never gives herself an opportunity to develop the skills associated with independent and original thought and composition. Instead, by plagiarizing, she merely becomes more proficient at copying the compositions of others.

In summary, the key moral harms associated with plagiarism correspond with four principal "victims" to the act of plagiarism: (1) The plagiarizer may harm the original author of a work by "stealing" his or her "intellectual property." (2) The plagiarizer harms his or her audience by deceiving them and by encouraging them to give credit and reward that they would not otherwise have given. (3) The plagiarizer threatens the reputation and the integrity of the communities of which he or she is a member. And (4) The plagiarizer engages in self-deception and, thus, avoids addressing the implications of his or her own lack of original and creative thought and composition.

Conclusion

Plagiarism is hardly a new problem, but with our increased reliance on the Internet and other electronic databases for our research, the act of plagiarism has become easier than it has ever been in the past. At the same time, the development of plagiarism detection software has made it even more likely that the plagiarist will be discovered. With this combination of circumstances, it should come as little surprise that the past few years have seen an epidemic in reported cases of plagiarism.

Informed authors and informed audience members need to reflect on the ethical implications of plagiarism. In this essay, I have attempted to aid such reflection by suggesting a definition that focuses on plagiarism as a form of deception or fraud. I have also suggested that, in distinguishing between what is or is not plagiarism, we should take into account the audience's expectations regarding "originality" and "authorship." Finally, we should also take into account the moral harms associated with any particular case of plagiarism.

Notes

[1] The incident received widespread coverage, but see especially, David Zhou, "Student's Novel Faces Plagiarism Controversy," *The Harvard Crimson Online Edition* (4/23/2006) http://www.thecrimson.com; David Zhou, "Examples of Similar Passages Between Viswanathan's Book and McCafferty's Two Novels." *The Harvard Crimson Online Edition* (4/23/2006) http://www.thecrimson.com; Paras D. Bhayani and David Zhou, "Sophomore Novelist Admits to Borrowing Language from Earlier Books," *The Harvard Crimson Online Edition* (4/24/2006) http://www.thecrimson.com; and Deborah R. Gerhardt, "Point of View: The Rules of Attribution," *The Chronicle of Higher Education* 52: 38 (May 26, 2006), p. B20.

[2] These incidents have been discussed extensively. See especially, Peter Charles Hoffer, *Past Imperfect: Facts, Fictions, Fraud—American History From Bancroft and Parkman to Ambrose, Bellesiles, Ellis, and Goodwin* (New York: Public Affairs, 2004); Elizabeth Blanks Hindman, "Jayson Blair, *The New York Times*, and Paradigm Repair," *Journal of Communication* 55, no. 2 (June 2005): 225–241; Jon Margolis and Elaine Povich, "Biden Admits Errors, Drops Out; Plagiarism Furor Drives him from Race," *Chicago Tribune* (September 24, 1987), p. 1; and Richard L. Johannesen in "The Ethics of Plagiarism Reconsidered: The Oratory of Martin Luther King, Jr." *Southern Communication Journal* 60 (1995): 185–194.

[3] For example, in journalism, see Andy Berens, "University of Wisconsin *Badger Herald* editor fired for plagiarism," *The Daily Herald* (December 6, 2006); and Elizabeth Stone, "For Plagiarists, No Veil Over Past Mistakes," *The Chronicle of Higher Education* 51, no. 14 (June 17, 2005): B5. In science, see Marcel C. LaFollette, *Stealing into Print: Fraud, Plagiarism, and Misconduct in Scientific Publishing* (University of California Press, 1992). In computer science, see N. Kock, "A Case of Academic Plagiarism (Industry Trend or Event)," *Communications of the ACM* 42, no. 7 (July 1999): 96. In mechanical engineering, see Paula Wasley, "Review Blasts Professors for Plagiarism by Graduate Students," *The Chronicle of Higher Education* 52, no. 41 (June 16, 2006): A13; and Paula Wasley, "The Plagiarism Hunter," *The Chronicle of Higher Education* 52,

no. 49 (August 11, 2006): A8. In nursing, see Deborah Kenny, "Student Plagiarism and Professional Practice," *Nurse Education Today* 27, no. 1 (2007): 14–18. In marketing, see A. Stodart, "Creative Blues: The Controversy over Labatt's 'Street Hockey' Says More about Agencies than They Know," *Marketing Magazine* 103, no. 15 (April 20, 1998): 10. In business, see Denise Nitterhouse, "Plagiarism—Not Just an 'Academic' Problem," *Teaching Business Ethics* 7 (2003): 215–227.

4 Examples are plentiful, but see, for example, Thomas Bartlett and Scott Smallwood, "Just Deserts? Plagiarizing Professors Face a Variety of Punishments," *The Chronicle of Higher Education* 51, no. 30 (April 1, 2005): A26; P. S. Zurer, "NIH Panel Strips Researcher of Funding after Plagiarism Review," *Chemical and Engineering News* 67 (August 7, 1989): 24–25. See also "Edward Waters Loses Accreditation After Plagiarism Scandal," *Black Issues in Higher Education* 21, no. 23 (December 30, 2004): 24.

5 This definition is based on definitions offered by Richard A. Posner and by Laurie Stearns. See Posner, *The Little Book of Plagiarism* (New York: Pantheon Books), p. 106. See also Stearns, "Copy Wrong: Plagiarism, Process, Property, and the Law," in *Perspectives on Plagiarism and Intellectual Property in a Postmodern World*, Lise Buranen and Alice M. Roy, eds. (Albany: State University of New York Press, 1999), p. 7.

6 Posner, *The Little Book of Plagiarism*, pp. 50–51.

7 Peggy Whiteneck, "What to do with a Thought Thief," *Community College Week* 14, no. 24 (July 8, 2002), pp. 4–7; Scott Stebelman, "Cybercheating: Dishonesty Goes Digital," *American Libraries* 29, no. 8 (1998): 48–51.

8 Posner, *The Little Book of Plagiarism*, p. 19.

9 A recent example is described in "Niigata Nippo editorialist plagiarized Asahi Editorial," *Kyodo News International* (Japan). (February 21, 2007).

10 C. Jan Swearingen, "Originality, Authenticity, Imitation, and Plagiarism: Augustine's Chinese Cousins," in *Perspectives on Plagiarism and Intellectual Property in a Postmodern World*, Lisa Buranen and Alice M. Roy, eds. (Albany: State University of New York Press, 1999), pp. 19–30.

11 I am indebted to Dr. Janet Novak who, in a conversation, suggested Obama's speech as an example of the distinction between literary allusion and plagiarism.

12 Posner, *The Little Book of Plagiarism*, p. 20.

13 William Safire, quoted by Lois J. Einhorn, "The Ghosts Unmasked: A Review of Literature on Speechwriting," *Communication Quarterly* 30, no. 1 (1981): 43.

14 Augustine, *On Christian Doctrine*, D. W. Robertson, trans. (New York: Bobs-Merrill, 1974), p. 29. Quoted by Swearingen, "Originality, Authenticity, Imitation, and Plagiarism," p. 21.

15 See Swearingen, "Originality, Authenticity, Imitation, and Plagiarism." For another important historical example of this issue, see Tilar J. Mazzeo, *Plagiarism and Literary Property in the Romantic Period* (Philadelphia: University of Pennsylvania Press, 2007). And for a famous case in the twentieth century, see Johannesen's analysis of Martin Luther King's plagiarism in "Ethics of Plagiarism Reconsidered."

16 See Thomas Tedford and Dale Herbeck, *Freedom of Speech in the United States*. 5th edition (State College, PA: Strata Publishing, 2005), chapter 12. Also, for an intriguing analysis of copyright and plagiarism codes as applied in higher education, see Bill Marsh, *Plagiarism: Alchemy and Remedy in Higher Education* (Albany: State University of New York Press, 2007).

17 Stearns, "Copy Wrong," p. 10.

18 Jonathan Malesic, "How Dumb Do They Think We Are?" *The Chronicle of Higher Education* 53, no. 9 (December 15, 2006): C3.

19 John Taylor Williams quoted by David Mehegan in "Harvard Novelist's Book Deal Canceled: More Signs Emerge of Duplications," *The Boston Globe* (May 3, 2006).

Preview to "Covering Tragedy: Media Ethics and TWA Flight 800." As readers and viewers, we have become accustomed to intensive, extensive, and sometimes intrusive newspaper, radio, and television news coverage of disasters, violence, and accidents. News coverage focuses both on ordinary citizens and public figures as victims or relatives in such traumatic events: car, plane, or train crashes; terrorist bombings of planes, ships, or buildings; mass shootings of innocent victims by both adults and children; rape and child abuse; and natural disasters such as floods, forest fires, tornadoes, and hurricanes.

Using both personal experience and scholarly research as bases for her argument, Martha Cooper examines four issues central to ethical news coverage of victims of tragedy: whether to cover a particular story; how to get the story; what aspects of the story should be told; and journalist accountability for decisions. For each of these four issues, she illustrates journalistic practices that are unethical or ethically suspect. Her goal, in part, is to sensitize present and future journalists to the importance and implications of each issue. Her discussion also is an aid to citizens in evaluating the ethics of news coverage of tragedy. In her conclusion, Cooper refers to the revised 1996 Society of Professional Journalists code of ethics (discussed in chapter 10) as a step in the right direction. In 1999 Jay Black, Bob Steele, and Ralph Barney published the third edition of *Doing Ethics in Journalism: A Handbook with Cases* (Boston: Allyn & Bacon). They explicitly discuss aspects of the SPJ code that Cooper deemed a positive step (pp. 27, 40–43, 48–50; also see pp. 105–107, 222–225, 235–236; 240, 261–263).

In 2000 a book was published that deals head-on and in-depth with the ethical issues raised by Cooper: William Coté and Roger Simpson, *Covering Violence: A Guide to Ethical Reporting About Victims and Trauma* (New York: Columbia University Press). Had she lived to read it, I am sure Martha Cooper would have welcomed it. Coté and Simpson draw upon research about trauma suffered by direct and indirect victims of tragedy and violence and also on their experiences at two universities as journalism educators who developed training programs for journalists in news coverage of victims and trauma.

Some of the questions raised by Coté and Simpson (p. 3) echo the thrust of concerns raised by Cooper: "What are the personal and professional costs of trading in the injuries and hurts of other humans? Do such stories need telling? If the stories need telling, how can a reporter get a better purchase on their parts: the people, what they go through in violence and loss, how they recover, what the traumas of violence and disaster mean for them and for the rest of us." The values they advocate for journalistic excellence include "caring for the people in the story and others close to them, respecting the voices of people at the center of the event," and "doing no harm" (pp. 3–4). To the traditional ethical obligations for journalists, they add a crucial one—"the obligation to justify to oneself, to the editor, and to others a decision not to intrude in the suffering of others." This decision, they argue, "takes precedence over news value or competition because of a strong moral factor—the choice between preventing harm and causing harm" (p. 10). For example, they explore an option unthinkable for most journalists: "Should I not do this interview at all" (p. 9)?

Coté and Simpson avoid much of the abstraction and ambiguity of many journalism ethics codes that Cooper condemned. Throughout their book, they provide numerous detailed examples of situations and issues. They offer concrete sugges-tions for ethical journalistic practices in covering the scene, reporting with pic-tures, interviewing, and writing the story. For example, in their concluding overview chapter they suggest questions for interviewing. "Three opening com-ments always will be appropriate: 'I'm sorry this happened to you'; 'I'm glad you were not killed'; 'It is not your fault.' Do not ask, 'How do you feel?' That enrages or stuns more victims than any other question reporters ask. Instead, ask what the person needs" (p. 226).

Covering Tragedy: Media Ethics and TWA Flight 800*

Martha Cooper

1995. Oklahoma City. The image of a firefighter cradling an infant, badly burned and dying, is etched into my memory and probably in yours. I was riveted to the television coverage of this tragedy of domestic terrorism. In 1996, just a lit-tle over a year later, I found myself in the midst of, and personally involved with, another tragedy: the explosion of TWA Flight 800. I was visiting my sister and her family and my mother in Montoursville, Pennsylvania. My niece, Cheryl, had been saving money for months to join her high school French Club in a week-long trip to France; she was aboard the doomed jetliner; she died July 17, 1996. I will never again watch, or read, or listen to the coverage of a tragedy in quite the same way.

Perhaps it is because for several months prior to the tragedy I had been work-ing intensely on a project about postmodern communication ethics, or maybe it was because two months after the death of my niece my brother-in-law asked for my help in holding journalists to account, but whatever the reason, my experi-ence being close to the scene of this tragedy leaves me wanting to make a differ-ence in how media professionals cover tragedy. It is in that spirit that I tell this story.[1] It is a story of some of the ethical issues surrounding the coverage of the explosion of TWA Flight 800. Really it is several smaller stories: four moments within the larger story; four moments during which I, or someone close to me, articulated an ethical impulse about the situation; four moments that entail four distinct ethical concerns for media professionals who cover tragedies.[2]

Moment 1: You know, the media will be here in the morning.
                    —I to my partner, about 1 A.M. July 18, 1996

My partner and I were just getting to the edge of Montoursville after the eight-mile drive across winding roads from the farm. It was about one in the morning, and we were headed in to tell my mother, Cheryl's grandmother, what

*This essay is slightly revised by Martha Cooper from a paper she presented at the annual con-vention of the National Communication Association, Chicago, November 21, 1997. It is reprinted with her permission.

had happened. We'd spent the last four hours with my sister and her husband, trying to get through to the emergency numbers flashed on CNN, trying to call the numbers listed in the materials left behind about the French Club trip, being quiet, praying, hoping that somehow someone might have survived the fiery crash we saw intermittently on the big screen TV at the farm. As we entered the village, it dawned on me: *"you know,"* I said, *"the media will be here in the morning."* I felt absolute dread at the thought, just as I was certain it would happen.

Tragedies get coverage. The top news story in 1995, according to the Associated Press, was the bombing of the Federal Building in Oklahoma City. In 1996, TWA Flight 800 was the biggest story; the ValueJet crash was voted number three (O'Neill, 1996). The photographs from stories like these are what win the awards. Pictures of victims and survivors of personal tragedies are staples in Pulitzer prize competitions (Padgett, 1985–1986, p. 54). Fifty-six percent of all award-warning photos and stories are of this type (Brown, 1987, p. 76). The human interest angle would bring reporters and their camera crews to Montoursville. How could they resist? Twenty-one victims, all from the same small town, a picturesque town that was only four hours from New York City in one direction and Philadelphia in another (two major media markets within easy striking distance) guaranteed the upcoming invasion.

What happens when hundreds of journalists and media professionals descend on one small town (in the last census, Montoursville had about 5,000 residents)? CNN first reported that students from the French Club were onboard the flight at about 3 A.M. By 7 A.M. the first out-of-towners had arrived. Within 24 hours of the crash, there were over 30 satellite dishes for uplinks in the high school parking lot. The main street was crawling with photographers, camerapersons. A similar invasion was, of course, occurring on Long Island as reporters rushed to cover the recovery effort and investigation of the crash. At both locations, media coverage invaded the privacy of those involved in ways that interfered with the grief process.

In Montoursville, there were countless episodes of broadcasters attempting to interview grieving friends and acquaintances as they sought to attend a funeral, to view the impromptu memorial at the high school, or otherwise to pay respects to the dead. The photographs of grieving students that graced the cover of *U.S. News* and the story pages of *Time, Newsweek* and countless newspapers bear witness to the omnipresence of the camera and the microphone in the midst of what would otherwise have been private or semi-public circumstances. Journalists injected themselves into events that would otherwise have been private or open only to friends but not strangers, thereby creating publicity in spaces usually reserved for private action and reflection. For example, a photographer from a New York newspaper trespassed on cemetery property in order to catch my sister and brother-in-law on film as they selected a burial plot for their daughter. My family stole into the town's memorial service under cover of a rental car from New Jersey and entered the school's gymnasium through a back door in order to avoid the lights and cameras of the media on hand. Later, local police and friends were stationed at both entrances to the church to make clear that photographers were not welcome at the funeral of my niece. Others, however, were not so sheltered. According to a sound technician with whom I spoke during the editing of a video obituary compiled by ABC News, a prize-winning photographer had appeared at one of the first funerals in Montoursville and taken pictures in the church within inches of the faces of grieving relatives.

In addition to these direct invasions of privacy, more subtle invasions occurred as well. In these cases, private documents were publicized. The most notable example comes from *Time*'s coverage. *Time*'s cover story on July 29, 1996, dealt with the TWA tragedy. The first paragraph of their cover story included the following as the fourth sentence:

> Out of a camera bag fished from the waste came a list in pencil, in what seemed to be a young girl's handwriting. *Amy: light pink, size 8. Corry: dress. Steph: orange or hunter green*—the plan for a spree in Paris, transformed into a haiku of loss. (Chua-Eoan, 1996, p. 31)

My brother-in-law recorded the heartbreak this created for the parents who first read their daughter's shopping list in *Time*. The camera bag had floated ashore on Long Island. Who opened it? How did *Time* obtain the list they recast as haiku? How did this private list become a matter of public record?

Invasions of privacy like those just described are not without effects; they interfere with the grief process. Cheryl Aspy, an associate professor of family and preventive medicine, commented on her experience following the Oklahoma City bombing:

> . . . part of the healing of the psyche is grieving privately. When your loss becomes a public loss, the media heightens the pain. When all the cameras are gone you have to grieve all over again, which makes the situation more traumatic. (cited by Foster, 1996, p. 37)

Hence, media coverage can heighten the pain for survivors during and immediately after the tragedy when the media glare is brightest.

Media coverage can also interfere with the grief process in the longer term. Once national and international media attention is focused on a particular site, that site becomes public whether intended or not. The cemetery in Montoursville where many of the French Club students are buried has become something of a tourist attraction, a place to visit, like the nearby Little League Hall of Fame, when strangers come to town. So busy has the cemetery become that family members must carefully time visits to the graves of their departed loved ones in order to avoid being photographed or questioned by ordinary people as well as reporters. I understand this situation developed about three months after the funerals; I experienced it nearly a year after the tragedy. Because bereavement occurs over a lengthy period in cases of sudden death and man-made disaster (Kohn and Levav, 1990), the publicity effects of media coverage can be particularly important.

Both in the short term and in the long term then media coverage creates public sites out of private sites and thus inhibits the possibility of private mourning for those close to the victims. Such an invasion of privacy inhibits the grief process. The ethical issue that should be at stake here is *whether or not to cover the story*. Given the impact of coverage, media professionals should worry about this question very intentionally.

Moment 2: These are the people you teach, right?!

—My nephew to me about 2 P.M., July 21, 1996

I recall my family's experience with ABC News. Along with the other families of members of the French Club from Montoursville who were gathered at the Ramada Inn in New York on Sunday (four days after the explosion), they were presented an advance viewing of a video-obituary that ABC planned to run on the evening news. After viewing the segment, my sister objected to its broadcast on the grounds that only some of the students who had been aboard the airliner were shown (only those for whom there was ready film footage from their performances as interscholastic athletes) and that even for those shown the footage was misleading. For example, my deceased niece was shown as a basketball player; although she did play basketball for a couple of years, she was never a star and rarely entered the game until the last few minutes; on the other hand, she had excelled as a dancer and had been dancing for over 10 years. Many of the other students had talents other than in sports that were more representative of their lives than the scraps of sports film that the network had spliced together. After considerable objection from the parents, ABC's field producer reluctantly agreed to reedit the segment with more appropriate pictures, as long as the families could provide photographs, home video, or other appropriate materials to the producers on location in Montoursville (4 hours away by car) within an hour. The time frame necessitated frantic calls to people like myself who were asked to rush valued pictures or home video to a local hotel where the crew was putting together the segment.

My nephew and I, who were trying to take care of matters at the farm while the family was in New York were happy to be of help, but what about those families for whom the deadline and parameters of the network created real hardship? When we arrived at the local hotel where the field production team was working, we offered the tape of my niece's most recent dance recital, asked them to make a copy so that we could return home, and offered to identify Cheryl from the host of girls dancing on stage. Their response was curiously insensitive. We were told "they would get the tape back to us," admonished that "people not in the business just didn't understand about deadlines," and shuffled out of the room as quickly as possible. I persisted in explaining that we would wait for them to dub a copy of the tape and that they would need our assistance in identifying Cheryl. We waited in the hotel lobby. It was there that my nephew turned to me and said: *"These are the people you teach?!"* I was just as frustrated as he with their behavior.

In about 45 minutes, the crew returned; they'd decided they needed our help in identification after all. My nephew joined them in their truck in the parking lot, while I chatted with the sound technician. It turned out they were a freelance crew, mostly from Chicago, who'd been called over from a job in Philadelphia to produce for ABC Nightly News. After a bit, the field producer asked me to join them in the truck to verify my nephew's identification of Cheryl. I did so, but explained that I was not completely sure as the material with which we were working was home video, filmed from the back of an auditorium, shooting a dozen girls all dressed in identical costumes and looking very similar. As we left the parking lot with my sister's camera and tape safely in hand, my nephew turned to tell me about his interaction with the producer in the truck. He said that as he was having difficulty identifying Cheryl, the woman had scornfully reproached him: "can't you even identify your own sister?!" I queried, "how did you respond?" John replied: "I said, 'Oh, she's the one in the purple outfit and the white shoes.'" I was appalled by the insensitivity of the field producer, impressed by the quick wit of my nephew; all I thought to say was: "How did the editing-guy respond?" John said he laughed. I wondered if this was an isolated incident.

When I returned to the farm to field more phone calls from newspaper and television reporters I learned it was not. While most callers were respectful—expressing their sympathy, asking if the family was ready to talk, and politely closing the conversation when I responded that the family was dealing with the matter privately—others were rude in their relentless interrogations for details, hasty hangups, and general unpleasantness. Later I learned that even those reporters who had been polite on the phone had really refused to take "no" for an answer. When family members declined to speak or share photographs, reporters and others from the same news organizations simply pursued the story through other means, stalking the high school and questioning friends, acquaintances, and others. They offered unsuspecting high school students $50 for their yearbooks, another $50 if they would identify the victims. Perhaps it was just such hawking for pictures and copy that resulted in a variety of inaccuracies in the media coverage. *U.S. News and World Report*, for instance, published a picture of the school's German Club rather than the French Club. Similarly, in the often-published yearbook picture of the French Club, in which the victims were circled, one victim was misidentified, probably as a result of the rush to publish and broadcast about the victims.

Probably the worst infraction of this type occurred in New York, where reporter Tonice Sgrignoli went undercover for her story. Sgrignoli impersonated a grieving family member in order to gain access to the Ramada Inn where TWA and the FBI had provided a "safe place," shielded from the press, for grieving family members. After several days, when Ms. Sgrignoli was discovered, numerous observers denounced her behavior as "irresponsible to the extreme" and as "clearly crossing the line of ethical conduct" (Giobbe, 1996, p. 18). Were Sgrignoli's actions an isolated case, they might be easier to dismiss; however, her impersonation is simply one among others in similar cases. For example, during the search for survivors in Oklahoma City a year before, another reporter had impersonated a rescue worker in order to cross the police line and get the story (Retsinas, 1995). While not all members of the press are willing to cross boundaries of public decency, clearly some are during any given tragedy.

The ethical issue at stake in these instances concerns *how to get the story*. When news routines put deadlines and scoops ahead of respect and integrity for those whom the story is about, those subjected to media coverage are likely to feel used, disregarded, betrayed and violated. My nephew's comment to me underscored my own responsibility for making sure media professionals know how to treat their subjects in addition to knowing how to get the story.

Moment 3: "We can't let them see this right now; would you put it somewhere they won't find it, at least for a while?"

—I to my partner, about 2 P.M. July 24, 1996

Wednesday, exactly a week after the tragedy, I collected the mail from my sister's country mailbox. It consisted of four stacks of cards banded together and stuffed tightly into every available space (probably 400 cards) along with the usual fare of bills, advertisements, and magazines. Among them was *Newsweek* with a cover story on Flight 800. I opened to the article and was immediately jarred by a two-page spread showing a naked corpse being loaded aboard a boat involved in the "rescue." I moved to the story and read the following lead paragraph:

> The dead do sometimes tell tales, if you know how to look for them. . . .
> The body of a person killed by a bomb looks different from the body of a
> victim in an ordinary plane crash. The flesh of bomb victims is shredded
> and may be singed by chemicals. (Death, 1996, p. 29)

Just a few paragraphs later: "There were legs and internal parts floating around. It smelled like rot" (p. 30). I quit reading, rolled up the *Newsweek*, turned to my partner and said: "We can't let them see this right now; would you put it somewhere they won't find it, at least for a while?"

What I was recoiling from in *Newsweek* is what numerous scholars and critics have dubbed the "pornography of grief" (Brown, 1987; Goodwin, 1983). Its characteristics are graphic descriptions that disregard its subjects while positioning viewers or readers as voyeurs. Like traditional pornography it preys on the desire to see or hear that which is forbidden and in the process treats those who are seen or heard with an obvious lack of dignity and an exploitative gaze. Most of us can recognize these pornographic images without formal training. Three hundred readers contacted *Newsweek* about their "disrespectful, insensitive, and unnecessary photo" (Protesting, 1996). The editorial response to these objections was telling. *Newsweek* wrote: "In fact, we rejected several even more graphic images. But we felt this exclusive picture, while admittedly upsetting, made a powerful journalistic statement about the horror of the tragedy and difficulty of the rescue search that words could only approximate" (Protesting, 1996). The words quoted above certainly seemed horrendous to me. But clearly, *Newsweek*'s intention had been to convey horror and to use their "exclusive" picture.

We can compare the decision of *Newsweek* about what pictures and words to publish with a similar decision by those who were on the scene on Long Island during the recovery and identification of the victims. According to several accounts, "from the beginning, families were protected from learning the hideous condition of the victims' bodies" (Russakoff, 1996). According to Chief Medical Examiner Charles Welti, of the first 100 bodies recovered, less than ten were viewable. How did he make this judgment? According to one report, the medical examiner's office "believed viewing the remains would magnify, not soothe the grief" of parents and other relatives (Russakoff, 1996). Welti's judgment is supported by other research on victimology that indicates sensational and inaccurate media coverage "compound and complicate the grief process" for survivors (Knapp, 1986, p. 103).

While the pornography of grief plays on the voyeuristic impulses of viewers and readers it magnifies the horror and disorientation of those involved with the tragedy. Loss of a loved one, especially in a sudden and violent way, creates a terrible feeling of violation. Concurrently is a considerable desire for control—a wish to exert control over the situation in at least some small way. Small details, such as which picture of the deceased is published or which details of his or her life are put on display for the world to see, become important in coping with the situation. Consider the care that families often give to the construction of an obituary; or in those cases where death is expected, the care given by the soon-to-be-departed. These intentional actions underscore the felt need to have some control in these situations. A pornography of grief completely disrupts any sense of control. The worst, the most gruesome, the juiciest details, regardless of taste, and absent any intentions of those closest to the victims, are broadcast and published. The result: a heightening of pain for those afflicted and a general increase in fear and anxiety among those closely involved as well as those more removed from the situation. Some research documents that graphic coverage of victims reinforces "mean world syndrome," a condition marked by higher degrees of fearfulness, anxiety, and uncertainty about the world (Wilkinson and Fletcher, 1995).

What is at stake ethically in the moment I have just described is a question about *what kind of story will be told*? Will this be a story of horror and anxiety, a story with only victims? Or will this story feature agents and actors who have some choices over their lives, some dignity in their presentation, some function other than as objects for the gaze of the curious?

> **Moment 4:** "What has really struck me is how little discussion there is, even in those places where professionals are ostensibly concerned with ethics."
> —I to my sister and brother-in-law in a letter dated October 11, 1996

In late August, my brother-in-law phoned to ask if I could help him. He wanted to send a letter to someone at ABC and maybe to someone else to complain about various invasions of privacy and insensitive intrusions he thought the family had suffered at the hands of the press. "Can you help?" he asked. "Can you tell me who to send the letter to? Are there any ethical codes I can refer to?" I said "sure," confident I would get back to him with the necessary information by the next day. About a week later I called with some information. Over the next two months, he and I spoke several times about how to hold journalists accountable for their insensitive actions. In one of the last letters I faxed to him, I wrote: "What has really struck me is how little discussion there is, even in those places where professionals are ostensibly concerned with ethics."

I had consulted my friend and colleague Dick Johannesen who I was sure could provide me the information I needed immediately. He did give me copies of several ethics codes right away and opened his personal library on media ethics to me. I was astounded at the paucity of information about ethics relevant to covering tragedies as I perused the material. I had mused about how journalists could be so insensitive, had wondered, "don't journalists have families, too?" In the textbooks and the codes I began to find the answer to these questions.

First, there appeared to be little to ground any training about how to cover tragedies for journalism students. A quick look at media ethics books revealed little to no discussion of how broadcast or print journalists should cover tragedies. In the books I reviewed, none had an entry on "tragedy," "disaster," or "grief" in their indexes. Occasionally there was a brief comment about such situations. The following was typical:

> . . . how to handle pain and grief? How to avoid what columnist George Will calls the "pornography of grief," the brutal exploitation of the grief and pain of others?
>   The camera—television's or a newspaper's—is the worst offender; it intrudes, it catches and exploits the tears on the cheek, the tremble across

the lips. But word journalists who crowd around the grave, who push into the church as the dead are eulogized are part of the problem too. When covering grief, you must judge whether it belongs in public view or is one of those stories that should not be published. If you must publish, move in with sensitivity, get your story and get back out as quickly and gently as possible. (Fink, 1995, p. 52)

That's it; that's the sum total of advice on this matter from a standard textbook on media ethics for aspiring journalists. One question is answered by a short paragraph. Is it any wonder that practicing journalists covering TWA 800 were insensitive, disrespectful of privacy, and distasteful?

The pedagogical gaps that encourage ethical negligence in the coverage of tragedies were mirrored by a second problem—ambiguous and incomplete codes of ethics. After searching ethics codes for what might apply in this instance, I found only two that were at all relevant. Article 4 of the Radio/TV News Directors Association Code of Ethics addressed the general topic of respect in the following way:

Broadcast journalists shall at all times display respect for the dignity, privacy and well-being of persons with whom the news deals. (Fink, 1995, p. 314)

Which times such respect is advised was not elaborated in the code. Tragic situations, incidents of violence and grief were not addressed in this code.

Article V of the ethics code of the Society for Professional Journalists came a bit closer to the mark. It read:

Fair Play: Show respect for the dignity, privacy, rights, and well-being of people encountered in the course of gathering and presenting the news.

. . . guard against invading a person's right to privacy

. . . don't pander to morbid curiosity about details of vice and crime. (Fink, 1995, p. 311)

Although SPJ's code addressed the issue of pandering to morbid curiosity, it did so in the context of "fair play," not in the context of tragedy or grief and thus probably provided less guidance to those confronted with covering an event in the heat of the moment.

There wasn't much to go on in launching an ethics charge from these codes, but I sent my brother-in-law what I had found and hoped it would provide some backing for his claims. Determining just whom he should contact turned out to be a more difficult problem. I talked with colleagues in broadcast journalism and media studies to ask who my relatives should contact. To a one, these colleagues began their answers by suggesting that making contact was probably pointless because of the nature of the industry. I was told that news routines, ambitions, arrogance, and the drive for audiences and profits all worked against anyone paying too much attention to the needs of people like my family when there was a big story to tell. I was informed that in the past complaints might go to a "Standards and Practices" division or committee. However, my colleagues continued, there weren't many of these left—it seems these committees were considered an expendable part of operations after the FCC Act was amended several years ago and in economic hard times for news divisions that accompanied increasing concentration in the media industries. Ultimately, I suggested that my brother-in-law send his complaints to the news directors and field producers involved in the stories of concern. He did that, but he also sent his concerns to journalistic celebrities like Peter Jennings of ABC Nightly News. After weeks without any response, he contacted *USA Today* and arranged to have his letter of complaint published there. About the same time, Peter Jennings contacted him to talk about these matters.

The ethical issue at stake in the moment I have been describing is: *How can the media be responsible and accountable for their ethical decisions?* In my experience, textbook treatments and ethical codes provided minimal help in this regard, and the industry provided zero guidance for how to launch a complaint or seek redress. Ultimately, the only effective means for holding the press to account required just the sort of public act and eventual publicity that had been at the root of the complaint in the first place, an agonizing "catch-22" for anyone who wanted to press for journalistic accountability.

Conclusion

Shortly after the fall term began in 1996, one of my journalism colleagues gave me the Internet address for the Society for Professional Journalists and mentioned that there was a lively discussion going on within that organization as they debated a new ethics code in light of the TWA tragedy. Within a couple of months, and during the time I was corresponding with my brother-in-law about the insensitivity of the media, SPJ passed a new ethics code that included language more to the point about covering tragedies than any code to date. Among the statements in the new code are the following:

Minimize Harm

Ethical journalists treat sources, subjects, and colleagues as human beings deserving respect. Journalists should:

- Show compassion for those who may be affected adversely by news coverage.
- Be sensitive when seeking or using interviews or photographs of those affected by tragedy or grief.
- Recognize that gathering and reporting information may cause harm or discomfort.
- Recognize that private people have a greater right to control information about themselves than do public officials.
- Show good taste. Avoid pandering to lurid curiosity.

The Code goes on to say:

Be Accountable

Journalists are accountable to their readers, listeners, viewers and each other.

This new code is somewhat reassuring because it addresses some of the concerns I have catalogued in this essay concerning privacy, sensitivity, taste, and accountability. However, a new ethical code alone probably will not prevent the ethical infractions catalogued here from future repetition. While it is certainly a step in the right direction, the new code retains a preference for abstraction over concrete reality. Terms like "sensitivity," "taste," and "accountability" are of course subject to multiple interpretations. There will always be grounds for arguing, as *Newsweek* did, that a particular photo or story was really necessary, didn't really offend, wasn't a matter of poor taste. However, by making future journalists more aware of the consequences of their decisions and actions through narratives like this one, we may help media professionals to adopt an alternative ethical stance toward the coverage of tragedies.

Using concrete experience that emerges from narratives like this one may provide an alternative to both unexamined news routines and ethical decisions based on abstract reasoning applied to and from extant ethical codes. Certainly this conclusion is supported by theorists who encourage casuistic approaches to communication and journalistic ethics, approaches that emphasize the importance of analyzing moral issues in the context of case studies in order to develop general but not universal ethical guidelines (Boeynik, 1992; Miller, 1996). It is my hope that narratives such as this one may help in two ways. First, by focusing on the moments in which ethical impulses arise, practicing or aspiring journalists may find a guide for gauging just when they might consider ethical questions in their coverage (i.e., whether to cover the story, how to get the story, what story to tell, and how to be accountable for the story). Second, narratives such as this one may provide practicing or prospective journalists a basis for understanding how their decisions about covering tragedies may affect their subjects, viewers, and readers and thus provide a gauge for *what* constitutes ethical coverage. In the stories I recounted earlier, I suspect readers had little trouble evaluating the media ethics involved. As Sandra Davidson Scott (1993) has observed, when journalists empathize instead of rationalizing, these matters are not very complicated. We often "know" what is or is not ethical. Moreover, there's probably a fairly high degree of reliability in these judgments; a Newseum/Roper poll showed that 82 percent of adults think journalists are generally insensitive in reporting tragedies (Reporting, 1997, p. 2). However, if media professionals are preoccupied with *getting* the stories they will report and never listen to the stories of those whom they report about, then journalists may not be well equipped to empathize. And without such empathy, there seems little hope that split-second ethical decisions in the heat of the moment of covering a tragic story will comport with many professional codes of ethics. Moreover, without training that goes beyond abstract values and generalized advice, it is unlikely that journalists will find any grounds for establishing accountability and minimizing the harm of their professional activities.

Notes

[1] This essay is best read as an auto-ethnography, a genre of academic research that foregrounds personal experience and does not attempt the more traditional distancing of a scholar from that which is studied. I was neither a casual viewer nor a detached observer of TWA Flight 800. Instead I write as an involved participant in the event. For a similar treatment of another plane crash, see Ellis (1993). Ellis explores the methodological implications for individual scholars and for the social sciences of blending personal narrative with emotional sociology. For another example of the use of first-person narrative to explore media ethics, see Coleman (1987). Coleman discusses the ethical issues surrounding everyday decisions confronting a street photographer in terms of narrative accounts.

[2] I am orienting my discussion of ethical issues around four moments of self-reflexiveness in which I experienced a very clear concern for ethics, for an impulse toward ethical action. I have argued elsewhere (Cooper, 1998), following Levinas, that ethics occurs when we experience a "call to conscience," an impulse toward moral action, obligation, or responsibility. Michel Foucault (1984) initiated his studies of ethics by defining ethics as "the relationship you ought to have with yourself," thus emphasizing the importance of self-reflection to moral action. His own studies of the genealogy of ethics incorporated a particular concern for ethical impulse, for how one is incited to experience ethics as an issue. The incidents that I recount in this paper are thus best understood as moments of articulation of that ethical impulse. They are, quite literally, spoken or written statements that occurred during the tragedy that caused me to ponder what was going on ethically in the media coverage of the event. They are recalled both from my memory and from my personal journal from that time.

References

Boeynik, D. (1992). Casuistry: A case bound method for journalists. *Journal of Mass Media Ethics, 7*, 107–120.

Brown, J. E. (1987). News photographers and the pornography of grief. *Journal of Mass Media Ethics, 2*, 75–81.

Chua-Eoan, H. (1996, July 29). Terror on flight 800. *Time*, 26–39.

Coleman, A. D. (1987). Private lives, public places: Street photography ethics. *Journal of Mass Media Ethics, 2*, 60–66.

Cooper, M. (1998). Decentering judgment: Toward a postmodern communication ethic. In John M. Sloop & James P. McDaniel (Eds.), *Judgment Calls* (pp. 63–83). Boulder: Westview.

Death on flight 800. (1996, July 29). *Newsweek*, 26–33.

Duffy, B. (1996, July 29). TWA flight 800: Blown away. *U.S. News & World Report*, 22–27.

Ellis, C. (1993). "There are survivors": Telling a story of sudden death. *The Sociological Quarterly, 34*, 711–730.

Fink, C. C. (1995). *Media Ethics*. Boston: Allyn & Bacon.

Foster, S. (1996, September). Sudden death, slow answers. *Counseling Today*, 37.

Foucault, M. (1984). On the genealogy of ethics: An overview of work in progress. In Paul Rabinow (Ed.), *The Foucault Reader* (pp. 340–372). New York: Pantheon.

Giobbe, D. (1996, August 3). Over the line. *Editor & Publisher*, p. 18.

Goodwin, H. E. (1983). *Groping for ethics in journalism*. Ames: Iowa State University Press.

Knapp, R. J. (1986). *Beyond endurance: When a child dies*. New York: Schocken Books.

Kohn, R. & Levov, I. (1990). Bereavement in disaster: An overview of the research. *International Journal of Mental Health, 19*, 61–76.

Miller, R. B. (1996). *Casuistry and modern ethics: A poetics of practical reasoning*. Chicago: University of Chicago Press.

O'Neill, H. (1996, December 26). TWA explosion named top story. Available: Internet.

Padgett, G. E. (1985–86). Codes should address exploitation of grief by photographers. *Journal of Mass Media Ethics, 1*, 50–56.

Protesting a picture. (1996, August 19). *Newsweek, 19*, 12.

Reporting or exploiting? (1997, March 24). *The Freedom Forum News*, pp. 1–2.

Retsinas, G. (1995, May 6). Reporter's deception denounced. *Editor & Publisher*, pp. 16, 39.

Russakoff, D. (1996, August 12–18). The dilemma of flight 800. *The Washington Post National Weekly Edition*, p. 29.

Scott, S. D. (1993). Beyond reason: A feminist theory of ethics for journalists. *Feminist Issues, 13*, 23–40.

Wilkinson, Jeffrey S., and James E. Fletcher. (1995). Bloody news and vulnerable populations: An ethical question. *Journal of Mass Media Ethics, 10*, 167–177.

Video and Internet Resources

VHS and DVD on Communication Ethics

"Advertising and the End of the World." Media Education Foundation. 1998. 46 min.
Does advertising in our consumerist society really promote personal happiness and satisfaction, our collective as well as private interests, and long-term as well as short-term decisions?

"Business Ethics on the Job." Available from Insight Media. 2003. 25 min. VHS & DVD.
A series of live-action scenarios sensitizing viewers to issues of honesty, loyalty, integrity, confidentiality, and respect for others.

"Business Ethics and Social Responsibility." Available from Insight Media. 2003. 20 min.
Ethical failures of corporations and individuals are examined through discussion of ethical theories, codes of ethics, ethical decision making, and corporate social responsibilities.

"Business Ethics: Truth in Advertising." Available from Films for the Humanities & Sciences. 1997. 28 min.
Explores the commercial competitive frenzy that forces devaluing of concern for truthfulness in advertising. Helps consumers to separate fact from fiction and half-truth.

"Deadly Persuasion: The Advertising of Alcohol & Tobacco." Media Education Foundation. 2003. VHS 60 min. DVD 60 min. plus 30 min. abridged.
Jean Kilbourne examines marketing strategies and advertising tactics that capitalize on the psychology of anxiety and addiction to create and reinforce life-threatening dependencies.

"Do Unto Others." Part of the PBS *Ethics in America* series. 1988. 60 min.
Excellent on interpersonal communication ethics: duties; loyalties; consequences; ethical character; whistle-blowing; changes in judgments as elements in relationships change.

"Doublespeak." Available from Films for the Humanities & Sciences. 1988. 28 min.
How euphemisms, jargon, gobbledegook, and inflated words are used to distort, obfuscate, cover up, or replace meaning in private and public discourse.

"Dreamworlds 3." Media Education Foundation. 2007. 55 min.
Sut Jhally's critique of the exploitation of female sexuality in music video.

"The Ethics of Journalism." Available from Insight Media. 1995. 2 parts, 30 min. each.
Explores how journalists deal with such ethical issues as honesty, thoroughness, objectivity, privacy, covering disasters, and conflicts of interest.

"End Game: Ethics and Values in America." PBS (available from Insight Media). 2002. 60 min.

A scenario with professional actors is presented in several stages with opportunities for response from audience members, viewers, and experts. An honored educational activist faces a decision whether to report a fatal accident she caused. Questions discussed: Is she doing the right thing? Does the end justify the means? Would *you* report yourself to the police? Should her friend turn her in? Would *you* turn in your best friend? Scenario raises issues of lying and whistle-blowing. Experts are: David Kaczynski (who turned in his brother, Ted, the Unabomber); Michael Josephson (founder of the Josephson Institute of Ethics); Jackie Joyner Kersee (Olympic track star).

"Ethics and the Legal Profession." Available from GPN Educational Media. 2002. 30 min.

The attorney-client confidentiality privilege. Lying. Defending immoral clients.

"Ethics and Media Professionals." Available from GPN Educational Media. 2002. 30 min.

Privacy vs. people's right to know. Media ethics in business and advertising. Role of the media in a free society. Deception, conflict of interest, and photojournalism.

"Faces of the Enemy." Available from Insight Media. 1987. 58 min.

Documentary on how people and nations dehumanize their enemies as subhuman or non-human. Excellent illustrations (visual and verbal) of the process of "moral exclusion" where "they" are symbolically placed outside the boundaries where normal ethical standards apply to "us."

"Game Over: Gender, Race, & Violence in Video Games." Media Education Foundation. 2000. 35 min.

Examines the images of masculinity, femininity, race, and violence represented in video games.

"Government Ethics." Available from GPN Educational Media. 2002. 30 min.

National security issues. Administrative dilemmas. Moral mazes in public administration.

"Introduction to Professional Ethics." Available from GPN Educational Media. 2002. 30 min.

Principles of applied ethics. Analyzing professional ethics. A framework to evaluating ethical dilemmas. Doing the right thing.

"Killing Us Softly 3." Media Education Foundation. 2000. VHS & DVD. 34 min.

Latest edition of media critic Jean Kilbourne's presentation in which she examines hundreds of ads and commercials to critique advertising's image of women.

"Liar, Liar, Pants on Fire." Available from Films for the Humanities & Sciences. 1999. 30 min.

Explores issues of truthfulness, reasons for lying, and degrees of deception in politics, business, and private life.

"Media Ethics." Available from Films for the Humanities & Sciences. 1998. 28 min.

Examines problems of media honesty and fairness, of coverage of the private lives of public officials or citizens thrust into public view, of commercial influences on ethics, and of the societal impact of film, video, and rock/rap lyrics.

"Michael Josephson." Part of the PBS *A World of Ideas with Bill Moyers* series. 1989. 30 min.

An interview with the founder of the Josephson Institute for Ethics. Relevant to leadership, organizational ethics, legality versus ethicality, character or virtue ethics, and lying as coercion.

"Pack of Lies: The Advertising of Tobacco." Media Education Foundation. 1992. 35 min.

Evaluates advertising strategies for reassuring smokers, targeting women, and targeting children.

"The Perils of Whistleblowing." Available from Insight Media. 1998. 50 min.

Mike Wallace and a team of reporters investigate the methods by which companies attempt to discredit and smear employees who are whistle-blowers. Also examines the damage done to the lives of whistle-blowers.

"Politics, Privacy, and the Press." Part of the PBS *Ethics in America* series. 1987. 60 min.
Explores ethical issues in news coverage of the private lives of public officials.

"Public Trust, Private Interests." Part of the PBS *Ethics in America* series. 1988. 60 min.
Explores the relation of the private misconduct of public officials to citizen evaluation of their public service.

"Sexism in Language." 1982. 20 min.
Available from Films for the Humanities & Sciences. Analyzes examples of sexist language in everyday conversation, song lyrics, newspaper reports.

"Sissela Bok." Part of the PBS *A World of Ideas with Bill Moyers* series. 1989. 30 min.
An interview with philosopher/ethicist Sissela Bok. Relevant to issues of ends versus means, lying and deception as categories, and difficulty of keeping secrets.

"Social Responsibilities of Professionals." Available from GPN Educational Media. 2002. 30 min.
Integrating personal and professional responsibilities. Duties of professionals. Corporate responsibility. Professionals and the social contract.

"Speaking with Confidence: Ethics." Available from Insight Media. 1997. 30 min.
Stresses honesty, truthfulness, and responsibility in public speaking. Provides examples of ethical and unethical public speaking.

"Spin the Bottle: Sex, Lies, and Alcohol." Media Education Foundation. 2004. VHS & DVD. 45 min.
Jean Kilbourne and Jackson Katz examine the normalization of alcohol abuse in today's youth culture. Examples from Hollywood films, TV sitcoms, and commercial advertising.

"Truth About Lies." Part of Bill Moyers' *The Public Mind* series for PBS. 1989. 60 min.
Available from Films for the Humanities & Sciences. Examines lying and deception in public and private life. Relates to issues of ends justifying means, implied ethical agreements, ethical character, rationalizations for lying, and definitions of lying.

"Truth or Consequences: Communication Ethics." Available from Insight Media. 1995. 29 min.
A real-life case study of whistle-blowing focuses on issues of corporate loyalty, employee obligations, and repercussions and consequences.

"Truth or Fiction? Photography and Ethics." Available from Insight Media. 2001. VHS & DVD. 27 min.
Uses actual case studies of photographic manipulation. Discusses positive and negative influences of digital technology.

"Whistleblowers." Available from Films for the Humanities & Sciences. 1992. 24 min.
Two actual case studies (environmental pollution; the *Challenger* disaster) of diverse ethical issues in whistle-blowing.

"Why We Lie." Available from Insight Media. 2000. 51 min.
Experts examine uses of and reasons for lying. Demonstrations include polygraph tests, facial gesture analysis, and results from "lying diaries" kept by college students.

Video Source Web Site Addresses

Films for the Humanities & Sciences	www.films.com
GPN Educational Media	www.gpn.unl.edu
Insight Media	www.insight-media.com
Media Education Foundation	www.mediaed.org
Public Broadcasting System (PBS)	www.pbs.org

Web Sites on Ethics

http://ethics.sandiego.edu/index.asp
  many resources and links on ethical theory and issues
http://commfaculty.fullerton.edu/lester/ethics/ethics_list.html
  a directory of media ethics resources on the Web
http://www.scu.edu/ethics/links
  Markula Center for Applied Ethics. Over 250 links to other ethics groups
http://josephsoninstitute.org
  Josephson Institute of Ethics
http://ethics.iit.edu/codes/
  over 850 codes of ethics from widely varied organizations
http://jmme.org
  Journal of Mass Media Ethics
http://www.mediaethicsmagazine.com
  online version of *Media Ethics*. Analyses & commentaries; news; book reviews
http://indiana.edu/~appe/index.html
  Association for Practical and Professional Ethics. Numerous relevant links
http://poynter.org/research/me.htm
  media news ethics research and resource files of the Poynter Institute
http://www.rtnda.org/
  Radio-Television News Directors Assoc.—current code and issues
http://www.spj.org/
  Society of Professional Journalists—current code and issues
http://www.prsa.org/
  Public Relations Society of America—current code and issues
http://www.aaf.org/
  American Advertising Federation—current code and issues
http://www.aaaa.org/
  American Association of Advertising Agencies—current code and issues
http://www.bbb.org/
  Better Business Bureau—advertising ethics code and issues
http://www.theecoa.org/
  Ethics Compliance and Officer Association
http://www.adbusters.org/home
  Adbusters Culture Jammers Headquarters—attempts to counter the influence of ads

Sources for Further Reading

General Sources

Arneson, Pat. *Exploring Communication Ethics: Interviews with Influential Scholars in the Field.* New York: Peter Lang, 2007.

Becker, Lawrence C., and Charlotte B. Becker, eds. *Encyclopedia of Ethics,* 2nd ed. 3 vols. New York: Garland Publishing, 2001.

Benjamin, Martin. *Splitting the Difference: Compromise and Integrity in Ethics and Politics.* Lawrence: University Press of Kansas, 1990.

Bourgeois, Patrick L. *Philosophy at the Boundary of Reason: Ethics and Postmodernity.* Albany: State University of New York Press, 2001, chapters 1, 8–11.

Boss, Judith A. *Ethics for Life: A Text with Readings,* 3rd ed. Boston: McGraw-Hill, 2004.

Bracci, Sharon L., and Clifford G. Christians, eds. *Moral Engagement in Public Life: Theorists for Contemporary Ethics.* New York: Peter Lang, 2002.

Cane, Peter. *Responsibility in Law and Morality.* Oxford, UK: Hart, 2002.

Caputo, John D. *Against Ethics: Contributions to a Politics of Obligation with Constant Reference to Deconstruction.* Bloomington: Indiana University Press, 1993.

Copp, David, ed. *The Oxford Handbook of Ethical Theory.* New York: Oxford University Press, 2006.

Elliott, Deni. *Ethics in the First Person: A Guide to Teaching and Learning Practical Ethics.* Lanham, MD: Rowman and Littlefield, 2007.

Fischer, John Martin. "Recent Work on Moral Responsibility." *Ethics* 110 (October 1999): 93–139.

Gert, Bernard. *Morality: Its Nature and Justification,* rev. ed. New York: Oxford University Press, 2005.

Gini, Al. *Why It's Hard to Be Good.* New York: Routledge, 2006.

Greenberg, Karen Joy, ed. *Conversations on Communication Ethics.* Norwood, NJ: Ablex, 1991.

Hass, Aaron. *Doing the Right Thing: Cultivating Moral Intelligence.* New York: Pocket Books, 1998.

Ingram, David Bruce, and Jennifer A. Parks. *The Complete Idiot's Guide to Understanding Ethics.* Indianapolis, IN: Alpha, 2002.

Jaksa, James A., and Michael S. Pritchard. *Communication Ethics: Methods of Analysis,* 2nd ed. Belmont, CA: Wadsworth, 1994.

Jensen, J. Vernon. *Ethical Issues in the Communication Process*. Mahwah, NJ: Erlbaum, 1997.

Johannesen, Richard L., "Communication Ethics: Centrality, Trends, and Controversies." In *Communication Yearbook 25*, William Gudykunst, ed. Mahwah, NJ: Erlbaum, 2001, pp. 201–236.

——— "Perspectives on Ethics in Persuasion." In Charles U. Larson, *Persuasion: Reception and Responsibility*, 11th ed. Belmont, CA: Thomson/Wadsworth, 2007, chapter 2.

Jonas, Hans. *The Imperative of Responsibility: In Search of an Ethics for the Technological Age*. Chicago: University of Chicago Press, 1984.

Jonsen, Albert R., and Stephen Toulmin. *The Abuse of Casuistry: A History of Moral Reasoning*. Berkeley: University of California Press, 1988.

Kidder, Rushworth. *How Good People Make Tough Choices*. New York: Morrow, 1995.

———. *Moral Courage*. New York: Morrow, 2005.

Klumpp, James F. "Freedom and Responsibility in Constructing Public Life: Toward a Revised Ethic of Discourse." *Argumentation* 11 (February 1997): 113–130.

Kohlberg, Lawrence. *The Psychology of Moral Development: The Nature and Validity of Moral Stages*. San Francisco: Harper & Row, 1984.

Kroll, Barry. "Arguing About Public Issues: What Can We Gain from Practical Ethics?" *Rhetoric Review* 16 (Fall 1997): 105–119.

Langston, Douglas C. *Conscience and Other Virtues*. University Park: Pennsylvania State University Press, 2001.

Liszka, James Jacob. *Moral Competence: An Integrated Approach to the Study of Ethics*. Upper Saddle River, NJ: Prentice-Hall, 1999.

Lucas, J. R. *Responsibility*. New York: Oxford University Press, 1993.

Lynch, Michael P. *True to Life: Why Truth Matters*. Cambridge, MA: MIT Press, 2005.

McDowell, Banks. *Ethics and Excuses: The Crisis in Professional Responsibility*. Westport, CT: Greenwood Press, 2000.

Mackin, James A., Jr. *Community over Chaos: An Ecological Perspective on Communication Ethics*. Tuscaloosa: University of Alabama Press, 1997.

Makau, Josina M., and Ronald Arnett, eds. *Communication Ethics in an Age of Diversity*. Urbana: University of Illinois Press, 1996.

Miller, Richard B. *Casuistry and Modern Ethics: A Poetics of Practical Reasoning*. Chicago: University of Chicago Press, 1996.

Nash, Robert J. *Answering the Virtuecrats: A Moral Conversation on Character Education*. New York: Teachers College Press, 1997.

Neher, William W., and Paul J. Sandin. *Communicating Ethically: Character, Duties, Consequences, and Relationships*. Boston: Pearson/Allyn & Bacon, 2007.

Pojman, Louis P. *Ethics: Discovering Right and Wrong*, 5th ed. Belmont, CA: Wadsworth, 2006.

———. *How Should We Live? An Introduction to Ethics*. Belmont, CA: Wadsworth, 2005.

Pols, Edward. *Acts of Our Being: A Reflection on Agency and Responsibility*. Amherst: University of Massachusetts Press, 1982.

Rachels, James. *The Elements of Moral Philosophy*, 4th ed. Boston: McGraw-Hill College, 2003.

Strike, Kenneth A., and Pamela A. Moss. *Ethics and College Student Life*, 2nd ed. Upper Saddle River, NJ: Prentice-Hall, 2003.

Thomassen, Nils. *Communicative Ethics in Theory and Practice*. New York: St. Martin's Press, 1992.

Toulmin, Stephen. "The Recovery of Practical Philosophy." *American Scholar* 57 (Summer 1988): 337–352.

Weston, Anthony. *A 21st Century Ethical Toolbox*. New York: Oxford University Press, 2001.

———. *Creative Problem Solving in Ethics*. New York: Oxford University Press, 2007.

Wolfe, Alan. *Moral Freedom: The Search for Virtue in a World of Choice*. New York: W. W. Norton, 2001.

Wood, Allen W. *Kant's Ethical Thought*. Cambridge: Cambridge University Press, 1999.

Political Perspectives

Altman, Andrew. "Liberalism and Campus Hate Speech—A Philosophical Examination." *Ethics* 103 (January 1993): 302–317.

Applbaum, Arthur Isak. *Ethics for Adversaries: The Morality of Roles in Public and Professional Life*. Princeton, NJ: Princeton University Press, 1999.

Borgmann, Albert. *Real American Ethics*. Chicago, IL: University of Chicago Press, 2006.

Cody, W. J. Michael, and Richardson R. Lynn. *Honest Government: An Ethical Guide to Public Service*. Westport, CT: Praeger, 1992.

Denton, Robert E., Jr., ed. *Ethical Dimensions of Political Communication*. New York: Praeger, 1991.

———. *Political Communication Ethics: An Oxymoron?* Westport, CT: Praeger, 2000.

Dowling, Ralph E., and Gabrielle Grinder. "An Ethical Appraisal of Ronald Reagan's Justification for the Invasion of Granada." In *Warranting Assent: Case Studies in Argument Evaluation*, Edward Schiappa, ed., Albany: State University of New York Press, 1995, pp. 103–124.

Garofalo, Charles, and Dean Geuras. *Ethics in the Public Service*. Washington, DC: Georgetown University Press, 1999.

Gouran, Dennis. "Guidelines for the Analysis of Responsibility in Governmental Communication." In *Teaching about Doublespeak,* Daniel Dieterich, ed. Urbana, IL: National Council of Teachers of English, 1976, pp. 20–31.

Gutman, Amy, and Dennis Thompson. *Democracy and Disagreement*. Cambridge, MA: Belknap Press, 1996.

Haiman, Franklyn S. *Freedom, Democracy, and Responsibility: The Selected Works of Franklyn S. Haiman*. Cresskill, NJ: Hampton Press, 2000.

Johannesen, Richard L. "Haigspeak, Secretary of State Haig, and Communication Ethics." In *The Orwellian Moment,* Robert L. Savage, James Combs, and Dan Nimmo, eds. Fayetteville: University of Arkansas Press, 1989, pp. 109–118.

———. "An Ethical Assessment of the Reagan Rhetoric: 1981–1982." In *Political Communication Yearbook 1984*. Keith Sanders, Lynda Lee Kaid, and Dan Nimmo, eds. Carbondale: Southern Illinois University Press, 1985, pp. 226–242.

Johnstone, Christopher Lyle. "Reagan, Rhetoric, and the Public Philosophy: Ethics and Politics in the 1994 Campaign." *Southern Communication Journal* 60 (Winter 1995): 93–108.

Lewis, Carol W., and Stuart C. Gilman. *The Ethics Challenge in Public Service*. 2nd ed. San Francisco, CA: Jossey-Bass, 2005.

Ryn, Claes G. *Democracy and the Ethical Life: A Philosophy of Politics and Community*, 2nd ed. Washington, DC: Catholic University Press of America, 1990.

Thompson, Dennis F. *Political Ethics and Public Office*. Cambridge, MA: Harvard University Press, 1987.

Ulmer, Robert R., and Timothy L. Sellnow. "Strategic Ambiguity and the Ethic of Significant Choice in the Tobacco Industry's Crisis Communication." *Communication Studies* 48 (Fall 1997): 215–233.

Human Nature Perspectives

Arnhart, Larry. *Darwinian Natural Right: The Biological Ethics of Human Nature*. Albany: State University of New York Press, 1998.

Botan, Carl. "A Human Nature Approach to Image and Ethics in International Public Relations." *Journal of Public Relations Research* 5, no. 2 (1993): 71–81.

Bradie, Michael. *The Secret Chain: Evolution and Ethics.* Albany: State University of New York Press, 1994.

Brummett, Barry. "A Defense of Ethical Relativism as Rhetorically Grounded." *Western Journal of Speech Communication* 45 (Fall 1981): 286–298.

Campbell, Karlyn Kohrs. "The Ontological Foundations of Rhetorical Theory." *Philosophy and Rhetoric* 3 (Spring 1970): 97–108.

———. "The Rhetorical Implications of the Axiology of Jean-Paul Sartre." *Western Speech* 35 (Summer 1971): 155–161.

Casebeer, William D. *Natural Ethical Facts: Evolution, Connectionism, and Moral Cognition.* Cambridge, MA: MIT Press, 2003.

Degler, Carl N. *In Search of Human Nature.* New York: Oxford University Press, 1991.

De Waal, Frans. *Good Natured: The Origins of Right and Wrong in Humans and Other Animals.* Cambridge, MA: Harvard University Press, 1996.

Fouts, Roger, and Stephen Tukel Mills. *Next of Kin: My Conversations with Chimpanzees.* New York: Living Planet Books, 1997.

Gazzaniga, Michael S. *The Ethical Brain.* New York: Dana Press, 2005.

Goldman, Alvin I. "Ethics and Cognitive Science." *Ethics* 103 (January 1993): 337–360.

Guignon, Charles. "Existentialist Ethics." In *New Directions in Ethics: The Challenge of Applied Ethics,* Joseph R. DeMarco and Richard M. Fox, eds. New York: Routledge & Kegan Paul, 1986, pp. 73–91.

Haraway, Donna. *Simians, Cyborgs, and Women: The Reinvention of Human Nature.* New York: Routledge, 1991.

Jaggar, Alison. *Feminist Politics and Human Nature.* Totowa, NJ: Rowman and Allanheld, 1983.

Johannesen, Richard L. "Richard M. Weaver on Standards for Ethical Rhetoric." *Central States Speech Journal* 29 (Summer 1978): 127–137.

Johnstone, Christopher Lyle. "Evolution, Speech, and Morality: Toward a Rhetoric of Survival." *Dialogue and Universalism* 5, no. 3 (1995): 85–104.

McShea, Robert J. *Morality and Human Nature: A New Route to Ethical Theory.* Philadelphia: Temple University Press, 1990.

Midgley, Mary. *The Ethical Primate: Humans, Freedom, and Morality.* London: Routledge, 1994.

Nitecki, Matthew H., and Doris V. Nitecki, eds. *Evolutionary Ethics.* Albany: State University of New York Press, 1993.

Nussbaum, Martha. "Human Functioning and Social Justice: In Defense of Aristotelian Essentialism." *Political Theory* 20 (May 1992): 202–246.

Pinker, Steven. *The Blank Slate: The Modern Denial of Human Nature.* New York: Viking, 2002.

Savage-Rumbaugh, Sue, and Roger Lewin. *Kanzi: The Ape at the Brink of the Human Mind.* London: Doubleday, 1994.

Segerdahl, Par, William Fields, and Sue Savage-Rumbaugh. *Kanzi's Primal Language: The Cultural Initiation of Primates into Language.* Hampshire, UK: Palgrage Macmillan, 2005.

Sokolon, Marlen K. *Political Emotions: Aristotle and the Symphony of Reason and the Emotions.* DeKalb, IL: Northern Illinois University Press, 2006.

Stevenson, Leslie, and David L. Haberman. *Ten Theories of Human Nature,* 3rd ed. New York: Oxford University Press, 1998.

Thompson, Paul, ed. *Issues in Evolutionary Ethics.* Albany: State University of New York Press, 1995.

Dialogical Perspectives

Anderson, Rob, Leslie A. Baxter, and Kenneth N. Cissna, eds. *Dialogue: Theorizing Difference in Communication Studies*. Thousand Oaks, CA: Sage, 2004.

———, and Kenneth N. Cissna, eds. *The Martin Buber–Carl Rogers Dialogue: A New Transcript With a Commentary*. Albany: State University of New York Press, 1999.

———, Kenneth N. Cissna, and Ronald C. Arnett, eds. *The Reach of Dialogue: Confirmation, Voice, and Community*. Cresskill, NJ: Hampton Press, 1994.

Arnett, Ronald C. *Communication and Community: Implications of Martin Buber's Dialogue*. Carbondale: Southern Illinois University Press, 1986.

———. "What is Dialogic Communication? Friedman's Contribution and Clarification." *Person-Centered Review* 4 (February 1989): 42–60.

———, and Pat Arneson. *Dialogic Civility in a Cynical Age: Community, Hope, and Interpersonal Relationships*. Albany: State University of New York Press, 1999.

Atterton, Peter, Matthew Calarco, and Maurice Friedman, eds. *Levinas and Buber: Dialogue and Difference*. Pittsburgh, PA: Duquesne University Press, 2004.

Bergman, Shmuel Hugo. *Dialogical Philosophy from Kierkegaard to Buber*. Albany: State University of New York Press, 1991.

Cissna, Kenneth N., and Rob Anderson. *Moments of Meeting: Buber, Rogers, and the Potential for Public Dialogue*. Albany: State University of New York Press, 2002.

Czubaroff, Jeanine. "Dialogical Rhetoric: An Application of Martin Buber's Philosophy of Dialogue." *Quarterly Journal of Speech* 86 (May 2000): 168–189.

Friedman, Maurice S. *The Confirmation of Otherness in Family, Community, and Society*. New York: Pilgrim Press, 1983.

———. "Carl Rogers and Martin Buber: Self-Actualization and Dialogue." *Person-Centered Review* 1 (November 1986): 409–435.

———. *Dialogue and the Human Image: Beyond Humanistic Psychology*. Newbury Park, CA: Sage, 1992.

———, ed. *Martin Buber and the Human Sciences*. Albany: State University of New York Press, 1996.

Gurewitch, Z. D. "The Dialogic Connection and the Ethics of Dialogue." *British Journal of Sociology* 41 (June 1990): 181–196.

Gusdorf, Michael. "Alterity and Ethics: A Dialogical Perspective." *Theory, Culture, and Society* 13, no. 2 (1996): 121–143.

Hammond, Scott C., Rob Anderson, and Kenneth N. Cissna. "The Problematics of Dialogue and Power." *Communication Yearbook*, 27 (2003): 125–157.

Hyde, Michael J. *The Life-Giving Gift of Acknowledgment: A Philosophical and Rhetorical Inquiry*. West Lafayette, IN: Purdue University Press, 2006.

Johannesen, Richard L. "The Emerging Concept of Communication as Dialogue." *Quarterly Journal of Speech* 57 (December 1971): 373–382.

———. "Nel Noddings's Uses of Martin Buber's Philosophy of Dialogue." *Southern Communication Journal* 65 (Winter/Spring 2000): 151–160.

Kent, Michael L., and Maureen Taylor. "Toward a Dialogic Theory of Public Relations." *Public Relations Review* 28 (Feb. 2002): 21–37.

Kohanski, Alexander S. *Martin Buber's Philosophy of Interhuman Relation*. East Brunswick, NJ: Associated University Presses, 1982.

Lipari, Lisbeth. "Listening for the Other: Ethical Implications of the Buber-Levinas Encounter." *Communication Theory* 14 (2004): 122–141.

Murray, Jeffrey W. *Kenneth Burke: A Dialogue of Motives*. Lanham, MD: University Press of America, 2002.

Nealon, Jeffrey T. "The Ethics of Dialogue: Bakhtin and Levinas." *College English* 59 (1997): 129–148.

Sampson, Edward E. *Celebrating the Other: A Dialogic Account of Human Nature.* Boulder, CO: Westview Press, 1993.

Southern Communication Journal 65 (Winter/Spring 2000). Entire issue on conceptions of dialogue and communication ethics.

Stewart, John. "Martin Buber's Central Insight: Implications for His Philosophy of Dialogue." In *Dialogue: An Interdisciplinary Approach,* Marcelo Dascal, ed. Amsterdam: John Benjamins B.V, 1985, pp. 321–335.

———, ed. *Bridges Not Walls: A Book About Interpersonal Communication,* 9th ed. New York: McGraw-Hill, 2006.

———, and Karen Zediker. "Dialogue as Tensional, Ethical Practice." *Southern Communication Journal* 65 (Winter/Spring 2000): 224–242.

Thomlison, T. Dean. *Toward Interpersonal Dialogue.* New York: Longman, 1982.

Situational Perspectives

Cunningham, Robert L., ed. *Situationism and the New Morality.* New York: Appleton, Century, Crofts, 1970.

Edelman, Samuel M. "The Rhetorical Situation and Situational Ethics in the Symbol of the 'Refugee in the Israeli-Palestinian Arab Conflict." In *Conversations on Communication Ethics,* Karen Joy Greenberg, ed. Norwood, NJ: Ablex, 1991, pp. 167–177.

Fletcher, Joseph. *Moral Responsibility: Situation Ethics at Work.* Philadelphia: Westminster Press, 1967.

Martinson, David L. "Public Relations Practitioners Must Not Confuse Consideration of the Situation with 'Situational Ethics'." *Public Relations Quarterly* 42 (1997–1998): 39–43.

Pratt, Cornelius B. "Critique of the Classical Theory of Situational Ethics in U.S. Public Relations." *Public Relations Review* 19 (Fall 1993): 219–234.

Rogge, Edward. "Evaluating the Ethics of a Speaker in a Democracy." *Quarterly Journal of Speech* 50 (December 1959): 419–425.

Simons, Herbert W. "Persuasion in Social Conflicts: A Critique of Prevailing Conceptions and a Framework for Future Research." *Speech Monographs* 29 (November 1972): 227–247, especially 238–240.

Religious, Utilitarian, and Legalistic Perspectives

Christians, Clifford G. "A Cultural View of Mass Communication: Some Explorations for Christians." *Christian Scholar's Review* 7 (1977): 3–22.

Christians, Clifford G., and Robert S. Fortner. "The Media Gospel." *Journal of Communication* 31 (Spring 1981): 190–199.

Elliott, Deni. "Getting Mill Right." *Journal of Mass Media Ethics* 22 (2007): 100–112

Glover, Jonathan, ed. *Utilitarianism and Its Critics.* New York: Macmillan, 1990.

Hsing, Yun. *Being Good: Buddhist Ethics for Everyday Life.* New York: Weatherhill, 1998.

Hunt, Arnold D., Marie T. Crotty, and Robert B. Crotty, eds. *Ethics of World Religions,* rev. ed. San Diego: Greenhaven Press, 1991.

Hurley, Paul E. "Does Consequentialism Make Too Many Demands, or None at All?" *Ethics* 116 (July 2006): 680–706.

Jensen, Vernon J. *Ethical Issues in the Communication Process.* Mahwah, NJ: Erlbaum, 1997, chapter 2.

Kaplar, Richard T., and Patrick Maines. "The Role of Government in Undermining Journalistic Ethics." *Journal of Mass Media Ethics* 40, no. 4 (1995): 236–247.

Phelan, John M. *Disenchantment: Meaning and Morality in the Media.* New York: Hastings House, 1980, chapters 3 and 4.

Pojman, Louis P. *Ethics: Discovering Right and Wrong,* 5th ed. Belmont, CA: Thomson/ Wadsworth, 2006, chapters 1, 6, 7, and 10.

Rachels, James. *The Elements of Moral Philosophy,* 4th ed. Boston: McGraw-Hill College, 2003, chapters 4, 7, 8.

Shaw, William H. *Contemporary Ethics: Taking Account of Utilitarianism.* Malden, MA: Blackwell, 1999.

Scheffler, Samuel. *Consequentialism and Its Critics.* New York: Oxford, 1988.

West, Henry R., ed. *The Blackwell Guide to Mill's Utilitarianism.* Malden, MA: Blackwell, 2006.

Some Basic Issues

Adam, Alison. *Gender, Ethics, and Information Technology.* New York: Palgrave Macmillan, 2005.

Arnett, Ronald C. "A Dialogic Ethic 'Between' Buber and Levinas: A Responsive Ethical 'I.'" In *Dialogue: Theorizing Difference in Communication Studies,* Rob Anderson, Leslie A. Baxter, and Kenneth N. Cissna, eds. Thousand Oaks, CA: Sage, 2004, pp. 75–90.

Baird, Robert M., Reagan Mays Ramsower, and Stuart E. Rosenbaum, eds. *Cyberethics: Social and Moral Issues in the Computer Age.* Amherst, NY: Prometheus Books, 2000.

Bauman, Zygmundt. *Life in Fragments: Essays in Postmodern Morality.* Oxford, UK: Blackwell, 1995.

Best, Steven, and Douglas Kellner. *The Postmodern Turn.* New York: Guilford, 1997.

Cavalier, Robert J. *The Impact of the Internet on Our Moral Lives.* Albany, NY: SUNY Press, 2005.

Clarke, Roger. "Ethics and the Internet: The Cyberspace Behavior of People, Communities, and Organizations." *Business and Professional Ethics Journal* 18 (Fall–Winter, 1999): 153–167.

Cole, Terry W. "ACLU v. RENO: An Exigency for Cyberethics." *Southern Communication Journal* 64 (Spring 1999): 251–258.

Cooper, Martha. "Ethical Dimensions of Political Advocacy from a Postmodern Perspective." In *Ethical Dimensions of Political Communication,* Robert E. Denton, Jr., ed. New York: Praeger, 1991, pp. 23–47.

———, and Carole Blair. "Foucault's Ethics." In *Moral Engagement in Public Life: Theorists for Contemporary Ethics,* Sharon L. Bracci and Clifford G. Christians, eds. New York: Peter Lang, 2002, pp. 257–276.

Combs, James E., and Dan Nimmo. *The New Propaganda: The Dictatorship of Palaver in Contemporary Politics.* New York: Longman, 1993.

Cunningham, Stanley B. *The Idea of Propaganda: A Reconstruction.* Westport, CT: Praeger, 2002, chapters 7–9.

Gilchrist, James A., and Paula S. Gilchrist. "Communication Ethics and Computer Technology: The Case of Computer Monitoring." In *Responsible Communication,* James A. Jaksa and Michael S. Pritchard, eds. Cresskill, NJ: Hampton Press, 1996, pp. 107–131.

Goldzwig, Steven R. "A Social Movement Perspective on Demagoguery: Achieving Symbolic Realignment." *Communication Studies* 40 (Fall 1989): 202–228.

Gross, Larry, John Stuart Katz, and Jay Ruby, eds. *Image Ethics in the Digital Age.* Minneapolis: University of Minnesota Press, 2003.

Gunkel, David. *Hacking Cyberspace*. Boulder, CO: Westview, 2001.

Hassert, M. "Constructing an Ethical Writer for the Postmodern Scene." *Rhetoric Society Quarterly* 25 (1995): 179–196.

Hester, D. Micah, and Paul J. Ford, eds. *Computers and Ethics in the Cyberage*. Upper Saddle River, NJ: Prentice-Hall, 2001.

Jackall, Robert. *Propaganda*. New York: New York University Press, 1995.

Johnson, Lawrence E. *Focusing on the Truth*. London: Routledge, 1992.

Kienzler, Donna S. "Visual Ethics." *Journal of Business Communication* 34 (April 1997): 171–187.

Kizza, Joseph M. *Ethical and Social Issues in the Information Age*, 2nd ed. New York: Springer, 2003.

Kramer, Jana, and Cheris Kramerae. "Gendered Ethics on the Internet." In *Communication Ethics in an Age of Diversity*, Josina M. Makau and Ronald C. Arnett, eds. Urbana: University of Illinois Press, 1997, pp. 226–243.

Lester, Paul. *Photojournalism: An Ethical Approach*. Hillsdale, NJ: Erlbaum, 1991.

———. *Visual Communication: Images with Messages*. Belmont, CA: Wadsworth, 2003, chapters 6 and 7.

Madison, Gary B., and Marty Fairbairn, eds. *The Ethics of Postmodernity: Current Trends in Continental Thought*. Evanston, IL: Northwestern University Press, 1999.

Marlin, Randal. *Propaganda and the Ethics of Persuasion*. Peterborough, Ontario: Broadview Press, 2002.

Mensch, James R. *Ethics and Selfhood: Alterity and the Phenomenology of Obligation*. Albany, NY: SUNY Press, 2003.

Messaris, Paul. *Visual Persuasion: The Role of Images in Advertising*. Thousand Oaks, CA: Sage, 1997, chapter 4 and Epilogue.

Meyers, Diana Tietjens, ed. *Feminists Rethink the Self*. Boulder, CO: Westview, 1997.

Murray, Jeffrey W. *Face to Face in Dialogue: Emmanuel Levinas and (the) Communication (of) Ethics*. Lanham, MD: University Press of America, 2003.

Pinchevski, Amit. *By Way of Interruption: Levinas and the Ethics of Communication*. Pittsburgh, PA: Duquesne University Press, 2005.

Porter, James E. *Rhetorical Ethics and Internetworked Writing*. Norwood, NJ: Ablex, 1998.

Pourciau, Lester J., ed. *Ethics and Electronic Information in the Twenty-First Century*. West Lafayette, IN: Purdue University Press, 1999.

Pratkanis, Anthony, and Elliott Aronson. *Age of Propaganda: The Everyday Use and Abuse of Persuasion*, rev. ed. New York: Freeman, 2001.

Rooksby, Emma. *E-mail and Ethics: Style and Ethical Relations in Computer-mediated Communication*. London: Routledge, 2002.

Schrag, Calvin O. *The Self after Postmodernity*. New Haven, CT: Yale University Press, 1997.

Serban, George. *Lying: Man's Second Nature*. Westport, CT: Praeger, 2001.

Smeltzer, Mark A. "Lying and Intersubjective Truth: A Communication Based Approach to Understanding Lying." *Argumentation* 10 (1996): 361–373.

Smith III, Ted J., ed. *Propaganda: A Pluralistic Perspective*. New York: Praeger, 1989.

"Special Issue: Ethics and New Media Technology." *Journal of Mass Media Ethics* 16 (2001): 253–312.

"Special Issue: Virtual Reality and Communication Ethics." *Journal of Mass Media Ethics* 18 (2003): 153–307.

Spence, Edward, and Brett Van Heereken. *Advertising Ethics*. Upper Saddle River, NJ: Pearson/Prentice-Hall, 2005.

Taylor, Charles. *Sources of the Self: The Making of Modern Identity*. Cambridge, MA: Harvard University Press, 1989.

Taylor, Victor E., and Charles E. Winquist, eds. *Encyclopedia of Postmodernism*. London: Routledge, 2001.

Wheeler, Thomas H. *Phototruth or Photofiction? Ethics and Media Imagery in the Digital Age*. Mahwah, NJ: Erlbaum, 2002.

Interpersonal Communication and Small Group Discussion

Anderson, Rob, and George M. Killenberg. *Interviewing: Speaking, Listening, and Learning in Professional Life.* Mountain View, CA: Mayfield, 1999. Ethics sections throughout.

Baker, Barbara, and Carol L. Benton. "The Ethics of Feminist Self-Disclosure." In *Interpretive Approaches to Interpersonal Communication,* Kathryn Carter and Mick Presnell, eds., Albany: State University of New York Press, 1994, pp. 219–256.

Blum, Larry. "Deceiving, Hurting, and Using." In *Philosophy and Personal Relations,* Alan Monetiore, ed. London: Routledge and Kegan Paul, 1973, pp. 34–61.

Galanes, Gloria J., Katherine Adams, with John K. Brilhart. *Effective Group Discussion,* 11th ed. Boston: McGraw-Hill, 2004, pp. 16–18, 132–134, 154, 285–286, 380–382.

Cialdini, R. B. "Interpersonal Influence: Being Ethical and Effective." In *Interpersonal Processes: The Claremont Symposium on Applied Social Psychology,* S. Oskamp and S. Spacapan, eds. Newbury Park, CA: Sage, 1987, pp. 148–165.

Deetz, Stanley. "Reclaiming the Subject Matter as a Guide to Mutual Understanding: Effectiveness and Ethics in Interpersonal Interaction." *Communication Quarterly* 38 (Summer 1990): 226–243.

Englehardt, Elaine E., ed. *Ethical Issues in Interpersonal Communication.* Orlando, FL: Harcourt College Publishers, 2001.

Fulkerson, Gerald. "The Ethics of Interpersonal Influence: A Critique of the Rhetorical Sensitivity Construct." *Journal of Communication and Religion* 13 (1990): 1–14.

Gudykunst, William B., Stella Ting-Toomey, Sandra Sudweeks, and Lea P. Stewart. *Building Bridges: Interpersonal Skills for a Changing World.* Boston: Houghton Mifflin, 1995, pp. 89–100, 290–293.

Hardwig, John. "In Search of an Ethics of Interpersonal Relationships." In *Person to Person,* George Graham and Hugh Lafollette, eds. Philadelphia: Temple University Press, 1989, pp. 63–81.

Hawes, Leonard C. "The Dialogics of Conversation." *Communication Theory* 9 (August, 1999): 229–264.

Lumsden, Gay, and Donald Lumsden. *Communicating in Groups and Teams,* 4th ed. Belmont, CA: Wadsworth, 2004, pp. 42–49, 143, 146, 204–205, 321–325.

Meyers, Christopher. "Appreciating W. D. Ross: On Duties and Consequences." *Journal of Mass Media Ethics* 18 (2003): 81–97.

Spitzberg, Brian H., and William R. Cupach, eds. *The Dark Side of Interpersonal Communication,* 2nd ed. Mahwah, NJ: Erlbaum, 2007.

Stewart, Lea P. "Facilitating Connections: Issues of Gender, Culture, and Diversity. In *Communication Ethics in an Age of Diversity,* Josina M. Makau and Ronald C. Arnett, eds. Urbana: University of Illinois Press, 1997, pp. 110–125.

Wilson, Gerald L., Alan M. Hantz, and Michael S. Hanna. *Interpersonal Growth Through Communication,* 4th ed. Dubuque, IA: Brown Benchmark, 1995, pp. 282–292.

Zorn, Theodore E., and Lawrence B. Rosenfield. "Between a Rock and a Hard Place: Ethical Dilemmas in Problem-Solving Group Facilitation." *Management Communication Quarterly* 3 (1989): 93–107.

Communication in Organizations

Adams, Guy B., and Danny L. Balfour. *Unmasking Administrative Evil.* Thousand Oaks, CA: Sage, 1998.

Allen, Lori A., and Dan Voss. *Ethics in Technical Communication: Shades of Gray.* New York: Wiley, 1997.

Anderson, James A., and Elaine E. Englehardt. *The Organizational Self and Ethical Conduct.* Fort Worth, TX: Harcourt College Publishers, 2001.

Arnett, Ronald C. "A Choice-Making Ethic for Organizational Communication: The Work of Ian I. Mitroff." *Journal of Business Ethics* 7 (1988): 151–161.

Botan, Carl. "Ethics in Strategic Communication Campaigns: The Case for a New Approach in Public Relations." *Journal of Business Ethics* 34 (April 1997): 188–202.

Bracey, Hyler, Jack Rosenblum, Aubrey Sanford, and Roy Trueblood. *Managing from the Heart.* New York: Delacorte, 1990.

Brewis, Joanna. "Who Do You Think You Are? Feminism, Work, Ethics, and Foucault." In *Ethics and Organizations*, Martin Parker, ed. Thousand Oaks, CA: Sage, 1998, pp. 53–75.

Brown, Marvin T. *Corporate Integrity: Rethinking Organizational Ethics and Leadership.* New York: Cambridge University Press, 2005.

Cheney, George, and Lars Thøger Christensen. "Organizational Identity: Linkages between Internal and External Communication." In *The New Handbook of Organizational Communication*, Fredric M. Jablin and Linda L. Putnam, eds. Thousand Oaks, CA: Sage, 2001, pp. 231–269.

Cheney, George, Lars Thøger Christensen, Theodore E. Zorn, Jr., and Shiv Ganesh. *Organizational Communication in an Age of Globalization: Issues, Reflections, Practices.* Long Grove, IL: Waveland Press, 2003, chapters 7, 10, and 14.

Chonko, Lawrence B. *Ethical Decision Making in Marketing.* Thousand Oaks, CA: Sage, 1995.

Ciulla, Joanne B., Clancy Martin, and Robert C. Solomon, eds. *Honest Work: A Business Ethics Reader.* New York: Oxford University Press, 2007.

Clampitt, Phillip G. *Communicating for Managerial Effectiveness*, 3rd ed. Newbury Park, CA: Sage, 2005, chapter 10.

Conrad, Charles, ed. *The Ethical Nexus.* Norwood, NJ: Ablex, 1993.

———, and Marshall Scott Poole. *Strategic Organizational Communication: Into the Twenty-First Century,* 6th ed. Belmont, CA: Thomson/Wadsworth, 2005, chapter 12.

Cooper, David E. *Ethics for Professionals in a Multicultural World.* Upper Saddle River, NJ: Pearson/Prentice-Hall, 2004.

Crockett, Carter. "The Cultural Paradigm of Virtue." *Journal of Business Ethics* 62 (2005): 191–208.

Davis, Michael. "Some Paradoxes of Whistleblowing." *Business and Professional Ethics Journal* 15 (Spring 1996): 3–19.

Deetz, Stanley, Deborah Cohen, and Page P. Edley. "Toward a Dialogic Ethic in the Context of International Business Organization." In *Ethics in Intercultural and International Communication*, Fred L. Casmir, ed. Mahwah, NJ: Erlbaum, 1997, pp. 183–226.

———, Sarah J. Tracy, and Jennifer Lyn Simpson. *Leading Organizations Through Transition: Communication and Cultural Change.* Thousand Oaks, CA: Sage, 2000, chapter 6.

Dombrowski, Paul M. *Ethics in Technical Communication.* Needham Heights, MA: Allyn & Bacon, 2000.

Edgett, Ruth. "Toward an Ethical Framework for Advocacy in Public Relations." *Journal of Public Relations Research* 14 (2002): 1–26.

Eisenberg, Eric M., H. Lloyd Goodall, and Angela Trethewey. *Organizational Communication: Balancing Creativity and Constraint*, 5th ed. New York: Bedford/St. Martin's, 2007.

Englehardt, Elaine E., and DeAnn Evans. "Lies, Deception, and Public Relations." *Public Relations Review* 20 (1994): 249–266.

Fitzpatrick, Kathy, and Carolyn Bronstein, eds. *Ethics in Public Relations: Responsible Advocacy.* Thousand Oaks, CA: Sage, 2006.

Guth, David, and Charles Nash. *Public Relations: A Values Driven Approach.* Boston: Allyn & Bacon, 2000, chapter 6.

Guy, Mary E. *Ethical Decision Making in Everyday Work Situations.* Westport, CT: Quorum Books, 1990.

Hackman, Michael Z., and Craig E. Johnson. *Leadership: A Communication Perspective,* 4th ed. Long Grove, IL: Waveland Press, 2004, chapter 11.

Hall, William D. *Making the Right Decision: Ethics for Managers.* New York: Wiley, 1993.

Heath, Robert L., ed. *Handbook of Public Relations.* Thousand Oaks, CA: Sage, 2001, chapters 31–35.

Jaksa, James A., and Michael S. Pritchard, eds. *Responsible Communication: Ethical Issues in Business, Industry, and the Professions.* Cresskill, NJ: Hampton, 1996.

Jennings, Marianne M. *The Seven Signs of Ethical Collapse: How to Spot Moral Meltdowns in Companies . . . Before It's Too Late.* New York: St. Martin's Press, 2006.

Johnson, Craig. *Meeting the Ethical Challenges of Leadership,* 2nd ed. Thousand Oaks, CA: Sage, 2005.

Johnson, Roberta Ann. *Whistleblowing: When It Works—and Why.* Boulder, CO: Lynne Rienner Publishers, 2003.

Journal of Business Communication 27 (Summer 1990). Entire issue on ethics.

Journal of Mass Media Ethics 4, no. 1 (1989). Entire issue on public relations ethics.

Jubb, Peter B. "Whistleblowing: A Restrictive Definition and Interpretation." *Journal of Business Ethics* 21 (August 1999): 77–94.

Kirkwood, William G., and Steven M. Ralston. "Ethics and Teaching Employment Interviewing." *Communication Education* 45 (April 1996): 167–179.

Markel, Mike. *Ethics in Technical Communication: A Critique and Synthesis.* Westport, CT: Ablex, 2001.

Martinson, David L. "Enlightened Self-Interest Fails as an Ethical Baseline in Public Relations." *Journal of Mass Media Ethics* 9, no. 2 (1994): 100–108.

Mattson, Marifran, and Patrice M. Buzzanell. "Traditional and Feminist Organizational Communication Ethical Analyses of Messages and Issues Surrounding an Actual Job Loss Case." *Journal of Applied Communication Research* 27 (February 1999): 49–72.

May, Steve, ed. *Case Studies in Organizational Communication: Ethical Perspectives and Practices.* Thousand Oaks, CA: Sage, 2006.

McDaniel, Charlotte. *Organizational Ethics: Research and Ethical Environments.* Aldershot, UK: Ashgate, 2004.

McElreath, Mark P. *Managing Systematic and Ethical Public Relations Campaigns.* New York: McGraw-Hill, 1997, chapters 9 & 10.

McMillan, Jill J., and Michael J. Hyde. "Technological Innovation and Change: A Case Study in the Formation of Organizational Conscience." *Quarterly Journal of Speech* 86 (February 2000): 19–47.

Metzger, M., D. R. Dalton, and J. W. Hill. "The Organization of Ethics and the Ethics of Organizations: The Case for Expanded Organizational Ethics Audits." *Business Ethics Quarterly* 3, no. 1 (1993): 27–44.

Michalos, Alex C. *A Pragmatic Approach to Business Ethics.* Thousand Oaks, CA: Sage, 1995.

Miethe, Terance D. *Whistleblowing at Work: Tough Choices in Exposing Fraud, Waste, and Abuse on the Job.* Boulder, CO: Westview, 1999.

Murphy, Patrick E. "Character and Virtue Ethics in International Marketing: An Agenda for Managers, Researchers, and Educators." *Journal of Business Ethics* 18 (January 1999): 107–124.

Nash, Laura L. *Good Intentions Aside: A Manager's Guide to Resolving Ethical Problems.* Boston: Harvard Business School Press, 1990.

Nicotera, Anne Maydan, and Donald R. Cushman. "Organizational Ethics: A Within Organization View." *Journal of Applied Communication Research* 20 (November 1992): 437–462.

Northouse, Peter G. *Leadership: Theory and Practice*. 4th ed. Thousand Oaks, CA: Sage, 2007, chapter 4.

Paul, Jim, and Christy A. Strbiak. "The Ethics of Strategic Ambiguity." *Journal of Business Communication* 34 (April 1997): 149–159.

Pepper, Gerald L. *Communicating in Organizations: A Cultural Approach*. New York: McGraw-Hill, 1995, chapter 7.

Petrick, Joseph A., and John F. Quinn. *Management Ethics: Integrity at Work*. Thousand Oaks, CA: Sage, 1997.

Plamondon, Ann L. "Ethics in the Workplace: The Role of Organizational Communication." In *Organizational Communication*, Peggy Yuhas Byers, ed. Boston: Allyn & Bacon, 1997, chapter 4.

Pratt, Cornelius B. "Applying Classical Ethical Theories to Ethical Decision Making in Public Relations: Perrier's Prudent Recall." *Management Communication Quarterly* 8 (August 1994): 70–94.

Seeger, Matthew W. *Ethics and Organizational Communication*. Cresskill, NJ: Hampton, 1997.

Shulman, David. *From Hire to Liar: The Role of Deception in the Workplace*. Ithaca, NY: ILR Press/Cornell University Press, 2007.

Solomon, Robert C., and Clancy Martin. *Above the Bottom Line*, 3rd ed. Belmont, CA: Wadsworth, 2004.

Terris, Daniel. *Ethics at Work: Creating Virtue in an American Corporation*. Waltham, MA: Brandeis University Press, 2005.

Vardi, Yoav, and Ely Weitz. *Misbehavior in Organizations: Theory, Research, and Management*. Mahwah, NJ: Erlbaum, 2004.

Yuthas, Kristi, Rodney Rogers, and Jesse F. Dillard. "Communicative Action and Corporate Annual Reports." *Journal of Business Ethics* 41 (Nov. 2002): 141–157.

Formal Codes of Ethics

Black, Jay, Bob Steele, and Ralph Barney. *Doing Ethics in Journalism*, 3rd ed. Boston: Allyn & Bacon, 1999, chapter 2.

Blake, Richard, et al. "The Nature and Scope of State Government Ethics Codes." *Public Productivity and Management Review* 21 (1998): 453–459.

Christians, Clifford G. "Self-Regulation: A Critical Role for Codes of Ethics." In *Media Freedom and Accountability*, Everette E. Dennis, Donald M. Gilmor, and Theodore L. Glasser, eds. Westport, CT: Greenwood Press, 1989, pp. 35–53.

Condren, Conal. "Code Types: Functions and Failings and Organizational Diversity." *Business and Professional Ethics Journal* 14 (Winter 1995): 69–87.

Cooper, Thomas W., Clifford G. Christians, Frances Ford Plude, and Robert A. White, eds. *Communication Ethics and Global Change*. New York: Longman, 1989.

Courtright, Jeffrey. "An Ethics Code Postmortem: The National Religious Broadcasters' EFICOM." *Journal of Mass Media Ethics* 11, no. 4 (1996): 223–235.

Evers, Huub. "Codes of Ethics." In *Media Ethics*, Bart Pattyn, ed. Leuven, Belgium: Peeters, 2000, pp. 255–281.

Gordon, A. David, and John Michael Kittross. *Controversies in Media Ethics*, 2nd ed. New York: Longman, 1999, chapter 3.

Gorlin, Rena A., ed. *Codes of Professional Responsibility: Ethics Standards in Business, Health, and Law*, 4th ed. Washington, DC: BNA Books, 1999.

Hass, Tanni. "Reporters or Peeping Toms?: Journalism Codes of Ethics and News Coverage of the Clinton-Lewinsky Scandal." In *Desperately Seeking Ethics: A Guide to Media Conduct*, Howard Good, ed. Lanham, MD: Scarecrow Press, 2003, pp. 21–43.

Johannesen, Richard L. "What Should We Teach About Formal Codes of Communication Ethics?" *Journal of Mass Media Ethics* 3, no. 1 (1988): 59–64.

Journal of Mass Media Ethics 17, no. 2 (2002), entire issue.

Kaptein, Muel, and Johan Wempe. "Twelve Gordian Knots When Developing an Organizational Code of Ethics." *Journal of Business Ethics* 17 (1998): 853–869.

Matthews, M. Cash. *Strategic Intervention in Organizations: Resolving Ethical Dilemmas.* Newbury Park. CA: Sage, 1988, pp. 51–82.

Molander, E. A. "A Paradigm for Design, Promulgation, and Enforcement of Ethical Codes." *Journal of Business Ethics* 6 (1987): 619–631.

Murphy, Patrick E., ed. *Eighty Exemplary Ethics Statements.* Notre Dame, IN: University of Notre Dame Press, 1998.

Newton, Lisa H. *The Corporate Code of Ethics: The Perspective of the Humanities.* Fairfield, CT: Fairfield University Press, 1992.

Rogers, Priscilla S., and John M. Swales. "We the People? An Analysis of the Dana Corporation Policies Document." *Journal of Business Communication* 27 (Summer 1990): 293–313.

Spero, Robert. *The Duping of the American Voter: Dishonesty and Deception in Presidential Television Advertising.* New York: Lippincott and Crowell, 1980, chapter 10.

Stevens, Betsy. "Analysis of Corporate Ethical Code Studies: 'Where Do We Go from Here?'" *Journal of Business Ethics* 13 (January 1994): 63–70.

Feminist Contributions

Brabeck, Mary M., ed. *Who Cares? Theory, Research, and Educational Implications of the Ethic of Care.* New York: Praeger, 1989.

Brennen, Samantha. "Recent Work in Feminist Ethics." *Ethics* 109 (July 1999): 858–893.

Card, Claudia, ed. *Feminist Ethics.* Lawrence: University Press of Kansas, 1991.

Carse, Alisa L., and Hilde Lundemann Nelson. "Rehabilitating Care." *Kennedy Institute of Ethics Journal* 6 (1996): 19–35.

Evans, Judith. *Feminist Theory Today.* Thousand Oaks, CA: Sage, 1995.

Frazer, Elizabeth, Jennifer Hornsby, and Sabina Lovibond, eds. *Ethics: A Feminist Reader.* Cambridge, MA: Basil Blackwell, 1992.

Groenhout, Ruth E. *Connected Lives: Human Nature and an Ethic of Care.* Lanham, MD: Rowman and Littlefield, 2004.

Haas, Tanni, and Stan Deetz. "Between the Generalized and the Concrete Other: Approaching Organizational Ethics from Feminist Perspectives." In *Rethinking Organizational and Managerial Communication from Feminist Perspectives*, Patrice M. Buzzanell, ed. Thousand Oaks, CA: Sage, 2000, pp. 24–46.

Hallstein, D. Lynn O'Brien. "A Postmodern Caring: Feminist Standpoint Theories, Revisioned Caring, and Communication Ethics." *Western Journal of Communication* 63 (Winter 1999): 32–56.

Hamington, Maurice, and Dorothy C. Miller, eds. *Socializing Care: Feminist Ethics and Public Issues.* Lanham, MD: Rowman and Littlefield, 2006.

Hekman, Susan J. *Moral Voices, Moral Selves: Carol Gilligan and Feminist Moral Theory.* University Park: Pennsylvania State University Press, 1995.

Held, Virginia. *Feminist Morality: Transforming Culture, Society, and Politics.* Chicago: University of Chicago Press, 1993.

———. "Feminist Transformations of Moral Theory." *Philosophy and Phenomenological Research* 50 (1990): 321–344.

Houston, Marsha, and Cheris Kramarae. "Speaking from Silence: Methods of Silencing and Resistance." *Discourse and Society* 24 (1991): 387–399.

Jaggar, Alison M. "Toward a Feminist Conception of Moral Reasoning." In *Ethics: The Big Questions*, James P. Sterba, ed. Oxford, UK: Blackwell, 1998, pp. 356–374.

———, and Iris Young, eds. *A Companion to Feminist Philosophy.* Oxford, UK: Blackwell, 1998.

Koehn, Daryl. *Rethinking Feminist Ethics: Care, Trust, and Empathy.* London: Routledge, 1998.

Landau, Iddo. *Is Philosophy Androcentric?* University Park: Pennsylvania State University Press, 2006.

Larrabee, Mary Jeanne, ed. *An Ethic of Care.* New York: Routledge, 1993.

Lerner, Harriet Goldhor. *The Dance of Deception: Pretending and Truth-Telling in Women's Lives.* New York: Harper Collins, 1993.

Makau, Josina, and Debian Marty. *Cooperative Argumentation: A Model for Deliberative Community.* Long Grove, IL: Waveland Press, 2001, chapter 2.

Miller, Sarah Clark. "A Kantian Ethic of Care?" In *Feminist Interventions in Ethics and Politics: Feminist Ethics and Social Theory.* Lanham, MD: Rowman and Littlefield, 2005, pp. 111–127.

Noddings, Nel. *Philosophy of Education,* 2nd ed. Boulder, CO: Westview, 2007, pp. 213–235.

Parsons, Susan Frank. *The Ethics of Gender.* Oxford, UK: Blackwell, 2002.

Porter, Elisabeth. *Feminist Perspectives on Ethics.* London: Longman, 1999.

Robinson, Fiona. *Globalizing Care: Ethics, Feminist Theory, and International Relations.* Boulder, CO: Westview, 1999.

Scott, Sandra Davidson. "Beyond Reason: A Feminist Theory of Ethics for Journalists." *Feminist Issues* 13 (Spring 1993): 23–40.

Sevenhuijsen, Selma. *Citizenship and the Ethics of Care: Justice, Morality, and Politics.* London: Routledge, 1998.

"Special Topic: Caring and the Media." *Journal of Mass Media Ethics* 21 (2006): 99–214.

Starhawk. *Dreaming the Dark: Magic, Sex, and Politics,* new edition. Boston: Beacon Press, 1988, chapter 3.

Sterba, James P. *Three Challenges to Ethics: Environmentalism, Feminism, and Multiculturalism.* New York: Oxford University Press, 2001, chapter 3.

Sullivan, Patricia A., and Steven R. Goldzwig. "A Relational Approach to Moral Decision Making: The Majority Opinion in Planned Parenthood v. Casey." *Quarterly Journal of Speech* 81 (May 1995): 167–190.

Tong, Rosmarie. *Feminine and Feminist Ethics.* Belmont, CA: Wadsworth, 1993.

Walker, Margaret Urban. *Moral Understandings: A Feminist Study in Ethics.* New York: Routledge, 1998.

Walters, James W. *Martin Buber and Feminist Ethics: The Priority of the Personal.* Syracuse, NY: Syracuse University Press, 2003.

Wood, Julia T. *Who Cares? Women, Care, and Culture.* Carbondale: Southern Illinois University Press, 1994.

Intercultural and Multicultural Communication

Appiah, Kwame Anthony. *Cosmopolitanism: Ethics in a World of Strangers.* New York: W. W. Norton, 2006.

Blum, Lawrence. "Ethnicity, Identity, and Community." In *Justice and Caring: The Search for a Common Ground in Education*, Michael S. Katz, Nel Noddings, and Kenneth A Strike, eds. New York: Teachers College Press, 1997, pp. 127–145.

Browning, Don, ed. *Universalism vs. Relativism: Making Moral Judgments in a Changing, Pluralistic, and Threatening World.* Lanham, MD: Rowman and Littlefield, 2006.

Burger, Rudolf, Peter Brezovszky, and Peter Pelinka, eds. *Global Ethics: Illusion or Reality?* Vienna: Czernin Verlag, 2000.

Casmir, Fred L., ed. *Ethics in Intercultural and International Communication.* Mahwah, NJ: Erlbaum, 1997.

Christians, Clifford, and Michael Traber, eds. *Communication Ethics and Universal Values.* Thousand Oaks, CA: Sage, 1997.

Cook, John W. *Morality and Cultural Differences.* New York: Oxford University Press, 1999.

Cooper, Thomas W. "Communion and Communication: Learning from the Shuswap." *Critical Studies in Mass Communication* 11 (December 1994): 327–345.

———. *A Time before Deception: Truth in Communication, Culture, and Ethics: Native Worldviews, Traditional Expression, and Sacred Ecology.* Santa Fe, NM: Clear Light Publishers, 1998.

Cua, A. S. *Moral Vision and Tradition: Essays in Chinese Ethics.* Washington, DC: Catholic University of America Press, 1998.

Dragga, Sam. "Ethical Intercultural Technical Communication: Looking Through the Lens of Confucian Ethics." *Technical Communication Quarterly* 8 (Fall 1999): 365–381.

Gutmann, Amy. "The Challenge of Multiculturalism in Political Ethics." *Philosophy and Public Affairs* 22 (Summer 1993): 171–206.

———, ed. *Multiculturalism: Examining the Politics of Recognition.* Princeton: Princeton University Press, 1994.

Hall, Bradford 'J'. *Among Cultures: The Challenge of Communication*, 2nd ed. Belmont, CA: Thomson/Wadsworth, 2005, chapter 11.

Hopkins, Willie E. *Ethical Dimensions of Diversity.* Thousand Oaks, CA: Sage, 1997.

Johannesen, Richard L. "The Ethics of Plagiarism Reconsidered: The Oratory of Martin Luther King, Jr." *Southern Communication Journal* 60 (Spring 1995): 185–194.

———. "Diversity, Freedom, and Responsibility in Tension." In *Communication Ethics in an Age of Diversity,* Josina Makau and Ronald C. Arnett, eds. Champaign: University of Illinois Press, 1966, pp. 157–186.

Kane, Robert. *Through the Moral Maze: Searching for Absolute Values in a Pluralistic World.* New York: Longman, 1994.

Kirkwood, William G. "Truthfulness as a Standard for Speech in Ancient India." *Southern Communication Journal* 56 (Spring 1989): 213–234.

Kukathas, Chandran. "Explaining Moral Variety." In *Cultural Pluralism and Moral Knowledge,* Ellen Frankel Paul, Fred D. Miller, Jr., and Jeffrey Paul, eds. Cambridge: Cambridge University Press, 1994, pp. 1–21.

Küng, Hans. *Global Responsibility: In Search of a New World Ethic.* New York: Crossroads, 1991.

Lange, Heiko, Albert Lohr, and Horst Steinmann. *Working Across Cultures: Ethical Perspectives for Intercultural Management.* Dordrecht: Kluwer, 1998.

Makau, Josina M., and Ronald C. Arnett, eds. *Communication Ethics in an Age of Diversity.* Urbana: University of Illinois Press, 1997.

Marshall, Joseph M. *The Lakota Way: Stories and Lessons for Living: Native American Wisdom on Ethics and Character.* New York: Viking Compass, 2001.

Martin, Judith N., Lisa A. Flores, and Thomas K. Nakayama. "Ethical Issues in Intercultural Communication." In *Readings in Intercultural Communication*, Judith Martin, Lisa Flores, and Thomas Nakayama, eds. Boston: McGraw-Hill, 2002, pp. 363–371.

May, Larry, and Shari Collins Sharratt, eds. *Applied Ethics: A Multicultural Approach.* Englewood Cliffs, NJ: Prentice-Hall, 1994.

Morgan, Eileen. *Navigating Cross-Cultural Ethics: What Global Managers Do Right to Keep from Going Wrong.* Boston: Butterworth/Heinemann, 1998.

Nardin, Terry and David R. Mapel, eds. *Traditions of International Ethics.* NY. Cambridge University Press, 1992.

Okin, Susan Miller. "Feminism and Multiculturalism: Some Tensions." *Ethics* 108 (July 1998): 61–84.

Paul, E. F., F. D. Miller, Jr., and J. Paul, eds. *Cultural Pluralism and Moral Knowledge.* Cambridge: Cambridge University Press, 1994.

Ruland, Vernon. *Conscience across Borders: An Ethics of Global Rights and Religious Pluralism.* San Francisco, CA: University of San Francisco and Association of Jesuit University Presses, 2002.

Ryn, Claes G. *A Common Human Ground: Universality and Particularity in a Multicultural World.* Columbia: University of Missouri Press, 2004, chapters 5 and 9.

"Special Issue: The Search for a Global Media Ethic." *Journal of Mass Media Ethics* 17 (2002): 261–317.

Sterba, James P. *Three Challenges to Ethics: Environmentalism, Feminism, and Multiculturalism.* New York: Oxford University Press, 2001, chapter 4.

Ting-Toomey, Stella, and Leeva C. Chung. *Understanding Intercultural Communication.* Los Angeles, CA: Roxbury, 2005, chapter 13.

Ward, Stephen A. J. "Philosophical Foundations for Global Journalism Ethics." *Journal of Mass Media Ethics* 20 (2005): 3–21.

Wines, William A., and Nancy K. Napier. "Toward an Understanding of Cross-Cultural Ethics: A Tentative Model. *Journal of Business Ethics* 11 (1992): 831–841.

Wiredu, Kwasi. *Cultural Universals and Particulars: An African Perspective.* Bloomington: Indiana University Press, 1996.

Case Studies of Theory and Practice

Artz, B. Lee, and Mark A. Pollock. "The Rhetoric of Unconditional Surrender: Locating the Necessary Moment of Coercion." *Communication Studies* 48 (Summer 1997): 159–173.

Bailey, F. G. *Humbuggery and Manipulation: The Art of Leadership.* Ithaca, NY: Cornell University Press, 1988.

———. *The Prevalence of Deceit.* Ithaca, NY: Cornell University Press, 1991.

Barad, Judith, with Ed Robertson. *The Ethics of Star Trek.* New York: Harper Collins, 2000.

Bineham, Jeffery L. "Some Ethical Implications of Team Sports Metaphors in Politics." *Communication Reports* 4 (Winter 1991): 35–42.

Booth, Wayne. *The Company We Keep: The Ethics of Fiction.* Berkeley: University of California Press, 1989.

Boxill, Jan, ed. *Sports Ethics: An Anthology.* Malden, MA: Blackwell, 2003.

Burke, Kenneth. "The Rhetoric of Hitler's 'Battle.'" In *The Philosophy of Literary Form,* rev. abridged ed., Kenneth Burke, ed. New York: Vintage Books, 1957, pp. 164–189.

"Cases and Commentaries: The Unabomber." *Journal of Mass Media Ethics* 10, no. 4 (1995): 248–256.

Cohen, Randy. *The Good, The Bad, and the Difference: How to Tell Right from Wrong in Everyday Situations.* New York: Doubleday, 2002.

Crossen, Cynthia. *Tainted Truth: The Manipulation of Fact in America.* New York: Simon & Schuster, 1994.

Courtright, Jeffrey L. "'I Respectfully Dissent': The Ethics of Dissent in Justice O'Connor's *Metro Broadcasting, Inc. v. FCC* opinion." In *Warranting Assent: Case Studies in Argument Evaluation,* Edward Schiappa, ed. Albany: State University of New York Press (1995), pp. 125–152.

Deuze, Mark, and Daphna Yeshua. "Online Journalists Face New Ethical Dilemmas: Lessons from the Netherlands." *Journal of Mass Media Ethics* 16 (2001): 273–292.

Eakin, John Paul, ed. *The Ethics of Life Writing.* Ithaca, NY: Cornell University Press, 2004.

Good, Howard, ed. *Desperately Seeking Ethics: A Guide to Media Conduct.* Lanham, MD: Scarecrow Press, 2003.

Green, Mark, and Gail MacColl. *Reagan's Reign of Error: The Instant Nostalgia Edition,* expanded and updated. New York: Pantheon, 1987.

Gross, Larry. "The Contested Closet: The Ethics and Politics of Outing." *Critical Studies in Mass Communication* 8 (September 1991): 352–388.

———. *Contested Closets: The Politics and Ethics of Outing.* Minneapolis: University of Minnesota Press, 1993.

Johnson, Barbara M. *Cheating: Maintaining Your Integrity in a Dishonest World.* Minneapolis: Augsburg Fortress, 1989.

Katz, Stephen B. "The Ethic of Expediency: Classical Rhetoric, Technology, and the Holocaust." *College English* 54 (March 1992): 255–275.

Lutz, William. *Doublespeak. From Revenue Enhancement to Terminal Living: How Government, Business, Advertisers, and Others Use Language to Deceive You.* New York: Harper & Row, 1990.

Mackey-Kallis, Susan, and Dan Hahn. "Who's to Blame for America's Drug Problem?: The Search for Scapegoats in the 'War on Drugs.'" *Communication Quarterly* 42 (Winter 1994): 1–20.

Markie, Peter J. *A Professor's Duties: Ethical Issues in College Teaching.* Savage, MD: Rowman & Littlefield, 1994.

Marsh, Bill. *Plagiarism: Alchemy and Remedy in Higher Education.* Albany: State University of New York Press, 2007.

Mitchell, Gordon R. *Strategic Deception: Rhetoric, Science, and Politics in Missile Defense Advocacy.* East Lansing: Michigan State University Press, 2000.

Mitroff, Ian I., and Warren Bennis. *The Unreality Industry: The Deliberate Manufacturing of Falsehood and What It Is Doing to Our Lives.* New York: Oxford University Press, 1993.

Moore, Mark P. "Rhetorical Subterfuge and 'The Principle of Perfection': Bob Packwood's Response to Sexual Misconduct Charges." *Western Journal of Communication* 60 (Winter 1996): 1–20.

Oakes, Guy. *The Soul of the Salesman: The Moral Ethos of Personal Sales.* Atlantic Highlands, NJ: Humanities Press International, 1990.

Olson, Kathryn M. "Aligning Ethicality and Effectiveness in Arguments: Advocating Inclusiveness Percentages for the New Lutheran Church." In *Warranting Assent: Case Studies in Argument Evaluation,* Edward Schiappa, ed. Albany: State University of New York Press, 1995, pp. 81–102.

Parry, Robert. *Fooling America: How Washington Insiders Twist the Truth and Manufacture Conventional Wisdom.* New York: Marrow, 1992.

Shogan, Robert. *The Double-Edged Sword: How Character Makes and Ruins Presidents, From Washington to Clinton.* Boulder, CO: Westview, 1999.

Smith, David H. "Stories, Values, and Health Care Decisions." In *The Ethical Nexus,* Charles Conrad, ed. Norwood, NJ: Ablex, 1993, pp. 123–148.

St. Onge, Keith R. *The Melancholy Anatomy of Plagiarism.* Washington, DC: University Press of America, 1988.

Valenti, F. Miguel. *More than a Movie: Ethics in Entertainment.* Boulder, CO: Westview, 2000.

Vaux, Kenneth L. *Ethics and the Gulf War: Religion, Rhetoric, and Righteousness.* Boulder, CO: Westview Press, 1992.

Ward, Annalee R. *Mouse Morality: The Rhetoric of Disney Animated Film.* Austin, TX: University of Texas Press, 2002.

Weaver, Richard M. *The Ethics of Rhetoric.* Chicago: Regnery, 1953.

Whicker, Marcia Lynn, and Jennie Jacobs Kronenfeld. *Dealing with Ethical Dilemmas on Campus.* Thousand Oaks, CA: Sage, 1994.

Williamson, Larry, and Eric Pierson. "The Rhetoric of Hate on the Internet: Hateporn's Challenge to Modern Media Ethics." *Journal of Mass Media Ethics* 18 (2003): 250–267.

Wilshire, Bruce. *The Moral Collapse of the University.* Albany: State University of New York Press, 1990.

Ethics in Mass Communication

Aucoin, James. "Implications of Audience Ethics for the Mass Communicator." *Journal of Mass Media Ethics* 11, no. 2 (1996): 69–81.

Baird, Robert M., William E. Loges, and Stuart E. Rosenbaum, eds. *The Media and Morality.* New York: Prometheus, 1999.

Baker, Sherry. "Applying Kidder's Ethical Decision-Making Checklist to Mass Media Ethics." *Journal of Mass Media Ethics* 12 (1997): 197–210.

———. "Five Baselines for Justification in Persuasion." *Journal of Mass Media Ethics* 14 (1999): 69–81.

Becker, Marilyn. *Screenwriting With a Conscience: Ethics for Screenwriters.* Mahwah, NJ: Erlbaum, 2003.

Bertrand, Jean-Claude. *Media Ethics and Accountability.* New Brunswick, NJ: Transaction Publications, 2000.

Bivins, Thomas. *Mixed Media: Moral Distinctions in Advertising, Public Relations, and Journalism.* Mahwah, NJ: Erlbaum, 2003.

Black, Jay, Bob Steele, and Ralph Barney. *Doing Ethics in Journalism: A Handbook with Cases.* 3rd ed. Boston: Allyn & Bacon, 1999.

Borden, Sandra L. "Choice Processes in a Newspaper Ethics Case." *Communication Monographs* 64 (March 1997): 65–81.

Bugeja, Michael J. *Living Ethics: Developing Values in Mass Communication.* Boston: Allyn & Bacon, 1996.

———. *Interpersonal Divide: The Search for Community in a Technological Age.* New York: Oxford University Press, 2005.

Christians, Clifford G. "A Theory of Normative Technology." In *Technological Transformation: Contextual and Conceptual Implications,* E. F. Byrne and J. C. Pitt, eds. Dordrecht: Kluwer Academic Publishers, 1989, pp. 123–139.

———. "Review Essay: Current Trends in Media Ethics." *European Journal of Communication* 10, no. 4 (1995): 545–558.

———, Mark Fackler, Kim B. Rotzoll, Kathy Brittain McKee, and Robert H. Woods, Jr. *Media Ethics: Cases and Moral Reasoning,* 7th ed. New York: Pearson/Allyn & Bacon, 2004.

———, John P. Ferre, and P. Mark Fackler. *Good News: Social Ethics and the Press.* New York: Oxford University Press, 1993.

———, and Kaarle Nordenstreng. "Social Responsibility Worldwide." *Journal of Mass Media Ethics,* 19 (2004): 3–28.

Cooper, Thomas W., Clifford G. Christians, Frances Ford Plude, and Robert A. White, eds. *Communication Ethics and Global Change.* New York: Longman, 1989.

Cote, William, and Roger Simpson. *Covering Violence: A Guide to Ethical Reporting About Victims and Trauma.* New York: Columbia University Press, 2000.

Craig, David. *The Ethics of the Story: Using Journalism and Writing Techniques Responsibly.* Lanham, MD: Rowman and Littlefield, 2006

Day, Louis A. *Ethics in Media Communications: Cases and Controversies,* 5th ed. Belmont, CA: Thomson/Wadsworth, 2006.

Elliott, Deni T., ed. *Responsible Journalism.* Beverly Hills: Sage, 1986.

Englehardt, Elaine E., and Ralph D. Barney. *Media and Ethics: Principles for Moral Decisions.* Belmont, CA: Wadsworth, 2002.

Fink, Conrad C. *Media Ethics,* 2nd ed. New York: Allyn & Bacon, 1995.

Funiok, Rudiger. "Fundamental Questions of Audience Ethics." In *Media Ethics,* Bart Pattyn, ed. Leuven, Belgium: Peeters, 2000, pp. 403–422.

Gordon, A. David, and John Michael Kittross, eds. *Controversies in Media Ethics*, 2nd ed. New York: Longman, 1999.

Gross, Larry. John Stuart Katz, and Jay Ruby, eds. *Image Ethics: The Moral Rights of Subjects in Photographs, Film, and Television*. New York: Oxford University Press, 1988.

Gunkel, David J. *Thinking Otherwise: Philosophy, Communication, Technology*. West Lafayette, IN: Purdue University Press, 2007.

———, and Debra Hawhee. "Virtual Alterity and the Reformatting of Ethics." *Journal of Mass Media Ethics* 18 (2003): 174–194.

Harcup, Tony. *The Ethical Journalist*. Thousand Oaks, CA: Sage, 2007.

Harvill, Jerry. "'Oikonomia': The Journalist as Steward." *Journal of Mass Media Ethics* 3, no. 1 (1988): 65–76.

Hausman, Carl. *Crisis of Conscience: Perspectives on Journalism Ethics*. New York: Harper Collins, 1992.

Hulteng, John L. *The Messenger's Motives: Ethical Problems of the News Media*, 2nd ed. Englewood Cliffs, NJ: Prentice-Hall, 1985.

Iggers, Jeremy. *Good News, Bad News: Journalism Ethics and the Public Interest*. Boulder, CO: Westview, 1998.

Johnstone, Henry W., Jr. "Communication: Technology and Ethics." In *Communication, Philosophy, and the Technological Age,* Michael J. Hyde, ed. Tuscaloosa: University of Alabama Press, 1982.

Journal of Advertising 23 (September 1994). Entire issue on advertising ethics.

Journal of Mass Media Ethics (every issue).

Kieran, Matthew. *Media Ethics: A Philosophical Approach*. Westport, CT: Praeger, 1997.

Knowlton, Steven R. *Moral Reasoning for Journalists*. Westport, CT: Praeger, 1997.

Lambeth, Edmund B. *Committed Journalism: An Ethic for the Profession*, 2nd ed. Bloomington: Indiana University Press, 1992.

Land, Mitchell, and Bill Hornaday, eds. *Contemporary Media Ethics: A Practical Guide for Students, Scholars, and Professionals*. Spokane, WA: Marquette Books, 2006.

Leslie, Larry Z. *Mass Communication Ethics: Decision Making in Postmodern Culture*. 2nd ed. Boston: Houghton Mifflin, 2004.

Limburg, Val E. *Electronic Media Ethics*. Boston: Focal Press, 1994.

Mason, Richard O., Florence M. Mason, and Mary J. Culnan. *Ethics of Information Management*. Thousand Oaks, CA: Sage, 1995.

Merrill, John C. *The Dialectic in Journalism: Toward a Responsible Use of Press Freedom*. Baton Rouge: Louisiana State University Press, 1989.

———. *Journalism Ethics: Philosophical Foundations for the News Media*. New York: St. Martin's Press, 1997.

Patterson, Philip, and Lee Wilkins. *Media Ethics: Issues and Cases,* 5th ed. Boston: McGraw-Hill, 2005.

Pattyn, Bart, ed. *Media Ethics: Opening Social Dialogue*. Leuven, Belgium: Peeters, 2000.

Phillips, Michael J. *Ethics and Manipulation in Advertising: Answering a Flawed Indictment*. Westport, CT: Greenwood, 1997.

Preston, Ivan. *The Tangled Web They Weave: Truth, Falsity, and Advertisers*. Madison: University of Wisconsin Press, 1996.

Pritchard, David, ed. *Holding the Media Accountable: Citizens, Ethics, and the Law*. Bloomington: Indiana University Press, 2000.

Sanders, Karen. *Ethics and Journalism*. London, UK: Sage, 2003.

Seib, Philip. *Campaigns and Conscience: The Ethics of Political Journalism*. Westport, CT: Praeger, 1994.

———, and Kathy Fitzpatrick. *Public Relations Ethics*. Fort Worth, TX: Harcourt Brace College Publishers, 1995.

———, and Kathy Fitzpatrick. *Journalism Ethics*. Ft. Worth, TX: Harcourt College Publishers, 1997.

Smith, Ron F. *Groping for Ethics in Journalism*, 5th ed. Ames, IA: Blackwell Publishing, 2003.

Wilkins, Lee, and Renata Coleman. *The Moral Media: How Journalists Reason About Ethics*. Mahwah, NJ: Erlbaum, 2005.

Wurlinger, Gregory T. "The Moral Universe of Libertarian Press Theory." *Critical Studies in Mass Communication* 8 (June 1991): 152–167.

Ethical Character and Virtue Ethics

Athanassoulis, Nafsika. "A Response to Harman: Virtue Ethics and Character Traits." *Proceedings of the Aristotelian Society*, 100 (2000): 215–221.

Copp, David, and David Sobel. "Morality and Virtue: An Assessment of Some Recent Work in Virtue Ethics." *Ethics* 114 (April 2004): 514–554.

Crisp, Roger, ed. *How Should We Live? Essays on the Virtues*. Oxford, UK: Clarendon, 1996.

Doris, John M. *Lack of Character: Personality and Moral Behavior*. New York: Cambridge University Press, 2002.

Foot, Philippa. *Natural Goodness*. Oxford, UK: Oxford University Press, 2001.

Herrick, James A. "Rhetoric, Ethics, and Virtue." *Communication Studies* 43 (1992): 133–149.

Jacobs, Jonathan. *Choosing Character: Responsibility for Virtue and Vice*. Ithaca, NY: Cornell University Press, 2001.

Kupperman, Joel J. "Tradition and Community in the Formation of Character and Self." In *Confucian Ethics: A Comparative Study of Self, Autonomy, and Community*, Kwong-Loi Shun and David B. Wong, eds. Cambridge, UK: Cambridge University Press, 2004, pp. 103–123.

Levy, Neil. "Good Character: Too Little, Too Late." *Journal of Mass Media Ethics* 19 (2004): 108–118.

Oakley, Justin, and Dean Cocking. *Virtue Ethics and Professional Roles*. Cambridge, UK: Cambridge University Press, 2001.

Pfiffner, James P. *The Character Factor: How We Judge America's Presidents*. College Station: Texas A&M University Press, 2004.

Quinn, Aaron. "Moral Virtues for Journalists." *Journal of Mass Media Ethics* 22 (2007): 168–186.

Swanton, Christine. *Virtue Ethics: A Pluralistic View*. Oxford, UK: Oxford University Press, 2003.

Taylor, Richard. *Virtue Ethics: An Introduction*. Amherst, NY: Prometheus, 2002.

Index

Abdicated responsibility, 144
Abuse of Casuistry, The, 239
Accessibility in organizational communication, 164
Accountability
    in journalism, 198–303
    media ethics and, 294–303
    organizational, 156, 161, 165–167
    political communication and, 26
    in public service, 270
    secrecy and, 120–121
Adkins, A. D., 250
Advertising. *See also* Commercial advertising, truth standard in
    codes of ethics in, 184–185
    intentional ambiguity in, 107
    photojournalistic ethics and, 115–118
    poetic properties of, 110
    politics and, 93–94
    suggestive, 37
    truth standard in commercial, 110–111
Advertising Age, 110
Advocacy, addressed in formal ethics codes, 188
After Virtue, 255, 265
Aldrich, Virgil, 245
Alinsky, Saul, 74–76
Allen, Anita L., 5
Alter, J., 248
Altheid, David, 173

Altman, Andrew, 233–234
Ambiguity
    in advertising, 107
    in codes of ethics, 192, 301
    ethics of, 106–108
    intentional, 106–108
    in organizational communication, 173–174
    of political candidates, 107
Ambrose, Stephen E., 283
American Advertising Federation
    Advertising Principles of American Business, 184–185
American Association of Advertising Agencies (AAAA)
    code of ethics, 184–185
American Association of Political Consultants
    Code of Professional Ethics, 194
American Demagogues, 115
American Society of Newspaper Editors, 195
Amorality of business practice, 174
Anderson, James, 124
Anderson, Rob, 65, 125
Anecdotes, misuse of in Ronald Reagan's rhetoric, 258–259, 272
Apel, Karl Otto, 141
Ardener, Shirley, 210
Arguer-as-lover metaphor, 61–62
Argumentative function of ethics codes, 182–183